To Soften the Blow

To Judy,
with love
from Looneybird

This first US edition published for Judybird Publishing

Copyright © Lynnie Vessels 2012

Printed and bound in the USA by CreateSpace. This book is available electronically on Amazon kindle and Barnes and Noble nook. To order in print, visit Amazon.com or www.lynnievessels.com.

Library of Congress Control Number: 2012905234

ISBN: 978-1479143160

Many names have been changed.

To Soften the Blow

By Lynnie Vessels

Even though
I did not hear the gun
go off that night,
everything I've done since
has been to soften its blow.

Introduction

On the evening of January 20, 1967, my father shot my mother with a twelve-gauge shotgun at a three-foot range across our dining room table. All of us, their six children, were present in the house when the gun went off. My three brothers, who my father had gathered at the table to watch the event, fled when the gun exploded. We three girls, ages five, seven, and nine, remained in the house while my father pointed the gun at my whimpering mother, trying to shoot her one more time - to finish her off. For *thirty minutes,* my nine-year old sister stood between my parents, her face inches from the barrel of the gun, shouting one word repeatedly at my father.

As I screamed, I shifted my gaze between this horrific scene and the eyes of my five-year old sister. The prolonged pain became too great. I had to make a choice between continuing to stare at the reality before me or into the loving eyes of my sister, eyes that transported me to a place that felt more real than the nightmare I was living. This single choice molded my life, crystallizing for me that all that exists between perceiving something as negative or positive is a choice. My older sister eventually found more words and resolved the conflict. Her words saved my mother. In that moment I learned a simple truth: if the words of a nine-year old girl can bring down a maniac, the right words can solve any problem.

The gun blast shattered my mother, literally, and our family, figuratively. I was simultaneously traumatized by the horrific act and enlightened by the miracles I experienced in the aftermath. I returned to my second grade classroom with no counseling. I solved my conflicts the only way I knew how – with violence. For seven years I did not say a word about the shooting. Eventually, my rage-filled body could take it no longer. One day, a very intuitive principal altered the course of my life in twenty minutes by looking me in the eye, giving me space to cry, and speaking the right words. I learned once again that all that exists between perceiving a situation as negative or positive is a choice. His continued attention sustained me and allowed me to enjoy my teenage years.

Although I was no longer violent as an adult, I was brought to my knees in the midst of my divorce. Realizing my deplorable lack of communication skills, twenty years after the shooting, I finally sought professional help. I could run from my past no longer. Gandhi said, "The only demons are those running around in our own minds and that is where our battles must be fought." I began to battle my demons, and, as a warrior replaced the victim in me, I came to understand the spiritual implications of violence.

I did no technical research for this book. I am not an expert on posttraumatic stress. I tell about the shooting and my parents' divorce at a time when divorce was extremely rare and shootings in suburban neighborhoods were virtually unheard of. I have always known I was meant to do something in response to being shown so much love in the midst of so much horror. This book is my something. My life and the people I reached out to, constitute my research.

I'm not a perfect person. Writing this has been a humiliating experience, as I have cringed writing the good about myself just as much as writing the bad. I have tried to give a complete picture of one human being struggling with posttraumatic stress.

A trauma or an act of violence is often retold in a single sentence. He was injured in a car accident. She was raped in the stairwell. They lost a child. A soldier lost his leg to an IED. Their parents divorced. A bomb went off in the square. The tornado destroyed their home. We lost our friend when the towers fell. I was bullied in school. He was fired. My sentence is, "My father shot my mom." Five words.

To the person who experiences a trauma and feels its effects, the event has far greater impact than words in a sentence can convey. In fact, it can alter a person forever. It can, and often does, lead to a life of resentment, anger, bitterness, fear, shame, and more violence. We can become bitter or choose to become better. There is no way to take away the trauma, but there are ways of managing responses to it so it does not destroy virtually every relationship a person has. I began to heal my anger using the miracles I saw on the night of the shooting: eye contact and words.

My discussions with those coping with posttraumatic stress, particularly soldiers and those abused, made it clear to me that anger and negative attack-thoughts were the most destructive elements. If not dealt with, the anger becomes rage, and the person begins to hurt others. If a person does not want to be angry, change is possible. A commitment is needed because it can be a long and arduous task. Change comes in lightning bolts of zigging and zagging. Zigging: moving three steps ahead. Zagging: moving two steps back.

There is great difficulty in being the angry person, whom I label "A." Although this person wants to be transformed into a happy person, whom I label "Z," he hasn't the foggiest idea how to make the journey, which I refer to as B through Y. These are the steps no one really shows a person how to take, and this is what makes change seem so unattainable.

Everyone wanted me to change; I wanted to change – to be different, but no one could show me how, and worse, when I tried, I felt shame for doing it wrong. I groped in the dark without an instruction book to guide me, trying to understand how to simultaneously purge the anger I carried while managing the conflicts in my present-day life. Although managing posttraumatic stress is a life-long process, I have documented my initial eleven-year journey of B through Y.

The most challenging time of all came after admitting I needed help. If you, too, are an "A" and are trying to become a "Z," you are welcome to use any parts of my B through Y as a roadmap for your own personal healing. There is value to the struggle, living the ups and downs - great joy and great pain – as you journey. I used all the resources I could find, every educator and healer. Every step, no matter how ugly the struggle, was worthwhile.

This book is not meant to be a tell-all story about anyone but me. I have written stories about my being bullied and the bully I was, from my perspective alone. When my father left, we children continued his legacy of abuse inside our household. In spite of it all, we ultimately succeeded in developing into fine and decent human beings. My siblings are the most important people in the world to me. Because I know their stories,

I have more respect for them than any humans on earth. When all is known, all is forgiven. Nothing in my words is meant to hurt anyone, especially them.

My story is extreme. Yours may not be. It may be more so. Or perhaps you were neglected and, therefore, cannot pinpoint an important event in your life, but feel traumatized all the same. Pain cannot be compared or measured; only the one who suffers can feel it. However, others can share in and witness the healing process.

I did not learn about the natural responses to grief, which include shock, anger, bargaining, depression, and acceptance, until twelve years after the shooting. I spent those twelve years believing something was terribly wrong with me. Learning this valuable information was enlightening, but realizing I'd lived without it for so long was devastating. We all suffer traumas, big and small. Children need to be taught the stages of grief early, *so they know when they are in them*. They need to know these responses are normal and natural. We adults know our suffering during a loss will end, but teenagers struggling with suicide have not had enough major losses to know their depression will lift and acceptance will come. It is up to us to cultivate this emotional intelligence in our young people.

Whether you are a person who has posttraumatic stress, loves someone who does, or just has had drama, trauma, and stress in your life, it is important while reading this not to compare yourself *out*, saying, "Oh, this has nothing to do with me." Rather, compare yourself *in*, by trying to find yourself in these pages. If I follow this practice, I find myself in everyone's story. I become a less judgmental, more tolerant and forgiving person. I soften.

The Blow

"No!"

Mom's tortured knocks on the door and simultaneous screams lift and pull me mechanically from the bathtub. The knocking comes from way, way up, at the top of the door. Maybe she has her arm over her head. Her knuckles rap and she shrieks, "Go get the Bolts! Go get the Bolts!" Whatever it is, she is alarmed to a frantic degree and I spring from the tub.

Judy scurries with me. *Why is she calling for our neighbors, the Bolts?* Wrapped in towels, we open the door, and step out into the urgency of Mom's calls. With our first steps, something jars us to a stop. We look down to see our feet, our toes beneath us, curling up from the deep puddle of blood pooled on the brown speckled linoleum floor. It is the warmth of the blood that is striking, spilling over our wiggling toes.

I swing my head to see the commotion in the living room. To my left is the picture that becomes ingrained in my head for the next twenty-one years, the most significant picture of my life. My mother is crouching on the hearth of the fireplace, almost in a ball, her head feeble and her body shaking. Her face is turned so I can only see one eye that I later describe as a "scared little bunny rabbit's" eye. It is bulging upward, fastened on the back of my nine-year old sister, Mary, who is standing in front of my mother, locked in a face-off with my father.

My father, panting, with the stiffest of arms wrapped around a long shotgun, with a maniacal look in his eye, is agitated, motioning his arms forcefully to his right while he roars at Mary, "Get out of the way! I'm going to kill your mother, you kids are going to an orphanage, and I'm going to jail for ten years!" He has already shot Mom once. She is squatting behind Mary, bleeding profusely.

Mary stands before him, her body stretched out, leaning forward, her chin jutting upward, three inches from the barrel of the shotgun. Her eyes are squinting, glaring straight into his. With her meanest might, she snarls, "No!"

He swerves the gun again to his right in a quick and forceful motion, "Get out of the way! I'm going to kill your mother, you kids are going to an orphanage, and I'm going to jail for ten years!"

From her same stance, same squinted eyes, same snarl, she gives another resounding "No!" with her chin jutting upward, holding steady, her eyes never leaving his.

"Get out of the way! I'm going to kill your mother, you kids are going to an orphanage, and I'm going to jail for ten years!" he roars down the barrel of the gun.

With one leg outstretched behind her, the other bent, slanting herself upward, her adrenaline is pumping. Her lungs are heaving, panting with breaths, her mouth is closed, and air is shooting from her nostrils. Mary does not move, except to sling this one word, once again, "No!"

"Get out of the way!" Using the exact same words he has each time, "I'm going to kill your mother, you kids are going to an orphanage, and I'm going to jail for ten years!"

It does not end. It is exactly the same, over and over. In the exact same angry, grizzly-gorilla stance, motioning the gun in a half moon circle to his right, he screams these exact same words of murderous intent.

Mary's defiant "No!" is exactly the same. The same stance, foot behind her, the same chin jutting up the barrel of the gun, the same three inches away, her same fierce eyes, trying to match his grizzly tone. Digging from the deepest parts of her little body, she shouts the same word, the only word she has.

Judy and I have stepped from the hallway into the living room, and are standing on the edge of the dining room. Judy is in front now, but she is turned, facing me. I am facing the three of them. I am watching all of this. Judy is watching me. Like a mirror of me, the two of us are facing each other with crinkled up, red faces, screaming with all our individual might. I can see her eyes, though her lids are wavering with her screams. She is staring straight into my eyes. I see her. I see her terror. I am looking back and forth, at this horrific picture of a violence I cannot comprehend, and then into Judy's green eyes. Wisps of blond hair are around her forehead, like mine, I am sure, so I can see my own wisps in her reflection.

There is no change in what is happening. My father makes the same motions, with his firm and fierce arms. He is eager to kill. Mary yells the same "NO!" straight up the barrel of the gun.

I do not know it then but a miracle is happening. I am watching a terrifying event, but I am also looking into Judy's eyes. Her face is moving but her eyes are not. They are crystal green. Her face is crinkled, but her eyes are not; they are steady. Her scream is shattering, but her eyes are still. She is wide-eyed now, frantic, as am I, but her eyes never leave mine. I do not know it then, but I am grounded in her eyes. Although her eyes are confirmation of my terror, when I look down into them I begin to see a peacefulness. Her eyes say, "Yes, this is happening! Here - see it in my eyes?" And I can. But I see something else. I know exactly what is happening before me. I am in present time. I cannot get away from this savage act. There is no pull to take me away, only the crystal clear mixture of calm and fear I see in her eyes. I am her. The picture of who she is, what I see, becomes who I am, how I see myself looking in those moments - in terror, but at deep peace at the same time. We know we are shaken to the core by what is happening, but there is something in her eyes, some place that is pulling me in and toward it, telling me this, what I am seeing in front of me, is not all there is. My mouth is open, I am screaming with her; my face is red and wrinkly, too. It must be, we are the exact same picture, reflecting back to each other what the other is seeing. She is my mirror.

"Get out of the way! I'm going to kill your mother, you kids are going to an orphanage, and I'm going to jail for ten years!"

"No!"

They repeat this dialogue fifty times. It is the length of time that will have the largest impact on me. Standing and screaming at the top of my lungs puts a stress on my body I cannot imagine, but the same space of time gives me the opportunity to see clearly that I can make a deliberate choice about where I want to be in these moments. I can be here with the violence, or I can stay grounded in Judy's eyes.

"Get out of the way! I'm going to kill your mother, you kids are going to an orphanage, and I'm going to jail for ten years!"

"No!"

I would say it was mechanical and rote, if it were not for the fury and murderousness of his eyes. His stance, his demonic state is anything but robotic. He is growling.

"Get out of the way! I'm going to kill your mother, you kids are going to an orphanage, and I'm going to jail for ten years!"

"No!"

Judy and I are still screaming, clenching our towels, our fists are rubbing each other's. Our eyes are connected. I'm glancing to my left, at this scene. My mother never changes either. She is whimpering; her eyes are bugged and bulging. His arms never lose their stiffness. His determination does not wane.

Then another miracle happens.

Mary changes her words. She is now exhausted, no longer forceful, as she says, "Daddy, look what you've done! I used to love you, but now I hate you! Look what you've done to my mommy. Look what you've done! I hate you. Look what you've done to my mommy. Daddy, I used to love you. Now I don't love you anymore."

Her eyes are softer and she is questioning. She does not say it, but her tone is "Do you *see* what you have done?"

There is a break in the tension that has held this scene together, a break in the maniac holding the gun. The glazed look is suddenly gone. His tight arms slacken, his elbows bend. There is an awareness that comes over him; he cocks his head to one side and he looks into Mary's eyes as she speaks. It is the moment of a miracle. Her eyes have not left his. She is giving him time to realize what he has done.

The magnitude sets in. How can it not? There is blood splattered everywhere. His wife is faintly shivering yet rigid and stiff, her eyes are wide open with alarm. Judy and I, who have been screaming non-stop, are now choking on our withering screams, our thick tongues. He squats and drops the gun. I hear it clank.

It would be years before I realized the third miracle that happened in this moment. In the deepest core of my being, this scene crystallized for me an utter faith that, if a little girl could bring down a maniac, any conflict could be resolved. Simpler than could ever be imagined, the most difficult of situations could be resolved with the right words and tone.

My mother is quaking. Her eyes are still bugged. It is the saddest picture I have seen. He goes to my mother and immediately begins wrapping his arms around her. He is picking her up but her legs are bent and wobbly and she is shivering. He is half carrying her; she is half walking.

Her bugged eyes dart around. I want her to look at me, but she does not.

He walks her around to the kitchen, past where Judy and I have been standing in the dining room. He leans Mom's right side onto the refrigerator. She is standing now, her body leaning on the refrigerator. He is frantically on the phone. The phone is attached to the wall, but has a long cord so that he can reach my mother. He calls his father. I hear him say, "I just shot Frannie." He hangs up. He calls the police. "I just shot my wife. Come get me."

While he is on the phone, Judy and I are in the same place we have always been, our feet planted on the floor of the dining room, only having moved slightly as my father passed by from the living room to the dining room, and into the kitchen with our mother. I am watching my mother lean on the refrigerator; I am aware of her breath. Her right arm is shredded like stretched chicken skin, a dangling rope hanging behind her; her right hand is attached to the end of these shredded pieces of roped skin. It is lying lifeless on the floor in front of Judy and me. I am staring at it. It is still. Her hand is dead.

While my father is on the phone, I am listening to my mother breathe as I take in this new scene. Then I do not hear her; I do not see her moving. She is still standing, barely, but her body is now slumped and still, her head now more a part of her shoulders. My father is reaching one arm out to hold her up, but I know now she is dead, like her hand, her body is lifeless. Her air is gone.

Then, like a little puff of fairy dust, her head pops away from the refrigerator, a fraction of a fraction of an inch, to the left. It is the most minute of movements, but not to a little girl who is watching for the slightest of any movement, knowing the stillness means certain death for her mommy. She has come back to life! Mom would later tell me in that moment she remembered her two thirteen year-old twin sons needed two number two pencils to take a test the next morning so they could get into the local Catholic high school.

My father is off the phone and wondering what to do. He lowers her to the floor in front of the stove. He realizes she is bleeding profusely. She is a nurse and she speaks to him. She is telling him to get towels, to apply pressure to the bleeding. She knows she has lost too much blood. He runs. He comes back with sheets. He is squatting now and I see him wind up her arm like a garden hose. He then presses the whole bundle of skin to her right side, where her arm is supposed to be, where the blood is coming from. He is wrapping the sheets around her and pressing them to her. I see her try to reach around with her left arm to apply pressure, but her attempt is weak and there is little strength in her. They are half lying, half sitting on the floor now, his arms around her. My dad is calmer. My mother is breathing in short crying huffs, trying to sit up, but her head slumps and she is swaying backwards as if she will fall. He holds her, rocks her.

We know it is a life or death situation. They are not aware of us, but we three girls are still standing in the dining room, and have been inching our way closer to watch the struggle to save her life.

There is a commotion at the front door. People are entering. Things begin to happen fast.

It is the police. My father reluctantly leaves Mom as they pull him away. They handcuff him from behind and walk him out the front door. His body is upright, and he is glancing behind him toward the people who have now gathered around my mom. The once white sheets are now masses of dark red.

Two men lift my mom, holding her up as if to take small baby steps. Her red corduroy house robe hangs, draping her in tatters. It looks like a Halloween costume that is cut for a hobo or scarecrow to wear, only this has not been cut. The gun has done this on its own, blowing it to bits, and I am immediately embarrassed for my mom that people are seeing her skin, her bra, her underwear.

Men in uniforms are flooding in and out of the doorway now, and medical personnel are on either side of Mom, walking her out to the ambulance. I see her hang her head. The feeling I get in this moment is that she is ashamed that her husband has shot her. Maybe she is just weak or has any of a hundred thoughts in her mind at this time, but the image of her head hanging down, as if not wanting to be seen, stays with me for many years, as if this, being shot and having police here, is something to be ashamed of.

I am back in my bedroom now. I am binding up a sock and leaning down to roll it up my foot when a policeman opens the door wider and says to us girls, "Put your clothes on. Everything is going to be okay." I will never forget the gentle tone of his voice. It was piercingly kind, but at the same time, I remember being embarrassed that our bedroom, with the clothes piled high atop the dressers, was a mess.

Having thoughts of being embarrassed about my mother's nakedness and about my room being messy in front of strangers always comforted me later. It informed me that even in the middle of this out-of-the-norm event, I must have still been a little bit normal. These were the very real flashes of thought running through the mind of a seven-year old in the midst of chaos.

A Blow of Another Kind

Soon we three girls are reunited with our three brothers at a neighbor's house, the Gentry's, where they have gathered after fleeing our house. I am sitting on the couch while everyone is scurrying about. There is clamor, talk, movement - the house is abuzz. Surprisingly, I feel safe. My brothers are there. Anywhere my brothers and sisters are is where I want to be. But the strangest feeling comes over me. Even though I am acutely aware of how secure I feel being here with my siblings, in a familiar house, I have a foreboding feeling I cannot shake. No matter how I try to convince myself I am safe and the worst is over, I know it is not.

How I knew, I cannot say, but if I had been asked by someone what I was thinking while I sat there on the couch at the Gentrys, I would have been able to say, "Something terrible is about to happen." As if it already hadn't!

Something terrible *was* coming.

Sure enough, soon my grandparents, our father's parents, are there to take the three of us girls to their home, six miles down the highway, and a thousand miles from this feeling of safety. The boys are old enough to remain with the neighbors. If only we are able to choose, we will surely pick staying with our brothers. Where we belong.

My memory of my life becomes crystal clear on this night and every day forward. I begin to remember the details of my life in living, vivid color, down to the exact words spoken, a dialogue I can script. But, although I remember the drive to my grandparents' house, I cannot remember the words said. Mary does. We three girls are crying in the back seat, while my grandparents in the front seat, hiss, "Stop crying!" I think my terribly foreboding feeling must be consuming me during this drive.

We are in their house. We three girls are sitting in the dark on the couch in the living room. Mary is between Judy and me, with her arms around us. I can feel her warmth, her love, her tenderness and worry, her still-panicked sense of urgency to protect us. She is shaking along with us. We are one entity as we quiver. Straight ahead is the long, living room, so dark I cannot see the other side; no lights are on. It is the blackness I stare into. To the right, the dining room is darkened, too, only there is a light shining into it from the archway door of the kitchen. This light is shining directly onto the ornate carvings of the mahogany buffet table on the left wall of the dining room.

Through the kitchen door, I see my relatives. My grandparents must be seated at the kitchen table, but I cannot see them because my aunts and uncles are standing around them, leaning over, listening to all that is being said at the table. It is the exact same stance I've seen many times, when these relatives play pinochle. I only hear mumbles, I do not know what is being said, and much time goes by. We little ones are shaking, whimpering. No one has come to us, no one has touched us, no one has hugged us, no one has cooed soothing words to us. We are in the very dark room. Mary is working hard to soothe us while the shock is setting into our nine, seven, and five year old bodies. I can see our six legs stretched out and dangling over the edge of the couch. We still have dried blood on us.

I am in shock and waiting.

Although not the worst to come, what happens next changes my life forever. My Uncle George, standing behind my grandparents who are seated at the dining room table, all at once, throws his head back, laughing wildly at something that is said.

Now that I am grown, I do realize that in times of enormous stress or sad events like funerals and wakes, when enough time goes by, adults begin to talk about things other than the crisis at hand. This fact I do not know as a seven-year old who has just seen my mother blown to tatters, bleeding on the floor, being carried away. I am still reeling from the pictures in my head. None of this – about adults gathering - do I know.

I only know that the moment I witness my uncle's head go back and hear his uproarious laughter, I turn to stare at the ornate carvings on the middle drawer of the buffet table. In this moment I say to myself, "I will never respect an adult just because that person is older than I am."

I feel an inkling of the rock I am to become.

It is time for us girls to go to bed. The relatives are gone now. Not one of them stepped into the darkened room where we sat on the couch. They came in the back door and went out the back door. I am confounded by this and, filling with venom, I begin to feel the poison of hate creep through my veins. I am running the water in the bright lights of the bathroom that separates my grandparents' bedroom from the guest bedroom where my sisters and I will sleep. I can see the water running down the drain as I wash myself. We three girls crawl into the bed, lying side by side. Maybe we doze off to sleep.

And then it happens.

What I see next will be a picture that haunts me for years to come. It will be years before I speak to Mary about this. When I do, I find she remembers seeing exactly what I see in these next moments.

Sometime, in the deep, dark dead of night I look up to see a black figure, silhouetted in black, walking toward me through the bedroom doorframe. It is black on black, but I see it vividly. There is not a sound in the night. It is my father. He walks into the guest bedroom and crawls into bed with the three of us girls. I freeze, scared my breathing will be heard. I remain frozen, not moving an inch for the rest of the night.

I do not know what jail is or what "being let out on bail" is. I do not know any of this. All I know is the dark figure coming toward me is the angry man who has hurt my mommy.

He has been let out on bail. And where does one go when he is bailed out of jail after shooting his wife? I guess one goes to his parents' home. That is what my father has done.

Mary is lying on the side of the bed closest to the door; I am lying in the middle. Judy is next to the wall, fast asleep. I do not know Mary is awake, I only learn this later. She, too, has become a frozen statue as my father lays his body down next to hers and falls asleep.

I do not sleep that night. I lie in complete horror. If I know fear, it is here we met. This is the night we become intimate. We are together in an endless standoff with each other. I cannot sleep or it will leap into me and keep me. As it is, its grip has me, but I do not know how much of me it has. I only know my life depends on my staying awake.

Sleeping soundly, my father does not wake. He does not molest us; he does not touch us inappropriately in any way, on this night – or any other. But if molestation is a violation of one's body, this incident in my bed caused me to relate to all others who have been encroached upon by a violator.

As ferocious as Mary had been earlier this evening, her body is now spent. There is nothing left in her with which to protest. I'd watched her become a wet noodle and turn back into herself after my father put down the gun. Anyway, how would two little girls know they had the right to sit up in bed and scream, "Get out! Get out!" loudly enough for people to come running and chase my dad and his crazy thinking away?

In these fear-sick hours of the night, while I wrestled with how utterly wrong this was, I lost the ability to protect myself. I would fail miserably at becoming appropriately angry for the next two decades. If my father did not know enough to protect us, or my grandparents did not know enough to protect us from him, how was I ever to learn how wrong this was? It only *felt* wrong. In the long hours that passed that night, I came to surrender a piece of myself to this wrong and helpless feeling – and in the exhaustion of it all, my victimhood was sealed.

My father left the next morning. There was talk of what to do with us.

Turns out, the police had asked my mother while she was on the operating table what she wanted to do – did she want to prosecute? This, they say, is something that should not be asked of a victim on the very night she is victimized. It would be many years before laws passed to protect the victim, relieving her of the responsibility to make decisions in a state of shock. Having come "back to life" to care for her children, my mother's first thoughts were of us. "Let him out so he can make money and feed the children."

He was let out, but he would never make money, and with that, he would never again have the privilege of feeding his children.

From the time my father was handcuffed at the house, taken away to jail for a few hours, and released the same night, was the only time he was incarcerated for this crime.

My father went to a mental hospital in town for one month. For the next five years he lived in Los Angeles, then Boston. He never sent child support, although we did get cards for birthdays with dollar bills inside. For the most part, he was out of our lives for good. At least physically.

Beforehand...
It would take years to piece it all together, but fitting together the puzzle

pieces of my life became something I was driven to do.

For the next ten years, I had no memory of my life before I stepped out of the bathtub on the night of "the shooting," as it was referred to in our family on the rare occasion it was mentioned. It was near the end of my high school years before memories and pictures from before the age of seven came back to me. It would be another ten years, when in therapy, that I began interviewing everyone I knew, who knew us, who knew anything at all about my parents, the shooting, beforehand, or afterwards. The smallest of details became beneficial to help me create the most complete picture, so I could somehow make sense of it all.

I do remember vividly several hours before the shooting, my mother picking us up from Brownies in the parking lot of the church. We girls were laughing and giggling with her because she had a new hairdo and we were saying our mother was the most beautiful woman in the world! My mom, whose brown hair was normally flat to her head, had it teased into a beehive! The sun bounced off of it and she was all smiles.

My mother was having a date with my father that evening. Before he came to get her, she told him over the phone that she had a surprise for him. The surprise was her new hairdo. When he arrived that night and found out it was only her hairdo and not dropping the divorce like he'd hoped, he told her he had a surprise for her.

But let's go back a bit.

My mother was an only child, born to a German immigrant father and a Lithuanian immigrant mother who settled in Northern Virginia, across the Potomac River from Washington, D.C. My grandmother had left her first husband who abused her, and my grandfather, who was very much in love with her, waited seven years for her divorce to become final before they could marry. My mother was their only child, born to them in 1928, in their later years. When my mother was five years old, her mother was finally, after many years of mental instability, taken to a home for the mentally ill, where she would remain for the next 47 years, until she died. My grandfather had done everything he could to keep the woman he loved in the home with them. When she took a log from the fire and threw it under the bed, he knew it was too dangerous to keep her there. The stress of losing her made his hair turn completely white. No one knew exactly what happened to her, what kind of illness she had, but soon after she was institutionalized, she became catatonic and remained that way until her death.

Our granddaddy was such a loving man that I later believed the love in our family must have trickled down from him. We grew up with his saying, "I see God in every blade of grass." Mom remained with her father for two years, going to public school, but not being cared for properly, while my grandfather worked. The next-door neighbor woman and my grandfather became lovers, and she suggested putting Mom into a boarding school several miles and a world away from my grandfather. Even though she felt truly loved by her adoring father, Mom was essentially raised by nuns in a Catholic boarding school in Washington, D.C. She loved the nuns and got a tremendous education but was never able to heal the effects of the double abandonment she'd suffered.

Mom studied hard and became a competent nurse.

My father was the middle child of five – two older sisters who became nuns, and two younger sisters who married and had children. His mother was a stern woman with thick ankles who was rarely affectionate. I remembered my grandfather as a cheerful man for the most part, always playing a game with the toothpick in his mouth: did he swallow it or not? It would disappear for long stints and then, uh oh! There it was again.

My mother and father met in the late 40's at Catholic University in Washington, D.C. Mom had not had much experience with men, just a few beaus. She and my father broke up once, but just when my mother felt she was over him, he came back into her life, asking to marry her. They married in Washington, D.C., and remained there until the twin boys, Carl and Jeff, were born; soon after, they moved to my father's hometown, Louisville, Kentucky.

Whenever I have spoken of the shooting and people learn I am from Kentucky, I can see them conjuring up backwoods people with bare feet, out in the boonies and mentally jumping to *Well, that's what those kinds of people do in Kentucky.* But my parents were highly educated people, raised in cities, then living in the suburbs in the 50's and 60's in Middle America. My father wore a suit and tie to work each day. One friend was surprised when he saw early pictures of my brothers wearing suits and ties and us girls wearing fancy dresses and hats. He assumed we'd always been very poor, which was definitely the case after my father left, but not before.

From the time my brothers were very young, my father was a harsh disciplinarian. He believed in heavy spanking and, when my mom begged him not to, he told her that *he* had been raised in a family, not she, and he would show her how a family was run.

Next, Aaron was born, then Mary, then me, and then Judy – all of us were two years apart.

If there were only one word to describe my father who had been an English and philosophy major in college, it would be charming. Everyone loved him. He was intelligent, talked to anyone about anything, and laughed often and with gusto. Until he came home.

To simply state it: my father was a raging alcoholic. He drank. He

raged. He beat his children. Once, in my late twenties, I was sitting at my older brother's kitchen table. I said to him, "Jeff, how often did our father beat us?"

He stopped abruptly, head tilted down, his soupspoon half way to his mouth, glaring at me over his glasses. "You're kidding, right?" as though I needed an answer to something completely obvious. Without dropping his spoon, his eyes steadily on mine, he very slowly said, "He beat us every single day."

Since Jeff was one of the oldest, he got beaten daily for nearly thirteen years. I was the fifth of six, so my memory was not as good as his.
I knew to take his word for it. The standard punishment meted out by
my father was that if someone did something wrong, he lined us all up,
oldest to youngest, took a belt and went down the line. Every time I see
the captain blow his whistle and line up his children in "The Sound of
Music," I think of my father. My father used a belt, a board, a switch, a
wooden spoon, a tree limb, whatever was handy.

I can see all six of us kids, walking around the living room, searching
the floor; I can feel the fear, his control over us as we look for any shred
or speck of dirt, his mantra being, "If you can see it, it's too big for the
vacuum." Our job was to make the floor "spotless" before vacuuming.
Another of his sayings was "You can get the jelly into the peanut butter,
but you can *never* get the peanut butter into the jelly." God help one of
us if we got the peanut butter into the jelly. When he asked a question
and we stammered, too afraid to answer, he stomped forward and yelled
in our faces, "Yes? No? Pee in your ear? Which one is it?" Whatever that
meant.

We children were united in a constant state of fear. When my father

was present, there was a sucking in of air among us, as if we were holding our collective breath, mentally communicating to each other not to make any quick or sudden movements, not to raise our eyes upward so as to disturb the heaviness of the load we so evenly balanced. There would be no tattling in this house. No child could have survived the guilt of knowing he had brought onto a sibling the hand of my father's wrath.

Usually we were hit together, while in a group, but there were times he singled out a child. One act of cruelty I could not think about for years without sobbing was the day he told Aaron, "If you do that one more time, I'm going to get a switch and whip you 100 times." Well, Aaron, being the little boy he was of about eight or nine, sure enough, did it again. My father flew out the door and got the thinnest, longest branch from our willow tree in the front yard, peeled off the leaves, and headed into the boys' bedroom. I heard my father whip and begin to count. "One! Two!" The cries coming from the room were so horrifying that I went to the door and opened it a crack. I saw little Aaron running around the room like a squealing pig, jumping up and over the top of the bunk bed and sliding down the wall behind it, running round and round the room as fast as he could while my father caught him with his whip on all sides of his body. He whipped and counted. "Twelve! Thirteen!" Knowing he would not stop until he reached one hundred, I closed the door and sat outside listening to Aaron's high-pitched, before-puberty screams and squeals. It was the saddest sad and the clearest love I ever felt toward one of my siblings.

There were times when my father was so displeased by something the boys had done, he pulled the car over and told the boys to get out and pull their pants down to their knees. There on the highway with cars passing, he whipped them for all to see.

Aaron told me, when we were older, of two occasions when he, my father, and my other two brothers were walking in the woods. My father beat Aaron until he was unconscious. He forced his two older brothers to leave him there on the path, high up on the ridge of our land, as the three of them walked away, back to our campsite down the hill. Aaron woke up alone.

One day I opened the medicine cabinet in my parents' bathroom, only to have the box of baking soda tumble out, spilling baking soda over the sink and beyond. I was so terrified that I did not spend the time to clean it up. Thinking that I would be caught in the process, I ran. Later, when my father saw it, he lined us up and asked for a confession from the culprit. He wanted to give a "demonstration" to the others, of what would happen to them if they also did something "bad." I could not speak; I remained still. I was terrified he would beat me mercilessly in front of my siblings. My silence caused all of us to get hit with the belt. In my guilt, I never told anyone what I'd done.

Often when my father got mad and was clearly moving to whip one of my brothers, I heard the brother beg, "Please, Daddy, just give me a demonstration!" The meaning was clear: if the child got a "demonstration" or a preview of "what was to come," it would cause him or her to stop doing whatever it was that bothered my father, so as not to get "the real thing."

The clearest first memory I have of making someone laugh, is the day my father saw me do something "wrong" while I was out on the screened-in back porch. I do not know what I did. I only know that to him it was wrong. He said, "Come here!" I, of course, was terrified and froze in my tracks. He came closer. I backed away. Again, he said, "Come, here!" as he was coming toward me. I backed away squatting, cowering in the corner and said, "Please, Daddy, oh, please, Daddy! Just give me an invitation!"

He burst out laughing and spun around to my brothers who'd been watching. Shirking off whatever I'd done, still laughing and shaking his head, he walked away. I'd meant, "Please, Daddy, give me a demonstration." Those older than I got the "joke." I did not. All I knew was I made my father laugh and the beating that I was about to receive had now vanished into thin air - like magic! This must have made quite an impact on me, because I later became a class clown and tried to wiggle my way out of things with humor. At the very least, I learned that one word, phrase, or sentence - said at the right time - could be very powerful.

When my mother's Aunt Stella died and left Mom money, my dad went to Canada to settle the will. I remember vividly my brothers gathering around my mother under the cigar tree in the backyard begging her to make our father leave. I could hear her saying to them, "So, you would like it like this all the time?"

"Yes, Mom, please," the boys begged. "Make him go away!" I did not know then what I was to learn later in life: if a father beats his son long enough, one day the boy will turn on the man and lash out at him with greater violence. It makes me wonder now if my brothers were afraid of what they might do if my father were to stay and continue beating them. There must have been so much going on in their thirteen-year old minds.

Where was my mother during all of the beatings? Whimpering to the side. Always there, not far off, whimpering, crying, and pleading for my father not to hit his children. But he did and there she stood. Crying. And into her arms we fled after a beating, crying.

I think my mother knew the time was right. She had to do something.

It is true that my mother was clearly a codependent, a term used for the person who enables the other to continue his raging alcoholic behavior. She should have left him early in their marriage, as the children came. But I will give her this: she tried. I don't think one can ever underestimate the power one's religion holds over some people. My mother was a devout Catholic. Her own father lived with another woman, yet would not divorce his still mentally ill wife, who by then had lived in an asylum for over thirty years. My mother was raised by nuns in a Catholic boarding school. She was awakened by nuns in the morning and put to bed by nuns at night. She studied with the nuns and she played with the nuns. Her best friend grew up and became a nun. Mom went to a Catholic nursing school. We went to church every Sunday and she enrolled her children in Catholic school.

My mother went to priest after priest to tell each one of them of my father's brutality and that she wanted to leave him – which, of course, meant divorcing. Each priest told her the same thing: if she divorced, she, along with her children, would be banished from the Catholic Church, from all she'd ever known. I believe it was more than my mother could endure.

But on that day in the back yard, I could see my mother's eyes taking in the expressions on my brothers' faces. They were begging. Begging to have the beatings end. Maybe she, too, sensed the two thirteen-year-old boys were reaching the place where their suppressed anger from years of abuse could get the best of them. Apparently, my father had already received a broken rib from a "playful" wrestling match.

And so, though fearful of my father's rage and the prospect of being banished from the church, my mother told my father she wanted a divorce.

He moved out of the house – the house he bought, the house where he sat at a desk working from home, doing much of his insurance work when he wasn't at the office, the house where his wife lived, the house where his six children lived, the house where he'd lived for twelve years.

Now living away from us, my father had fits of rage where he stalked us, driving up and down the street. My mother packed us all into the car and took us to drive-in movies night after night. I can still smell my fear as I am sitting on the floor board of the car behind the driver's seat, my knees balled up to my chin as we are leaving our driveway. My father is lurking about; I am told to stay down.

Moving from this state of fear, literally to a state of joy where I watched Julie Andrews' portrayal of Mary Poppins in the movie of the same name and Maria, the singing nun, in "The Sound of Music," had

a significant effect on my life. Even today while I am singing and dancing in my classroom, I feel her presence. She was just a character in a
film, one I saw after escaping a brute, but to me, she was reality. After a
summer full of fleeing our father, pulling into a graveled parking space,
sitting on the hood of the car or in chaise lounge chairs, watching these
happy movies, I sensed the difference between good and very bad.

Sometimes a lie can hold back danger. Most summer nights at the
drive-in were a dollar fifty a carload, so we were able to afford that, but
on regular nights the price was $3 for adults and kids under twelve were
free. One "regular price" night driving through the gate, the ghost of fear
keeping us all company, we kids heard the ticket taker ask if there were
any kids over twelve in the car. "No," our mother lied, and the ache it
gave to each of us as we drove through the entrance, having listened to
our saintly mother, was almost palpable. We each knew then that it was
either lie, or turn the car around and be back "out there" where he would
surely find us. But for now, we were safe among strangers, here to enjoy
our family's brief respite from reality. Lying was wrong, but I learned
sometimes it was a dire necessity.

Even though my father was living outside the house now, the priests
encouraged my mother to "date" him and try to work things out for the
sake of their marriage and the children. Part of that working out was
going to meetings – AA for him and Al-Anon for her. He picked her up
for a "date," they went to their meetings, out to eat afterwards, and then
returned home where he dropped her off.

On that particular night, the night of the shooting, my mother, after
seeing all of us so thrilled about her new hairdo, told my father on the
phone that she had a surprise for him when he picked her up.

When he arrived before she had finished dressing for the evening, my
mother came out of the bedroom in her fine-lined, red corduroy robe,
and showed him her hairdo. When he realized that the "surprise" she had
for him was only her hairdo, he became very angry. Possibly he'd been
expecting her to "drop" the divorce proceedings. He gathered my three
brothers and my mother around the dining room table and told them he
had a surprise for them.

My mother thought his surprise for her was that he was going to give
her the record album, "Camelot," a film they'd seen together.

He went back into my parents' bedroom and found a gun under the

1-21-67

Husband Charged With Shooting Mother of 6

A mother of six children was wounded last night with a blast from a 12-gauge shotgun. Her husband was charged with the shooting.

Mrs. ███████ Vessels, 38, of ███████ Drive, was reported in fair condition today at General Hospital. She suffered wounds in her right arm, right side and chest.

Her husband, ███████ Vessels, also 38, was charged with malicious shooting and wounding, and is to appear Monday in Quarterly Court. He is in Jefferson County Jail.

Police said Mrs. Vessels was shot at her home about 7:25 p.m. The couple's children, ranging in age from 5 to 13, were in another part of the house, police said.

Louisville Courier Journal article January 21, 1967

wrapping paper of the closet floor, the only gun my mother had not removed because she thought it was a BB gun. He reappeared with a 12-gauge shotgun. When he got back to the dining room table where the four of them had faithfully remained, he perched the gun up on the table, in a fashion that led Jeff to believe he was going to give them a lesson in cleaning a gun.

It all happened in a matter of seconds. My father announced to the boys, "I'm going to kill your mother, you kids are going to an orphan-

age, and I'm going to jail for ten years!" With that, he raised the gun and pulled the trigger.

My mother had been seated directly across from him, in fact, in my seat at the dining room table. He lifted the gun and pointed it at her chest. As she realized what was happening, she immediately stood and turned to her left to run. The force of the blast went through the right side of the middle of her body, blowing up her arm and torso. Shotgun pellets were driven into the dining room walls, into my brothers, and into all parts of my mother's body.

My brothers ran. My nine-year old sister, Mary, was down the hall, in my brothers' room, ironically, watching "Gunsmoke." Running, Carl burst into that room, frantically locking the door. As he jumped out the window, my father kicked the door down. He stood in the doorway, holding the shotgun at the ready, but his prey had fled. Our mother stood behind him, holding her side, saying, "Don't hurt the children!" Distracted by our mother, he ignored Mary.

Each brother sped off to a different neighbor's home – one to the Gentrys,' one to the Thatchers,' one to the Chathams.' And, interestingly enough, my mother called out the name of the Bolts,' yet a fourth neighborhood home. We knew all our neighbors well, and the four of them instantly thought of four different families. What this signified to me later was that, similar to our church parish, we were very closely connected to our neighbors. My mother was a pied piper to all the children in the neighborhood and a friend to all the adults. She was known as one of the most loving people that many in our neighborhood and church had known. The shooting devastated them.

As far as the sound of the "blast" of the gun that night, I did not hear it. Whenever I was in the bathtub as a child, whoever I was with, we played underwater. We were always having contests to see who could stay under the longest. We went down side by side and then turned our heads sideways to open our eyes, blow bubbles, and come up laughing. Judy and I even kissed underwater and hummed songs to guess which ones they were. Since I was only one wall and five feet away from the blast, I think I must have been underwater at the time.

Neighbors heard it in all directions and reported the gunshot sounded like a tin trashcan being thrown against a brick wall. My first memory was my mother's knocking on the door and her screams, "Go get the Bolts!"

Those words and screams I heard, and the pictures I saw next stayed in my head every day from that day forward. At some point in my life I heard people say that advertisers filtered pictures of popcorn and fizzling colas into movie frame pictures – so fast that no one could consciously notice them – so that moviegoers would jump up and run to the concession stand. Subliminal persuasion it is called. No matter where I was beyond that night, no matter what I'd been previously thinking or enjoying, the "blood scene," as I'd later call it (to distinguish it from what I called the "bed scene" that same night with my father), was to "pop up" in my head several times a day. For no rhyme or reason, it was there. And it did not leave. Each and every day for the next 21 years, I was visited by the vision of my mother squatting and whimpering on the hearth, her eyes bugged out like a scared rabbit's, Mary's little body leaning in, her chin jutting up the barrel of the shotgun that was held so forcefully by my fierce and maniacal father.

My Script
And so, at the age of seven, my script was written for me. It went some-

thing like this: when a man loves you, you cannot leave him. If you try, he will stalk you. If you really decide to leave, he will blow you to shreds, not get in any trouble for it, and will come back to your bed and sleep with you. Then *he* will leave *you*.

This could very well have become my belief system had I not been slapped into present time by the peace I found looking into Judy's eyes that night. In the midst of all the horror playing out in front of the fireplace, demonstrating on an intimate level the craziness this world could produce, I found a place to go that told me none of what I was seeing was real. As I looked into the ocean of Judy's eyes, the vastness there was like traveling in suspended animation through space. I never left the room, but I was being shown a world much bigger than mine. Had this time holding her eyes been a few moments, it might have been only a glimmer, a glance of recognition this love existed, then vanishing into thin air, and thus from my memory. But I now believe it was because of the length of time of this ordeal that this force was able to take hold of me and pull me to it, pull me into believing it. Screaming, my eyes flashed back and forth as if playing a game of eenie, meenie, miney, mo, moving from the standoff at the gun to Judy's eyes. This happened quickly at first, until my eyes began to slow down and settle in one place. It was as if I was being asked to pick. One force was going to extinguish me, the other sustain me. I picked what I saw in Judy's eyes.

I'd never asked a question, but was given an answer. It was as if I was being fed a lie, yet simultaneously being shown the truth. My life was impacted in such a way I became keenly aware of these two worlds, narrowing my focus like a laser beam on the cruelties and kindnesses of others. Examining them would become my life's work.

It was going to take gallons of ink and years of editing, revising, and rewriting to carve out a brand new script, but I had a touchstone: Judy's eyes.

What a Rascal!

Sometimes love transcends all else. From my grandparents' home, we three girls were taken across town to my Aunt Mary and Uncle Joe's house. They were not really our aunt and uncle, more like cousins. They had five children who were actually our second cousins. We lived with them for the first three weeks after the shooting, while the boys remained

Judy and Lynnie

at home with neighbors. Being with these relatives was much different than being in my grandparents' home. I felt safe with them. Uncle
Joe was a firefighter who worked 24 hours and then came home for 48
hours. All of us kids would be in the living room watching television
when Uncle Joe came home exhausted. He'd take off his shoes and put
his feet up on the ottoman. It was the worst odor anyone ever wanted to
smell, and all of his children yelled, "Peeueww, Dad!" harassing him and
running from the room screaming. It was a wonderful feeling to see kids

who could harass their dad for something that truly was disgusting, all in good humor. Uncle Joe just laughed and took it in stride. Too tired to move, he now had the room to himself.

Aunt Mary took us in like we were her own. She was kind, loving, and strong. She had a unique voice that was easy to listen to. She was the ruler of the house, a disciplinarian, and all in a good way. Living with her, I never felt like I was in the way or unwelcome. In fact, I sometimes heard her making it clear to her own children that they were to treat us with kindness and respect, not that they would not have, but she was making sure we three girls were comfortable. It must have had an effect on me, too, knowing that one of the five children was not their biological daughter or sister, but someone they had lovingly "adopted" because she needed a home. Watching how she fit in so readily and easily to this family made it easier for me to feel at home.

The sweetest thing that happened to me in those early days after the shooting was Uncle Joe sneaking each one of us girls, one by one, up to the hospital room to visit our mom. Children were not allowed in the ward where my mom lay in her bed. This gentle and kind man knew, more importantly than any hospital rule, these little girls who had last seen their mother bleeding to death, needed to see her in person. No voice over the phone would lessen the questioning or prove to them more than seeing her in the flesh that yes, she was alive and that yes, she would survive. There he was, motioning for us to be as quiet as possible, hiding us under his trench coat, carrying us onto a crowded elevator, walking calmly down the hallway, entering our mother's room, gently closing the door. All so that we could see her lying in her bed, hear her breathing and her sweet voice cooing to us, and feel her soft kisses on our lips. The wisdom he showed in that one act created a place for him in heaven, in my seven-year old mind. I can still feel the bounce of his step and the beating of his chest, hear the rumbling of his coat, and smell the patient determination in his soul as he broke an administrative rule. In those moments, I came to value and understand the rascal in every one of us.

Hmmm… this must be different…
Aunt Mary was a third grade teacher at a Catholic school nearby. Judy had not started school yet, I was in second grade, and Mary was in

fourth grade. Mary wanted to stay with Aunt Mary in her third grade classroom. Judy stayed with them and played at the tables in the back of the classroom. I chose to go into the second grade classroom. Even though we only stayed three weeks with our aunt and uncle, none of us knew in advance how long we'd be there.

My strict nun teacher would not allow us to talk to each other in class, although one little girl smiled at me with inviting curiosity. The hallway to the lunchroom was narrow and dark. The playground was walled-in brick. Outside on the playground that first day, the same little girl tossed me a ball and said, "Why are you here?"

"My father shot my mom," I replied.

The little girl, tickled by this, rolled her eyes, threw her head back while swatting the air and laughed, "Oh brother!"

She did not believe me. I froze.

It would be seven years before I'd utter those five words again.

In wanting to fit in, I laughed it off, too, and went on playing ball with her.

That very afternoon I started a relationship with myself, really with my eyes, that remains today. I went into my aunt's attic, one with a multitude of dusty old household items, the kind of attic that was a delight to play inside, only on this day, it was not that kind of day. I sat down, cross-legged, at the base of a full-length mirror. I leaned in very closely and looked straight into my eyes, conscious now of the eyes that Judy had been looking into just days before, during the horror of the shooting.

I looked very carefully this time; I studied my eyes. I took my time. This was now myself I was talking to, no words just yet. I searched my eyes. I thought and thought. I wondered if I could find in *my* eyes, the peace I'd seen in Judy's. The conversation started - words, thoughts, and ideas were spinning in my head, spilling out from my eyes, there in the mirror. My eyes reached into their upper right corners, searching the room around me for an answer to one thought that kept repeating itself. *Hmmm… Hmmm… this must be different… Maybe everyone doesn't have a father that shoots her mother… This must be different… Hmmm….*

The little girl laughed at me when I told her the truth. I was keenly aware of the fact that I did not want to be laughed at. The essence of the conversation in my head after that was how I was going to handle this in the future. The answer I decided was that I would just not talk about it.

When I think of that day and those moments and what that decision later meant, I see that that was the perfect time for someone to sit down with me and ask me what I was thinking. Today in our society, counselors step into the lives of victims and encourage them to talk at crucial times. This was my crucial time.

Instead, I had this conversation with myself, and the choice I made that day only caused me to become more and more sick. I learned later the expression "We are as sick as our secrets." I kept my secret whenever I was away from my family, and it was all to prevent anyone from ever laughing at me again.

Life in the Fog

The strict routine at my Aunt Mary's Catholic school was brief and uneventful and, I think, the structure was good for the beginning of what I call the "fog" of my life. For the next seven years, I only saw the fog in front of me. There was no horizon, no imagining the future, no arms-up-running-wildly-into-the-future kind of thinking or acting. I can best describe it as a thick, dense state of being, one that weighed me down. My future and my past were shown to me, step by step, the past weighing me down with the flickering "blood scene," the future only appearing in glimmers of what could be around the corner, never far away. Whatever future of mine stood on the other side of this fog was blocked off. Getting through a day was like trudging through a muddy swamp.

Severely traumatized, I would not breathe a word of it.

No one mentioned the shooting. No one asked me a question about it. It was as if it never happened. All the while, the blood scene and bed scene repeatedly fired off in my head, no matter where I was, no matter with whom. These were my pictures now, and I could share them with no one.

It was a beautiful and sunny day, the day we girls came home from Aunt Mary and Uncle Joe's house. I had missed the familiarity of my brothers. The separation was painful, and now we were all back home. But our home was much different from the time I'd left it. The police had gathered and walked us out through the blood and turmoil as we passed the watching eyes of our neighbors. Quickly, our neighbors and the men and women of our church stepped in to wash away the ghastly night. Cleaner than clean, many objects in my house that had never caught my eye did so now. Above the kitchen cabinets, my mother kept her punch bowls and shiny glassware, wedding presents. As I walked through the kitchen, each one sparkled brightly, much to my delight.

The walls were clean, puttied, sanded and painted white. No more pellet holes that had sprayed the walls of the dining room and kitchen. The floors shone. The linens were clean. The whole house smelled new.

There was no blood anywhere. No bright red, warm, splattered, puddled or drag-marked blood anywhere. Its wretched smell was gone. Washed clean.

It is hard to explain the overwhelming feeling of gratitude I felt as a little girl of seven upon seeing this. I know now how it feels as a grown woman when I am tired and feel like I cannot do one more thing, let alone an enormous task, and a companion or co-worker comes along and recognizes that I need help and reaches out to do the entire task for me. I know that feeling of relief and the feeling of being loved and the love I feel for that person in that moment.

The feeling as a little girl living in a fog already, as someone who could not have seen that far ahead, had never even thought one way or the other about what to expect when I walked back into the house, but with stunning clarity I felt the importance of this homecoming present. Others had the forethought for me. How utterly kind and excruciatingly compassionate. It was the first of many of the strong, full-of-impact moments of kindness the people of our parish bestowed on my family and me.

I wanted to know exactly who made the punchbowl sparkle. I walked around at church activities for years wondering, *Was it her?* And then looking to someone else, *Hmmm… maybe it was her?* In all of the silence and sadness I would have after that, I thought it would be so comforting to just be able to walk up to a woman in my church and say, "Was that you who cleaned up my house? I just want to thank you." Whoever she was, surely she would sense my depth of gratitude. I just wanted so badly to connect with someone who'd seen what I'd seen. Surely I would see the horror in her eyes that I'd felt at seeing all the blood. She would look at me and we would shake our heads and just know. We wouldn't have to say much. But I would have someone who knew that part of me.

It was the beginning of my longing for someone to know that part of me.

On this day another pattern began – one of experiencing deep joy and deep pain within, deep joy at the kindness of others, deep sadness and pain over cruel acts of others. The joy I could stand. The cruelty or sadness, I responded to with anger.

Shortly after returning to my home on this first day, I stepped back onto my front porch. Walking through the grassy gully of my front yard were two neighborhood boys. They stopped to talk in a whisper. They looked up at me and continued their whispering. I felt my body harden like a rock. My fist clenched. And then, the unthinkable happened. They looked back at me and laughed.

It was as if my life had been threatened by two little birds and I was now a Tyrannosaurus rex. I did not flinch; it was primal. I was running at a pace with such force, they did not stand a chance of getting away. They ran, but only got to the hedge that divided my yard from that of our neighbors. I caught the first one, and in an instant I was on top of him, my knees on either side, beating him in the face with my fists, pummeling hard with no let up in sight.

There was blood when I finished. I walked away calmly with no remorse. There was a sentence in my head that spoke to me like an oath: *No one laughs at my family.*

To this day, I do not know if the boys were discussing my family or me when they laughed. I only know that this is how the world was colored for me now. Laughing at someone else's pain was a crime.

Welcome Back

I went back into my second grade classroom and to my teacher, Sister Conchedda, Sister Cheddar Cheese to us kids. Never a word was said to me regarding the shooting. That is how it remained over all my school years. Yet one thing did happen that made me sense Sister Conchedda felt for me. Each day a child, not necessarily a different child, was allowed to wash the chalkboards. It was considered the highest honor to be asked because it was the task each child wanted desperately to do. It was now almost March and I, along with many others, had never, as yet, been chosen to do this task. At the end of the first day I arrived back in class, Sister Conchedda asked me if I'd wash the board for her.

It was a small thing, but a sweet gesture coming from a woman one would hardly call sweet. The next day she asked me to do the same thing and I did, and after that, the chore went back to another child. At the end of the year there were still several children who were never asked to wash the board. I knew it had been Sister Conchedda's way of saying, "I know you have been through a hard time and I want you to feel special for a day or two. Welcome back." She never spoke those words and she did the best she could, but it was one of the first omissions of words by an adult that had a profound effect on me. I sensed there was something terribly wrong when a tall and powerful adult was not able to say words to a tiny child who could have used them so badly.

I began to wonder about words after that. Just what would create an inability in a person to say them, when they, to me, were so clearly needed?

Mom was home from the hospital, and the seven of us were living in the same house again. Years later I learned that several of my mother's college buddies had offered to adopt one or two of her children. I did not see it at the time, but I did witness my mother's re-telling of her response to the offerings by her friends. To see the look on her face turn into that of a fierce lioness was truly a sight. *No one* was taking her children. No doubt about it, our mother loved us.

Mom came home in a cast she wore for the next two years. Believe it or not, before long she went back to school to get her RN degree, cast and all. We went on food stamps for one year and my three older brothers worked at the local grocery stores and car washes. The church, specifically the Saint Vincent de Paul Society, helped us with needed items, and the canned-food drive items collected at schools were directly funneled to our house. We were together, and we got by, thanks to our own hard work and the constant generosity of others.

On the night of the shooting, my mom's arm had been damaged beyond use. Two famous hand surgeons had been flown in to work on her arm and hand. She was eventually given the first artificial elbow they created. She was their guinea pig and she became quite a celebrity in the "arm" world. Mom would have over three-dozen surgeries in the next three decades. I stopped counting at forty-three surgeries.

My First Dot

As I grew up after the shooting, I recognized other people's kindnesses as profound acts. They were, in fact, so powerful that in my adulthood I began to refer to them as "dots." With every verbal or demonstrative kindness bestowed on me, it seemed like my whole internal world slowed down, just so I could take in every inch, every morsel, reliving every second of it as often as I could. It was much later that I realized I began to build my life on the kindnesses, the "dots," of others. And so I began to refer to it as "connecting the dots" to build my life. No matter what pictures remained in my head, always seeming to pull me backwards, it was these dots that pulled me forward, just like I was pulled into Judy's eyes. It was the power in the dots that convinced me they had to be more real than any bad pictures that remained in my head.

Because her wisdom had such a dramatic impact on me, I think of Mrs. Warren as my first dot.

Whenever school was in session, and my mother was having another surgery, I stayed with Mrs. Warren. She and her family were members of our church, and it was easy for me to get to and from school from her house. There was a Mr. Warren and two older, teenage children. Since Mrs. Warren did not work and my world then was so different from that of teenagers, I spent most of my time just with her. By now, during my stays with them, I was eight, nine, and ten years old.

It happened on the first day I arrived at her house for one of my stays. Her house was big, with a basement and long, uncluttered countertops in the kitchen. Everything was in its place. On that day I walked into the bathroom and saw electric toothbrushes. In my fascination, I must have wanted to try one out!

I was standing in the middle of her living room when Mrs. Warren approached me. She was beautiful – dark, black hair, ruby red lips, the sweetest eyes. She leaned from the waist and stopped at eye level with me. Between our two sets of eyes, she held up the electric toothbrush. It was covered in Oreo cookie crumbles, the snack she'd fed me earlier.

As soon as she held the cookie-crumb-filled toothbrush in front of my face, I froze. She looked into my eyes and then back at the bristles of the brush and said, "Lynnie, did you use this toothbrush?" She looked me straight in the eyes. My fear was intense. I looked straight back into her eyes and shook my head, without blinking. I could tell she saw an eerie fear in me that, up until this point in her life, she may not have seen. Confused, she pressed on, "Are you sure you did not use this toothbrush?" And with every certainty that my little body could muster, I shook my head in the direction of "No" again.

I do not think she was even mad when she approached me, but I do think she was out to get a confession, similar to the likes she'd surely gotten from her own older children. What I do know is in me she saw something that changed her mind. She saw a child who'd been beaten, and who was fearful that a beating was coming. I sensed she saw that the fear of being beaten was as hard for me as living through it, and in that intimate moment she saw with clarity the essence of who I was: a little bundle of fear. It was the first real intimate moment I'd ever had with someone who was not a member of my family. She looked at me, and I looked at her and in those very brief moments of time, I knew that she knew that I knew that she knew my story.

She lowered the electric toothbrush to her side, and she let it go.

A funny thing happened. In the moment she let go of her desire to get a confession, I let go of something, too: not everyone in this world is going to hurt me if I do something wrong.

And if the power of that moment had not been enough, its full force was laid upon me on my next trip to the bathroom. There in the mirror, I had Oreo cookie crumbs all over the outside of my mouth and in my teeth.

To this day, her act of letting go is my definition of kindness.

Our Church Community

Our church was called Our Lady of Consolation, or OLC for short. In 1967, when the shooting occurred, few around us had heard of a couple divorcing. Certainly there had been no "shooting" any of us had ever known about. In our community, we were the first.

I do not know how others cope with this sort of thing now. Certainly divorcing and shootings are much more prevalent in our society. I only know that in the fog where I lived for so many years afterwards, there were figures of all kinds stepping in to lend a helping hand. When a finance company came to our house with a moving van and began carrying out our bunk beds, our washer, our dryer, and other pieces of furniture onto the front yard, Father Dunstan came to stand on the sidewalk, his arms wrapped around my mother, holding her while she cried. I can see the frozen food being taken from the freezer and put into cardboard

boxes. The freezer and countless other items were being re-possessed. I can feel the humiliation of it all as the neighbors walked by in real or imagined curiosity.

But it was only a matter of hours before many of these items were returned. My Aunt Mary paid the finance company and my mom repaid her over the next several years. Phone calls were obviously made to others and the Vessels family was being helped by the Saint Vincent de Paul

Society and countless others who pitched in.

OLC was my school and my church. Each morning before school, Monday through Friday, we started the day by going to Mass. The routine and structure of a parochial school was very grounding and I received a solid educational foundation. I felt comfortable with all my teachers and these people were stepping-stones for me during my years in elementary school. Each Sunday and at church events I saw the same adults. I did not have to learn their names; I came to know them over time. That everyone knew and loved my mother was a great comfort and gave me an identity I needed since, while living in the fog, I had so few skills to identify myself.

Through these years, I labored, dragging my mud behind me, never able to escape the pictures in my mind. The endless barrage did not leave me alone. But I often stared into the sky and had wonderful thoughts, seemingly quite separate from whatever was going on around me. I felt the most remarkable amazement of life. Years later, a dear friend described this as "havingness." It is a feeling that comes over us, perhaps when seeing a beautiful sunset or an act of nature, when we feel like everything is right with the world. I'd often be filled with knowing - right then and there - I had exactly what I needed for all my life. There was no more wanting or wishing. I knew it was all there in a bundle of multitude. Joy.

One morning in the fourth grade while standing on the concrete playground, I had such a feeling. I looked up into the familiar white gray sky of winter with gratitude swelling up from within me. This time it was accompanied by words of utter clarity. "My father shot my mother for a reason and I am going to do something with this." I was bursting with joy in that moment. I find it fascinating that although my anger would later come cascading out of me, I was never bitter about the shooting. Someone once said of me, years into my adulthood, he'd never seen me as wanting pity.

I did not know my purpose yet, but I knew that each day of my life I was filled with both the intense pain of reliving the blood scenes in my head, and simultaneous joyful thoughts of havingness. Two very extreme emotions emanated from me. Each one I could feel to my core. Although I knew nothing of the spiritual implications of violence, I knew I was to do something with being shown so much love in the midst of so much horror. Of this, I was sure.

My spiritual beliefs have morphed from my early teachings in the church, and I no longer call myself Catholic, but I have only good feelings about its members. I'm not sure Our Lady of Consolation Church could have had a better name.

One Hour

I said I never had any counseling after the shooting, but that is not altogether true. I did have one hour. Perhaps because she'd seen me acting unusually, my mom took me to see a social services person named Mr. Walsh. He was simply a tall man with black hair in an office. We visited him when we went downtown to pick up food stamps.

On this occasion, Mr. Walsh asked me to sit in a long and deep dollhouse and play dolls. He and Mom talked between themselves. Unbeknownst to me, they were watching me interact with the dolls. This one hour of Mr. Walsh watching me play with dolls was the extent of my counseling after the shooting.

Finding Our Way

Mom went back to work, and the boys were left to look after us much of the time. Although there was a true sense of relief when my father left and we were free of his abuse at home, I can't say the abuse stopped there. We were three younger girls living in a house with three older boys, each boy having been subjected to heinous acts of abuse by my father before he left.

The boys were filled with rage. The abuse they had endured for so many years, my mother's inability to stop it, the witnessing of the shooting, the guilt in not having been able to save her, and having run from the house, left them angry. Survivor's guilt, my mom called it. No one blamed the boys for what was the natural thing to do. The fact that they were different from their peers and now had to work to help support their family, to put their dreams such as sports and recreation on hold while we eked out an existence, had to be stressful for my brothers.

It's not surprising that there was a lot of controlling and abusive behavior meted out as the days and years went by, each of us trying to piece together a life that had already been shattered inside our home.

Using the two words, "the shooting," was the extent of our reference to that night, but if it was ever talked about beyond that, it came from the three of us little girls in questions directed toward our mother: "Are you mad Pops shot you, Mom?" "Do you still love him?" "Do you wish you never married him?" "Do you hate him?"

Her answers were always the same: "Your father is an alcoholic, and this is what the disease of alcoholism can do to a family" and "I do not love him anymore in the way I did when I married him," and "If I had never married him, I would never have had you, and I would not trade you for anything in the world," and "I could never hate someone who gave me you. Your father is a part of you, and I love you with all my heart."

Amazing.

This provided much comfort and peace in our family, as it did not bring on the outward rage that each of us might have felt at the thought of what he'd done. I did learn later in therapy that it would have been better for my mother to model some healthy anger toward my father after the shooting, part of the natural progression of grieving the loss of her husband, her arm, their livelihood, and family dreams, but that was not who she was. One afternoon I was at my girlfriend's house and heard her mother refer to her husband as a "prick." With her spewing that one word about a man who I saw as such a loving husband, father, and provider, I came to appreciate the mother I had.

While there was a lot of joy in our household – lots of talking at the dinner table about all kinds of topics, particularly whatever was on the news that night, sitting around laughing at the television, playing in the yard together, camping trips and trips to Washington, D.C. to visit Granddaddy and Grannie's – there was also lots of anger.

In our earlier days each boy had been assigned to look after a particular girl. Jeff helped Mary, Carl helped Judy, and Aaron helped me. They made sure we were bathed, clothed, and generally looked after, such as holding our hands when crossing streets. It seemed the boys resented that my father had been easier on the girls and so when he left, that was not to remain the case.

Now my mother worked long hours, many days the 7-3 shift and immediately the 3-11, as a nurse in a hospital in town. She hired babysitters for us, but they rarely stayed long, so my brothers watched us while Mom was at work. My brothers did the best they could with their own angry minds and brewing thoughts of how to survive as men in this world. But I would not know life without a constant threatening presence until the last brother moved from the house.

Mary was as fearless with my brothers, as she'd been with my father. When Carl came to attack her, she planted her two palms, fingers splayed, in his chest and shoved him across the room. With this same brother, I cowered in fear when he moved angrily toward me. It was these two different types of reactions I began to study as an adult. Mary had forcefully said no to the gun, and she was able to shove across a room any strong brother coming at her. I stood by screaming on that night and continued to feel that terror when threatened. I called that my victim stance, and it was something I later set out to consciously heal.

Jeff was the main disciplinarian. He had a terrific sense of humor, spoke in funny voices often, and had a hearty laugh. But when Jeff needed a reprieve from the annoyance of us three girls, he put us under the beds in our room. Judy and I went under the bunk beds, where we, at least, fit. Mary went under the separate bed that was hers, but with the springs being so low, she had to squeeze herself under there. This made it a hundred times worse because she was already being called fat. My brother left us there for hours, sometimes five or six. If that were not cruel enough, he came into the room and threw items at us, as hard as he could.

For some reason, I was the one he kept under the bed the longest. Maybe I was the most difficult for him to cope with, I do not know. I only know that after he let the other two girls come out from under the beds, and my mother was home from work, I lay under the bed for hours still yelling and screaming and begging to be let free. Even when I knew my mother could hear me, she did not come. I could only assume that the stress on everyone was so excruciating, that each person had to think only of him or herself. Still, I wondered why I was singled out. When I was under the bed, lying there all those hours, my tears long dried, I'd hear a voice. "It's okay, Sweetheart. I love you. Everything will be okay."

This happened so frequently, my being forced under the bed with my constant loud screaming, I began to have chronic throat problems as a child. In my adulthood, doctors pondered over my damaged vocal cords. I wondered if the stress on my throat might have even started on the night of the shooting, given the length of time I stood screaming.

Jeff was one of the twins, and my mom leaned on him more than any of the boys. We even heard the term "emotional husband" used about him among all the psychological terms thrown around our house when we were young. Jeff was the taskmaster, and we needed to do what he said. He took the lion's share of the responsibility in our family. When my mother cried, she cried to him.

All my years growing up with Jeff, without saying a word, he picked me up by the back of my arm, my triceps area, lifted me off the ground, carried me to where he wanted me, and threw me. Then he barked out a chore that I was to complete. He had total physical control of me and I was at his mercy. He carried Judy the same way.

There was one thing Jeff did, though, that I translated into his love for me. Once I was riding our pony bareback underneath our swing set with no swings; it was just a long bar. When I got right below the bar, I reached and hooked both my elbows backwards up over the bar. At once, the pony began to trot off, out from under me. My head swung forward and my legs flew backwards. I was just about to drop to the ground and land on my face. I let out a gasp and Jeff, who'd been raking leaves, threw down the rake and made a mad dash to catch me in mid air, saving me from certain harm. Whenever I wondered if he cared for me, I thought back to that moment. Funny, how his providing protection for me equaled love in my mind.

When once describing Jeff to a friend, in comparison to the other boys, Mary said, "He was the one who had the hardest time being mean to us."

If Jeff had the hardest time being mean, Carl had the easiest. He was the meanest of the three boys. When he told me to do something, it was with the threat, "If you don't, I'm going to knock every tooth down your throat." This was not hard to believe since he could have still harbored anger about a baseball bat once knocking out his front teeth during play. I felt sure he wanted someone else to also feel the pain he'd endured, and was just waiting for a chance to inflict it. I was conscious of every move I made around him. To this day, having heard that line so many times, I still imagine my teeth being knocked out of me.

It is hard to say who carried the greatest burden of the abuse in our household. Everyone had a difficult time, but I imagine we'd all agree that Mary's lot was the lot from hell.

Yes, she had stood up to the gun and essentially saved my mother's life, seemingly her largest task in life accomplished. But she was the oldest girl, and Grannie told her it was up to her now to take on the chores of the mother. Mr. Walsh, the social worker, told Mom to sit her oldest daughter at the head of the table "where she can get up and do everything." Not only did Mary cook the meals and make sure that the house was in order, she had the unique task of taking care of Mom. Mom had to be bathed, she had to be clothed, each piece of clothing going on one by one. Judy and I helped when we were around, helping Mom pull up her girdle, pull on her white stockings, zip up her white dress, tie her white shoelaces before she went off to work. But essentially, these constant chores fell to Mary and every detail was left to her. For nine years, until she went away to college, Mary tended to my mother's many needs.

It just about killed her. She was trapped inside the house all day. She sat at the end of Mom's bed waiting for the next task; her time was never her own. Everyone she encountered praised Mary to the hilt, but she was secretly resentful and angry all those years. To this day she cannot believe it when someone praises her - her guilt of feeling that hatred was so strong. My mother went through some terrible phases of depression and often wailed, "I wish I had died that night!" And there sat Mary, who'd saved her. Soon she, too, was wishing she'd let Mom die that night, her anger and resentment growing, day after day, year after year.

To make matters a million times worse, my brothers harassed Mary about her weight, calling her "Fat-ass" and "Fatty" and "Thunder Thighs" and "Fat Slob," and so on. It was true that she was a bit overweight, but nothing to warrant the bullying she suffered. It was the cruelest of cruel things to do to a growing teenage girl.

I later learned that depression directed outwardly is called an explosion and depression directed inwardly is called an implosion. Mary sat for years on the end of Mom's bed - imploding. Understandably, Mary had a bossy and irritable personality at home.

Although rough when wrestling around, Aaron was never violent. He was the good-natured brother who found humor in life. He was a "wild man" and still is. I believe Aaron suffered most from the violence dished out from the men in our family. I saw him shore himself up and move on from it many times. He was the most gregarious of the boys, very friendly, with an adventurous spirit. He was a good role model for how to re-think your life and laugh about the good in it.

Aaron – and all of my brothers, really – had a lot of friends. There were scads of neighborhood boys in our house at all times. Forever, I was walking in the front door and gingerly tip-toeing across an ocean of long legs, all stretched out in one direction, usually toward the television. Boy, boys, boys. One fence separated three families on one side of our back-yard, and the kids from those houses alone totaled 28. The neighbors on the other side of our house had three kids. That's 31 kids from both sides of the fence, including us. Out the back fence were thousands of acres of woodland. Out the front, we lived on a hill where a patched pothole was first base for a kick ball game we played in the evenings. In winter, when the street was filled with snow, we went sleigh riding. There were twenty pairs of gloves drying near the hearth when we kids took breaks to get warm.

Although Mom was handicapped, she always had a lot of people "on hand" to help her in her perpetual stream of generosity toward kids. She had a continuous pot of hot chocolate going in the pot on the stove, fill-ing it and re-filling it for new batches of kids. She made a bottomless pot of chili into which she added more and more pasta, making it go further.

Despite all of the horror that had visited our house previously, every kid in the neighborhood wanted to be in our home. My mother wel-comed everyone with a delighted open spirit. No one was turned away. She laughed and hugged each person coming and going, but there was one fact everyone knew before entering. "If you go in there, Mrs. Vessels will give you a chore before you can leave." That was Mom's rule and every kid followed it. She was the pied piper of the neighborhood.

I know now those chores my mother gave the neighbor kids gave them a sense of belonging, a message that we were all operating on the same level, but I did wonder at the time why anyone would come back for a visit if it meant doing chores!

I ran like a wild little creature through the woods behind our house. Later in my adult years, during a meditation, the instructor asked us to look at our feet and follow them through the earlier years of our lives. In almost every single phase of my life, under my feet was dirt or grass or leaves or mud or water or snow or rocks or sand. Everything I ever need-ed was outside - freedom. Living inside meant oppression and someone controlling my every move.

At home, I received a great deal of criticism. Along with having my hair pulled, being punched, pushed, shoved, picked up, carried and thrown, dragged on my back, sat on, and threatened, I was "wrong" or "bad" or "could never do anything right."

Once in my twenties, Mary visited me. I was showing her a new dress I'd just made. I showed her some dangly earrings that matched, but explained I did not have the confidence to wear the dangly earrings "outside." I told her that, for some reason, I was terribly afraid of "drawing attention to myself." My sister, in all her compassion in wanting to give me as much information as she could in the early days of my therapy, knew I was trying to piece together my life and make sense of it. She said, "Lynnie, that's because you could never do anything right. I was the angel. I was the good one, but you could never do anything right for anyone in our house. You tried and tried so hard, but it was useless. Everyone was always on you."

The moment she told me that, a cannon went off in my chest. Another piece of my puzzle solved as to why I'd felt so low about myself. I was ever so grateful for that piece of information, yet why, I wondered, was so much criticism directed at me? I would be in my late forties before I learned the reason. Back then, I was as confused as a person could be. With all the adults or older siblings running past me, with all the chaos going on, I was being barked at for the craziest of things. I remember my head spinning. *I can't be this bad. How could I be this bad? I haven't done anything with my life yet. I've barely been anywhere at all. I'm just a kid.*

The truth was I really had done nothing wrong. Yes, I might have done a chore wrong or not gotten something right the first time, having not even been taught how to do it, just told. But by then I knew right from wrong. I knew when I had bad "behavior," but this was something different. People were taking their anger out on me. I was pleased when Mary told me that I'd been the one who could "never do anything right." I finally could pinpoint a reason for my sadness; it made perfect sense.

We had a neighbor who in later years told me, "It's a wonder all you kids didn't go crazy, living in that house." I had a special secret. It's a secret I never shared with anyone until I got older and realized it was the reason I survived those young years. I had an inner voice. I suspect everyone has one; I'm not sure but I often think people must, or more people might commit suicide. I don't know exactly how other people have made it through their "stuff," but I know how I made it through mine.

Whenever I needed it, my voice spoke to me and, depending on what had happened, the words varied only slightly, saying, very, very slowly: "I love you, Lynnie. It's okay. Everything is okay. You are fine. Sure you made a mistake, but you will do better next time. I am here. I will help you. I will help you learn a better way. I love you. I forgive you. Everything is okay." In almost these exact same words, every single time, these were the words I heard. When I saw the blood scene flash into my head, I heard, "It's okay. I love you, Lynnie. I am here. I am here with you. You are fine. Everything is okay. I love you." I heard it clearly and I still hear it clearly today. It calmed me.

No matter how bad things looked on the outside, I still had this voice that was like the answering of a prayer. It was not a booming voice; it was more like a thought. The tone might have been loving like my mother's since she was the only one I knew who talked in that tone, but the words were from somewhere else. I thought of it as God since it came to me when I needed it. But then, sometimes I wondered if I just thought the words myself when I needed them. Whatever it was, I had an inner life. When I was in nature, walking in the woods, my inner life and my outer life matched.

When I entered the world of people, I would not feel this nearly as much. Among people, the thing that impacted me most was the tone of their voices and the words that came out of their mouths. When a person made harsh or thoughtless comments, I saw that person as separated - very far - from his inner voice. I assumed he had one. I could not have been alone on this. When hearing loving comments from someone, whether said softly or firmly, I assumed this person to be very close to his inner voice and, like me, could hear it.

Judy

Each one of us took the brunt of something and Judy's came from being the youngest. She was a beautiful, sweet, kind little girl. Whenever a visitor came to the house, including our boyfriends in later years, Judy grabbed the person by the hand and took him outside to show him something fascinating in the back yard or beyond. The innocence about her was remarkable and everyone saw her bright light. She was the most giggly, filled-up-with-laughter little girl. Until she got angry. Judy had received the "trickle down" effect of five siblings' rage. When she was angered, she picked up the nearest item, chased someone down and, as hard as she could, threw it into the face of her victim. There was no reasoning with her. I'd say, "Judy, you may seriously hurt or kill someone." This did not affect her. I realized that, in her anger, she wanted to hurt someone. She made no apologies for it.

Judy played with toys. None of us had many toys growing up, but as the sixth and youngest child, Judy seemed to have and enjoy toys. We joked that she would be asking for a talking telephone when she was twenty-one years old. She had a doll named Drowsy that was always getting broken. Our mom sent the doll back to Mattel regularly to have it replaced with a brand new one. Judy even had me playing Barbie dolls with her when I was fourteen and she was twelve. By then, we'd become really good at designing dollhouses with Tupperware and tissues that covered the entire living room. One day from her little-girl mind, Judy christened me Looneybird and I've been that to her ever since. On the same day, Mary became Murraybird. Go figure.

Judy was my best friend, my laughing buddy. To put it simply: she was my best time. I adored her. And we thought we were SOOO funny! Walking home from the bus stop with our books in hand, we leaned inward at an angle, on each other's shoulders, and called it "Dead man walking on a dead man." When we traveled by car we made faces at passersby. When we walked downtown in Washington, D.C., we made up foreign languages, hoping others would stop to listen and wonder where we were from, just as we'd listened to them and wondered where they were from.

But Judy got hurt just like I got hurt. She got picked up and thrown, put under the bed, threatened – all of it. But Judy had one thing more to deal with than I had – she had me to deal with. Yes, I was mean to Judy, and yes, I hit Judy, but mostly, I controlled her. She adored me and would do whatever I said. I was her leader and she followed me. In this way, I was able to manipulate her, to get her to do what I wanted, the majority of the time. In the neighborhood, there were no girls my age, only one Mary's age who was her best friend, and others only Judy's age and younger. I had no one to hang out with, so Judy's friends all followed me!

There was a gorge in the woods just off the creek that had a great mud hole. Red, soft mud. Judy and I frequented the mud hole and, one at a time – because we were keenly aware of the danger – sank our toes, pointing them, into the mud. Down and down one of us went, the other looking into the eyes of the descending one. We each pretended we were Johnny Weissmuller in Tarzan, sinking in quicksand. Finally, when one of us sank up to our chests, we pulled the other to freedom. Caked and covered in mud, almost from head to toe, we sat on the banks of the creek and let the mud cake and dry. Oh, how cool that was! Then, off into the creek we scampered to clean ourselves. It was either just the two of us or Judy's friends watching, but they were too afraid to "sink" in the mud themselves. It was clearly dangerous, but we were daredevils. I remember once being down in the gorge when some strange kids happened by. One looked down at us from the top and said, "Does your mother know you're doing this?"

We proudly replied, "Nope!" We were free in a Huck Finn sort of way.

Judy also watched more cartoons than any of us and she loved singing the tunes from these. "Oranges poranges… who said? Oranges poranges… who said? There ain't no rhyme for oranges!" Because of one cartoon, she named a place in our woods "Lillyput." This was a magical place of soft, cushy, lush green leaves that rolled up and over the rocks and logs beneath them. Very few people traveled into this spot, but it could be seen from the trail. It was weird going into this vast expanse of undulating leaves because who knew what was beneath all that? But Judy didn't care. To lie on her back in the lush greenness was her goal and she got me in there every time.

I have two big regrets about my relationship with Judy. Something in me just could not stand to have her beat me at rummy, so I cheated. She was younger and more naïve and I took advantage of her youth. When it was my time to draw a card, I distracted her and pulled three cards off the top of the deck. Pretty soon, I had many runs spread out, and she marveled at how good I was. To this day it pains me to think that she trusted me, and I betrayed her trust. She thought I was so much better than she was. I can only think it was my way of keeping control over her admiration of me, or keeping at bay the feeling of being laughed at. I couldn't stand for her to beat me. Still, when I look back on how my insecurities may have diminished her self-esteem, I am ashamed.

The other thing I regret with Judy happened one day when I was talking on the telephone. She would not leave me alone. She kept bugging me, and since she and I, having several older siblings, were champions at pestering, she was doing a very good job of it. Even though she was being funny and cute, I lost my temper and cracked her over the skull with the telephone receiver. Now, this was not the lightweight telephone receiver of today. It was the old fashioned, very heavy kind, and I hit her with a big thump. She immediately yelped and a bump quickly rose. Although Judy was okay and said it did not hurt, I have never really been able to come to grips with the fact that I hit her so hard. It's something I can never take back.

When someone dies or goes away, I guess your regrets about them are magnified. Judy is not dead, but she has "gone away," and now that she is gone, I often wonder if I contributed to it.

Camp Merry Ledges

There was no better place on earth for kids. I knew it then. I know it now. One of the saving graces of my life was that for the same seven years I was in "the fog," I got to go to Camp Merry Ledges. It was a chance for underprivileged kids from Louisville to spend ten days with 100 other kids on Blue River in Indiana. We'd always been a family of campers, but this place was different. The large timber lodge with stone fireplaces had paths emanating out in all directions. They led to the girls' and boys' units of tents on wooden platforms, the flagpole, the singing tree, the river, the docks, and the bathhouses. We ate in the large dining hall where "runners" from each table picked up the meals and ran them to our tables.

Every day there were long lists of activities to do such as arts and crafts, building furniture, painting, and hiking. We developed skills there – were certified in swimming, boating, archery, and caving, but we also got to experience, at a young age, swinging from a rope into the river, swamping canoes, having shaving cream fights, winning races, learning new dances, watching roaring bonfires, being able to have crushes on boys, and a secret ritual once a year - skinny dipping in the river with girls in the middle of the night. Our camp counselors were children of the 60's and taught us all the words to their songs. When they sang, it was with a depth I admired. It seemed that each counselor I had over all those years was a loving person, a minister of peace in some way.

The first summer after the shooting, only Mary and I went, as Judy was too young. Although Mary was more shy than I, we were still two scared little ones, off on a mysterious adventure. Each year, no matter how old I was, when the bus pulled away and Mom stood waving, I had the sharpest pain stab through my heart. It did not let up until we were about thirty minutes away. Even though we both really wanted to go, it was the most frightening of experiences to be separated from our mother, surely reminding us of a darker time. I could see that Mary, and later Judy, felt the same way I did each time, sitting speechless, for the first part of the drive.

A great plus about this experience was that the kids were equally black and white. This gave us a chance to become very good and life-long friends with African Americans from downtown Louisville. But the first summer we were playing together, two girls, one black, one white, were tenting together and calling each other sisters. Innocently, Mary said, "You can't be sisters because one of you is black and one of you is white." Everyone fell silent. These two girls took it upon themselves to exclude Mary for the rest of the day, even though she tried to apologize.

It broke my heart in sixteen places to see Mary hurt. Ostracized, she sat outside and away from the tent. I sat with her all day, each of us saying very little to the other, but being loving and gentle. We had been raised to respect all people. Because I know the exact nature of my siblings' sufferings, there is a part of me that feels any hurt they might endure due to embarrassment or shame.

The next day all was forgotten, but Mary and I both knew to tread lightly on the race issue. We learned to be sensitive to those who'd suffered such prejudices. It would be something Mary and I would spend the rest of our lives doing: coming to understand the plight of those oppressed, whether it was for women or other minorities. We came to know that upon initially meeting us, our scars of oppression or our wells of compassion could not easily be seen from the outside.

Brother David

The other saving grace in my life was Brother David. My mother became friends with him at the hospital while he was being treated for depression, on leave from the monastery. Brother David had come to Saint

Meinrad, the largest Archabbey in America, to study to be a monk when he was a wayward boy of thirteen. He was in charge of the vineyard, baked the bread for the abbey, and was the caretaker of the beautiful rock garden. Mom brought him home for dinner when I was ten years old. For the three of us little girls, it was love at first sight. He held open a brown grocery bag, threw an imaginary stone into the air, and caught it on its way down, secretly flicking the bottom of the bag to make a noise. He took pipe cleaners and bent them into little stick figures, gifts for each of us. He had a smile that lit up the world, but Brother David's finest quality was that he was the essence of forgiveness.

How can someone be that, you may ask? What had I done at ten years old that he was supposed to forgive? How does one know the essence of a human being? His tone of voice, his mannerisms, his laughter, his eye contact, his glide, his whole demeanor housed forgiveness. There would never have been a thing I would have been ashamed to tell him. His love and his compassion for three little girls was such that it could be felt for years and wherever on earth we traveled. We visited Brother David often and, when we were away from each other, he wrote to me in calligraphy by candlelight. His letters are some of my most cherished keepsakes.

Brother David was only in my life for seventeen years. At the age of 48, he died of colon cancer just as I reached the age of 27. On a visit home, Mary and I called him to say we were driving up to see him. When we arrived on the Abbey grounds, he came to us with open arms, in his flowing black robes, gliding like an angel. The three of us sat on a bench, talking. He laughed and asked us questions about ourselves. I noticed the tubes to the colostomy bag hanging beneath his robes.

Then an amazing thing happened. The bells for the next prayer session rang. He stood, and, to my horror, began to say good-bye! *How could he be leaving us? He just got here. We just got here! We came for a visit. Mary's home from Australia! He can go to any prayer session – the next session! We haven't seen him in so long and won't be seeing him again for so long. He may die before we see him again.* All of this was on our faces, I'm sure, and he touched our cheeks and kissed us softly. We knew that, although we were deeply important to him, his ritual of prayer was more so. Who could argue with that? That is who he was. It was the last time we saw him alive.

Our last moments with Brother David

We watched him walk away, down the sidewalk, to the abbey chapel, the skirt of his black robe swaying.

Here are some of the excerpts from the letters I have from Brother David:

For my birthday: "Soon we will be celebrating your birthday. Happy the day on which you were born! The world is a better place because of it and certainly more beautiful. May the freshness and joy of springtime be yours and may God's peace fill you."

At Christmas: "We celebrate his coming and his presence. May there be a deep and quiet joy in your heart."

And as he became sick: "As I get older (or feel that way) the energy and enthusiasm of the young appears more and more amazing. They take it for granted – which it is – while their elders realize only too well how much it is a gift for a season."

"Healing is a gradual process. No matter what kind of sickness a person might have, we all want to be made well right away. But time seems to be a necessary ingredient. Is that perhaps to make us appreciate health the more? It is a blessing but one that we tend to take for granted.

"The days ahead are uncertain, but I am trying to take just one day at a time. At times, that is quite enough, but also, as you've probably noticed, when we try too much to see what's coming, we often miss what is at hand."

And the last letter from him: "So often my thoughts go back to that afternoon this summer when you came to see me. It was only a short time that we had together, but how glad I was to see you. It was good to see how you've grown and that that which was so beautiful in you has become even more so. You leave such pleasant memories."

He always signed them "With my love, Br. David."

We girls were just a few of the many flowers he tended in his lifetime. If ever a life could be a teacher, it was his.

Boy Crazy

In fifth and sixth grades, I seemed to always be in trouble with authority. On top of that, a curious phenomenon began to take hold of me. Around all of the boys, "it" started happening. I'd be talking to a boy I'd literally known all my life. All of a sudden I'd catch his eye and the "it" thing happened. There. Boom. I was gone. All of a sudden, I was "in love," and this poor, unsuspecting boy whom I'd played, argued, and worked with for so many years, was done for. I never spoke to him again. I was officially in love.

"It" had struck. Puberty.

From then on, he – the boy - was this entity that floated around in the classroom. Someone I'd known so well, was now an enigma. All of a sudden, I loved his hair, his eyes, his laugh, his look, every mannerism. He was my future husband. For the next two weeks. Then the feeling somehow went away and my crush was transferred to a new boy. It started with Mark. Then there was Mike and George and Tony and Jack and Rueben and Terry and another Mike.

On one particular day on the playground, it happened to be Tony. I was stealing his hat, and then he came back and took mine! Each time he stole my hat, I yelled, "Mrs. O'Connell!" Well, I must have yelled it once too often because my fifth grade teacher yelled, "That's enough! To the office with you!"

I walked straight toward the office, but I passed it by and walked across the parking lot instead. I was so mad, I was going home! I was almost off the school grounds when the principal, Sister David, came out to holler my name to return. I did and I was given detention. Detention number one.

And that was the beginning of trouble. Boys and trouble or just plain trouble.

At the end of sixth grade I went to my first boy/girl party at Tony's house. Tony was dreamy – dark skin, dark hair, and dark eyes – and had a ton of rascal in him. We played spin-the-bottle and my first kiss was with Rueben. But Tony was the boy I really wanted to kiss, and when my chance finally came, it was during the "the longest kiss" contest! I was happy to compete for the prize. Just lips, no tongue, but it was kissing and the intrigue had begun.

Wild Child

Between the ages of ten and thirteen, the restlessness inside me became overwhelming. Little did I know the fog was lifting and a great rage was to replace it. I wouldn't have described this time as "wanting to be cool," as others did, but I did *not* want to be boring. I was living on the edge. I wanted to be seen as someone who'd already done things. I was doing things I was far too young to be doing, but the beauty was by the time I was older, I could say I'd "already done that."

On the extreme opposite end of boring is dangerous. I was smoking at twelve. I began shoplifting with my friends. I heard one brother talking about hitchhiking, so I began to do that, too. I was fighting. When I fought, it was with my fist straight into a person's face, and I never lost – outside my home, that is.

It was around this time that my oldest brother Jeff said to my mom, "If you don't get her a horse, she's going to be pregnant and married by the time she's sixteen."

That one line was to have a significant effect on my life, good and bad. The bad part: in that statement I heard my brother calling me a whore. He wasn't, of course, but that is what I heard. The good part: because that is what I heard, I vowed I would never give him or any man a reason to call me any such thing.

I was twelve and living in Kentucky and many girls my age had a horse. Mom could see I wanted one, but I did not think to ask for it, knowing we did not have the money. We'd had a pony given to us many years before, and I'd been riding horses for years. I spent my days at the barns of friends. My brother's advice won out and Mom bought me a horse for ninety dollars, paying five dollars a month.

If my horse was meant to be a deterrent, a deterrent he was. Red, short for Red Rider, became my best bud. I kept him in the stall my brothers had built in the backyard for the pony we'd had. The farmer behind our house let me graze my horse in his fields. I was content riding my horse and I sat in the stall talking to him for hours on end. Red was the only one I talked to about anything important. Though the pictures in my head haunted me incessantly, I never spoke of them. My loneliness was becoming unbearable. I vowed, *I will never forget how painful it is to be thirteen.* There I was, sitting in the straw curled up in the corner, listening to the rain pound outside, my horse standing over me, his nostrils snorting, feeling safer there than in my house.

I was a popular kid, but I still had not had a true friend in my life.

Because I was into my wild phase, I stayed out until all hours of the night. Since my mom worked long hours, there was no one checking on me. I heard a girlfriend say once that she had a curfew and had to get home. My first thought was a little boastful. *Huh! Not me!* And then thinking about it, *Gee I wish I had someone who knew – or noticed – when I came in.* Judy played, Mary worked, and I roamed. After my chores were done, I left the house to run wild in the woods.

I wondered why Mary did not leave, too. I did not realize the heavy emotional and psychological burden that kept her there. I am ashamed of myself now that I did not help her more. Mary was Cinderella and, although I was not mean to her like the stepsisters in the story, I was mean by omission. The more I left the house, the more Mary had to do.

Whenever I stepped into the kitchen or lifted a lid off a pot, Mary yelled, "Get out of the kitchen!" I took it literally and got out of the whole house. I did not learn how to cook until much later in life and, even then, felt very insecure about my skills. My life was outdoors.

All my friends had horses and we rode daily. We took our horses to the store, to each other's homes, swimming, blackberry picking, and galloping on long runs. I had a reputation for managing feisty horses and probably fell off over 100 times, but I became very coordinated and athletic from the challenges. I chose to ride my horse bareback most of

Lynnie at age eleven

the time, so I regularly had blisters on my rear end. My legs and the rest of me got strong and my confidence and self-esteem heightened from handling horses well.

I have vivid memories of riding my horse at midnight on the mountain behind my house, meandering through the moon-drenched woods singing, "The hills are alive with the sound of music," at the top of my lungs. It was not really a mountain, just a very, very tall hill, but I like to call it a mountain because it sounds more cowgirly, and I was one wild cowgirl. The feeling this freedom gave me was indelibly marked in my soul. Like a touchstone, I would use it to guide me back to who I was whenever in my life I found myself being controlled by another person.

There is a saying that if you want to know who a woman really is, look to her at ten years old, before the posturing for boys or the competing among girls began. Watch in your mind's eye how she behaved, how she spoke in her environment, and you will know her. If I am anyone, I am that girl on that horse, on that mountain, singing that song to that moon.

Sleeping

As much as the outdoors healed me, I still had to come home. As I was growing up, every night when I went to bed, this is what I saw when I closed my eyes: skinny, red spaghetti-like noodles all knotted up, floating in black ink-like fluid. I could not fall asleep until I meticulously untangled every single strand of spaghetti. No matter how long it took, I had to work at each one. If I went the wrong way, I'd have to move it back, another way, this way then that. All with my mind.

When one knot was untangled, it would then flow in a horizontal line, floating like a gentle wave in the still sea of black ink.

Sometimes this process took hours. I now believe the number of knots might have been equal to the number of problems I perceived around me at the time. There were never fewer than twenty knots. Some were very difficult to unwind, but each success cleared the way for another.

When I was finished, the spaghetti noodles had flattened out to be more like fettuccini and they were all flowing horizontally in the black fluid. A little fluid would splash up on top of one once in a while, to let me know the current was below, but when they were all flat and flowing horizontally, Boom! I was out like a light.

Once when I was young and camping with all the scouts next to a river, everyone was sitting around the campfire at dusk telling stories. I stood up calmly and, with no announcement, walked to the tent to find my bed to go to sleep. As I entered the tent, I heard one of my brothers say, "Boy, that Lynnie. You never have to tell her to go to sleep. She just gets up and goes without a fight." My eyes bugged to hear this. *Had someone noticed something about me? Were they talking about me? Was this something positive? Yes, it was!* It was a nice thing said about me in my family. I was stunned and delighted, thinking that yes, it was true. Most kids had to be prodded into going to bed. I was thrilled, and I decided right then and there that I was always going to get the "prize."

No one knew the real reason I went to bed early. I had work to do. I remember days when I was tired from staying up so late in bed, trying to untangle the knots. I began planning to go to bed earlier in order to get good sleep. The actual time I fell asleep was much later than anyone realized. Sometimes I wanted to cry, I was so exhausted. I knew I could not sleep until I finished. I would feel myself whimper and then my voice would say, "Just a little bit more, Lynnie. You can do it. I love you, Sweetie. Everything is okay. We'll get there."

I never spoke about this phenomenon of my spaghetti to anyone until I was well into my thirties, and now it makes me recognize just how remarkable the human psyche is. There were a lot of problems in my little world to be fixed, but I could only fix them in my head. One spaghetti noodle at a time.

Trouble

Our church school, OLC, had been a wonderful place for us, and we'd gotten reduced tuition and lunches, but now it was time to move to middle school. Some of my friends were going to the girls' Catholic high school, but we could not afford that, so along with many of the students from OLC, we went to the nearby public secondary school.

Being a teacher now, I often kid about the fact that coming from a parochial school, the minute I hit public school, my education stopped. That is not altogether true, but I was the quintessential incorrigible kid let out of a cage to run amok in the public school.

I started out slowly and worked my way to bigger trouble. Thank goodness before all of the trouble started, I found something to ground me. I began taking art in the seventh grade, I loved being creative, and I got recognized for my talent. But, ever the instigator, in my P.E. classes, when we were asked to run the trail behind the school, I organized a group to run over the massive hill to go to my house for peanut butter and jelly sandwiches. We'd get back just in time for showers.

My English teacher was very old and not very energetic. When she wanted our attention, she banged the stapler on the side of her desk. I had no respect for her. I did whatever I wanted in her classroom, which looked like this: I talked constantly, I got up and moved about the room whenever I wanted, and, in fact, I climbed up on the free-standing wooden closet and sat up there one entire class period. She could not coax me down and so, resigned to that fact, continued to teach class. Now, that is bizarre behavior. You'd think that someone would have noticed.

Uncontrollable, I was sent to the office repeatedly. My name was for-ever being called on the loud speaker. I can't say I was proud of it, but everyone knew who I was.

I was a regular in the office. My principal was Mr. Taylor, the assis-tant principal was Mr. Nixon, and the counselor was Mrs. Oyhler. There were rows of chairs sitting in the hallway just outside their offices. I spent a good part of seventh grade sitting in those chairs. Each time I was sent there, Mr. Taylor took out his paddle and paddled me. Afterwards, I sat waiting for one class to end and the next to begin. The next class it might start all over again. They called my mom many times, of course, but she was working pretty much non-stop, and my oldest brother, Jeff, had gone off to the navy by then, so she did not have him to discipline me. My other brother, Carl, was out a lot because he was in college and, truthfully, he may have taken too much pleasure in disciplining me; besides, he did not seem to care much, one way or the other. Aaron, by then was so involved in working outside the house, by his senior year, he had five jobs at one time. To him, our house was a hotel. If it's true everyone finds her niche, mine was trouble.

Popping Back Into Our Lives

Pops returned to Kentucky after living out of the state for five years. The way my mother acted, you never would have known what he'd done to her. She welcomed him back into our home for visits. She wanted her children to have a father. I later learned that one reason she did not press charges was she did not want her children to have a father in prison.

During the five years my father was gone, when he returned, and until I was about fifteen years old, *every* single time I spoke to him by phone or in person, my very first question was, "Daddy, why did you shoot Mom?"

"Oh, Honey, I was very, very sick," he answered.

"Are you sorry you shot Mom?"

"Oh, yes, very much so. I'm very sorry I did that," he replied. "I'm very, very sorry." I could hear in his voice he was, indeed, very sorry.

"Do you still love her?"

And his answer was, "Yes, I do."

"Do you want to be married to her again?"

"Well, I do not think that is possible anymore."

The questions rolled off my tongue just like that, every time. I asked almost the exact same questions, and every time I got almost the exact same answers.

Never did he brush my questions aside. Never did he appear annoyed or bothered by my questions. In fact, he'd sometimes say, "Is there anything else?" Satisfied, I'd say "No" and begin talking to him about what I was doing.

With my questions, I seemed to be paving a safe place for myself. If he was coming back into my life, even for a few minutes, I needed reassurance. The vision of his aggressive stance with the gun was in my head each day. His words, "I'm very, very sorry," were comforting, especially when the pictures flashed in my head. I did not know this at the time, but hearing those words over and over again, also paved the way for me to forgive him.

When Pops came to visit our home, the boys literally ran for the hills. They made a joke of it, and could not tumble over each other fast enough to "get out of Dodge." It was quite comical. Mary made herself scarce. Judy and I, still needing and wanting a daddy, stayed. We'd been the youngest, and suffered the fewest years of abuse from his hands. He was just simply our dad. When every other kid has a dad and you do not, then one day, Presto, you do, it is quite an intriguing phenomenon.

When he came over, he let us sit in his lap at the driver's seat in the car and drive up and down the driveway. He was funny and laughed heartily. He had scratchy whiskers and smelled of Old Spice.

The Rock

If the grief process moves from shock to anger, I became the poster child for anger. By the age of twelve, my rage was spilling out in full force. The fog had lifted now, but the pictures in my head remained. They never lessened or increased over time - about three times a day was standard. They remained a constant, unpredictable flickering that flashed at any given point, day or night.

The trouble was, I could never determine when they would come and I could not will them to leave. They were like invisible houseguests. If I was sitting with others and I got a "visit," it was not like I could say something aloud. No one else saw them, but someone may as well have come running through the room dragging a trail of blood. The sadness that overcame me was as if a thief had run through the room and stolen the image of normal I was trying to be.

If I was standing in line to get an ice cream cone, and someone said, "What flavor are you getting?" *What flavor ice cream am I getting? Is she kidding?* It sounded so trivial. *Can't she see the pain I'm in? Who cares about ice cream flavors? I'm looking at horrible blood stuff right now. Can't you see? What's wrong with you people? Don't you know what I see in my head? What's my favorite color? Who cares! Why is everyone so preoccupied with little things? Don't you know there are bigger things to be dealt with?*

I was disgusted with the stupidity of adults around me.

The biggest shock of the shooting was that no one ever talked about it. But I was forced to think about it; I saw it in living color. There was my dad with the gun, Mary jutting her chin up its barrel, Mom squatting at the hearth, and her dead hand. I saw Judy and her little wrinkled face, mouth open, screaming, mirroring me. Seeing her face in my mind, I saw mine. In some ways I never stopped screaming. Only now the screaming was from the inside.

Often Mom's still hand popped onto my screen. Just the hand lying there, dead. *There's a dead hand in front of me. Does everyone know my dad killed my mom's hand? Hello?* Mom had lost the use of her right arm. She'd never use it again. It was painful to watch.

Who could I tell? I'd see someone preparing a chicken, pulling the bones apart, stretching and ripping the skin, and think, *Hey, that's exactly what my mom's arm looked like when she was leaning on the refrigerator!* These opportunities to speak passed. I was living my life wanting to say many things, but stopped myself every time.

Mom's favorite show was "M*A*S*H," and we'd often sit together and laugh, but we took one particular daily job very seriously. My mom's skin inside her cast itched badly, so each night, one of us girls took turns lying on the couch with her, using a stick of some sort to reach up into the cast and scratch her itch. For several years, we took lotion and rubbed the inside of her curled-up fingers, hoping to stretch her fingers out enough to be used again. But the skin grew tight and we could see that the constriction of her fingers was permanent.

One day I handed a note of excused absence to my shop teacher. He looked at my Mom's handwriting and chortled, "You expect me to read this chicken scratch?" He held the paper in front of the other teacher's face so he could read it. Both of them laughed as the first one crumbled it up into a ball and threw it into the large gray trashcan in shop class.

How does one say to a teacher what I felt? *Hey, my mom lost the use of her right arm. The hand that she used to write with died. If you want, I can show it to you here in my mind. It's right here, see? It's not a lie. I'm not making this up. She had to re-learn how to write. This is the best she can do. She works hard at it. She goes to work every day and people read her handwriting every day. Because they try. I'm proud of her that she can write at all. Oh, and by the way, she used to have the most beautiful handwriting. We still have remnants of it in our scrapbooks. You should have seen it! But she lost it, along with so many other things. Her handwriting is just the start of what she lost. You really shouldn't laugh at things you don't understand like this. And, I still need to show that note to my other teachers, but you've thrown it into the trashcan now. How do I tell them you did not believe my mother's handwriting? How do I tell them that yes, it does look like chicken scratch, but I'm just glad she's here? How do I tell anyone why it looks like chicken scratch?*

It would have been the perfect time for someone to take me aside and ask, "Who wrote this?" or, "Why does this writing look like this?" because I would have been glad to say why, in private. But publicly, as the whole class looked on? This only fueled my rage.

Instead, I heard their laughter and then I saw the ornate piece of furniture in the dining room, lit up by the light that streamed out of the archway of the kitchen door on that night. In my mind, I was listening to my Uncle George's wail of laughter, and just hardened myself even further, continuing to make the decision for the umpteenth time that I would never respect an adult just because that person was older than I.

I remember my math teacher being frustrated with me. I wanted to learn the concepts she was trying to teach me, but I could not. She stood over me angrily. This was not the best approach. I remember looking up at her with a scowl. *Lady, until you give me some inkling that you have any idea what is going on in my head, what I have been through, I am not doing anything for you.*

All I wanted was for someone to know what kind of pain I was in. Heck, I would have settled for anyone else just talking about the pain they were in. Just something to let me know that people around me were like me in some way, to let me know I was not some alien from another planet.

I vowed I would not be an adult like these people.

I did not know how sick I was. I did not know that a child like me should never have gone through the shooting without counseling. Although I did know I was lonely, I did not know how desperately I needed someone to talk to. Through those years of silence, the anger just built up. By the time I got to middle school, I was a holy terror. Deep down, I was pissed off, and I was filled with hate. On the surface, I was a ball of laughs with a bubbly personality and lots of superficial friends. I was a leader and people followed me. "The trouble with trouble is it begins with fun." I was the tour guide for trouble, always looking for mischief. But living on the edge meant fun was not enough. I was not the kind of person any teacher wanted others to follow.

Naturally, I acted disrespectfully to adults I did not respect. And naturally, I could only respect adults who were telling me the truth. I looked around me. I saw no one telling me the truth. Not one adult around me in all those years had taken the time to ask me about the shooting, or even how I felt. I'd been around adults at school, at church, in my neighborhood, even at home, who knew exactly what I'd been through.

Why has someone not helped me? Can't they see how much I am hurting? What's wrong with me? Why is everyone moving about? It's like it just happened for me. Does anyone know? Does anyone care? It still hurts so badly! The years have not passed for me....

Decisions

I decided, before being swayed into anyone's clutches, I was not going to do drugs. I also decided I was going to wait for a long time before I ever did anything sexual with a guy.

I'd seen the devastation of drugs on my family, and my mother had raised us girls with the saying "Sex is the most wonderful thing in the world with someone you love." What I liked about that was Mom did not have the requirement of marriage attached to sex. Instead, she attached love, proceeding to teach us about real love. Although it would take years to understand the kind of deep love she meant, and the precise value of just what I would be giving of myself in sex, I think her simple statement was enough. Somehow, it left enough room there for me to feel respected for my choices. Later, I applied that respect to myself when the time came to make my decisions, not just the first time, but every time in the years ahead. As an adult, before engaging in sex, I asked myself if I felt respected and loved. I used that as my guide. Of course, what my brother had said earlier, was also a determining factor in my choice making.

Speaking of sex, my mother, being a nurse, had answered every question my sisters and I ever had about it right there on the spot, using terms like vagina, penis, and sperm. She was as forthright as a parent could be. She educated us well; I did not need to learn about sex outside the home. My mother did such a thorough job that my curiosity was quenched and further explanation was not needed. All I needed to do in that area was wait. Her response to our one question helped, too. "Mom, what would you do if we ever got pregnant?" She replied, "Well, we would find a way to raise the baby as a family."

If anything was going to keep us from getting pregnant, it was that. *What? She's not going to kick us out? We would stay here and raise the baby together? No way! Live with our mom forever, raising a baby?* Now, that was birth control! No need to rebel under those circumstances. Worse than any threat, her method of telling us the truth did the deed. My mother was brilliant.

Watching the Pros

My family knew hard work. From my three brothers I learned how to be a good worker. My brothers embodied the real definition of my all-time favorite word: ingenuity. We did not have money to fix things, so when something broke down and Mom worried, my brothers went into action rigging up devices. Without instruction, complaining, whining, or hesitation, these teenage boys came up with solutions nobody would have imagined. Watching them go to work and get a job done was a sight to behold.

My father's parents bought our family 200 acres for two thousand dollars when we were all very young, saying the land was meant for the kids' college fund. When we were not camping away with the scout groups, we camped on our cherished land, nicknamed "The Two Hundred." My brothers knew how to work the land, building tree houses, and surviving in the woods.

Each of my brothers felled trees to split wood for firewood and sold it. Aaron made a business of it, working his way through college. He'd wake us up gingerly and lovingly at 4 A.M., with the smell of bacon and eggs beckoning us from the kitchen, asking us to please come help him "do firewood." We three girls got up, ate, and the four of us rode in his 1967 pickup truck with "Keep on truckin" on the side. At the top of the steep hills where he'd cut a tree into round pieces, we'd squat, pick up each piece, and heave it down the hill. Again and again. We needed to do this many times just to get one log down the hill. It was heavy, honest-to-goodness hard work. At the bottom, Aaron split the wood. We girls loaded it into each other's arms and stacked it into the back of his truck.

Those runs with Aaron were some of my favorite times growing up. Everyone loved Aaron. He made friends easily, and he was a real character. He made everyone laugh and he made us feel good about ourselves. We were invited into some very nice homes to sit around the fire and drink hot chocolate.

This was tremendous physical work. Days in the snow we worked so hard, we were dripping with sweat inside our clothes. The snow in the woods was beautiful, and Mary and I learned something that Judy was too young to realize. The more you moved, the warmer you'd stay. When Judy became too cold, she sat in the front of the truck and cried because she was freezing.

I had bigger muscles than any boys my age.

The Rock's Bottom

In eighth grade the bar on trouble was raised for me. Smoking, shoplifting, hitchhiking, and fighting all kicked up a notch. Let me just start by getting one thing out of the way. I had detention hall with Mr. Garrison in Room 101, every single day in the eighth grade. I was smoking one to two packs of cigarettes a day, mostly at my friend Jane's house. We sat at her dining room table playing cards for hours. Her family of thirteen kids was a riot to be around, and all of the kids started smoking young, so I fit right in. Outwardly, I was wild. Internally, I had no boundaries either. It was as if each emotion I had flowed into another. One splashed over the first, overlapping and extinguishing it, quickly trying to take over as the most important. Then a bigger wave came and did the same thing to the new emotion. I was a tumultuous sea.

I often went downtown and visited Mary Kay, a great friend from summer camp. We strolled into stores and put whole cartons of cigarettes down our knee-high socks, which were well concealed under our huge bell-bottoms. We stole jewelry and make up from stores. Of course, these were things I could not use because, Duh, they were stolen! Mary Kay and I made up concoctions of dishwashing soap and went out in the middle of the night and sprayed cars with it. For what reason? For kicks. We thought it was funny. Now I cannot tell you why. Mary Kay was older and prettier, with a wild streak even longer than mine. Daring as I was, hanging out with her was sure to lead to bigger escapades.

I also shoplifted clothes and jewelry with another friend. I only wore them when I was with her. Then I heard of someone getting caught shoplifting. That did it. No material things could wipe away the embarrassment I knew I'd cause my family if arrested. As tantalizing as it was on the edge, the fall was too steep.

I hitchhiked downtown a few times, until once when my brother Aaron saw me on the side of the road with my thumb out. That ended. For a while.

Fighting. It happened. It pains me to say I was violent. I could be so violent, it was scary. By now, I was filled with tremendous anger, though masked by a bubbly personality and shenanigans galore.

I'm sure my principals and counselor tried to get through to me in those two years of middle school, but they couldn't. As soon as I got to the office, I was light and playful. In my eighth-grade year they began putting me to work, giving me odd jobs in the office. I was comfortable there, worked hard, and whatever I'd done to get booted out of class was forgotten.

I remember the assistant principal, Mr. Nixon, giving me a ride home one day in his Volkswagen. I could not bear for him to see where I lived. I do not think it was because I was ashamed of where I lived. It was because it felt too intimate. Literally, "too close to home." The life I led at school was different from the life I led at home. I was tough at school. I was cool. At home, I was controlled by others.

A light in my life was Mr. Gossett, my eighth grade English teacher. He had us diagramming sentences and playing word and sentence games on the board. I was good. Very good. I had my Catholic education, and I was smart in English. Mr. Gossett was young, kind, and respectful. When I was in his class, I felt special.

Everyone was starting to get boyfriends in middle school, but not me. I was red-haired and freckled. I looked at my face in the bathroom mirror one day, from every angle, and decided I was not pretty or cute - until I smiled. Then, I wasn't so bad. I decided I was going to smile.

Besides the fight I'd had with the neighbor boy the day I returned home after the shooting, there had only been one other incident of fighting before middle school. It happened at camp one year. A tall girl in the next unit yelled something provocative over to my unit of girls such as "You guys are gonna lose!" I marched right up to her and punched her in the nose as hard as I could. She was stunned. She opened her eyes widely and started to cry. *Task accomplished.* I never heard another word about it.

I had a friend named Lizzie, with whom I spent the night on several occasions. While I was with her in the country visiting her grandparents' farm, we went to their country church to listen to the very animated sermons. We got such a kick out of watching the congregation's responses. We'd double-dated with two boys in a car. One of them let me drive down winding roads in the country. I went around a curve so fast all four wheels of the car came off the ground. We landed in a cornfield and needed a tow. Lizzie and I had some wild experiences and were good buddies, until one day she did something prissy that angered me. We arranged to meet out in the "smoke hole" after school to fight. I punched her in the face several times, but she did not hit me once. I was proud. Lizzie later moved down to the farm and I never saw her again.

I did have one best friend growing up. Sherri and I were close, both wild and crazy fourth graders when we met. We had a lot of fun together, memorizing the words to songs, going to visit her grandmother "Mama Stell" downtown, creating an alphabet sign language, and goofing off in elementary school. One day when we were in the sixth grade getting ready to take a test, our teacher, Miss Berne, had positioned the desks in a circle. Sherri and I had previously been in much trouble with our "alphabet signing." Taking the test that day, Sherri lifted her head (to think, I assume), and I lifted my head at the same time. Our eyes made contact for a split second, but long enough for Miss Berne to look up at the exact same time. She marched over to each of us, took our papers, and tore them right down the center. We did not even create a fuss, not because we knew we had not cheated, but because we knew that we were not the straightest pins in the pincushion at other times.

Sometime in the eighth grade when Sherri and I weren't as close, she told a boy I liked him, something I'd told her in confidence. I was mortified. I did not hesitate to punch her in the face, right in the hallway.

That night, Sherri's friend, the toughest girl in the school, a tenth grader named Carla, called my house several times. Each time she said, "We're going to kill you tomorrow."

Now I was scared. On many different levels. Yes, I was scared for myself, but I was mostly scared for them. *Don't these people understand how much anger I have inside me? They don't want to mess with me. I will hurt them. I have more anger in me than all of them put together and I will surely kill one of them if they come on too strong.* I knew the minute someone tried to hurt me, it would touch every hurt I'd ever had. I knew no one was a match for that. I did not want this volcano of anger to erupt because I had no idea of its depth and power.

I walked around my house. This was the first time since that day sitting at the base of the mirror in my aunt's attic that I was undeniably aware of the fact I needed someone to talk to. My family members were going about their business, not noticing me. But I needed someone, never more than now. My life as the hood at school was so different from my family, our church, our mother, and my siblings. I was the different one. How would anyone understand that I had truly fallen into crowds that were really – I thought - going to kill me? I looked around my house. I had five siblings and a mother, a house teeming with people and activity, but I was alone. That was the first moment I understood loneliness. I did not know what to do.

I went to my mother's medicine cabinet, opened it, and touched the front of each bottle. Was I seriously thinking of killing myself? *Yes. I will kill myself before they kill me, before I am forced to kill someone.* I stood there touching the bottles for a long time. *Now what 'exactly' would be strong enough to kill me?* Never actually picking up a bottle from the shelf, I closed the cabinet door and turned away. I lay on my mother's bed and cried just knowing I felt sad enough to want to kill myself. Somehow I went to sleep that night, and somehow got up and walked to school on the path through the woods. When I came out into the clearing, I could see my sister, Mary, and her group of girlfriends walking in a pack on the far away sidewalk. I longed to be like Mary in those moments. Watching her - chit chatting her way to school with all of her good, wholesome girlfriends, all smart and together, made me feel empty.

When I got close to the school, I saw a large crowd gathered out back. They were waiting for me. *Here goes. Don't they know how badly I can hurt them? Don't they know how much anger is inside me? Don't they know all I see is blood in front of me every day? Please,* I pleaded from within, *walk away from me. I do not want to hurt you.*

Simultaneously, I was afraid of killing and being killed.

I did not feel the fear from the night before as greatly, but I was not without it. I walked across the parking lot and onto the worn-off grass that was hard solid dirt. The crowd gathered around me. Carla, so mean she was ugly, with her curly black hair and all of her anger, yelled at me. "We don't like what you did to Sherri." Carla's pack of hoods was standing beside her. Sherri was standing behind them with a purple and black eye.

A crowd of a hundred had gathered, many yelling. In the midst of the storm, I heard a voice of an angel. In the smallest, sweetest, and most confident voice, "Come on, Lynnie." It was Mary. *Saved.* I turned around to her outstretched hand. I took it and walked away with her through the tunnel of the crowd. I heard Carla say to Josey, her gang member, "Get her!"

Josey jumped on my back. I fell straight to the ground, on hard dirt that might as well have been concrete, directly on my nose. The impact put a permanent bump on my once ski-sloped nose, but I did not feel it after the initial hit, and I knew what I had to do. Josey never got a punch in. I pulverized her. If people had come for a fight, they got one. The wrath I unleashed on her was ugly. She limped away, stunned, with two black eyes, a bleeding face, and her yellow shirt ripped off.

When I turned to leave, the shop teacher was there to escort me to the office. I remember telling Mr. Taylor I had not wanted to fight. "Lynnie, if people know you *will* fight, they will keep coming at you, wanting to beat you, and you can bet that is what they are after." That stuck with me. *Continuing to fight?* I did not want this. Somehow, I kept a low profile after that, my fifth fight, and my fighting days were over. I thought.

I read *Shane* by Jack Schaefer, a novel about a superb gunfighter. He was so good, men wanted to "test" their abilities, by tracking him

down and challenging him to a gunfight. He never lost and consequent-
ly killed many men. Because he did not want to kill anymore, he "hid"
out and even backed down from fighting which caused the young boy
in the novel to think him a coward. Shane knew exactly why he backed
down and was comfortable with it. He did not want to hurt anyone else.
I could relate.

The Fence

I was starting to bite off more than I could chew, putting my safety in
jeopardy. I had already made the decision about staying away from sex
and drugs, but no one told that to sex and drugs. Making the decision
was not good enough, I soon realized, because sex and drugs were everywhere. No matter how I tried to stay away from them, they came stalk-
ing. Except for having made that very valuable decision, I was vulnerable
prey. Now I had to figure out how to be "in and amongst it" without
becoming "involved." Not an easy task being a wild young girl in the
seventies.

I still wanted to have fun, but I was quickly learning that older people's ideas of fun involved sex and drugs. Especially older people who
would allow a young girl to join them. *Ugh.* Because of this simple fact,
acting older was not all it was cracked up to be. I simply was not emotionally equipped for all that I could possibly encounter, for all that *could*
go wrong.

The rule in our house was that I wasn't supposed to date until I was
sixteen. That was the age we girls could get our ears pierced, too. I let my
older neighbor pierce mine when I was thirteen. My first date was in the
eighth grade, with a very popular sixteen-year-old boy. He took me to
see the movie "Easy Rider," and then to cruise McDonald's. Everyone in
our town cruised McDonald's. Around and around they'd go, until they
thought they had sufficiently seen and been seen by others. We left to go
parking on top of a large hill in town. As soon as he turned off the car,
he leaned over to kiss me, putting his hand on my breast. I immediately
slapped him hard and told him to take me home.

One night, my friend and I sat in the gully across the street from my
house and drank vodka. I only took a few sips, as I really did not like the
taste, but we sat there until five in the morning. No one in my family
noticed I was gone. There was a corner house down at the intersection

that had fairly new people living in it. Through the night we watched as many cars drove in and out of the driveway. People stood laughing, yelling, and talking in the yard. They were clearly old enough to be out of high school.

Intrigued by this, wanting to know more, I later ventured into this circle, and found myself invited into their house. The woman was young, had a husband, and two small children in bed. She was very friendly, though I was obviously at least ten years younger. Again, people were coming and going, through the door and down the hall. Red lights were the only ones on in the house. A fellow came up to me and sat down. I recognized him to be the way-too-much-older boyfriend of my wild classmate. Soon enough he put his arm around me, and leaned in for a kiss. I said, "What about Penny?" He was surprised I knew anything about her, and backed off. All the while, probably twenty people had pulled into the driveway, been heartily greeted at the door, and then enthusiastically led down the hallway into a bedroom. Soon enough, they were back out again and gone.

Uh, oh. Sex and drugs. I got myself out of there quickly, went home, and for days afterward I felt myself quivering in my own skin. Here I had been so close to a situation that could have led me down a road I did not want to go down. *What was I to do?* I could tell I was developing now and at fourteen, boys – some much older – were looking at me differently. *What if he'd tried more? How would I have responded?* He was much older and bigger, and though I prided myself on taking risks, *that* feeling of danger was more than I could handle.

It was then my psyche put me on a fence.

For about a month, I was walking it, tiptoeing gingerly. In my mind's eye it was a two by four beam, laid flat, so that I was walking the four-inch wide strip. But it was wrapped in barbed wire. I had to be very careful not to trip on the jagged wires that wound the post. I saw myself on it every day, walking carefully. Each day, I shook and quivered, as if I were really walking it, wobbling, trying not to fall.

I did not know what to do. I needed someone to talk to, but about what? My fear of falling to the other side? One side of the fence represented my family: my sweet and kind mother and my struggling siblings, the blood, sweat, and tears of hard work we had put into our family's survival. On that side was our church and all the people who'd helped keep us afloat so that we could survive the devastation of the shooting, go on to college, and make something of ourselves. How was I to let them down? Say sorry, thanks, you did a great deal for me, but it was not enough? Your efforts were in vain? It was like a slap in the face to my family, to everything I knew I had the power to become.

Or did I? The largest part of me believed I was destined to be this hoodlum, which surely meant becoming a criminal. When my thoughts traveled further than that, I knew that would not be acceptable to me. I did not want to remain this violent, scared person with no one to talk to. I'd probably have to kill myself or be killed. So, essentially, the other side of the fence meant a spiritual or literal death.

I walked that fence with these thoughts ever present in my mind. I went about my work at school and home. I was careful not to do any of my usual foolishness. The school year was ending soon. I had accumulated enough detentions to last until the very last day, as there was nothing more to do with me.

The biggest reason I did not want to engage with others is that I did not want to tumble. Something told me that if I should fall on either side, I would only be given that one landing, and there I would remain. There was a good side and a bad side. The good side was my life with my family, where I was the person I thought they barely knew. I did not know how to fit there, how to be myself, whoever that was. The bad side was a life I had lightly experienced but one that scared me. That was not the person I wanted to be. But how was I to decide? It seemed that neither worked for me, so on the fence I tiptoed.

You know that jittery feeling of being super, duper stressed out when your body's tied up into knots? Then something happens, and you just fall apart? Well, my body had finally become the full-fledged rock it had been destined to become on the night of the shooting. Every day I saw my Uncle George's head fall back laughing hysterically, and every day I saw that piece of mahogany furniture, the birthplace of my rock. By now, my hatred from that moment was magnified many times over.

Outside I was a rock. Inside, I was quivering and quaking. I was physically shaking now. Everywhere I went. I was trying desperately to keep myself up on that fence, lest I fall unsuspectingly. My body shook so much, I thought others could see it, but they could not. The stress inside me wanted out. My body was not large enough to contain it for so many years. I felt I was bursting at the seams. Terrified.

Then came the day I fell off the fence.

The Farmer

In all his wisdom, Mr. Taylor, who'd been my middle school principal for two years, said, "Let's go for a walk." The courtyard at my school separated the middle school from the high school, with the gym and cafeteria in the middle, and the library above the covered courtyard.

And so we walked, he in his suit and I in my fence-walking attire. When we got to the other side, he opened the door for me and said, "There's somebody I want you to meet."

We walked into a typical high school office with a large waiting area in front of a long counter covered with various forms, with secretaries' desks and ringing phones behind it. Mr. Huggins was standing on the other side of the counter when we walked in. Mr. Taylor motioned for him to come around to our side of the counter. Mr. Huggins joined us in the large waiting area. Both men were very relaxed, and Mr. Taylor said to Mr. Huggins, "Here's somebody I want you to meet. I'm afraid if we don't help her, we're going to lose her."

Those were the truest words I'd ever heard spoken by an adult. Finally, someone I could respect. My eyes flashed upward when he said it. I was stunned. He knew what I knew!

With that, Mr. Huggins said to him, "Is that right?" as they both looked down at me, noticing the deer-in-the-headlights look on my face. Then to me, Mr. Huggins said, "Okay, come on back," letting Mr. Taylor know he'd take it from there.

As he held open the hinged door for me, Mr. Huggins said, "Follow me." As he passed his secretary, he said, "Hold all my calls."

He held the door to his office open for me. I walked in and he closed the door. He turned down the blinds on the window of the door. He motioned for me to sit down in the chair across from his. He walked around his desk to sit in his chair, lifted the telephone receiver off its hook, and laid it on the desk. *He already said 'No calls'!* Then he put his feet up on his desk and clasped both hands behind his head. With an upward motion of his shoulder blades and a very relaxed look on his face, he looked me directly in the eye. In an easy tone, he asked, "What's wrong?"

Caught. Red handed. Here I was alone in a room with a man who'd given me the illusion of having all the time in the world for me, looking me directly in the eye. I'd had a lot of attention in the previous years, but this kind of attention was frightening. It had never happened. I could only look into his eyes for a second, but in that heartbeat of a second, I broke. I flung my head down hard and began to cry. I cried and cried, to the point of heaving and sobbing. Somewhere deep inside me a valve released and with every heave, tears literally poured out of me. The floodgates had opened. My nose was running into my lap in long clear strands of string. I could see it, but I could *not* lift my heavy head, and I could *not* stop crying. I did not stop. I cried on and on, convulsively.

There was no movement in the room, no rush to the door, no touch that came to my knee, no hug, no box of tissues thrust under my nose. There was only a witness giving me eye contact and space to be who I was and feel what I was feeling. At last. Space. With another human being, looking me in the eyes, not flustered by the sight of me before him.

I'd venture to say that I stayed in that position crying for twenty minutes. My body drooped; my head was dangling like a bowling ball. My shame was unbearable and into my lap it puddled. As I realized there was going to continue to be "space," and no rushing in of an ambulance to cart me off to the insane asylum, or paddy wagon to send me to jail, I began to relax in the quiet this man provided. With that relaxation, came my ability to lift my head.

Slowly I did lift my head, and when I did, Mr. Huggins was in the exact same spot. Legs down, hands in his lap now, his eyes were looking directly into mine. He'd not budged.

With his question still lingering in the air, I lifted my head fully. I looked him dead in the eye. Out of my mouth came the words that had been on the tip of my tongue for seven years. "My father shot my mom, and I'm mad!"

With that, I hung my head once more and cried on. This time not as hard, but the heaving did come. When it did, I coughed and spluttered. The words were out. The rock had crumbled.

Again, Mr. Huggins said not a word. Today, I marvel at that. He had virtually not moved. It seemed the wisest move I'd ever seen someone make - was not a move at all. He did not speak until I lifted my head fully the second time and was looking him in the eyes. He leaned forward and said, "This is all fair and good. I'd be mad, too. Now, how are we going to educate you?"

Had he not heard what I'd said? Surely he did because he said he'd be mad, too, but how can he be talking about educating me after that? Say what?

I did not understand, because it was the first time I'd experienced grand emotions coupled with an educational outlook. The concept befuddled me. One day I'd learn about this technique, but now all I could do was feel how it affected me. I looked at him in bewilderment. *Educate me? What? How? Why? What on earth are you talking about?*

And then he said, "You have so much energy!" He thrust out his long arms to one side and said enthusiastically, "Right now, all your energy is going into negative things." I stared at his long arms that, while apart, created a channel. "We have to find some way to have you pull your energy back from negative things and funnel it into positive things." He yanked his arms back to his torso, turned slightly and propelled his arms out in front of him in the other direction. Again, I could see the "channel" he spoke of.

The fence! He's showing me what is on either side of the fence! Yes! That is what I've been trying to do! Yes! Yes! Show me! How can I live on this... 'positive' side?

I was stuck on the word positive. I did not know what it meant. I was fourteen years old. My mother was a walking dictionary, my father had been an English major in college, and I had a wide vocabulary. How, then, had this word escaped my knowledge thus far in life?

Even though I did not know exactly what he meant, I got the gist of it. And, I was fixated on *how* he said, "You have so much energy!" That was different. How he said it. It was said with so much enthusiasm, in a tone I'd never heard before when spoken about me. Previously, the nicest thing I ever heard said about me was from a counselor at camp when he said, "Lynnie's not a bad kid. She's mischievous, but she's not bad."

That day in front of Mr. Huggins, I only knew this "energy" business sounded much better than anything else I'd heard said about me. He had a happy tone in his voice. That one sentence turned my world around. "You have so much energy!" Five simple words, but it was the *tone.* His tone was loving and kind, unaffected by "where" or "into what" my energy had gone. I just *had* it.

Later I realized the loving tone of his voice and the words he said matched my inner voice, the one that had guided me to this point. He was the first person I ever met who came *close* to matching my inner voice. After that it was as if his words were drawing me to them. The force was strong. It was as if my T-shirt was being pinched at the sternum, and being pulled forward, dragging me along. I did not know why then. I only knew that I liked it. I felt more whole being around someone who spoke kindly and in a loving tone, like my inner voice spoke to me. When my inner and outer voices matched, I felt like all was right with the world.

As if my body was like the soldiers at Buckingham Palace who make sharp turns, I made a complete switch in a different direction that day.

Mr. Huggins explained that my feelings were very important and that I needed to get them out, but my education was equally so. Therefore, I had to work on both in equal amounts of time. He handed me a blank, wide-rule, spiral notebook, and said, "Here, take this, write down your feelings, and bring it back to me. I will read them."

I said, "Okay." I got up and went to class.

I had a friend. For the first time in my life, I'd made a real friend, someone who knew the deepest part of me.

In one version of "The Ugly Duckling," I think of Mr. Huggins. When the ugly duckling is shunned by her flock, she flies away. Awkward, naïve, and unknowledgeable, she drifts for a long time, not being able to find her way. One winter day, very tired, she sits down in the water, too young and uneducated to know that at night the water will freeze. The next morning, sure enough, she is stuck – her bottom has frozen onto the lake. She cannot budge. She sits there in frustration for a long time, wondering if she might die in this position when along comes a farmer who sees her predicament. The farmer goes away and comes back with his tools. Down at the side of the lake, he pulls an ice pick from his toolbox, and carefully, carefully, walks out onto the ice where the scared duckling is trapped. He begins to delicately chip away at the ice, knowing full well that if he chips away too hard, he and the duckling are bound to fall into the frozen lake and die. He must be careful, too, not to pierce the body of the little duck, so as not to kill it. Soon enough the duckling is set free, and when she walks across the frozen lake, she wiggles her bum to get off the residue of ice. The farmer is pleased and the duckling is grateful. The farmer takes the duckling home to sit by the fire, to rest up for the long road ahead. There is an understanding that although this may be the man who freed the duckling, he may not be the one to whom the duckling belongs; the duckling must be able to seek and find her own kind. After a month, the duckling, educated more about the ways of the world, has found a friend along her path, and is ready to begin her journey anew.

I had found my farmer.

My mentor, my therapist, my father, my friend

I do not remember if he said, "Bring it back to me when it's full," or "Bring it back to me when you want." I do know that in two days, I'd filled the entire spiral notebook with my unbridled thoughts and feelings. The valve had been released, the cork in the bottle let out, the plug in the dike removed.

I dropped off the notebook and two days later Mr. Huggins called me to his office. When I sat down, he handed back the notebook. I opened it. To my surprise and mortification, he had indeed read every page – and he had corrected in red ink every grammar and punctuation mistake I'd made!

What? These are my feelings? How could you? I did not write this to have it be critiqued in this way! How dare you take my thoughts and mark through them like this! Who cares about grammar? I wasn't even thinking about my grammar when I wrote this. I thought I could just write to you freely. These thoughts went through my head in a matter of seconds and then Bingo! I remembered what he'd said. *Oh, I see, this is how you will teach me. You said I needed to give equal weight to my feelings as to my education. Oh, I get it. I can let my feelings out until the cows come home, but in the meantime, I am to study and learn. I am to build a life from where I am now.*

I knew right then and there I had a mentor. On the right side of the fence.

I did not speak a word of this to Mr. Huggins. I was mute in his presence. If ever anyone was meant to be molded, it was I. Mr. Huggins was the potter and I was his clay. In the same meeting when he handed back my notebook and told me to continue writing, he said, "Now, we have got to get you into something, a sport, an activity where you can put all of this energy!" I was all ears. "I want you to run for a class officer."

"What's that?" He explained what the student government was and that I would have to be elected by my peers.

"And a sport. I want you to think of a sport to do, something you're good at. You don't have to know now. Just think about it and we'll find one for you in the fall."

All this could be done. None of this was scary to me. Maybe I was well known enough to win an election. Maybe. I was athletic. Maybe I could find a sport. I could do this. For the first time in my life, I was looking ahead with that positive attitude he spoke of.

I never described the details of the shooting to Mr. Huggins. In fact, after that first sentence rolled off the tip of my tongue, we never spoke of it again. I didn't cry again, either. Every conversation we had after that was either present or future related. It would be many years before I'd speak of or write about the pictures in my head.

From this time period with Mr. Huggins, I learned the value of directly telling someone what TO DO. So many times I see an adult asking a child, "Well, what do you think you should be doing?" and then wait for an answer, as if he's going to get one. If the child knew what TO DO, he'd probably already be doing it. I was one big, black hole. I needed someone to guide me out of it.

In between my studies, I continued to write my thoughts and feelings down in spiral notebooks. I continued to give them to Mr. Huggins, and he continued to hand them back, my mistakes marked in red ink. Writing was an assignment. It was the tool Mr. Huggins used to reach me. Little did I know that my writing to him in these early days would form my habit of reaching for a spiral notebook and pen in all times of stress. It is no coincidence I am an English teacher today.

B Through Y

Anyone who has tried to make great changes is familiar with the lightning bolt of change, meaning you take three steps forward and two steps backward, and so forth. The zig and the zag, I call it. Although I was on my way and knew I didn't ever have to go back to walking that fence, I now had to figure out how to live on this side.

From the moment Mr. Huggins asked me what was wrong, my life changed. What I've learned about change is that it is very tricky. I have come to use the alphabet as an analogy for change. For instance, you are A and A is really, really bad. It is something others do not want you to be; *even* you do not want to be. A goes against the norms of society and you have decided that yes, you want to change. But Z is where it's at! That's where others are, the ones who frown upon your being A. So, you set out to be Z. Heck, you'll settle for W, X, or Y. You just want to get close.

But here you are at A. B does not look far off, so you attempt to make changes in your life.

Without ever knowing how to be a Z, I can tell you from experience, B through Y is ugly. You don't have to be a rocket scientist to know that anyone who attempts to change her life to the degree I needed to change, is going to fail, again and again. Failure hurts. It brings up fear, embarrassment, humiliation, shame, and guilt – all of the ugly emotions. But it is these emotions that need to be felt, walked through, to get to the other side. You start the best you can, you look for a steppingstone to place your feet, and you leap.

B through Y is every experience you have when you want to speak up where you have usually been silent, knowing that your speaking up may change your relationships forever. B through Y is stopping yourself from talking too much when you know you have said enough. B through Y is finally telling someone who has treated you badly how you feel. B through Y is saying you're sorry to the person you know you have been using or been unkind to or one you have been talking about behind his back. B through Y is when you do the thing that you fear because you think it will make you a better person. B through Y is saying goodbye to someone you love because you know that person is not good for your personal growth, despite the big bursts of laughter, excitement, familiarity, or history you share. B through Y is when you begin hanging around with different people because they are better for you, though at first they may seem boring. You feel awkward and clumsy and do not know how to respond. B through Y is learning how to take criticism well, learning how to trust the giver. B through Y is learning how to be laughed at without resorting to violence, being kind where you used to be harsh, being firm where you used to be a marshmallow. B through Y is telling the truth to someone in spite of the cost.

Navigating B through Y is a very hard thing to begin in your teenage years, yet it was to be my life if I was to learn how to walk a straight path.

I have heard many sane people talk about the fact that they will not allow themselves to "go there," to make big changes, open up their emotions, to get too angry, because they are fearful that once the plug is let out of the dike, they will not be able to control their anger. Or their fear of humiliation is so great, they prefer not to take the risk.

Meeting Mr. Huggins let the steam out of my pressure cooker, so I was able to put my anger on the back burner. Now, I had to learn how to live. Where were role models for what I needed? It seemed that most people were already at Z and happy there. I didn't see people let out their real feelings, so how was I to know how to do it?

The road to good, solid health was going to take a lifetime to achieve. I was at the beginning stages of just learning not to hit, and a far cry from learning how to resolve conflicts with words. One thing I did have going for me was that I'd witnessed a maniac be brought to a calm, with honest words. I knew it could be achieved. If I could only get there – to speak without fear in the midst of conflict. Mary had done it. Problems could be resolved through using words. Little did I know the firestorm I'd have to walk through to find the courage to use words, especially the word "No!"

I knew nothing about posttraumatic stress disorder, nothing about the responses to grief. I'd not seen effective communication modeled. Had it been explained to me in advance that this was going to be a very long, difficult, and extremely painful road to travel, it might have been easier. I did not understand there were phases of healing trauma that I would have to walk through, that there was an end to each phase. Up ahead of me, Mr. Huggins held a light. It was my job to navigate the rocks below, never knowing if or when I'd fall, trying desperately to think my way through the process of becoming a person with appropriate feelings.

Zigging and Zagging

Although I was now on the side of the fence where I wanted to be, it was not going to be without its ups and downs. I was still scared, but felt calmer, connected. One time I attempted to open the door about the shooting with Mary. I wanted to have a conversation, to find out what was in her head, what pictures she carried. Was she still suffering inside, like me? I wrote in her high school yearbook that she was my hero (for saving Mom), but when she read it, she just rolled her eyes and snapped, "Oh, Lynnie, you're so dramatic!"

I thought I must be crazy for bringing up something that was so long ago and seemed not to matter. But how could I explain to people that those pictures were with me every single day? Fresh. Like yesterday. If I could not explain it to Mary, who was there and part of the pictures, how could I approach someone else?

It was now the summer of my fourteenth year and I was leaving for camp. My father came to see us off at the bus, along with my mother. He came around to the backside of the bus and asked me if there was anything I needed. "Yes! A carton of cigarettes!"

"Really?"

And, half kidding, I said again, "Yeah! Will you go get me a carton of cigarettes?" He nodded and scurried off. I really did not think he would go get them, much less be back in time. But he did and he was. He handed me a carton of cigarettes, all smiles, through the back bus window that was facing the street. Cigarettes were legal to have at camp since they gave us smoking breaks after meals, but something seemed so sad and pathetic. It made me feel dirty somehow and that I'd used him because no father in his right mind would do that for his daughter. That's when I realized that no one is in his right mind when he's desperate to be loved. The reason it felt dirty was it was simply wrong to put him in that position, when all he wanted was love.

In the early days of Camp Merry Ledges, the directors were fun, free, and frolicking. Then along came a new director, Miss June, a former nun, who was very strict. Not such a good mix with the wild fourteen-year-old I was. Camp activities were already established, so she was not able to interfere with our ability to enjoy what we loved.

My own mother had been overly permissive. A pattern in my life became not faring well with strict women in authority, especially those who, in my mind, were trying to take away my fun. In fairness to them, to gain control of a group that has an uncontrollable person in it, that person must be squashed to have order. I wasn't into being squashed. Miss June and I were on our fourth summer together. She was looking for a reason to kick me out of camp for good. It was not long before she found one.

Some of us rode to town to go to Mass. On Sunday night a new counselor drove my buddies and me there in a station wagon. We filled up the back pew of the church, except for the counselor who went to the front. It had only been a few minutes into Mass when my buddies and I decided to leave. We walked around the small town and found ourselves sitting on the grass under the shade of a tree. I suggested that we ask the next car of guys who drove by to get us some beer. That's just what we did, and, within minutes, they brought us a six-pack of beer. I did not even drink beer! None of us really drank, but drinking beer had to be the ultimate in pushing the envelope. It was definitely pushed too far when someone suggested we try to sneak the beers back into camp. I did not think that was such a good idea, but someone put the beers into the bottom compartment of the station wagon.

We were back in the pew to catch the tail end of church. As we pulled out of the church parking lot, the beer bottles rattled and clashed. The counselor was confused and one girl let out a sputtering laugh. We were doomed.

The counselor had to tell the director. We were all scared, but that night we allowed some kids from other units to visit our tents anyway. Part of the fun of being an older camper was sneaking around at night visiting other tents. We discussed what had happened and wondered our fate out loud. Basically, we were saying our goodbyes. We knew this was serious.

Sure enough, the next morning all our parents had been called, and we were expelled from summer camp. My brother Aaron made the drive to pick me up, mad as a hornet that he had to do so, but madder still that I'd gotten into this kind of trouble when Mom was just out of the hospital, recovering from a surgery. He did not want this to upset her, so *he* put me on restriction. I could not go anywhere for two weeks. Aaron drove an ice cream truck that summer and came back to the house now and again to check on me. I was there.

As if getting kicked out of camp was not enough that summer, I almost burned down the kitchen. Weeks later, preparing for a picnic, Mom was frying chicken on the stovetop. I had been given the task of taking the last three pieces out of the oil when they were done. Mom, Mary, and Judy went to Mom's bedroom to read the Sunday paper. Envious, I joined them a few minutes later. I closed the door to Mom's air-conditioned bedroom. Several minutes later, I opened the door to find a perfectly straight line of the blackest black smoke, parallel to the floor at mid-thigh level, stretching across the living room and down the hall. The chicken was on fire. To see anything, we had to scamper on the floor to the kitchen. We were all panicked, trying to reach the flames. Mom finally put a lid over the chicken, and Poof! The fire was out.

It took me six months to clean all the places the dirty, black, soot had reached. It was everywhere! I had to re-paint the whole kitchen, including the cabinets.

My friend Jane and I spent much of the summer together. She was a gymnast and thinking of going out for cheerleading. I thought about it, too. One day we were sitting on the hill on her front lawn, smoking cigarettes. Her older sister, in a hurry to accomplish a task, asked us to go to my house to get her a certain pair of scissors. We ran as fast as we could, got the scissors, and ran back. But the scissors were the wrong type. We ran back to my house to get the right pair, and then back to Jane's house where we handed them to her sister. Jane and I sat on the hill again, huffing and puffing. For the first time in my life, I was having difficulty breathing. Remembering Mr. Huggins suggesting I join a sport in the fall, I looked at Jane and said, "You know that cigarette I just smoked?" And without waiting for an answer, I continued, "That's the last one I'm ever gonna smoke." And it was.

When fall came, I was ready. I decided to run for my freshman class vice president. The week of campaigning was to begin. The banners were hung. While making last-minute touch ups, taping up my posters, I just happened to see my eighth grade math teacher who at that very minute glanced at the posters and learned I was running for an office. As soon as she read my poster, she approached Mr. Huggins in the same hallway and said, "You cannot let a girl like that run!"

He put up both his hands, with palms out and facing her, looked her in the eyes, and snapped, "She's running." He dropped his hands, but continued to look at her a second or two more, as she drank in what he'd said, before continuing on his way.

Someone in high places was pulling for me. *Wow!*

Because I'd gone to a parochial school that produced a lot of smart kids, and because I'd spent the last two years in the junior high smoke hole, which produced many hoodlums, I pretty much knew everyone and everyone knew me. I won the election.

When I told everyone at home I'd won the election, the response was, "Okay, so what? Get back to your chores!" I was a little surprised at first because I'd never heard of anyone in my family doing anything like this, running for office. But, just about that fast, my thoughts turned to: *This is probably good that everyone is acting like this is no big deal. That way, I'll never be conceited.* I was happy with that thought, because at that age, it seemed like being called conceited was the worst insult. It was decades before I realized that some families actually took their child out to dinner to celebrate this kind of win.

I had a ball being a class officer and worked my tail off in the position. The only real trouble I caused that year was not really trouble, just performing dare-devilish antics. Our freshman class had a car wash to raise money and we got out of class for an hour or so to pitch in. I finagled a way to stay out there all day. I went around to all the teachers and asked them if they wanted their cars washed. When they said yes, I took each set of car keys, proceeded outside to drive each car up to be cleaned, and then parked it back in its spot when finished. The trouble was, I did not have a driver's license. No teacher knew that I was the one driving. No one asked, and I did not say.

I'd been driving various cars for years, here and there, and had already wrecked two cars by age twelve – one belonged to a boy in our neighborhood, another belonged to the boy in the country. Now, I was a seasoned driver at fourteen.

Vice president or not, I still had a little rascal in me.

Choosing a Clear Path

I was coming into my own; I could feel it. Mr. Huggins was giving me tasks, and I wanted to be responsible for him. I was finally getting a chance to be who I thought I really was. I loved people. I talked and laughed with everyone. I was so happy people had voted for me and had, essentially, given me a job. It was more than that. I was grateful. I took it seriously. From then until the end of my senior year, I got to know something about everyone. I asked people their names, I sat in on conversations, and I made it a point to know things about people. I began to find joy in making people happy, just by being friendly and striking up conversations.

What I noticed is that a lot of people were surprised to be talked to. Many were shy, but I found those were the people who often had unique perspectives and flat out honest comments. I sought out those people. I was never in a clique, never wanted to be. Too constraining. I always loved being included in people's circles, and I moved around them easily. But I saw that others did not have as easy a time. I sensed they felt excluded. I knew those kinds of feelings didn't just come out of thin air. I became a detective. I started to notice the actions of others that might make people actually feel excluded. Here I was, working so hard to help people feel good. I was fighting a battle with something invisible.

I noticed that mostly, exclusion was done with proximity or words. Someone walking into a crowd saying to only one person, "We're going to the pizza parlor tonight. Wanna come?" or "I'm having a sleepover on Friday night. You're invited!" or comments directed to someone close about someone across the way, "Did you see what she was wearing? I'd never wear that." Or in bragging, "I never shop for sales. My mom spends full price on me."

I decided many words and actions excluded people, or made them feel inferior, less than. This was unkind. I had a nagging inner sense. I began to pick up the other ways that people abused each other, on a regular, more acceptable basis, *with words*.

Inside my house, I'd seen blatant bullying. Outside my house, and now out of the fog, bullying never escaped me. It was the subtle bullying I began to take a deep interest in, watching the acts as if they were movies being played out in front of me. There was no measuring the two; blatant or subtle, bullying was wrong.

I deflected so much of what was said. Whenever something negative was said, I did not attach much significance to it and thought worse of the person who'd said it. But that did not seem the case with everyone. I noticed people actually *following* the person who made the mean comment. To my surprise, others were buying it! I wondered if it was to avoid being ridiculed themselves.

When comments like these were made I noticed the corners of mouths turning up slightly, ready to laugh at the cruel words, but realizing that this was somehow not funny. I'd see in their down-turned eyes that they quickly realized it was a mistake, but it was too late – the laugh was out. Or I noticed the slight puff of laughter that popped out of someone's mouth, only to be followed by eyes darting around to see if others had been impacted as well. Then more down-turned eyes.

I noticed how words could turn the air into something else, could change the chemistry of a room. I'd seen enough of this at home, from subtleties to ugly words to violence, the senseless harm that only pulled a person backwards. Probably because I'd been so rough, I was not bullied at school, but when I saw the down-turned eyes of those ridiculed, something in me wanted to step in. There had to be another way.

I was going to include people. I was going to be kind. I would never have used the word kind in those days, but that is what I'd call my choice today. Somehow, I had a real knack for it. I'd had a bubbly, gregarious personality before, during and after my hoodlum days, but something was different. I sensed my changes were noticed. The real smart people may have wondered if I was really changing, and my old smoke-hole buddies seemed to be sending me messages like "More power to you, Lynnie!"

In seventh and eighth grades, with my girlfriends, I remembered flicking other kids with rubber bands in a catch-me-if-you-can sort of way, or kicking boys in the ankles on purpose during square dancing class. We'd all laugh, but it was definitely bullying. I'd been a bully myself.

Understandably, I may still have been a little intimidating and unpredictable to some. I decided to use that position, though, as a means to protect others from this subtle bullying. If I ever noticed anyone bullying, I stepped in readily to divert the conversation. It was a way for me to manage the anger brewing inside me. I used the leader in me to help others. I could not protect myself at home. The victim in me was alive and well there and my steady anger still seethed, but I could protect others at school because I now had someone there to protect me.

I started volunteering regularly for the Red Cross in the blood bank downtown. This was a job I loved for years and it made me feel good about myself.

Being kind worked for me. It was the essence of who I was. My well of compassion for people was deep; it was my natural response. Protecting others from harsh words would be a challenge, especially when I learned that some had perfected this kind of bullying to an art form. The highest price for this art went to those proficient at subtleties.

Subtleties are the nuances only some get. When a person has said something ever so subtly, often its full effects are not realized until after that person has left. It is as if the person has walked through the room or conversation with a razor blade and gone slit, slit, slit and vanished. And slowly, suddenly, you start to see little droplets of blood on the victims, and the hurt and suffering from the words has begun.

It's like that feeling of wishing you'd had a comeback to a nasty remark, and then thinking of it later, and wanting a repeat opportunity. But it's more than that. Often the most brilliant words strung together for a comeback neither overcome, nor restore the damage that has been done by the most cunning words. It is the bully for whom there is no comeback who is most damaging. Or worse, for whom no one but you noticed the need for a comeback. *This* bully is greatest at her craft. She will rise in popularity among a crowd of girls whose insecurities are so well hidden they may lie years and layers deep. And on top of that, there may be nothing there when the layers are removed. Followers.

Maya Angelou once said she believed one day science would be able to measure the effects of words on people. She said the expression "throwing a dart at someone" from across a room had more meaning than we realized, that the chemical make-up of our bodies actually changes in the face of harsh, or loving words.

After being traumatized by a rape when she was seven years old, Maya Angelou remained totally mute for seven years. She came away from her life experiences with a deep understanding of the power of words. I felt a closeness to her. The shooting had happened when I was seven and I did not talk about it until I met Mr. Huggins at fourteen. It may seem strange to some, how one would come to know the power of words when she does not possess them. I liken it to freedom. When one does not have it, one realizes its importance.

The Present

For a very brief period of my life, I made a new friend. Midge had been shipped around from foster home to foster home and somehow landed in our neighborhood for a year. She was a tall girl with brown hair and a deep, raspy laugh who enjoyed just spending *time* with us. She, Judy, and I got along wonderfully and we did just that: spent hours in our bedroom talking, playing, and laughing.

I sensed our house was a refuge for Midge, one she'd longed for all her life. It was from her I learned how utterly devastating it would have been for me to have moved from place to place without a parent, had we lost Mom. Although our family was dysfunctional, we remained in one house my entire life growing up, which, given what we'd already been through, I believe contributed to my well being in untold ways.

I intuitively knew that the depth of Midge's pain, although different from mine, reached as far. One indication of this was that she always wanted to have fun and laugh. She did not have to *go* anywhere to do it. It was as if any pain she'd suffered, she knew was not real and what was real was experiencing joy in all its simplest forms. Although I never spoke of this to her, her wisdom touched me deeply.

In November, Midge told me she had to move back to California. I felt a cannon go off in my chest. The thought of losing her caused a deep and piercing pain. The sharpness of the initial impact lessened, but the pain in my chest did not go away for a month.

When Christmastime came, Midge gave me a present. It was a tape dispenser for labeling, that when clicked, embossed letters onto the tape. I could click out words onto the tape and stick the tape on my note-books or drawers. It only came with a certain amount of tape, so I had to be careful not to make mistakes.

On Christmas Eve day, I was lying in my bottom bunk. I heard a sound. "Click, click, click." I thought nothing of it. This sound went on for a very long time, and became part of the rhythm of the rest I was having, drifting in and out of sleep. Then all of a sudden, I realized with certainty exactly what the clicking sound was. I ran out into the living room and saw Carl, clicking on the tape dispenser, the same letter, over and over. The used tape wound around and around itself. When he saw my disbelief, he chuckled, proud to have provoked me.

I flew into a rage. "Give me that!" I yanked it out of his hand and stood there with an evil face spewing curse words, one after the other. This was something I'd never done but had seen Mary do many times. It was my first time standing up to my brother. I went overboard on the cursing. He stood up, raised his right hand over his head and, with all his might, brought it down crashing onto the left side of my face. The right side of my face slammed onto the floor, knocking me unconscious.

Coming to, I felt my mom and sisters dragging me into the bedroom. I was crying, beet-red, with both sides of my face and ears burning and throbbing. It was the hardest I'd ever been hit.

My sister was telling Mom to make Carl leave. My mother, of course, was whimpering and crying. From the first whimpering gasp that came from her, I knew. My psyche had seen this movie many times. Carl would not be going anywhere. The flash of despair I felt in that moment, realizing it would take a hit worse than this one, in order for Mom to demand him to leave the house, sent a chill through me. *How much worse than knocking me out cold on Christmas Eve would it have to get?* I knew he was capable of hurting me much worse. Was my mother really willing to allow him to stay and chance this?

In that moment I experienced the depths of despair my brothers must have felt toward my mother who'd allowed my father to stay for so long – too long. All I knew for sure in that moment was that I was going to be hurt again. A wave of humiliation crashed over me as I realized my mother was going to allow it.

I was supposed to go to dinner that night to meet the family of my first, real boyfriend. We'd been having so much fun going out to movies in his car. I did not want to go to this dinner, truly ashamed of how I looked and felt. But the girls in my family encouraged me to go. Two hours later, I walked out of my house all dressed up. I sat at the dinner table with his family in their very attractive home. I remembered the dinner well – in color, people, decoration, and food - but the next day, I could not recall what had been said.

I was in shock.

Midge moved to California and we wrote letters regularly. The only thing that seemed to soothe the hurt of her move was our promise to see each other again someday.

Teenage Roller Coaster

I continued to date my boyfriend, but after six months he wanted more than just kissing and hugging. Since I'd already decided that was not going to happen until I was much older, he broke up with me. He told me in the stairwell at school. He said he needed more time with friends, which I thought was fishy because he was always with his friends. My first real break-up crushed me. Weirdly, just then the announcement came over the speakers that I'd won the election to be my sophomore class president for the following year. Still standing in the stairwell after receiving the news, everyone came to congratulate me. I tried to smile.

That afternoon, I was lying on my bottom bunk. Mary, seeing how hurt I was, said in the sweetest voice, "Come on, Lynnie. I'll take you to a movie." She took me to see "Serpico." I will always remember that day for the kindness she showed me when I was so down. Surprisingly, it really did help.

A day later, again in my bunk, Mom slipped me a note written in her own hand. Although her handwriting was hard to read, I made out what it said, "If you love something, let it go. If it comes back to you, it is yours. If it doesn't, it never was." That made a lot of sense and I was able to come out of it, just in time to see my now old boyfriend with a new girl. I heard from a reliable source that this relationship started before ours ended. Sure enough, in the high school yearbook two years later, their anniversary of dating was two days after we'd broken up.

During the year, every so often, Mr. Huggins sent a message to my teacher, asking for me to be sent to his office. This did not seem peculiar to any of my teachers, given my feisty personality and the fact that I'd always been in trouble in the past. No one knew the real reason I went to the office. I think most assumed I was still making trouble – somewhere.

When I got to the office and sat down, Mr. Huggins said, "So, how are you?" Off I'd go, a hundred miles a minute, telling him every detail I could possibly think of that had happened to me since last we'd spoken. I was a true motor mouth, and what was wonderful about this, was he never cut me off. He listened and laughed, as I did not hold anything back. He let me talk until he saw I was winding down, and he'd write me a note to go back to class.

For my four years in high school, Mr. Huggins called me to his office just like that. I told him everything. These sessions lasted at least an hour and occasionally two. I never told anyone why I went to the office, but this man was certainly my first therapist.

Years later when I asked him, "Why did you let me just go on and on like that?"

"Because I was fascinated by everything that came out of your mouth." He told me my words were unbridled and unmeasured and, although I never ratted anyone out, through me he gained a unique perspective of the inner workings of the school, something an assistant principal is not normally privy to. Because of that knowledge, he said, I'd made him a better principal.

He also said I gave him insights on how to raise his own children. His first child was exactly ten years behind me, so as I moved up in my high school years, he was continuing to have children, until the fifth and last child. He was later to call me his adopted daughter and said he developed and refined a lot of his child-rearing skills from rearing me first.

During that ninth grade, I was in another fight. My horseback riding buddy, and self-proclaimed spoiled brat, drove me to school each day in her little MG sports car. She wasn't always kind to me. One day in art class she walked by as I was painting a picture. She made a smart-alec remark and purposefully flicked her paintbrush on my painting, ruining it. I leapt out of my seat and beat her up, art materials flying everywhere. We both failed art that semester.

I knew I'd disappointed Mr. Huggins with the two steps back, the zag of my lightning bolt of change. I continued to zig forward and zag backwards over the years, desperate to zig and hoping against hope not to zag.

Something to Cheer About

Mr. Huggins and I talked about which sport I wanted to join freshman year, and I decided to try out for cheerleading. Me, the hoodlum. Hopefully, those days were behind me. I had to try out in front of two thousand students. I won a spot to be a junior varsity cheerleader the following year – tenth grade.

I was new to the cheerleading business, and quickly found that others were old hats; they'd been doing this since little league. I didn't even know what little league was. I learned too, that my coming into the fold along with another new girl meant two other cheerleaders from past years had been squeezed out. I did my best to fit in, but then every so often something happened that made me feel like I was living amongst aliens.

We had cheerleading practice about a mile and a half from my house. I walked, round trip each time, from my neighborhood of shingle-covered houses through the woods, across the school campus, and into the neighborhood of brick houses. We practiced in the yard of another cheerleader who lived in a large house with a long, winding driveway. Her father was a doctor, her mother a nurse, and the house was spacious and comfortable. Just to go into the kitchen to get a drink of water made me feel special. We all seemed to get along very well. One rainy, miserable day, a cheerleader's mother was picking her up. She offered me a ride, which I gladly accepted. When we had driven two blocks and were stopped at a stoplight, the girl turned to me in the back seat. "Well, this is it. We're going that way to Dixie Manor," pointing to the right. To the left was my house, less than five minutes away. It was pouring rain. This girl had always boasted that her mother took her shopping each weekend, which is where they were headed now, so I had to get out.

There is a moment in time when you make decisions about people and no matter what else they do from that point on, nothing can change the decision you've made. You've seen a part of someone that has caused you to realize who they are, deep down inside. I made no protest. I got out quickly and watched the car drive away. I shook my head in bewilderment at the character of both the mother and daughter. When I go to my high school reunions, sure enough, to this day, this woman talks about shopping as if it is her job. Funny, I've known her since first grade and, even though I love her, I find it difficult to respect her.

One day, Aaron needed our help to clear some of our land to build a cabin. By this time in our lives, my sisters were no longer tempted out of bed by Aaron's scrumptious breakfasts. I'd listen to them moan and roll over as he tried to rouse them, but when he came to me, my heart broke at the thought of him going out into the snowy woods by himself. I respected Aaron, and I loved him. I followed him and worked side by side with him throughout the winters. But on this summer day, he needed "all hands on deck" and his friend and we girls pitched in to work.

Aaron had a quality that dreamers and risk takers have: impulsiveness. Sometimes impulsive people make mistakes. Well, Aaron had made a doozey of a mistake. He really did not know how to clear land. He should have cut down each tree and dragged it away separately before he cut down the next one. He did not do that. Aaron cut them down, all at once, one on top of the other, so that what we were left with was a colossal game of pick-up sticks, only on a grand scale with massive trees, each with their limbs intertwined. It was going to take a strong army to fix this problem.

We woke up very early and headed to The Two Hundred without the proper tools, in the summer heat. With the swarming bugs, into the thicket we went. We worked from early morning until four in the afternoon. All day long it was tree limbs, branches, brush, dirt, saws, lifting, dragging, walking, and sweating, while getting scraped and cut. It was the hardest work I'd done to date. On the way home, Aaron and his work crew dropped me off at cheerleading practice. Driving up the circular driveway, I saw the group of seven girls standing there. It occurred to me then that I'd just worked harder in one day than the seven of them probably had with their lives combined. I did not feel less than these girls, nor did I feel better, but I did feel a very deep sense of pride. I knew how to work hard. I knew I had that in me.

Being a loner from a poor family, there still lived in me a small part that dared anyone to question my right to be in this supposedly elite group of girls. We went to cheerleading camp together at the University of Kentucky and I got to experience a whole different kind of camp! It was fun and I was beginning to really enjoy this cheerleading business.

That same summer, despite my fight in art class and my rough-around-the-edges demeanor, my art teacher – who'd given me the F - saw the leader in me and recommended me for leadership camp. I was in my fifteenth summer and felt very lucky to be selected. While there, I met my new boyfriend, Luke, who was going back to school in the fall to be the senior class president of his Catholic high school. His was the same school my two older brothers attended. You know, the one giving the entrance exam that Mom came back to life for, to make sure they got what they needed to take the test - two number two pencils to take the entrance exam? That school.

One day while at the leadership camp, we girls were dressing and undressing in our cabin when I glanced up at the screens that circled the highest part of the walls, just below the ceiling. There was a boy up there, looking into the cabin – watching us undress! I marched out, found him, and punched him square in the nose, knocking off and breaking his glasses. I walked back in as if nothing had happened. In my mind, nothing had happened. Someone did something very wrong, and I punched him in the nose. Simple. His parents found out what he did and had to bring him a new pair of glasses. I did not get in any trouble, although it was suggested to me by a camp counselor that I could possibly have handled it a bit differently. Remember, I was in leadership camp. Still, I had no words.

Helpless in the Dark

That fall I was my sophomore class president, had a boyfriend who was also his class president, was a cheerleader and was soon to be on the gymnastics team. It was to be a big year. At home, I was being tortured. I was not put into a dungeon and hung by my toenails and starved. I was not beaten. I was no longer being pushed, shoved, kicked, having my hair pulled, or made to stay under the bed for hours on end. My torture was a radio.

My older brother, Carl, did not go off to the navy or to college like my other two brothers. He stayed in town to attend a prestigious school. He worked all day and stayed up all night studying. He was mean, angry, and irritable. And silent. He did not yell, but he smirked and growled. The less he said, the more I feared him.

I was afraid for my life when I was around Carl. When he blew up, it was a silent, violent fury. He studied all night at the kitchen table, the only table we had, his books and papers covering the entire octagon where we ate dinner each night. He did not clean up his books when he went off to work, seeming to dare us each day to clean up and pile his things in another place in the house. We did just that and each night he came home, the same scenario occurred. Who could possibly have had the gall to remove his things from the table? Who exactly had done it? He wanted to know. That is when Mary stepped in, no matter who had been the actual one to stack the pile and prepare the table for dinner that night. She blasted him right back with angry words to match his, and he grumbled and walked away. I really admired her for that.

His expectation was that his papers should stay on the kitchen table exactly as they'd been placed, and we would not move them. Something was very wrong with his thinking.

Carl studied all night with the radio turned up. Our house was only 1,200 square feet, so everyone heard the loud radio. I was still untangling my knots. Each night, I endured all I could and, when I finally mustered the courage, I'd ask Carl to please turn down the radio. He just laughed at me, as if he took the utmost pleasure in the fact that yes, his radio had finally driven someone out of her bed to come and beg for something he could deny with pleasure.

It was physical and mental abuse. It was unbearable. Today, I am still triggered by people making noises when I am sleeping, having to reas-

Carl holding one-month old Lynnie

sure myself they are not doing it on purpose.

There was one battle I did attempt on my behalf. We had a very small entrance to an attic and I was the only one who ever went up there. One day, without telling a living soul, I took Carl's radio, wrapped the cord around it and crawled up into the attic. Plywood boards laid on one half of the attic floor, but there were only beams going down to the other end. No one, as far as I knew, ever went to that side. Thinking I might be the first, I took the radio and placed it behind the brick fireplace that went up that side of the house.

And came back to win an Academy Award.

Who had taken the radio? I was as dismayed as everyone else, secretly watching and mimicking the reactions of those who really did have no idea where or with whom the radio had gone. I feared getting caught, but I slept well for a few nights until Carl got another radio. I lived a good portion of my high school years with sleep deprivation.

My one saving grace was the story mom reminded me of regularly. Carl was six years old when I was born, and he'd been so proud of me. He rolled me around in the stroller for all the neighbors to see. He picked me up to hold me and show me off. As a baby, I'd spent a lot of time in his arms. There is even a picture of Carl holding me, wearing a big grin.

There was no wondering, *What happened to him?* I knew. The years of being abused had undermined everything he would have ever wanted to be as a man, had he even been given the chance to decide. I was hoping there was still time.

There is an eerie sort of forgiveness that happens around violence that perhaps others cannot understand. It may even be the force that keeps people together in relationships that are abusive. In the case of my brothers, in the moments I was most hurting from the abuse they were dishing out to me, I could feel the pain they had once suffered from the hands of our father. My cries were *their* cries that I still heard ringing in my ears.

No matter how much I feared my brothers, I never hated them or even lost my love for them. All I wanted for Carl was for him to be able to feel that love again, the love he'd felt when he was six, if not for me, then for someone else.

So instead of just living with abuse at home and going to school each day, I was now living two lives: abuse at home and utter happiness at school. Home became just a place where I did chores and where everyone seemed to walk around dull and gloomy. School was my refuge from that darkness.

And then along came Nem.

A New Kind of Pain

Let me introduce you to Nem or Nemi. I'm naming her this because it's short for Nemesis. It is the closest vocabulary word I can find for someone who, for me, was my exact opposite. In the dictionary, nemesis is something that a person cannot conquer, achieve, etc… or an opponent or rival whom a person cannot best or overcome. But none of these definitions feel quite right. In the thesaurus, nemesis is defined by one word: bane, which means a person that ruins or spoils. I suppose this would best describe what Nem, my nemesis, was for me. A spoiler.

I first saw Nem in the halls in middle school. She was cute, had long hair, and walked down the hall with another long-haired girl. I'd heard their names around the school, but had never met them. They meant little to me.

It was not until ninth grade, when I was a class officer that I was officially introduced to Nem. Neither of us knew at the time, but we were to begin a four-year teammate relationship as class officers and cheerleaders, both of which were yearlong positions. We would be working side-by-side, daily. My first impression of her was neutral. Still, she meant very little to me.

When I say very little, I mean she did not stand out in any way, one way or another, until she started standing out in "another." It was not one thing she did but little by little I began to notice her word choices, her tone of voice, especially how loudly she talked. It was as if she was conscious that everyone was watching her every move, as if on a stage. Most telling was how she manipulated a crowd. Her guise was caring, her tone less credible. Her spirit felt empty to me.

I watched as Nem talked about others not present, as if she cared for them, all the while, revealing their painful, private circumstances and how sorry she felt for them. "Oh, poor Katie. Her mom and dad got into... blah, blah, blah..." or "Oh, I heard that Justin's girlfriend broke up with him. He must feel so bad... blah, blah, blah..." or "Did you hear about Casey? Her dad lost his job and no one is sure what will happen... blah, blah, blah...." These were clearly new and raw issues of others she somehow took excited pride in finding out about first. It was the fact that she spread the news about the pain of someone she barely knew, under the guise of compassion that, for me, was manipulation to the hilt. I did not buy a word of it. What I heard was how she was putting down the people she spoke of, so as to make herself appear larger, better. Plain and simple: it was gossip. She did it very, very well.

Throughout my life, I'd heard from my mother: "Don't listen to gossip and don't get involved with people who speak poorly about others, because you know the minute they get mad at you and you walk away, they will speak poorly about you as well. You can bet on it."

It was a smart piece of advice. I certainly did not want this girl to have any information about me. I knew pain very well, and for her to talk about others' pain as if it was her right, made me sick. Right when I was trying to stop hiding behind my secrets, I was required to be with a person I had to be on guard with. It did not seem fair. I had no tools to work with here, only my intuition. I felt empathy and compassion in my heart, and as I listened to Nem talk about others, something did not ring true.

The story of the shooting in my family was no secret from my schoolmates, yet was simply not talked about in front of me. I knew for certain, had I been less than who I was, that story would have been fodder for

Nem's gossip and myself a candidate for the pity train she loaded with passengers. Although it had been years, my pain was still raw. Imagining Nem talking about my story as she did with others' stories was unfathomable.

I loathed everything about the character she was. Betty Davis came to mind. I cringed when I was around her. I was a leader among my classmates, and I took that job seriously. She was the center of her universe and I cannot say I ever heard anything of substance come out of her mouth. Even being the rascal I was, the fighter I'd been, even cheating on some tests, I knew what no integrity looked like. Kindness was what I valued above all else, the way a person treated others. Her lack of real concern for others would have made me cry if it had not instantly provoked a fierceness in me.

Because I did not respect Nem, she continued to mean very little to me until, of course, I became the subject of her gossip. I was never aware that she spoke poorly of me. Having come out of my fog, gossip was the most inane thing I could be subjected to. I abhorred it in every way. I literally did not hear it. I was too busy managing the great things unfolding for me.

By our tenth grade year, I'd given many speeches to my classmates and always loved making everyone laugh. I had a multitude of friends and felt loved by my peers. I had also, by that time, gotten to know who Nem was: the stereotypical cheerleader. I was naïve to think she would not target me.

We had "TV classes," where over a hundred students were put into a classroom to watch the teacher on the television for thirty minutes. We had a live instructor for the remainder of the class. Often we class officers went to the front of the room to give short speeches about activities. Almost everyone knows the feeling you have in front of an audience when you feel accepted or rejected. Making people laugh, for the first time in my life, I felt totally accepted. I was in my element.

One day we four class officers were working in the book supply room collecting money for a candy bar sale. We did this during lunch and now, we were "closing up shop," literally closing the window to the long counter where we'd stood. We began to talk about speaking to our classmates in our TV class about upcoming events. I was president, so I generally spoke to the class first, and the three officers added comments.

As we were discussing this, Nem said something to the group along the lines of "When we get up there, let's not make fools of ourselves by joking and making people laugh." This comment struck me between the eyes, because she could only have been talking about me.

I looked at her and said, "Are you speaking about me?"

Timidly now, she said, "Ah, yes."

I said, "Are you saying that I get up there and make a fool of myself?"

Again, not so timidly this time, she replied, "Yes."

"You bitch!" I said.

She cocked her head and spit the word back at me: "Bitch!"

Calling me a fool was the wrong thing to say to someone who fought her way out of conflicts and who was currently being tortured with sleep deprivation. It was the wrong thing to say to someone who stayed at school until seven o'clock most nights to keep from having to go home. It was the wrong thing to say to someone who was very sensitive about being laughed at. It was the wrong thing to say to someone who had just been dragged out of the darkness and into the light by the first mentor she'd ever had. It was the wrong thing to say to someone who was finally feeling admired for something she did well: getting people excited and making them laugh. It was the wrong thing to say to someone who, at that time, could only follow what she felt to be true: my classmates liked me. Now, she was telling me I was being perceived as a fool. From her perspective. Well, I'd already figured out her "perspective."

It was the day on the playground again, but this time, no one was going to shut me up. No, I'd seen her do this to others. Surely she had to have known my reputation from years before. Was this her way of crossing over to rope in *even* me, someone who lay in the outer reaches of her clutches? Was this her way of shutting me up, of buying more real estate in the neighborhood of let-me-see-if-I-can-take-them-out-one-person-at-a-time-and-show-them-how-much-better-I-am-than-them? Was she knocking on my door, testing the waters, seeing if I'd break like I'd seen her break others? Was she seeing if I was willing to buy property in her world?

I would not buy into the world where she lived. Having no words, I became violent. I picked her up by the collar and threw her against the bookshelves. Lifting her and holding her near her throat, I pummeled her face with my fists. I did not stop. She stood no chance.

I felt sorry for her as I had in the years before when I had worried that someone would start something with me and my anger would explode and cause me to hurt that person. The enormity of the anger that came out of me in that instant was equal to the pain of all I'd been through. Out poured the shame of what I'd tried to move away from. But there I was, the class president, ripping into someone's face with my fists.

There were two others present in the room that day and barely a word was spoken. In a strange way, it was an intimate moment for me. They bore witness to the depths of my pain. It was as if my flesh had been opened and peeled back, revealing not red muscles and blood, but all things black. Instantly, I was ashamed of my anger, of hurting Nem, and of having others see it. None of us deserved this.

When it was over, I was weary and shaky on my feet. Nem was bloody and beaten. It would be the last physical fight of my life. It was the ugliest I'd ever been.

There was no victory in this battle, only the realization of the long road ahead. If I was to live on this side of the fence, I knew this could not be the method by which I resolved conflicts.

Nem's mother took her straight to the hospital. Soon enough Mr. Huggins sat in his office with my mom and Nem's mom who was asking to have me removed from the cheerleading squad. Mr. Huggins' ultimate decision was to suspend me but to allow me to stay on the squad. It was a good decision for my life and me but, I would guess, a humiliating one for Nem. We remained cheerleaders together throughout that tenth grade year and to the end of our senior year in high school.

I was a hero to many in the school, as each one who congratulated me, evidently had experienced the subtleties of Nem's persona. To them, she was the typical mean girl and needed to be put in her place. I would much rather have had the words to "put her in her place," when she made her comments, but I did not have those words. Nem was an animal I might never understand.

She was, I'm sure, mimicking the life she knew. Unfortunately, so was I.

Sew Capable

Living at home, I needed something constructive to do, some place to put my energy. I found it in sewing. When I was eight, my mother sat me down at the sewing machine on our enclosed back porch and taught me how to make a fell seam, the double thick seam that runs down the inside leg of jeans. With an hour's practice, I was hooked. I made pair after pair of shorts – for me, my sisters, brothers, and even my neighbors! After that, I made virtually all my own clothes, all through high school. At sixteen, I began making money sewing cheerleading outfits, prom dresses, and later bridesmaids' gowns.

I was fast. I made five pieces in one night – two pairs of shorts, a pair of long pants, and two tops. With each finished product, I went into my mom's bedroom modeling it for her, waking her up in the middle of the night. "Look what I made, Mom!" She groggily looked up, nodded with a smile, and went back to sleep. I found tremendous joy in being creative and took great pride in my talent.

Sophomore Year

I dated Luke for nine months. I was aware that he wanted to have sex, so I suppose that is why he cheated on me. I found out one night when a slew of boys knocked on the door and came piling into my house while I was on the phone. When I turned around, all seven guys had gathered around our kitchen table. I hung up the phone.

"Lynnie, Lynnie!" The lead fellow panted. "We want you to help us play a trick on Luke. He's always at Pam's house or he's always at your house. We're getting sick of it, so we drove over to Pam's and told him we had you in the car! He chased us down the street, and doesn't know you weren't in the car. We want you to play along and say that, yes, you were in the car with us."

Pam? Pam who? What? But as they spoke, I figured out who she was. Pain shot through me. I sat there stunned as they laughed at the practical joke they had just played on their friend. I had no idea. This dawned on them, as they saw the look on my face. They thought they were being mean to Luke, but the butt of the joke turned out to be me.

Luke had been cheating on me for two months. I knew this because Pam put *their* anniversary date of the relationship in *her* yearbook. This break-up hurt even worse, and I was sad for a long time. Luke showed up on my doorstep asking for a second chance a couple months later, but I was going to the prom that evening – with another fellow. The answer was no.

Something else broke my heart that year. My mother threw a surprise sixteenth birthday party for me, inviting some schoolmates. I'd rarely had school friends into my home and this felt awkward. Within an hour, I was crawling out of my skin. I left to go riding around town with a friend. I was too wild, too embarrassed, too cool, and just too distant from my family to appreciate it.

I felt terrible for my mother that I left, but I could not stomach getting that kind of attention at home. Being abused in that house was nothing a party could erase. I did not even know how to smile when I was surprised. I had been so private with my thoughts there that when people were standing and looking at me, I felt naked. It was as if oil and water, separated for so long, suddenly mixed and were supposed to do well together, but clearly could not, and separated quickly. My face was numb. It wasn't until later that I realized what she'd done, the effort Mom must have put into throwing me a party. She never said so, but it hurt me that I must have hurt her feelings by leaving.

I was not close with my mother during my teenage years. I'd wanted to be, but once when I was having "boy problems" in middle school, I'd confided in her. On one of the nights she rolled me over to ask me how my day had been, she noticed I seemed sad. I'd confessed how hurt I'd felt about a boy and cried in her arms. The next day, while in my bedroom, I heard my mother talking on the phone to her girlfriend. She was laughing and giggling. I heard my name. I walked down the hall and heard my mother re-telling the story I thought I'd shared with her in confidence the previous night. I felt my rock, my hardness, in that moment. It was the last time for over a decade I was that vulnerable with my mother.

It was my sister Mary who was close to Mom. They were the best of friends by now. I listened in on many a conversation between the two of them, living vicariously through Mary. If I could not be close to my mother, I was glad she could. What I heard my mother say to Mary, I imagined her saying to me.

My mother had not known how to handle the wild child in me, so instead of stepping in to discipline me, she let others - my brothers and Mr. Huggins. She was probably afraid of my anger. Still, I was often confused by my mother's behavior toward me. I wanted so badly to be close to her, and although we were affectionate, she didn't try to break through my wall.

Anger at Home

As nice a person as I was at school, as good a person as I wanted to be, I was still often a moody, surly person at home with my siblings. It hurt to know I was two people. I went to school wanting desperately to feel normal. I walked back into my house and a depressed mood swept over me. Maybe it was the oppression of built-up stress that had long since been ignored. I just wanted to be out of it. Away.

I was a teenager living at home with angry people who did not know where to put their anger. As much as I did not want to be, I was one of them. At our worst, Mary was irritable and cranky, Judy had violent sprees, and I was unpredictably moody. Sometimes a cloak of hatred enveloped me. When this happened I was scary. I did not talk to anyone until it passed. On rare occasions, I was still violent at home, hitting Mary in the face twice while we were in high school. She and Mom criticized me behind my back constantly, something Mary apologized to me for years later. She realized that it had fueled my anger and she had not known I carried the disturbing pictures of the shooting.

I just wanted help, but I was too far gone in the anger department to understand the anger might leave one day. I wanted to be out on my own, believing that was the only way I would be rid of it. At the same time I wanted to have the support of my family.

I was caught in my inability to ask for help and in being so angry that no one really wanted to help me. I would have to make it on the outside, and so that is where I put my energy.

Donnie

Donnie was my lab partner in tenth grade biology. Something clicked for us that caused this quiet, calm boy and this loud and feisty girl to become friends for life.

Each day, we sat in the courtyard at lunchtime and ate pink mints, barely speaking a word. It was comforting to be together so consistently. When we did talk, I told him whatever I was thinking, but our relationship was the first one I ever had where I saw the value of being able to sit with another human being and not say a word. Although I never explained to him what was happening at home, I felt in that silence, Donnie understood me to my core.

He seemed to be the one person who drank in every subtlety that went on between Nem and others and Nem and me. We did not discuss this much, but I could tell he saw who she was and I respected his emotional intelligence that offered me unspoken validation. He could see what I was going through in my ups and downs trying to manage my exasperated feelings about her. But after a few minutes of sitting in his presence, they melted away. In a time of my life when I had no words for the turmoil inside me, I did not even need them with Donnie.

Busing in Louisville

If ever a cruelty existed, I saw it played out right before my eyes in prejudice against African Americans during my teenage years. Having spent so much time downtown with our friends, black and white, and because of the educated, open-minded mother we had, we kids had been exposed to all sorts of people. Each year at camp, we'd had boyfriends, and in my later years at camp, three of my boyfriends were black. My sister dated Claude, a black fellow from camp, for three and a half years in high school. Claude's mother, Tommie, babysat the three of us girls alongside her ten children and scads of grandchildren over the years. I always felt at home in her house downtown. Tommie accepted everyone, even the very flamboyant gay friend of the family's that sat at her table regularly. He seemed every bit of normal to me, loved like the rest of us.

Something happened in high school that caused my character to be tested. When I went into the ninth grade, we had five black people in our school of 2,500 students. Five. One fellow was Henry. He saw that I was completely open to him so we became great friends. Henry had a gentle, yet masculine voice. He was a lovely person. At one point, he admitted he loved me. I felt myself loving him, too, but became very frightened of getting closer to him.

I'd heard the verbal abuse neighbors and others heaped upon Mary over the years while dating Claude. I was not strong enough to withstand the criticism I'd encounter if I dated Henry. My rage, while now subdued, was too strong. I still did not have words for my anger, and anyone laughing at me or calling me the names that Mary and Claude were called, I knew, would only bring back the fighter in me. I had to protect the still fragile new me. With this temptation of Henry, I made a conscious decision not to date a black student in high school.

I am not proud that I failed this test of character. I wish I could say I threw caution to the wind, and let myself love a guy who treated me kindly. I pressed forward in a white world, not understanding why there was such prejudice for black people. I told no one of my decision. I felt like a coward. That option seemed better than continuing to get into fist fights. I put a smile on my face and made a difference with the strengths I had.

In 1975, the fall of my eleventh grade year, busing started in Louisville, Kentucky. White students from the suburbs and black students from downtown were selected by the letter of the alphabet and were to switch schools, by way of a massive busing system. Judy was bused to the downtown high school for ninth grade. Since I had friends downtown, had witnessed the poverty and lack of resources there, and had been enjoying what was an almost new high school, I could see the value in bringing impoverished students to our school. I was a very small minority.

One evening that summer, I was sewing on our back porch, but took a break and walked out onto the front porch. As I looked into the dark night sky, I saw a half circle-shaped glow covering the sky in one direction. A rumble accompanied it. Being an indifferent teenager, I ignored it. I later learned what I'd seen was a riot on the main highway, and the light was a multitude of bonfires. People chained themselves together to protest busing. Someone threw a brick through a car window, hitting a baby. From a friend stationed in the army in Scotland, I received a clipping of an article with a picture of this riot. It had made the front-page news. In Scotland.

I was not going to be bused, but had I been told to, I would have, just as Judy was preparing to do. Many parents put their children into private schools or finagled their way out of busing. Others were left to be bused. Nem's parents bought a second home near the school so she would not have to go to the new school in her re-drawn district.

Many boycotted school on the first day and attendance was low. When the downtown black students arrived, I greeted them warmly. I believed busing was going to be a good thing for many kids. My thoughts about this whole experience were positive. Mr. Huggins noticed that and put me on an advisory committee of students, both black and white who traveled downtown to discuss busing. We went to meetings at the school board and reported how we thought things were going. Because of how positive I felt about busing and because I was friendly, I was able to make friends very quickly with the black students who came to our school. I was told my leadership helped quell bad situations. Years later at reunions many of the bused-in students told me I had been their first friend and had helped them feel normal and safe.

But school was a scary place that year. There were riots and protests brought on by adults and there were fights among kids. Mr. Huggins had his nose broken while breaking up a fight. He was forever chasing kids and investigating turmoil.

One thing I noticed was that the inner-city students seemed to settle in far more quickly than the white students. They were so happy to be coming to a beautiful school. It seemed to lift their spirits and their self-esteem to be coming into a building that was painted in bright yellows and greens. I felt happy for them to be able to have the chance to experience our school as their own. The reverse was true at Judy's school. It was dark and dingy and many places were crumbling. She received no books and had no homework. It was another world. Judy immediately went out for cheerleading and was the only white girl on the squad. She brought her squad home where I made and fitted them with cheerleading outfits. It was a blast.

I could understand the initial anger and despair of having to leave a neighborhood school. It would have hurt me. But as angry as I'd been earlier, as a teenager, I could not understand directing it at anyone because of skin color. My family had setbacks and we had accepted a leg up to regain our footing. Without the sacrifice of others, it would have been almost impossible for us to make it in the world. It seemed natural that others would need the same.

Buddies

I wanted to be our senior class president, so I planned to wait it out a year and run. I felt enormous love for my classmates sophomore year. I wanted to preserve it. If I were senior class president, I could organize reunions and keep us in touch.

I did not date any of the boys at my school, and although I did have a crush on one or two, something told me not to go there. I was never going to give a boy a reason to cause me to feel ashamed if I were to see him in years to come. My mother taught me, without ever saying so, that the act of sex and your self-esteem go hand in hand, as if what I did with one would affect the other.

So the guys at school were my buddies. From the bleachers, I saw them pointing out my muscles to each other. Thanks to hauling firewood, when I drew my arms back, my biceps were hard baseballs. They called me Hercules. When a rival team's football players visited our school, the guys in the weight room said, "Hey, do we have a girl for you!" They'd come out to get me and drag me back to the weight room.

"Okay, Lynnie, show 'em."

We went through the same routine each time they wanted to show someone my weight-lifting abilities. I went around to the different machines and lifted whatever I could, and all the guys howled and screamed, shouting "Wow, look at that!" Then they pointed out all the guys who could not lift as much as I, and those guys feigned shame. I had never lifted weights, so I had no idea how much weight was considered a lot.

The guys knew, though, and I was their trophy.

The Night of the Pink Panther

Throughout my teenage years, I took my current boyfriends over to visit my dad in his apartment across town. I'd say to someone, "Hey, you wanna go visit my dad?" and off we'd go.

My dad had lung cancer, yet he smoked three packs of cigarettes a day. For the last five years of his life, every time I saw him, he coughed up crud into a handkerchief. In these last months of his life, the handkerchief was filled with blood when he brought it away from his mouth. He still walked and talked and was up and about like normal, except for the coughing.

Whenever we arrived at my dad's apartment he was thrilled to see me and meet my friend. Each trip to see him followed the same pattern. We'd walk in; he'd be bright-eyed and happy to see us. We'd sit down and have a wonderful chat – for about ten minutes. Then my dad brought out a bottle of scotch and began to pour a glass. I stood up and announced, "Okay, it's been great to see you!"

He smiled, was jolly, and walked us to the door. Every visit went exactly the same. I did not stand in judgment of him. His drinking was a reality and my cue to leave. I never wanted to see him drunk again.

I was never embarrassed or ashamed of my dad. Whether people knew of the shooting or not, it was not I who told them. No matter what he'd done, he was my dad, and that year I found out just how special our bond was.

In earlier grades, I'd gone to the Miss Spartan contest, a talent show and pageant named after our school mascot. I sat in the audience mesmerized, watching a girl sing, "Do You Know the Way to San Jose?" that had been sung by Dionne Warwick. The lights were out. Her dress was sparkling. I tingled all over and promised myself, *Someday I will be in*

With Pops

this contest.

In October of my eleventh grade year, I saw a poster on the wall advertising the Miss Spartan Pageant on May 7 – seven months away! Junior and senior girls were allowed to participate. *This is it. I'm going to be in this talent show.* I had no idea what I would do. The only performances I ever gave were the ones when doing the floor routine in gymnastics competitions. I'd always been told I sang well, and did so frequently, but the only words to a song I could imagine belting out on stage were "the hills are alive with the sound of music!" *I'll sing that and then step out of my skirt and start dancing, or doing gymnastics. How would that look? Dumb,* I decided.

By December I knew what to do: a gymnastics routine to the song "The Pink Panther." *"Da dun, da dun, da dun, da dun, da dun....da dun da, daaaaaaaaaaa da, da, da dun..."* I'd wear a pink leotard, pink tights, and a pink bow in my hair. Now all I had to do was make up the routine.

One night in early January, I was at my dad's apartment and saw a calendar on the desk. "Hey, Dad, I'm going to be in the Miss Spartan contest at school. Will you come?"

"Sure. Write it down on my calendar."

My dad had never come to any event I'd ever had – no game, no competition, no nothing. I never really expected either he or my mother to come. My mother only came to one game and one gymnastics meet a year. I figured he would not come to this, either, with his health deteriorating so badly, but I marked May 7, on his calendar anyway.

All through January, February, March, and April, I stayed at school late into the night, making up, practicing, and then performing my gymnastics routine to "The Pink Panther." My good friend and fellow gymnast helped me tremendously with my routine. Back then, one needed someone to put the needle on the record to begin the routine, and she did that for me.

It was 1976 and gymnastics was growing in America. Nadia Comaneci was famous. Because I was afraid I might do a back handspring into the cinderblock wall on stage, I asked if I could do my talent portion, my gymnastics routine, on the wrestling mat that we gymnasts used in practice each day. I promised it would not be too disruptive, that when it was my turn, the audience would just have to turn sideways. We'd need to turn down the lights and I'd enlist another friend, to shine a spotlight on me during the routine. Everyone agreed. All set. We contestants took a field trip to J.C. Penney's and picked outfits to wear.

The night of May seventh came. I took my gear back stage, curled my hair, and prepared to "do my thing" with the rest of them. We performed a skit together, had to walk around while someone talked about us, performed our talent, and wore eveningwear to walk some more!

I'd been a bundle of nerves, but performed my routine without a hitch.

The question I was asked by the MC was, "Who has been the most influential person in your life?" Immediately I thought of Mr. Huggins, and I could have spilled my guts right then and there, telling everyone how he had completely changed my life in a matter of twenty minutes. He was the person who stood by me, encouraged me, listened to me, and believed in me. But something told me that was not appropriate. It was the first time in all those years I ever had an awkward feeling about our relationship.

Lynnie with Mr. Huggins at a basketball game

I wanted to say, "Are you kidding? Mr. Huggins, of course! He gave me my life back! He saved me and opened the floodgates for me and now listens to me, and guides me and shows me, when I'm stuck, what to do next. I now have a wonderment and a zest for life I never had!"

It breaks my heart to think of all that could be denied another hurting child, if she, too, needed someone to talk to, but others were too concerned about what it "looked like" to listen to her. That's all it took, along with wisdom and a nonjudgmental attitude. How could anyone think this was inappropriate?

This was not the place to share our relationship – with an entire audience! I thought of all the wonderful things about my mother and what she'd taught me. With a quick save, I said, "Well, this may sound corny, but it is my mother." I went on to talk about her love for me. I thoroughly believed everything I said, and it was all true: I adored my mother, even though she and I were not close at the time.

The show was coming to a close. We girls walked back on stage in our formal wear. It was time to announce a winner. Now, this may be hard to believe, but it is true. Not once before this moment had I thought about winning this contest. In all the years of wanting to do this, of knowing I would someday, in all the months of practice, in all the fear of whether or not I could even do this in front of people, never once did winning

Lynnie's only picture with her mom and dad

cross my mind. All I'd wanted to do was perform. The fear of failure and that desire of moving through it was the reason I did it. It was a complete surprise to me when they said it was time to announce a winner.

What was different about this competition from others at school was that outside celebrities came in to judge the event: a local radio personality, a modeling agent, and some sort of television producer. The winner of this competition was judged on poise and talent, not on popularity, unlike being voted in by the student body for class officer or cheerleader.

I lined up on the stage with the rest of the girls. *Hey, I could win this!* Then, *Nah, that would never happen.* They announced the two runners up. When my name was not called for third or second place, I decided that was it for my chances.

And then they called my name as the winner.

I was completely stunned. Only minutes before, had I considered there would be *any* winner. There is a picture of me in my high school yearbook with the look on my face the exact moment they called my name. My expression is priceless.

Nudged out to the center stage, they draped a cape around me and gently placed a crown on my head. A dozen red roses were laid in my arms and a large, silver cup engraved with "Miss Spartan, 1976" handed to me. The MC took my hand and escorted me off the stage and onto the walkway that led out into the middle of the audience. I'd never once imagined any of this.

I stepped back onto the stage, the MC closed the show, and all the girls bombarded me, just like they do on television. The curtains closed and we girls were like a mob, everyone still yelling and screaming at the top of their lungs. I was now bawling, and when I turned around with tear-filled eyes and screams assaulting my ears, there stood my dad at the back stage door.

Everything else went away, as in a hush of a muffled, rumbling noise. I froze. He stood there surrounded by a bright and fuzzy white light, circling his entire being, just around the doorframe. Time stood still. I took in every detail of him in the mystical light. No one else knew what was happening. I knew my dad had just witnessed me doing something well. Crying with joy, I was so proud he saw me win.

Two huge surprises in a matter of minutes.

I gather it is difficult for some people to understand how some can still participate in a life with someone who has treated them so terribly. But my mother led the way to forgiveness of my father and I followed. Only much later did the irony occur to me that ten years earlier, he was a black-silhouetted demon coming through a doorframe, and now a glow of white fuzzy light had surrounded him at this door. Somehow, with the grace of God, this devil was now an angel, and I'd forgiven him.

Two More Gifts

The night of the Pink Panther was precious to me because my dad would be dead in less than four months.

Later that month he could no longer drive himself around, and asked me if I wanted to buy his car for thirteen dollars. It was a 1966 Dodge Dart and for which he'd paid fifty dollars years before. Once a man had struck him from behind and, rather than call the insurance company, he gave Pops all the money he'd had: thirty-seven dollars. My father thought he only needed to get thirteen dollars out of it. I gave him a twenty-dollar bill, never reminding him he owed me seven dollars in change.

My father's cancer was full on now and he spent much of the summer at the Veteran's Hospital in Louisville. On my last visit to see him, I went to the hospital with my current boyfriend, Todd. We'd just missed the previous visiting hours, which was only three times a day and only two people were allowed in the room. Todd and I waited three hours, sitting under the trees on the lawn.

When the next visiting hour finally arrived, and as we stood to enter the hospital doors, my Aunt Betty pulled up.

"Hi, Aunt Betty," I said. "I was hoping Todd could come in with me to see my dad."

"Nonsense. He needs to see family," she spat, uncharacteristically. This was my father's sister, the nun, who'd always been so kind. I could see she was a nervous wreck.

This saddened me because I'd been dating Todd for nine months and I knew my dad liked him. I did not know if I'd later marry Todd, so I really wanted my dad to see us together again. This was something my aunt did not understand. She came to visit him each of the three visiting periods of the day. *Couldn't she just forego this one?*

The moment I walked into the ICU, I took it all in. He was dying; he would be dead soon. My dad was very different now with his large head on shrunken-in shoulders. He was not a large man to begin with, probably about 5'8" and 150-160 pounds, but he was about 90 pounds now, skin on bones.

The instant I walked in, he lifted his head and, with a light in his eyes, said, "Did you bring Todd?"

See! I wanted to say to my aunt. *See how much he wants to see Todd?*

"Yes, I did bring him, but only two of us can come inside the room, so he is waiting just outside." My dad seemed comforted by this.

My aunt had sneaked in a water-soaked paper towel. She placed it on my dad's cracked and dry lips. He clamped down on it with his teeth and tongue and sucked feverishly at the water it provided. He was an animal, his eyes far off just then, intent on one thing: survival.

He was not supposed to have water because it made the cancer worse. But here he was, dying of thirst! They would not do this today. Cancer patients are made as comfortable as possible as they die, but this was not the case then. It was the saddest thing to see him sucking away, trying to get one drop. I was glad now for my aunt and her wet paper towel. He could not quench his thirst, of course, and I saw in his eyes how hard this fact was to accept. Leaning back, and with a sigh, his eyes came back to us.

It was easier to be with my dad on this day than it had been on any other day. We loved each other. There was a comfort level. Long ago my questions to him had stopped. I was satisfied. He was sorry.

I went to the right side of his bed and took his hand. I stood there looking at him lovingly, my Aunt Betty standing just behind me. There was nothing more to say to him. *Are they treating you right? How have you been? Are you okay? Does it hurt?* None of that needed to be said. That was small talk. I had the whole picture now and I was not going to waste a word on inane details. This was the end.

I held his eyes for a long time and said, "I love you." I could feel his body sink with a puff, as if in a sigh of relief. This was no ordinary "I love you." Into my well I dipped and with as much courage as I could muster, because I knew it would be putting a period on his life, I said, "I'm going to miss you."

Immediately, my aunt grabbed me and shoved me behind her and to the back of the bed. "What are you saying? He's not going anywhere!" She was furious.

But as I took another step to the back of the bed, to be directly in front of him, my father's eyes and mine, never left one another's. He and I were ignoring my aunt. Through his eyes I heard him say, "Thank you for acknowledging what is happening to me. I am going to die. Thank you for being realistic and cutting through this pretense that I am not. Thank you for saying so and for telling me that you will miss me. I feel it. I know I am going to die, and I do want to say goodbye."

This was the most poignant moment of my life.

The strength of forgiveness and compassion I felt in those moments for a broken man showed me who I was and just what I was made of. He needed to say goodbye. Standing there with my aunt, I was proud to give him what he needed.

My dad knew he had not lived a good life.

It is a re-occurring theme of my life that when someone is dying I can talk with him about it with great ease. It seems the most natural thing in the world to acknowledge what is happening. Most times I find the dying person desperate to talk about his death - to someone who will not break down.

When Tom Hanks' character was dying of aids in his hospital bed in the movie "Philadelphia," I watched a long line of people at his bedside say only goodnight to him. "See you tomorrow," was said, but not one person said goodbye, even for a "just in case." What harm would it do to say goodbye, *just in case,* several times? I think far better to say it ten times than none at all. I only got to say goodbye to my dad once.

Trying

Carl left the house at the beginning of my junior year, and with him went the doom and gloom. Never had I once had a conversation with my own brother. Our only communication: he snarled and I quaked.

When Mary left for college, I got my own bedroom, so I felt doubly wonderful when Carl left, but the fear of him returning lingered. I never let myself feel completely comfortable that he would not return. When I came to look back at my life with posttraumatic stress, I knew unequivocally, I'd been in a constant state of fear for the first sixteen years of my life.

That winter of our junior year, Nem and I accomplished quite a feat. Our cheerleading squad wanted new outfits, but we had no funds. We came up with an idea. What if we all pitched in our own money for material and I made the outfits for everyone? Nem and I bought the material, went to my house, and cut the fabric. I sewed and Nem organized everyone to come over for fittings. Voila! In no time, we had new handmade uniforms for basketball season, even wearing them in our yearbook pictures.

I was thrilled to work side by side with Nem on this project. I was hoping against hope we'd lay to rest any tension between us. As much as I wanted this, I felt she wanted it, too. Sometimes I had the sweetest feelings toward her, forgiving her for so much of the way she acted. I wanted to love her. I loved everyone! It seemed like for a little of my time with her on any given day, I'd be feeling comfortable, and then she'd say something that made me cringe. With a heavy heart and suddenly feeling bankrupt, I'd realize just how different we were. We lived in two worlds that would never come together. Her words were dripping with an arrogance of which she had no clue. Essentially, she was a bully, ever so sly. I had no idea what to do or say, so I did and said nothing.

As willing as I'd been to reach out, something told me her world was very dangerous and I would not survive in it. I do think deep down she knew I was not buying any of what she dished out. When everyone else seemed sold on her, I was the lone holdout. There was no pretending on my part. I shut off naturally and remained expressionless when she excitedly reveled in her escapades. What came out of her mouth was so shallow and inconsequential I was dumbfounded that anyone listened. I was not like this with everyone and it was not just the trivial that caused this reaction in me. It was the fact that it was laden with razor blades. Slit, slit, slit. I heard each hidden barb while others laughed and turned away, seemingly befuddled.

But the worst part of all was that during my moments of disgust, I remembered why I'd beaten her up. It hurt me badly to know the anger I'd sent underground could still flare up. I was not the only one she made angry. Some people at school rolled their eyes in utter contempt and called her "fake" and "phony" and occasionally looked to me for a response. I knew our fight spoke volumes to people about how I felt about her. I left it at that and said nothing. She was a fighter, too, except she was using a more acceptable weapon: words. Oddly, as quickly as my anger flared, a wave of forgiveness washed over me - for her and for me.

I have shortened her named from Nemesis to Nem, but she was no longer Nem. She had long since gone to "Nemi," because it sounded more "cheerleadery." She asked everyone to add the "i" to her name. I could not get it to come out of my mouth. She remained Nem to me.

Frequently, as I was walking down the hall, Nem yelled from twenty feet behind, "Hey, Lyyyynnie, when's cheeeeeerleading practice?" I turned slightly when I heard my name, but by the time I heard the words roll off her tongue, I rolled my eyes and could not get away from her fast enough. She knew full well what time practice was – the same time every day - and why on earth would she have to include the word "cheeeeeeerleading" to the sentence? Practice was practice. It was as if she had to constantly remind people of the favored position she believed she held.

I became a cheerleader because it was a year round, performance sport. Done right, it was a hard sport. Yes, one did get a lot of recognition for it, which I enjoyed. But I was so grateful for it, because it kept me out of trouble and gave me the structure I needed to harness my enormous energy. My relationship with Nem, and watching her flaunt the title of cheerleader, made me vow to be the exact opposite of the stereotypical cheerleader. I was ever so proud for years after that when people said to me, "Wow, you don't seem like any cheerleader I've ever known." And my close friends said, "Yeah, we'll let you ride with us (to this party or that), even though you're a cheerleader bitch." This term of endearment warmed my heart.

I'd lived in a house where I was not able to practice getting angry in a healthy way, and so was silent, which is one side of the pendulum. The other side was what had happened years before when I'd gotten angry with Nem and raged out on her in physical violence. I later learned that many people avoided getting angry because of the rage they feared might be inside them. They held it in and chose not to confront people because they feared the outcome. I could see why. I was still "A" in the A-Z category of conflict resolution, and Z was a long way off. I had to start with figuring out what my anger was about. What was it that made me want to communicate with Nem in all the ways I knew to be inappropriate? Finally, I landed on it. Exclusion. She could stand in a crowd and speak words with a smile, her words including some, excluding others, all at the same time, in the same sentence. The duty of the listener was to decide into which category she believed you fell. Some intrigued, some intimidated, people followed.

In fact, when I was down and vulnerable, she ever so subtly squashed me, excluded me. Soon Nem would show me her lowest low by allowing me to be stripped of a title I'd earned and deserved, one she'd coveted. She'd walk away with her head held high.

If That is What You Have to Do

That summer before my senior year, I was voted captain by the girls on the squad. The captain was usually a senior and only Nem and I were the seniors. I had a knack for rhyming and making up cheers and dances. I spent hours in front of my living room window, watching my reflection as I made up routines. When I had a new one, I taught it to our cheerleading squad. Because of this, our cheers and dances were unique. All of us cooperated and got along brilliantly, so we were very successful.

Each summer at cheerleading camp, ten squads were selected for the final competition, and one squad became that region's national champion. In years past, our school had not even come close to being in the top ten. Since it was my senior year and I thought we had a shot at it, I wanted to try. I asked the squad if they wanted to. They chimed, "Yes!" I explained if we did, practices would be grueling, sometimes two, maybe three a day, in the Kentucky summer heat, and I, being their captain, was going to be tough on them. They each agreed this was what they wanted, that I had a green light to push them. That is exactly what I did. We practiced until we physically couldn't.

By senior year, I was a leader in the school and a force to be reckoned with. Ms. Darby had been my cheerleading sponsor for three years, but I'd not had direct communication with her because I'd not been captain. Now, I was. Problem. Ms. Darby was never my teacher, but had a reputation for being mean. I never saw that side, but she had a peculiar way of communicating. She did not look me in the eye. She blinked a lot, looked around at others, but rarely spoke directly to me. Seeing her twice a week for three years, she never initiated talking with me and we never had a full conversation. I cannot remember her saying my name. Here I was, a teenager working on my communication skills, trying to work with a difficult adult. Instead of confronting me and working with me, however challenging I may have been for her, she made no attempt to build a relationship, and in fact, mostly ignored me.

The result of this was I reciprocated by ignoring her.

When I look back to see who should have taken the lead in this difficult situation, I have to say it should have been Ms. Darby. As a teacher, I consider it my job to address a student, confront him if necessary, and build a relationship. I wish Ms. Darby had attempted this with me. I did not dislike Ms. Darby, but I found it hard to respect her. Although there was not open animosity among us cheerleaders to Ms. Darby, many felt indifferent to her.

She and Nem had what appeared to be a wonderful relationship. Ms. Darby picked up Nem to drive her to each practice. Ms. Darby did not like the idea that we had so many practices that summer, because a sponsor had to be present. But this was our dream, and she came to most. Other practices, we had without her off campus. But whenever she was at practice, many of us felt slowed down by her constant input. Yet without her looking people in the eye, it was difficult for any of us to take her directions seriously. The tension between Ms. Darby and me was felt among the squad, but several girls had this tension with her. Life went on with all of this being very well ignored.

Ms. Darby had married somewhere in these years and changed her name. We said we had a hard time remembering it, so we stuck with Ms. Darby. As an adult, I see that is not altogether true. Had we had more respect for her, we would have put effort into remembering her new name.

We went to cheerleading camp that year and it was remarkable that when we ran out onto the field, most of us could do a round off and *many* back handsprings. Some of us could do upwards to twenty! I only reached eighteen at practice. We looked spiffy. This was rarely seen in those days of cheerleading and, in part, we were recognized for it. We did our best. We got into the top ten that summer at the University of Kentucky. I was so happy I sat down and cried when it was over. It had been a grueling summer, but we made our goal and it had been worth it. Anyone who says cheerleading is not a sport has probably never done it. We went home to rest up for a couple weeks before we were to report back to practice. It was a welcomed break.

On the Sunday morning that practice was to resume at school, we got a call that Pops had died. I walked over to school that evening to tell my squad what had happened and to not expect me at practice for a few days.

The girls consoled me and gave me their support, but this was the first time many of them had ever heard me talk about having a father. On many occasions growing up, when anyone asked me about my father, I simply said, "I don't have one." Since he was not there, I felt I really did not have one. It had been simpler to say that than to explain. It kept at bay having to talk about the divorce, hence the shooting, hence the pictures in my head. It felt okay to say this because my father was really more like a friend to me.

But the minute he died, all of a sudden, he was my father. Maybe that is why I wanted to tell my squad in person. Now, I did have a dad, and he was dead. The reality of that day, I came to find, was that he would be the only father I'd ever have.

I told my squad I'd see them after the funeral.

On Wednesday morning at 10:30, the phone rang. It was a squad member saying, "Lynnie, Ms. Darby says if you don't come to practice today, she's going to have us pick a new captain."

I replied, "Well, she will just have to do that, because right now I'm walking out the door to my father's funeral." I hung up the phone and drove my father's car to the church where I met my family, cousins, aunts, uncles and grandparents for Mass for Pops.

When I returned to practice the very next day, they'd voted Nem captain. I had not been there the day before, so I did not vote. But did that mean I was not eligible to be voted for? I did not know.

One girl told me later that she had voted for me. I wondered if the others did not vote for me because the memory of how hard I'd been on them at camp was still too vivid in their minds. If the vote was legit, this was the only explanation I could think of, since it had been very obvious who the leader of this crew was.

So this is the way Nem got me back.

There seemed to be a code of silence. I could not argue with it. I could not demand a recount. We could not re-vote to have my vote count. There seemed to be some kind of agreement between Ms. Darby and Nem to just ignore what was obvious: Lynnie left for three days and when she came back, there was a new captain and no questions were to be asked. Apparently, no new vote was to be made since the absent person did not get to vote. I was shocked and sad on two counts - losing the job I loved and the lack of respect shown for my father's funeral.

The other girls seemed to be acting in agreement, since no one seemed to acknowledge how painful this might be for me, although I later found out this was not true. But this was the path of dysfunctional relationships – ignoring what was.

Had I been healthy, I would have said, "Hey, this is not fair. I was captain. I was at a funeral! That's not only not fair, it's cruel! I was not even here to vote. My vote should count, too, as there are only eight of us! And who counted the votes, anyway? And why is it that I am not seen as the leader of this group anymore? What happened? Why was there even a vote? When I was voted in, it was for a year. Was my going away a convenient time to get rid of me? 'She stopped coming to practice!' Hello? Did anyone hear that I was at my dad's funeral? What if my dad had not died?"

But all, including me, were silent.

For my entire senior year, Nem got to say "Ready?" to start every cheer. Yes, it irked me since she was beginning cheers that were the babies I created. Every word, every motion had been my original. It felt like a farce, since it was the only way that anything had changed. She was not a leader I could follow.

This was nasty revenge. For the first time, I'd opened the wound and publicly announced I'd had a dad. Coming back after the funeral, it felt like someone pouring salt into… into my shame. *Well, yeah, I guess he wasn't that important… because he shot his wife. He could not have been a good person. But he was my dad. And he was the only one I had. I cannot help that he was that person. But he was my person. He was my dad. Everyone else has one. I want one, too. Why can't I have a dad? Why would everyone else's dad's funeral be important… but not mine? Because of what he did… Oh, yeah, he was a bad man. Look what he did. People know what he did. He was not worth anything. His funeral was not worth leaving for… But I loved him. Does that count?*

I did not need a title to be a leader. I'd hurt Nem. She'd hurt me. That's the way I saw it and accepted it. I assumed it had been a conspiracy cooked up between Nem and Ms. Darby, but if that is what she had to do to get a title I believed she did not deserve, so be it. That part was laughable and tragic and cause for me to believe my feelings of disrespect for those two were not rooted in fantasy.

Build Yourself Up

I kept the promise I made to myself and ran for president of my senior class. Unfortunately, my good friend, who'd been our junior class president, and for whom I'd campaigned for so vigorously the year before ran against me.

When I asked my mom for advice for my speech, she gave me the same advice she'd given me in years past: never put the other person down; always build yourself up.

Another boy in our class was running for president, too, and the three of us gave our speeches to our classmates. When finished, a friend rushed up and said, "Lynnie, did you hear what she said about you? Aren't you mad?"

What had she said? What are you talking about?

"You know the part where she said, 'Don't vote for someone just because they are funny or cute or popular.'"

"Oh, she was talking about me?" I was oblivious. I won the election and she did not speak to me for twenty years.

Like Jell-O

All my siblings reacted differently to my father's death. Mary went back to college, Judy cried, I was in shock, and Carl was calm. Aaron seemed indifferent and Jeff was businesslike, flying home from the navy to take care of responsibilities.

The result of the autopsy showed my father ultimately died of cancer of the pancreas, but he had cancer of the lungs and liver, too. The doctor said alcohol had destroyed one of my father's organs so severely that when he lifted it, it fell through his fingers like Jell-O.

Judy took Pops' death the hardest.

My mom had told the story of how happy she and my father were the year I was born. His business was going well and he was not drinking as much. But by the time Judy came along two years later, he accused Mom of having an affair because he could not remember having sex with her. Mom said it was because he'd come home too drunk to remember. She also knew he was accusing her of the very act he was committing. He was having an affair with a woman in our neighborhood. Because of this history, it was said that my father rejected Judy in ways I never saw or noticed, but when she was a teenager, her need for him and his rejection of her was deep. She went to his house to spend entire weekends. It began friendly, but soon she was begging him not to drink. Our father drank. Judy cried and cried about this. Seeing her desire to change him and never coming to realize she couldn't, was heartbreaking.

Relationships

I'd begun dating Todd in December of my junior year. I saw signs of his controlling behavior with his response to my going out with friends two weeks after we met. "You mean you'd rather be with them than me?" It was a red flag.

Todd was a freshman college football player, majoring in biology. He was big, muscular, cute, and smart - and he loved me. He bought a coupon book that offered half price on entrées, and he and I ate steak dinners all over Louisville. For a girl who'd not tasted her first Coke until she was twelve and ate potato chips only at Christmas, I felt like I was watching myself in a movie, sitting in a restaurant with a handsome date.

Todd and I had dated for over a year and, since my dad had known him, it was hard to think of not being with him. But Todd could be mentally controlling and my eyes were opening wider to that. We practiced sports together. He'd constantly said, "You're too skinny!" So I ate more and continued to train - and I gained weight. "You're too fat!" he'd harp.

I'd been terrorized, controlled, hit, and tortured by one man and three boys in my life, and even though I had Mr. Huggins, no mentor was strong enough to keep me from the road I had to travel to learn how to protect myself in romantic relationships. I did not know how. My father had not protected his children. My mother had not protected her children. My brothers had not protected their sisters. I did not protect Mary or Judy from my wrath.

No red flag I encountered seemed as bad as the abuse at home. I did not have any idea how good a relationship could be. If someone loved me and treated me better than I'd been treated at home, I used that as my measuring stick.

Believing I deserved nothing but the best in a relationship would take a lifetime to achieve. It would be years before my confusion about my place in my family lifted and I had many questions answered. Until then, my decisions about men were not clear-headed ones, and the zig and zag of my life with men remained. Learning how to protect myself physically, mentally, emotionally, and spiritually became a constant theme of my life with every relationship I had – male, female, boss, friend, lover, or colleague.

No Bigger Flag

For spring break senior year, I went to Florida with my wild girlfriends. They nicknamed me "Mama Vessels," because I was the one telling girls to slow down when they were driving eighty miles an hour, and I was staying in to keep from getting sunburned. I checked on everyone when we were coming in at four in the morning. I had time away to think, and it was in Florida I decided to break up with Todd.

Shortly after my return, I sat down on the edge of his bed while he was lying down, looked him in the eye, and told him I thought we should date other people. He, a former 198-pound class state champion wrestler, and a current weight-lifting, body building college football player, backhanded my arm, causing me to fly across the room and slam into the back wall of an open closet.

I had long, red finger-mark whelps on my upper arm. That was it. I broke up with him. A few days later I asked my best friend Donnie to go to the prom. He'd said, "Yes," and we made plans to go. In the interim,

Todd pursued me relentlessly. After several weeks, foolishly, I went back with him. I left Donnie in the lurch, telling him only a week beforehand that I could not go to the prom. It was the wrong thing to do. I was still the victim I never wanted to be and even though it was a long time ago, I can still recall the fear I had thinking about saying "No" to Todd. I was scared he would hunt me down and Donnie would be in the middle of it all. I went back with him against my better judgment. I knew someone who'd hit once would hit again. Not going to the prom with Donnie would be my biggest regret of high school.

Getting Real

Before graduation a task fell to me that showed me I had more than a knack for speaking in public. This would become a calling. I was to give the baccalaureate ceremony address. I had heard them before: the president summing up the four years of the "personality" of the class, the shenanigans that provided their best memories.

I was used to getting up and giving impromptu speeches at pep rallies and class functions, filled with information and laughs, sometimes writing a few words on a page, but this was a special, dress-up event. I even asked my brothers and sisters how I should go about this. My brother Aaron said, "Just be yourself."

Be myself? Who was that? The crazy person these people had always seen? The friendly person? The person who knew everyone by name and talked to everyone, no matter what? Or was I this other person, so ashamed of the pictures that crept into my mind? Ashamed of the things I could not say? Which one was I? The person who had loved them like my family because of what they'd given me? A home away from home? That's it. They had given me a home. A place where I could be exactly who I was: myself.

Sitting on the hood of my car, I meditated about the love I clearly felt and wanted to keep. Something else was clear to me. Through all my sufferings, I knew each one of them must have had their own. As much as I thought of myself as an island, I knew others thought the same of themselves.

I wrote five words on an index card, went to the microphone, and spoke directly to my 324 classmates. I had an introduction, and then I began naming familiar names of kids from seventh grade, ones no longer with us, telling funny stories about them. When I went up the years, I looked into the sea of faces and picked a person, named him or her by name, and told story after story about the people right in front of me. I do not know how many kids I made remarks about, but I do know I touched on someone from every possible group, and my classmates went from laughing to crying and crying to laughing and back again, several times. I watched as tears streamed down the faces of my classmates, male and female.

Their laughter gave me confidence. Their tears gave me confirmation I was telling the truth. I kept telling stories of staying out late, gathering in the parking lot, at football games, pep rallies, and pizza parties. I reminded them of who we'd been, who we were, and how we got there.

It was then I knew I had a gift to move people with speaking simple truths. Looking into the bleachers, I saw parents wiping their eyes with handkerchiefs, my mom included. It was here I learned two great truths about my life. The first: whoever I was when I was with my best friends, when I was laughing, joyous, and spontaneous, this was who I really was. I could be loud, funny, successful, obnoxious, yelling, screaming, loving, kind, wild and crazy. So it was true. With my classmates I could be myself. The other stuff was just a cloak that washed over me when I least expected it, trying to convince me I was some horrible person. Years later I'd see fully that the little girl filled with rage and shame was not who I was. She was a product of violence she'd witnessed and experienced. Secondly, my classmates had voted me most popular and there was no doubt in my mind why. If I wanted to be loved, I had to give it, be kind. First. I wasn't rich, I wore clothes I made myself, and drove a car with so many rust marks everyone called it "Spot." Years later I told my students there were two ways to be popular. One was to be intimidating. The other was to be kind. My motto to them was: if you want to be popular, be kind.

I still had a long way to go. Giving this speech was a zig, and along would come a big zag.

The Pay Back

Months before, some of my wild girlfriends who'd had Ms. Darby as their teacher, desperately wanted to "do something" to her for a "send off." It was suggested that we "pie" Ms. Darby after graduation. I was looking forward to it.

That's why one night after graduation, I reminded them of our plan. We went to a convenience store and bought four pies and let them thaw overnight.

The next morning, one girl picked us up one at a time. Among the four of us, it was decided that I was the one who could get her to come out of her classroom. I went to the door and motioned for her to come out. She did and two girls, each with two pies in her hands, smashed the pies in her face and on her body. All I saw and heard after that was bare feet slipping through pie filling and keys jangling. We scrambled back to the car and the driver, one by one, dropped us off at our homes, mine being the last. Mission accomplished.

As the driver and I sat in my driveway, we heard a screech of tires behind us. We turned to see Mr. Huggins jumping out of his car. He bolted up, leaned his head in the driver's window, and spit furiously, "I want to see everyone involved in this in my office in ten minutes!" He was gone.

I went to the phone and called Mom at work. "I think I'm in trouble."

"What did you do?" she asked. I responded, "We pied Ms. Darby."

"Oh."

"I think I'm really in trouble this time," I told her. "I need to go to the office now."

I was 18, so I was on my own with this one. It was more serious than it sounded when we'd planned it. The venom that was in the girls who threw the pies made it an act of violence and, once again, I was involved in traumatizing another human being. I told myself it was to exact revenge for what she did on the day of my father's funeral, but in the end, it was just more unnecessary violence. In his office, Mr. Huggins told us it was out of his hands and Ms. Darby was pressing charges.

That night after work, my girlfriend's father picked us up from the pool and told us the "pie-ing" of a teacher had been on the six o'clock news. She elbowed me in my side.

Only two of us went to court, since by then one had gone off to the military and the other was never seen by anyone and never ratted out by us.

We got dressed up to face the judge, as did about twenty girls, all of whom had either been cheerleaders or students of Ms. Darby, some still filled with hate. The hurt she evoked, I saw again, had extended far beyond my own. The case was dropped that day because Ms. Darby did not show. It was quite a disappointment to the girls who'd gotten all dressed up. This was the one statement of silent defiance they could make.

My hatred had passed with this final act.

Canned-food Drive

That summer before I left for college, I was a lifeguard and the head swim coach for a community pool. My schedule was noon to eight, perfect for partying with friends at night and sleeping in the next morning.

One night I was having a great time at a party. Two close friends and I were re-hashing our days together, keenly aware of the fact that these were our last days romping through the summer in high gear before we'd go our separate ways.

My friend since first grade, Kathy, turned and said, "Lynnie, I learned about giving through knowing you." I could tell she had something important to tell me, so I positioned myself to listen.

"When I was in the second grade, I walked into the kitchen to see my mom going through the cabinets, taking out cans of Spaghetti O's and Chef Boy-R-Dee Ravioli and corn, and all my favorite foods. She was putting them into a box – to give them away! Guessing what she was doing, I stopped her and said, 'No, no, Mom! Don't give away my favorite things. Give them these!' And I began pulling out cans of okra and beets and kale."

She went on, "My mom sat me down and looked me in the eye and said, 'But Kathy, you know Lynnie in your classroom? These will go to her. Don't you want Lynnie to have some of the things you love to eat?' I was still reluctant to give up my favorite foods to you." I sat very still as she told her story. Kathy continued, "Then my mother told me, 'Kathy, giving isn't real giving if it's easy. It is only when it is slightly painful that it means the most. It is easy to give someone something that you do not like, like a doll in the bottom of the toy box, but it is far more special to give something that is precious to you, such as a doll you still treasure. It is still of value to you, but now you can imagine the joy it would bring someone else. That is sacrifice. That is giving.'"

By the time she was at that point in her story, Kathy and I both had tears streaming down our faces, and our other buddy, was crying, too.

Then Kathy told me, after hearing what her mother said, and "getting it," she began to help her mom fill the cardboard box with all of her favorite foods for Lynnie. Not only that, but each time they went to the grocery store, Kathy pulled items off the shelves, ones she imagined I'd like, and put them into the shopping cart.

This, I never knew. In those ten years, I'd never heard a story such as this. Not a single soul had ever mentioned, or shown any evidence of knowing, what had happened to our family. It was lovely to hear that my fellow classmate and life-long friend had felt this love for me outside the classroom.

I was deeply touched by her lesson in giving, and years later, as a teacher, told this story to my students in November, at the beginning of the Thanksgiving canned-food drive. Every time I told the story, my students won the contest by over a thousand cans.

Tommy

My sister Judy briefly had a boyfriend named Tommy whom she wanted me to get to know. But Tommy had long hair, a ponytail, and an earring, and I was not interested in her dating him. In order to give their relationship no credence whatsoever, I just grunted as I passed through the room where they were. I regret this deeply now and I learned a valuable lesson. I thought if I ignored him, he would go away. He did.

When Judy left on vacation, Tommy shot himself in the head. Mom asked me to tell her when she returned. We all sat down at the table and let her tell us about her trip. When we got quiet, she knew something was wrong. I moved very close to her and said, "Tommy killed himself, Judy." As she took in these words, I slid over the newspaper article, announcing his death.

She sat looking at the article and blurted out, "I always knew he would do this. That's why I liked him so much. He needed me."

I never forget the shame I felt after Tommy's death. My stupidity was a great motivator in my future when I found myself judging others. I decided being a stuck-up bitch was not the answer to control what I wanted and certainly not the way to treat another human being. Here was Judy, one of the dearest people in the world to me, grieving a person she loved, a person who had obviously been in deep pain - and whom I had shunned while he was in it.

Wrong

People asked me where I was going to go to college. Since Todd had said he was transferring to wherever I decided to go, I waited until I knew he could no longer transfer before I made my decision known. I loved Western Kentucky University, Mr. Huggins' college. It just so happened to be practically the only college left in the state of Kentucky that none of my siblings had chosen. Thank goodness, the subject I wanted to major in – communications - was its specialty!

My mom took me to the campus on July 12, to sign up, which was not the usual date to sign up for college – six weeks beforehand. No one knew why I waited so long, not even my mom. I was too afraid of Todd to tell anyone. I had tried to use words to get away the first time. Now, I just had to get away.

Todd rode with my mom to drop me off. My going away *first* would begin a pattern of breaking up with guys. I knew what I wanted but could not seem to break away verbally. The time and distance put between us beforehand made the break up easier to bring to fruition. Away, I became clear-headed. Otherwise, in the enmeshment of my relationships, it was too difficult for me to trust how I felt and I was too easily swayed back in.

I "walked on" to my college gymnastics team. A "walk on" is just that, someone who just walks through the door and wants to be on the team. There were nine of us, six state champions on full scholarships, two on partial scholarships, and me, the "walk on." My skills were far inferior to those of the other girls, but they were kind enough to allow me to stay, and I was the only gymnast all year that competed in every meet without injuries. I loved the sport.

Todd came down in October to watch me in my first meet. I was thrilled with a capital T to be competing in a college gymnastics meet in the large red and white Diddle Arena, scoring points for the team. When the meet was over, I, in all my excitement, ran to Todd who was sitting in the bleachers. I plopped down next to him, ready to say with glee, "Did you see me? Did you see me?"

Before I could, he turned and said, "Do you want me to tell you what you did wrong?"

"No," I said. It was the last time I would let him deflate my spirit. I told him to take me back to my dorm. It was over. He called me for four years after that, asking me to get back together, but I was free of him. I'd become a victim to a controlling person and it was not until I got sufficient distance from him that I knew emphatically, "This is wrong."

While in the relationship with Todd or with others, whenever the man made far worse comments that I later learned to be mentally abusive, I had conversations in my head. *Wow, that hurt! How could anyone say something like that? That's mean. Surely he did not mean to say that. How could anyone say anything like that to someone? He says he loves me so he cannot possibly mean what he says…*

Away From Home

Elvis Presley died that August I started college. My roommate freshman year lived at her boyfriend's house, and left me with the freedom to play her stereo, something I'd never had at home. I was in heaven listening to Harry Chapin and Cat Stevens in the dark as I went to sleep each night. Brother David sent me posters from the Archabbey to decorate my dorm room. One poster read, "You don't have to know where you're going, as long as you're on your way." Another read, "Please be patient; God isn't finished with me yet." Another, "Bless the earth."

When I arrived at college, I had no idea how smart I was and no idea how hard it would be. I thought it better to assume others were much brighter than I, and it would be really hard. I stayed in and studied each night from 8 to midnight, went to sleep, got up at 8 a.m., ate oatmeal, and went to classes from 9 to 1. Then I went to gymnastics practice from 1 – 4, exercised for another two hours, and got home at 6:30. I ate my dinner that usually consisted of broccoli, tomato soup and Saltine crackers, hunkered down, and began to study at 8 p.m. I maintained this routine all year, only going out with friends on Friday or Saturday nights.

Turns out, I was an odd bird. Girls went crazy, begging me to come to parties with them, going out night after night drinking. No matter how much someone tried to entice me to go out during the week, I politely refused.

At year's end, I had a 3.0 grade point average but many girls had *much* lower grades. Some girls flunked out and had to go home, but those who stayed with low grades had to work triply hard for the next three years. Those years were easier for me.

It was in college and being out on my own that I realized I did not like the "panic energy" of stress. Those final exam weeks, I could see, were crazy, and the kind of crazy I did not need. By my sophomore year, when the professor gave me the syllabus on the first day of class, I went straight to the library and picked out over ten books on the research topic. I put them next to my bed for a month without looking at them, and then slowly, I picked them up one at a time. With some, I began to bookmark pages, and then later took notes. Over these months, I virtually composed the paper in my head. One day I sat down and wrote the paper, typed it, and turned in a completed paper sometimes a month in advance.

People thought I'd lost my mind when, in finals' week, I'd ask them to go play tennis. Little did I know then that making decisions not to wait until the last minute was the beginning of my stress management education that would save my life.

My brother Jeff came home from the navy and was a freshman in college, like me, so my mom had five kids in college at one time. Fortunately, I'd saved four thousand dollars beforehand working at McDonald's and waitressing. My father's military service and death provided me with a war orphan grant that paid my $300 per semester tuition. I applied for and received a basic equal opportunity grant from the government.

That Christmas of 1977 is my sweetest memory of being with my family. It also happens to be the last time we were all together. We were all home from college and we were all happy. That night, Judy and I, laughing and giggling like two goofy court jesters, took presents around to all our neighbors singing, "We wish you a Merry, Christmas; We wish you a Merry Christmas!" We were the happiest we'd ever been on that trek and we were the happiest we would ever be again. In the house there was laughter and love, the usual going to midnight Mass, and opening presents afterwards. Nothing in particular happened, but there was happiness in our home.

That winter I went back to college and traveled to weekend meets with the gymnastics team, often through heavy snow.

My Mom had repeatedly told us, "See the world! Go out there! Experience it all! Get in as much traveling as you can before you settle down. Go educate yourselves, not just in books, but travel!" I thought about being a camp director someday, so I applied to summer camps all over America. I accepted the only offer I got - at a Jewish kids' camp in the mountains of Massachusetts. I was thrilled.

I decided not to do gymnastics my sophomore year, so I tried out for cheerleading at the end of my freshman year. During my interview with the judges' panel, they asked, "What are your plans for the summer?" I rattled off my hopes and dreams of working at the summer camp. It was a perfect question, in perfect timing, to see enthusiasm from a would-be cheerleader. I got the slot.

To make extra money, I gave haircuts for three dollars and my dorm room filled with guys. Of course, the girls followed. One night, a graduate student and assistant basketball coach came up with the guys. Before I cut his hair, he took off his shirt. All the girls went crazy. His name was Rudy and he was darn cute. He asked me out and we began dating. I fell head over heels for him. He was charming and romantic and acted as if I'd hung the moon. One night a girl basketball player and friend sat on my bed and told me she thought Rudy was engaged. *That can't be true.* I never asked him straight out if it was true. Big mistake. My denial of this red flag my friend flew at me, "I think he is engaged," was nothing less than shocking.

For the last three months of my freshman year, Rudy and I played tennis every single night. He was older and well known on campus. It was our time alone that made me believe we were falling in love. He told me stories about his life, saying he'd never told anyone these things. I believed him. By the time that year was over, I just knew he loved me. If there had been another girl, she was long gone, because anyone could see he was nuts about me. When I went off to Massachusetts, Rudy called me frequently, telling me how much he missed me. I was in love.

Camp Not-so-merry

I spent a month traveling around New England before going to the camp. My brother Aaron encouraged me to hitchhike to meet him places – and to use it as a means of travel. I had that risk/danger factor playing out in my life. I was hitchhiking and meeting people, but mostly visiting friends and family.

I spent eleven days at Narragansett Bay, Rhode Island, with a college buddy's brother. Each day I hiked out to the cliff, sat on the rocks, and watched the waves crash wildly on the rugged boulders below. Although I'd seen scenes like this in movies, I'd never actually *been* to a spot like this. Those eleven days sparked in me the desire to meditate near water.

The kids' camp turned out to be a rigid experience. I saw it as the worst place for a child to be. A whistle initiated practically every move the kids made. They were marching soldiers, spoken to in harsh tones - until they were with me in the cabin! I had a cabin full of ten-year-olds and loved every minute of being with them. We laughed, played, and sang all day. I told them stories and took them from activity to activity until finally I tucked them in at night. My co-counselor, Alex from Northern Ireland, joined us in the evenings after her long hours teaching water skiing all day. Other counselors were from all over the world: Sweden, England, France, Ireland, Africa, and New Zealand, and we all had a ball together.

The kids were spoiled in their real lives, but not here at camp. They had the essentials they needed, except one thing: love from their parents. Camp lasted two months. On the only visiting day of the summer, some parents flew into camp on helicopters and shook their child's hand. I watched as they walked side by side with yards separating them.

Their housekeepers sent them letters and cookies that I kept in the "candy trunk," to be opened once a day – after rest/nap time. Other counselors saw the candy trunk as a nightmare because they did not have a "once a day" rule. Their kids were in and out of it all day long, which was controlling the counselors and creating chaos in the cabins. It was easy for me to say no to candy because I'd grown up with so little.

There was a pervasive air of tension in the camp. Girls and boys were kept separated all day. Everyone wore the same colored shorts and shirts. Every half hour a bell rang to alert them to go to their next "station." Kids were "forced" to do sports. I even saw one child crying and begging not to go when she was pushed off the dock to water ski (something I'd love to have done). At dinnertime we were all made to stand in silence for great lengths of time before being seated because of one child's misbehavior. This act, like so many others, was meant to control and demoralize the campers. It only angered me. As time went on, I began to feel by my standing there doing nothing, by not speaking up when the children were being spoken to in such harsh tones, I was giving the unspoken message I agreed with these leaders. The children looked at me. I had a hard time looking back into their eyes, not knowing what to say. My head began to throb. I became overwhelmed.

Each day I held a different soaking wet child in my arms. They were wet from sweating - from crying so hard. Hungry for affection, they were constantly leaping into my lap or following me so closely, I almost stepped on them. I felt like the kids were lonely for their families, and wanted to go home, something they had no control over. The realization of the emotional void of these kids was more than I could bear. Standing by doing nothing while I saw them demoralized made me want to jump out of my skin.

After one month, I went into the empty boathouse three nights in a row. I sat and cried for an hour each night. I did not know about post-traumatic stress triggers. I was triggered. I'd been one of those kids, hurt and demoralized, with no one stepping in to help me. I was not only being triggered by what I witnessed, but by feeling powerless to intervene. *No one* intervened. We young college kids watched day after day, as if we were statues with our feet glued to the floor, and our mouths zipped shut. When a leader did or said something unkind, we looked at one another and glanced down, into our frozen positions. I felt crazy.

On the third night, I called my mom. The moment I heard her voice, I could not control my crying. After listening, she responded, "Lynnie, it is not mentally healthy to stay where you are not happy." I resigned and went home. To Kentucky.

Walking Zombie

Rudy called me the entire time I was at camp, telling me how much he missed me. I called him to say I'd be flying home and asked if he'd drive the two hours to pick me up at the airport.

"Uh, my tires aren't very good on my car," he responded.

That's strange. I couldn't imagine why, if he liked me so much, he wouldn't do whatever it took to come see me after two months away. "I'll try to get another vehicle to make the trip," he said weakly.

I called my brother, Carl, and asked him to pick me up, just in case. Something told me deep down not to expect Rudy. Even so, when my brother was there, I looked around. No Rudy. I knew then I'd never see or hear from him again. I would not call or chase him. It was over.

I knew nothing about the stages of grief and the natural reactions the body has after a loss. I went numb and walked around in a coma, for the next several months.

That was the week my sister, Mary, became my friend.

Mary was going to Florida and asked me to come with her and her friends. I was impressed that she asked me. I could not figure out why she wanted me there with her, especially with the state I was in. I went, and once again, Mary's kindness melted my heart. Even though we were with others, our bond was powerful. We walked along the beach in silence. Sitting on driftwood, she sat with me as I stared into the sea. She was very respectful of the pain she saw in me. Later we danced the night away on the dance floor, unaffected by the guys trying to talk to us. It seemed like nothing was more important to either of us than the other.

Shored up somewhat, I went to Memphis, Tennessee, for cheerleading camp. I was not the same person they'd met in the spring.

When I came back to college in the fall, Rudy was not there. He'd gotten a job as a teacher in another part of the state. Within a few days, a friend came running up. "Lynnie, did you know that Rudy is getting married?" It had not been one month since our last conversation about picking me up at the airport. *He really had been engaged! The entire time we dated! Who could do that? What kind of person could do that?*

Being in a coma and being a cheerleader do not mix well. But there I was, in a deep, dark depression. I had no concept that one loss could bring up losses from the past. Grief, shock, triggers, PTSD – none of this was in my toolbox. I just thought something was terribly, terribly wrong with me.

Traveling with the cheerleaders was the worst. I was in a daze most of the time, driving in the van, sitting at dinner. I'd lost my bubbly self. Watching their disregard of people in restaurants and hotels brought my mood down further. I did not fit in.

When one cheerleader was not in the van, many berated him mercilessly. When he stepped into the van, all went quiet. In those moments my loneliness overwhelmed me. I found myself wondering what they might be saying about me. My demeanor had changed. My soul ached, but I did not know how to fix it. I had once been a leader, reaching out to others with kindness and compassion. Now, I needed someone to reach out to me.

What Could Be Stupider?

After meeting Mr. Huggins, I often exclaimed, "I went straight at fourteen." My wild days were behind me. Except for drinking alcohol. I spent four years drinking to excess, experiencing its dangerous effects until one day a lightening-bolt hit me.

I had tasted alcohol in those earlier days, but in my later years as a sophomore in high school, I began drinking beers with friends after games, and I only drank to get drunk. One night a week. We had contests to see who could drink the most beers. I won. Every time. I was proud of my title until I got sick my senior year. That did it for beer. Then I went to drinking wine with my senior year summer friends. My freshmen year of college, my drink on Saturday nights was some kind of whiskey with Dr. Pepper.

Something happened to snap me out of this. One glorious sunny October morning my sophomore year, we cheerleaders met to board a float for the homecoming parade. Afterwards, we were going to cheer at a football game, to be televised nationally. When we arrived, several guys said, "Come on you guys, let's go get some hooch!" This was a very high potent alcohol mixed in a punch bowl with a fruit drink. These were the same guys that wrecked their hotel rooms and were disrespectful to waiters. I took in the whole picture as several ran to follow them to the fraternity house around the corner.

I sat dumbstruck. *Now, what could be stupider? How much more thrill does a person need than a beautiful day, waving from a float, and cheering to fans on national television?* That was the moment I gave up drinking.

Little Sister

Judy came to visit me at college on a weeknight. I had class the next day, but we sat in my truck talking for three hours. Judy was two years behind me in school, but what a difference that made. She was into drugs and ran with a whole different crowd.

I made the decision early on not to do drugs in school. Whenever I was at a party in high school and someone passed me a joint, instead of saying, "No, thanks," I just took it in my fingers and passed it to the next person. It was the rare person who noticed I did not take a drag. I never made a big deal of it, because pot was everywhere. Mary had hung with a smart crowd and none of them did drugs. I hung out with a wild crowd, but I did not do drugs. Judy was hanging out with a crowd and *doing* drugs such as PCP and marijuana.

Judy with our dog Laddie before her illness

Once I'd gone home to watch Judy cheer in a varsity game. Seeing her was like looking into a mirror. I'd never taught her a cheer, never coached her, but there she was with her movements and her mannerisms - exactly like mine.

While seated in my truck outside my dorm, Judy and I talked as the rain poured down in buckets. She said she'd thought about killing herself several times. This broke my heart to hear, and before I could say anything, using her nickname for me, she said, "And you know why I didn't, Looneybird?"

"Why?" I asked.

"Because of you. Each time I think I can't do something, I look at you and see you doing it, so then I think I can. If you can do it, I think, so can I." She told me she was thrilled that I was "making it." She got a kick out of my being a cheerleader in college, describing it as "something we can tell your grandchildren." I did not tell Judy about the depression I was suffering. I don't know if I was aware of mine, sitting there in the truck. I certainly was not smart enough about therapy to know, had I told her of my own sadness and insecurities, it would have been a healing balm, a gift. I did not know that self-disclosure of that kind helped lessen the shame in another person. I was not handling my own depression well and I was in no space to talk about it. So the conversation remained about her.

Judy was in that dark place I would not recognize in myself until later: that place where she was so fully without life skills she couldn't imagine going on without help. She wanted to know how to do things right. She saw others doing them, but was completely blinded as to how to get there. Although she was stunted, she fully recognized support was vital to her survival. This was her cry for help. She'd come all this way to tell me. This was not the first time Judy reached out to me. While in high school, I spent a lot of time at Todd's house. She'd call me and ask me to come home. "I'll make you your favorite – frozen peas and mashed potatoes!" I rarely did.

Judy would be graduating from high school the following spring. I thought for days about quitting college and going home to help her through. I struggled with what to do. The thought of losing Judy frightened me, but I numbed myself to it and stayed. I blocked out Judy's cries for help and went on with my life. Even though now I see I did not have the tools to give Judy what she needed, I regret not spending more time with her, not coming home more for dinner. I could not stop her from doing drugs, but I could have come home more. There are many regrets when mental illness robs a family of one of its members.

Confronting a Lie

Rudy's friend came to me again that fall, gleefully describing Rudy's wedding in Pittsburgh, even handing me a favor from the wedding: a matchbook with the words "Lynne and Rudy" embossed in it. *Oh, my gosh! She even has my name!*

It had happened. I was not so shattered by the fact that a former boyfriend had chosen another woman, but more so by his "acting" that had been so convincing. I saw "charming" was another word for lying. *How could I have believed all those things he'd said to me? How could we have been so close and now he was gone? How could he have sat and cried and told me stories about himself, that to my thinking, he'd only felt comfortable enough to tell me? How could he look me in the eye? How could he have kissed me with such passion? How could he just up and walk away from the wonderful thing I thought we had?*

This was the fall my overeating started. I used food, particularly sugar as my drug of choice, to medicate the pain I was in. I was not educated in the family disease of alcoholism and I did not know that, if untreated, almost certainly each family member came out with a compulsion of some sort. Mine was overeating, and then to combat it, over exercising. The roller coaster had left the station, and no one was at the switch.

That second year of college, my roommate left school in October. Once again, I had a room to myself. Perfect for a depressed over eater. I could be alone in a dark room with my dark secret. It would be a decade before I learned about eating disorders. Then, I thought I was the only person in the world this miserable.

That fall, I was not at my best anywhere. I was becoming larger. I was not dependable for practices and I made C's in a couple classes. I decided to change my major. I'd thought I wanted to be a broadcast news journalist, but after working at the campus TV and radio stations, I discovered two things. I did not have the personality to "beat" someone out of a story; I could not chase someone down a sidewalk and shove a microphone into his face. Plus, it was awful that I was all alone in the TV station, except for the cameraman whose face I could not even see. My major felt obnoxious on one hand and lonely on the other. I changed majors.

That December, I was still in my coma. I went home for winter break, and my brother Aaron found me on my bottom bunk. I told him about my dating Rudy and his marrying another girl. Aaron immediately said, "So go see him. You need closure." The moment he said it, I knew it was the answer.

I'd been invited by my summer counselor friends to spend Christmas in England and Ireland. I'd be driving to New York the next day. I decided to start out early and drive to the school where Rudy worked. When I got there, I asked at the office if I could be taken to his classroom. A student helper walked me down to the room, and told Rudy he had a visitor.

He excused himself from his students and came out of his classroom. When he saw me, he fell backwards onto the lockers and put his hands to his chest in a display of shock. I said nothing. I just stood there. He began to babble. I still said nothing.

He looked at me, shook his head, and began apologizing. "I'm so sorry, Lynnie. I wanted to tell you. I can't believe I did this to you!" Finally, he became silent and we stood there, in the middle of the empty, locker-lined hallway, looking at each other.

When I finally spoke, I said, "I just wanted to see you. I just needed to see that this was true." I was not angry. In fact, I was the calmest I'd been in months. Aaron was right. It was not the first confrontation I'd ever had, but this was the one that told me that, instead of sitting on something for months, wasting my life, I needed to confront the person head on.

Rudy invited me to eat lunch with him and the other teachers. I wanted to take in the setting. At the lunch table sat the girl he'd dated before me. She had spent the previous semester in London, the semester Rudy and I dated. Rudy had helped her get the job. So here I sat with a newly married man and his old girlfriend who'd come with him to be a teacher at this very remote school in Kentucky.

I had all the information I needed. I had closure.

Keeping Kentucky

Little did I know how proud I was to be from Kentucky. I spent Christmas in Birmingham, England, with a camp counselor. My confrontation with Rudy had worked. It had shifted me, but my depression had not lifted fully. After Christmas, I took the ferry from Liverpool to Belfast, Northern Ireland, to be with Alex, my co-counselor, for New Year's. I had not exchanged enough money, so late that night, I stood in the galley counting my coins. The guys on the other side of the counter chatted to me and asked me where I was from. Kentucky. One fellow said in a very drawn-out Southern accent, "Kentuckyyyy Fried Chickeeeeen!!!!????"

"Yes, that's right," I replied happily.

Another guy said, "You don't sound like you're from Kentucky." Along with all my other broadcast journalism colleagues, I'd recently taken a "diction" course. It was designed to teach us to speak in a way that no one would know where we were from. My assignment was to practice this art – and I was.

In the moment the young Irish man said that, on this ship sailing through the deep, dark dead of night on the Irish Sea, it felt like the most ridiculous practice in the world. Why would I not want anyone to know where I was from? Here were these people, so clearly Irish and proud, and here I was - across the ocean - practicing an accent designed to conceal where I was from!

I decided then and there I'd never again practice speaking differently, something I never regretted. It felt so good to no longer put effort into changing something that so obviously made me, me.

Dark Colors

I wondered while crossing the Irish Sea that night why everyone on the ship was dressed in such drab colors of dark greens, blacks and browns. Before I'd ever been searched or had seen metal detectors back in the states, I experienced them in Ireland. When I got to Belfast, I found out why. There were still bombs going off regularly. Alex's boyfriend was a news broadcaster on the "telly." Each evening we filled our plates with dinner, sat on the couch, and watched him give the news. One particular night while watching, the television went blank with fuzz. The television station had three bombs go off in it that night. No one was hurt.

On New Year's Eve, Alex and I were at a party where I met a girl who invited me to her home. I accepted. On the night I was to go, Alex drove me to a wide intersection somewhere in the city. The girl was parked on the other side of the intersection. I got out of the car, walked across the street, and got into her car. We drove away and had a wonderful evening filled with Irish pancakes and her family. When the evening visit was over, we went through the same ritual in order to get me home.

That was Belfast Northern Ireland in 1979. Alex was Protestant. My new friend was Catholic. Alex knew I was Catholic, and I could tell she did not care, but somehow, living in this town, there was a line drawn. Alex did not know how to explain the conflict, and I could tell she was embarrassed by the obvious secrecy of carting me back and forth. Those drab colors? The color of war.

Powerful Knowledge

I returned to the states after a month of traveling, with Rudy not looming so largely in my mind. On my return, at age nineteen, twelve years after the shooting, some blessed soul gave me the book *How to Survive the Loss of a Love* by Peter McWilliams, Harold H. Bloomfield, and Melba Colgrove. It changed my life. I'd never heard much of what I read in this small book with the left-side pages describing the biological effects of loss, and the right-side pages filled with poems – feelings that might coincide with information given on the opposite page. The book explained the stages of grief: shock, bargaining, anger, depression, and acceptance. In each section facts were given along with the possible feelings a person might have while in each stage. A loss was described as something as small as losing a tooth to losing a loved one after a thirty-year marriage. I cried all the way through it - and read it again and again.

Reading about how natural it was to go into shock after a loss was a relief. Then to see how the mind spins around and questions: *What could I have done differently? What if I'd done this? Suppose I had done that?* Being angry was a natural response to loss. Being depressed was natural after loss. This was something a person could not control and found almost impossible to hide. With the Rudy loss, I'd skipped over the angry phase and went straight to depression. Knowing I would get through this phase, and acceptance was on its way, was a relief.

Learning grief was natural and normal lifted me up. Reading this caused me to think about past losses and how I'd walked through them. If I'd not been so happy to receive this information, I might have been angry. *Why had no one told me about this when I was younger? Normal? Natural? Biological? How does a human get this information, and why does it have to be after devastation hits? In my case, why so long after?*

Every child has trauma, albeit most not as extreme as mine, but some much greater than mine. It felt like I'd had valuable information withheld from me that could have facilitated my emotional intelligence far earlier in life. After the shooting, it seemed I spent my whole elementary years in shock, my high school years in anger, and now my college years in depression. I'd spent ten years of my life alone, thinking something was terribly wrong with me. All that time lost, for what? Lack of knowledge? This felt like a crime.

Body Expression

With the experiences I'd had on my traveling adventure – plus the insights I'd gained reading, I was changing. One unfortunate change was that I returned to the states heavier than ever. Having eaten my way through these countries, I was now a not-so-entirely-depressed cheerleader. Just one harder to lift!

Once, while standing in line at a restaurant, someone commented on my crisp, new haircut. My cheerleading sponsor, a man about thirty-five years old, said, "Yeah, now if she can just do something about her weight."

In a flash, a fellow cheerleader stepped in to defend me. Perturbed, this tall, big-boned cheerleader who obviously weighed more than I did, turned to him, "She looks just fine. Let's talk about my weight. Do you want to know how much I weigh, too?" I loved her chutzpah. But his comment was out. My weight was a now talked-about issue in public. Lovely.

My sister Mary went to my college's archrival, Eastern Kentucky University. Our teams were fierce enemies, but Mary and I were closer than ever. One night in February, we were playing her school's basketball team. During the big game, my fellow cheer mate, said, "Look, Lynnie. There's Rudy!" I saw him and felt nothing; that's when I knew I was better. While in the stands at half time, Rudy came to me, put his hands on my shoulders, looked me straight in the eye, and told me he'd made a terrible mistake, that he should have chosen me.

I said, "Yep," and walked away. The creep had been married all of four months. I felt sorry for his unlucky wife.

My team lost in a controversial last buzzer throw, but Mary and I went out to have a good time. My college mates were mortified that I was not back at the hotel, grieving our loss to Eastern. I had more important things to do, such as having a blast with my sister!

Little did I realize then what having a sister was going to mean in this lifetime. I was beginning to feel the strength I drew from my relationship with Mary. We had a ball. We enjoyed each other's humor, but it was more than that. I was beginning to sense a depth to our relationship. In my extremes of feeling deep pain and great joy in my life, here I was with another human who knew exactly where my pain stemmed from. The feeling of happiness I had when I was with Mary came from some place deep in my core. There was a peaceful respect between us. The higher I rose out of my depression, the more I realized how much I'd learned about myself while in it. *Hmmm... learning from depression? How could that be?*

Touched

I decided to drive across the country to California with Dana, a girl from my dorm, to look for a summer job. After finals, we each went home for two weeks to prepare, she to Atlanta, and I to Louisville. I had no topper on my truck, so her brother made us a locked box to store our belongings. We were going to load my bicycle, our camping gear, and our luggage into the bed of the truck. We set a date for leaving and I worked a job for those two weeks to make gas money.

On the morning of the day I was to leave on my cross-country journey, I awoke to my mom whispering in my ear, "Lynnie, are you really going to go to California without a topper on your truck?"

"Yes, I can't afford one," I replied, half asleep.

"Come on, get up. I'm taking you to get one."

Anyone else might not understand why this was such a big deal. My mom was going to spend money on me. It would be money she could not afford. We just never had any money. Nothing for extras. The topper only cost $200, but it was $200 I did not have. This was an extra, and something I was going to go without, but to have this topper would make all the difference in our comfort and safety levels in our travels.

Realizing early my family did not have any money for extras, I bought my first pair of shoes when I was twelve. I never asked Mom for money. I'd been working jobs and making my own clothes for years. This would be the first money I could remember my mother spending on me. Funny, all of a sudden, instead of a usual pang of guilt, and since she was so adamant about buying it for me, it felt right to accept this money from my parent. I was touched.

Two Girls and an Ocean of Possibilities

Dana and I had a grand ole time camping, going to a rodeo in Colorado, sleeping at the edge of a rippling creek in Durango, Colorado, seeing the Grand Canyon for the first time, and getting caught by campus cops while sleeping in the truck in a parking lot of the University of Arizona. I ate tuna fish out of a can from the tailgate while she wanted to go to restaurants. Her father had lots of money; still, she budgeted her money, which I admired.

Our first stop in California was to see my long-ago friend, Midge, whose move away at thirteen years of age, had been so painful. After five years of letter writing, we'd kept our promise to see each other again. It was wonderful.

Dana and I settled in Santa Barbara. I immediately got a job as a cashier in a restaurant. We needed a place to live so we drove to the low-rent college town of Isla Vista. We had heard that on some campuses, it was possible for college kids to rent empty dorm rooms for the summer. At the campus of UCSB, we went to ask. A guy with a towel on his head was pushing a cart along the sidewalk. We thought that was a bit strange until we realized all the kitchen staff wore the same towel on their heads! We asked him from a distance, "Hey, do you know if they will let people live in the dorms on campus for the summers?"

He said, "Uh, I don't think so, but you can ask in there."

"Thanks!"

He turned away, paused, and turned back, "Are you guys looking for a place to live?"

"Yes!" we smiled and off we went to inquire at the desk about living in the dorms for the summer. The answer was no.

When we walked out of the building, the same guy approached us, "Are you guys *really* looking for a place to live for the summer?"

"Yep."

"Well, my roommate and I are looking for two roommates for the summer. If you don't mind living with two guys, we don't mind living with two girls."

That is how we came to live with Jack and Doug for the summer. I started my job and rode my bike twenty-six miles round trip on Santa Barbara's bike path, much of it with an ocean view. Dana's father furnished her with enough funds so that she did not have to work. When I got home, she was ready for anything. The guys worked on campus. Many nights the four of us had dinner at the kitchen table. Almost every meal was burritos. We got along smashingly.

There were drugs everywhere. A frequent visitor to the apartment sat for hours saying, "Come on you guys. Let's just sit around and be bored. Being bored is so cool." Dana and I stayed very active and stood out because of it. We were even laughed at for doing dishes straight after dinner! Lots of kids smoked pot, but Dana and I did not. We roomies went to a few parties together where Jack warned us not to drink the electric punch. People liked to spike it with drugs, then sit back and get a kick out of the unfortunate souls who drank it. When some girls got smashed, they stumbled over, telling me how they wished they'd never started on this drug or that.

The summer was ending and although we'd already been to Sequoia National Park, Disneyland, and the San Diego Zoo, Dana and I still had one more adventure on our list: seeing the "Johnny Carson Show." We spent the night on the sidewalk and got tickets. Johnny was wonderful and his guest was the star of "M*A*S*H," Alan Alda. When we got back to Isla Vista, Dana had a stomach bug, which delayed our trip for three days. That first night, while Dana was sick as a dog, Jack asked if I wanted to go play tennis. "Okay," I said and thought nothing of it. As we were riding our bikes to the courts, I realized I'd never really had a conversation with just him. I wondered if we'd have enough to say to each other, but we talked freely.

The next night, Jack asked if I wanted to go watch the sunset. "Sure!" Nothing seemed out of the ordinary. We lived two blocks from the beach, and sunset watching had been a ritual among all of us throughout the summer. We sat down and before long, Jack said, "I've been watching you all summer. At first I thought you were some spoiled girl whose daddy gave her a truck and said 'Have a nice summer!' but I can see you are more than that. You are the real deal. I've watched how hard you work. You're different from anyone I've ever met." He said he'd noticed me riding my bike to work, my diligence at work, and my ability to be happy without spending a lot of money. I was not surprised to hear this, because I knew I was different from the girls who'd come up from the LA area.

Jack asked me questions about myself, where I'd come from, how I was raised. We sat on the cliff for three hours. Near the end of that time, he turned to face the ocean. Staring into the breeze that blew back his long black hair, he said, "I think I'm going to marry you someday."

I was shocked but said nothing. As we got on our bikes to ride the short distance home, I remember peddling down the dirt path, tingling. *I think this is the man I'm going to marry.* There was something very intriguing about a man who, unbeknownst to me, was watching me while I had been totally myself.

We did not kiss that night, but now there was something between us. We said our goodbyes the next day and Dana kept saying, "What's going on with you and Jack? Did I miss something?" *A whole lot!* If she hadn't gotten sick, though, I wondered if I'd have missed it, too.

Maybe I Will, Maybe I Won't...

Back at college for my junior year, I got a call from friends KB and Cheri asking me to go skydiving the next day. I said I'd go with them and take the course. *Maybe I'll jump, maybe I won't.*

At the site, our daylong lesson included jumping off a platform and rolling on the ground a ga-gillion times to prepare for landing, punching out our reserve parachutes, and learning the ins and outs of skydiving. Watching the faces of the other members of the training group, I was amazed. *Wow. These people look serious. They look like they're really going to jump!* I was impressed they had the courage. Me, I had not yet made up my mind. *Maybe I will, maybe I won't. We'll see...*

It was almost sunset. Since my friend KB had spent the whole day flirting with Bob, the jumpmaster, he rode in the plane with the three of us. We dressed up in gear so weighted down we could barely walk. I had not shared with anyone all day that I might not jump. *I'll decide when I'm up there. No one is pushing me into this. If I'm too scared, I just won't jump.* We were in the plane and off we flew!

When we were up, the jumpmaster, Bob, began to prep Cheri. The plane was really loud, so he had to cup his mouth with his hands and yell. Cheri got ready. *Oh, my! She's really going to do this!* I was scared for her. Even though she'd been given specific instructions, Cheri did not follow them. From the back window, I watched her jump. She went twirling out of that plane like a rocket, the fastest thing I'd ever seen, with her hands clamped to her helmet, her legs in a seated position. It was frightening.

I froze. Bob, the jumpmaster, came crawling close to me and, with hands cupped over his mouth, looked into my eyes. "Lynnie, Cheri didn't do it right!" *No kidding, that was anything but right.* As he was speaking, I was tickled. *This guy really thinks I'm going to jump. Ha!* The "Maybe I will, maybe I won't" had turned into "I won't!"

But he did not know that, so I decided I'd just go up there and look out the door. You know, while I was there and all. I stuck my head out and felt the breeze. *Hey this isn't so bad, kind of like sticking your head out of a car window.* I looked down into the white clouds that showed open-

Cheri, Lynnie, and KB

ings of green grass. Bob said, "Lynnie, put your left foot on the pedal." I looked down. *Well, that can't hurt.* So I did. My right leg was still inside and both my arms were on either side of the doorframe. I was safe. Then he yelled and pointed, "Put your right hand up on the wing." I looked up at the wing. *That can't be too bad. I'll try it.* I reached out and up, placing my right hand on the wing.

Instantly, a pang of realization shot through my entire body.

I had my left foot on the pedal, my right hand on the wing, and my whole body was slanted to the right, with my right leg dangling in mid air. It took me all of one second to figure out I was trapped. I knew enough about physics and athletics to know I had absolutely no leverage anywhere that would allow me to push myself back into that plane. I had no choice. I had to jump. The *Maybe I will, maybe I won't* mantra was literally out the window!

Bob knew none of this, so when he tapped my calf and counted, "One, two three," I stepped off the pedal and arched my back, stomach to the ground, with a great force. In that fluttering force, I could see Bob's smile and his ten fingers wiggling to me. I had jumped! And, I had arched!

In the entire day, nothing had really prepared me for this because I never really thought about the actual jump. *Duh!* I just never got past the fact that I might *not* jump. Falling from the sky with such force was a doozey of a jolt, a shock, and the biggest physical thrill I'd ever had. Yet it was more than that. The fact that I did not flinch – really, *could not* flinch - in the face of taking that step made a huge rush of power shoot through me. I'd had courage. I filled with such pride, I was crying and screaming with joy at the same time. And breathing heavily. *Lynnie, shut up! Listen!* I listened to the absolute nothing and soaked in the beauty.

All of us made it down safely and headed home in one piece. I considered my friends very brave because they'd *planned* to jump – and did. But I was certainly not feeling like a coward because I had learned I could do something very scary without flinching.

"When I'm With You..."

I was full on into my major and excited about my studies. Jack wrote me letters constantly, far more than I could respond to adequately. He loved to write and I came to see he was gentle and bright. He was honest and our views were similar. I began to love him.

Now, I was not really into the whole drug/pot scene in California, so I never really kept tabs on peoples' habits, and this was true of my observations of Jack. I had seen Jack smoke pot at times, but never logged it. When he arrived in Kentucky to spend a month during our winter break, he did not smoke pot at all, announcing, "When I'm with you, I don't need drugs!"

Naturally, I thought, *Well, if we are going to be together, he won't need to do drugs.* That is what he said, wasn't it? In my mind, case closed.

But he could not be with me all the time. When Jack was back at school, he continued to smoke pot, drink, and do other drugs. When he was with me, he didn't at all. He acted as if he had no need to do so. Call me dumb, but I took at face value that once he and I were together permanently, he would not do drugs. Big mistake.

During that break, Jack and I drove to Atlanta to see Dana. As we drove, he told me the stories of his childhood: his angry father, his parents' divorce, his mother struggling to survive and raise her kids as a waitress, finding his mother on the floor when he got home from school several times after her having attempted suicide, her getting pregnant and the whole family sitting down and agreeing they would all help raise the baby, and the boys' club leader that took advantage of him.

Wow. This guy's family, in some ways, is stranger than mine. I no longer felt like a freak.

For the first time, I told him about the shooting. At one point, he became so sick, he asked me to pull the car over so he could vomit. *That's it! This is love. He has felt my pain.* We were bonded. And he was still there. He had said we would marry and that was that. No matter what red flags I saw after that, it seemed nothing could sway us from following through.

Judy and the Knife

"Mental illness is the result of unresolved grief." Unknown.

My junior year at college was Judy's freshman year at hers. Although she made good grades, she was beginning to act strangely. She had developed facial tics and behaved in an irritable and aggressive manner, cursing loudly, and speaking disrespectfully to her boyfriend. Then, suddenly, she'd become Judy again, and everyone seemed to forget these odd episodes. I said it was more than that. I knew her too well. Something was clearly wrong. During finals' week of Judy's first full year of college, Mom got a disturbing phone call. The director of the dorm could not get Judy to come off the roof of the building. She had been up there for more than a day.

That is where we mark the beginning of Judy's illness. The previous summer, Mom had moved from our home into a new house downtown, our dog of fourteen years, Laddie, died, and Judy had gone off to college. Just before that, my father had died and Tommy had killed himself. In those years, Judy had easily been swayed into experimenting with drugs. It was too much stress for a young person. All these traumatic events had occurred in a space of two important years when kids come of age and find themselves. Judy didn't stand a chance.

Even more than the stresses Judy had had in recent years, one important fact could not be denied when considering Judy's well being. She could not remember the night of the shooting. Not a single detail. It was as if she'd not been there. Once in our teenage years she asked me to tell her a little about it and acted as if it was so strange that I knew anything. I kept saying, "You were right there with me." She could not retrieve any of it, and just kept shaking her head saying, "Really? Really?"

Judy faced away from the horrific scenes that night, but, if I was looking into her eyes, she was looking into mine. Even though Judy could not remember, I knew if she were ever to retrieve a memory, she would first have to recall the stark terror in my eyes.

Years later, in my studies of psychology and the development of the brain, I learned people process traumas differently at different ages. It made sense for Judy, at five, to block out what she saw. It made sense for me, at seven, to remember the details. Mary's complete disassociation from her body in the face of tremendous violence and potential death was explained, too.

Whenever I left our family home, Judy began following me out the door, picking up rocks and throwing them at me, my car, and particularly my windshield. I hurried as fast as I could to get in my car and drive away. For several years, this was my send-off. I imagined she was angry because I was leaving yet again. As the years progressed, the rocks became bigger and bigger.

When I came home from college in May, I noticed more of Judy's facial tics. One afternoon, I was preparing to pick up passengers to drive across the country, dropping them off in Las Vegas on my way back to spend the second summer with Jack in Santa Barbara.

Out of the blue, Nem called our home. It had been three years since I'd spoken with her. Judy was cutting carrots with a butcher knife in the kitchen. She took the call and passed me phone. I walked into the dining room and she followed me as I said, "Hello."

Curious, Judy asked, "Who is that?"

I briefly turned to her and whispered, "Nem."

"Why are you talking to that bitch?" she yelled loudly. I cringed, knowing that no one could have missed that.

I said, "Sorry," to Nem. In all my years of not feeling comfortable with Nem, I had not referred to her as that, nor did the women in my family use that word casually. Judy was recalling my years past with Nem, tension that was long since over. This was unusually aggressive behavior for Judy. She listened as I talked casually to Nem, as if we were friends. Judy had only thought of Nem as a hurtful person, and that was where she'd remained in her mind.

I was embarrassed and felt sad for Nem to have to hear that. She shrugged it off, saying, "Oh, that's okay."

We spoke for a bit, and when I hung up the phone, I went back into the kitchen. I said, "Judy, that wasn't necessary to say."

Judy's face instantly transformed. I knew to run.

She tore out after me, gritting her teeth and waving the butcher knife. I ran through the hall, around the corner, and into the one guest bedroom of my mother's house. It had no lock on the door. The force of Judy's first hit on the door knocked it open enough for her to get the butcher knife through the crack. I had my back on the door. As she banged harder and harder waving the knife, the door opened several times before I could forcefully shut it. Finally, Judy and her knife were on the other side of the door.

Judy stood there slicing the butcher knife into the slit of the door-frame yelling, "Come out, I'm going to kill you."

I held the door as steadfast as I could. I heard my mother standing just behind her saying, "Judy, stop! Stop!" She would not.

I kept yelling over the two of them, "Mom, call the police! Please call the police!" She would not. She stood there whimpering, crying, and begging.

For nearly two hours Judy stayed on the other side of that door.

Many years had passed since my fighting days, but I remembered well the pent-up anger I carried, my fear that somehow it would be un-leashed, and I would hurt someone seriously. Now, here was Judy with her pent-up anger waiting for me. She was nineteen-years old and had been abused all her life, in one way or another, and had never gotten the chance to unleash it. I knew this kind of anger and was keenly aware her strength could be superhuman. I had to be on the alert the entire time. Since I was an athlete, I was strong, but I didn't take for granted the fact that she could outpower me the instant I let my guard down.

Judy rested several times to regain her strength. I heard her panting like a cougar on the other side. I didn't know when she was going to take a deep breath and again heave her body into the door with full force.

Had Judy gotten though the door that evening, she would have done her best to kill me. Judy was not Judy. This was not the little girl who'd been my best friend throughout my childhood, my helpmate, and my comedy buddy. It is true, we had not been close recently; we'd grown apart after boys came into the picture for both Mary and me. Judy want-ed to stay young and play. Mom told us to go out and live our lives, but

Mary and I grew up too fast for Judy. Things around her changed - too fast. I was leaving once again. She had little control over the people in her life.

My mother, who had stood behind Judy in all that time, could not stop crying. She did not call the police, even though I'd begged her repeatedly.

Finally, Judy was spent. Mom and I sensed the spell she'd been under had passed. She walked away. I did not know if my passengers were still at the bus stop waiting, but I was going to find out, and drive away from that house as fast as I could.

I prepared my things. "Go talk to her before you go, Lynnie," Mom said. "She looks up to you. Go tell her things are all right. Tell her you're sorry." This seemed like a dream. Why was my mom saying this? I was bewildered, but went to the kitchen and looked out the back window anyway. Judy sat on the concrete porch, her feet dangling off the ledge, rocking quickly back and forth. Mom said again, "Please go sit with her, Lynnie. Tell her everything is going to be all right. She loves you, Lynnie. She looks up to you."

Wasn't I the one who'd been in danger? It seemed I was the one to whom an apology was owed. Knowing nothing about denial, how thick it could be in a family such as ours, I followed the victim stance my mom taught me. It felt creepy.

I went out to sit near Judy, about four feet away. She was talking to me now, rocking back and forth methodically, "I almost did it. I could have killed you. I *would* have, too. You would be dead right now. I wish I'd killed you. I would gladly go to jail for the rest of my life if I'd killed you. I'm sorry I didn't kill you. I would live the rest of my life happily in jail."

Judy was no longer physically violent, but her mental state was extremely so. As she talked, the more vicious her voice became. Her words reminded me of the words my dad had said the night of the shooting. The gist was the same, as if she knew in her mind she'd be going to jail if she'd killed me. She had already resigned herself to it. What was eerie about that was Judy had no recollection of the shooting. Now I knew, somewhere in her psyche, it must be lying dormant.

Judy in California

The people were still waiting for me at the bus station, and we drove across the country. I did not sleep the entire two-day journey. For the next year, I'd have nightmares about Judy's knife scraping at the door-frame.

I got an awesome job as a groundskeeper at a horse showgrounds in Santa Barbara that summer, this time riding my bike only 16-miles round trip. Jack and I were now living in our own room in the apartment, and Doug shared the other room with a new guy.

Even though this business with the butcher knife had happened with Judy before I left Kentucky, Judy and Mom had plane tickets to come to California. I picked them up in Los Angeles. Mom had just had yet another operation on her "good" hand and had a steel rod, the size of a thin straw, still sticking out of it about two inches. The first day, I'd planned to let them watch the rodeo while I worked the concession stand at the showgrounds. Before we left, Judy got in a verbal fight with Mom and shoved her. I'd never seen her be physical with Mom, and with Mom having an open wound, I was shocked seeing this behavior. I was not going to allow anyone to hurt my mother. I yelled at her briefly, but remembered her violent temper and stopped short. We left for the rodeo.

While I was working the concession stand, Judy came to stand in line to buy something. When she ordered from my co-worker and found out we did not have what she wanted, she ranted. "So why is it up there on the menu? If it is up there, you'd better have it! I'm going to stand here until you get it for me! Even if you have to go out to the store and get it! You should not have it written up there if you do not have it. You should have taken it off the board if you didn't have it."

I wanted to crawl into a hole.

Judy continued to badger the people in the concession stand. I knew not to step into the conversation, as I feared I'd set her off. Instead of experiencing wariness from my co-workers about the situation, I felt their compassion toward me, which supported me in my tremendous task ahead.

Decisive, I spoke to my boss, left work early, drove Mom and Judy back to the apartment, and went in to pack Judy's things. I said, "Come on, Judy. Let's go." I drove the two hours south to LAX and got her a direct flight home. Judy was lying on a bench with her eyes closed when

I left, but I washed my hands of her.

I went back to Santa Barbara and proceeded to show my mother California, from LA to San Francisco, by way of the coastal highway. Jack's family lived in the Bay Area, and we all had a great visit. I thought no more about Judy. At summer's end, I went back for my senior year of college.

Leaving Crazy

That Christmas, Mary came home after a year of traveling and working in Europe. She walked straight into the bathroom and gave me a big hug. In her ear, I whispered, "Thank God you're here. You can help me deal with this crazy family." She later told me that was that moment she decided to go to Australia. She worked two months at home and off she went to Australia, never to return.

Mary found a place to live in a country that was as far away from our family as a person could get, without going to the moon.

Public Half Speaking

I was soon to graduate with a speech and communications major with minors in mass media and psychology. I had wonderful professors, but one stood out. He laughed the entire time he taught – at his own jokes. The great part was, we laughed, too. I never saw anyone have so much fun in front of a podium as that guy. He was getting paid for this? He lived the quote, "Find a job you love and you'll never work a day in your life." That professor paved a way for me. I was going to find that kind of bliss someday.

By senior year, I'd given many speeches to my classmates. My last semester, I was assigned to give a persuasive speech, so I decided to persuade others to be a Big Sister or Big Brother. I was a Big Sister to a little girl my last two years of college. Her father had been stabbed to death with an ice pick through the forehead. During the actual speech, standing in front of my peers, when I talked of the difficulties this little girl faced, my voice quivered. The crowd stilled itself to catch each word. As I spoke of her life, I felt every morsel of it, and somewhere in that speech I felt myself talking about me. Every eye was on me, waiting to hear more. As I proceeded, I felt confident and strong, especially glad to be past the part about the little girl. When I finished, my classmates stared at me with wide eyes. No one ever asked me how I could speak of the little girl's feelings so deeply. It was the closest I'd come to speaking about what lay sealed in a vault in the cellar of my core.

Cross Country

After my graduation, I rode a bus out to California to Jack's graduation. We drove Jack's vintage car cross the country to my brother's wedding. We arrived at Jeff's wedding where I was to sing "The Wedding Song." He married a wonderful gal and I knew he was in love. When I first sang the words, "Do you believe in something that you've never seen before?" I cried. I knew Jeff had the same role models I'd had, and I admired him for believing he could do a better job than our parents. His marriage was a testament that a person could still fulfill a promise, even if the one given him had been broken.

Jeff did become a solid man in his community and when I visited him years later, I asked him, "How did you become the man you are?"

He responded, "Well, I went to Boy Scouts once a week and saw Mr. Clarke. Then I went home to our dad. Then I went to Boy Scouts and saw Mr. Clarke. Then I went home to our dad. Then I went to Boy Scouts and saw Mr. Clarke. One day I just looked at Mr. Clarke and said to myself, 'Hey, I want to be him.'" Jeff pointed his finger to an imaginary figure.

For him, it was as simple as that. Thank goodness for men like Mr. Clarke!

Jack and I rented a house in Louisville for the year before we were to marry the following June. I got a job as a youth program worker in a maximum-security detention center for juveniles. Kids were there for everything from running away from home to murder. It was at this point in my life I decided to try pot. I was working with kids who did drugs and felt I could not understand their experience. I tried it. No big deal. I did smoke it a few times after that, maybe once every six months over the next few years, but like drinking, it held little appeal for me. It only made me want to eat. *Ugh.* The last thing I needed.

I started walking three miles a day to work, taking the bus home. I'd continued to ride my overeating, over exercising roller coaster through-out my college years. Being away from the college scene now, I began to manage my overeating much better. The weight I gained in college began falling off.

Jack did not find a job for several months but finally signed on to be a manager of a restaurant in town. During the time that Jack had not worked, he'd spent time playing basketball and made friends with guys who smoked pot. I was disappointed. *If he could just make friends with people who did not smoke pot, things would be okay.*

Jack and I planned a wedding for late June and a honeymoon bicycle trip up the east coast.

The 911 Voice

In the early eighties, before real-life crime shows and 911-recorded calls were televised, I saw a scene played out on my mother's kitchen television. The camera moved through a house, showing still pictures of double French doors and sheer curtains. I heard a woman's voice on a 911 call. "Help me, he's going to kill me! Help me, please! He's outside! Come now! He's here and I know he's going to kill me! He's here. He's in the house! Help! He has a knife. Help me, please! He's going to kill me!" It was obvious by the next sounds he killed her mid-phone call.

I stood staring at the television and the next thing I knew I was kneeling in the front yard of my mother's home unable to stop screaming.

Jack stood behind me while Mom tried to console me. I went home and slept it off. Jack never mentioned it and I was able to stuff down whatever had tried to come up for another several years.

The Affirmation Confirmation

It was now five years after I'd graduated high school and a beautiful thing happened. Nem called. It had been two years since that last phone call. She asked to come over to the house where Jack and I lived. I showed her around and soon we were talking. This was unusual for us, because we didn't have a social relationship. She said she'd come specifically to ask me something. *What could it possibly be?*

Nem told me she'd been very much in love with a man who'd broken up with her. He'd told her, "Nem, you don't know the meaning of humility."

"I've thought about this word humility for a long time. I've asked other people what they thought it meant. I read the definition in a dictionary, but I still don't understand what *he* meant. I thought if anyone knew the definition of humility, it would be you. Maybe you can explain it to me in a way that I can understand."

It was as if the heavens and earth opened and I was filled with "havingness." All of the silent suffering was lifted from our relationship and the love and respect I had for her then was everything I'd ever wanted between us. The full value of the best reason to experience pain was brought home in that moment. As painful as our relationship had been, in that moment, I could not have loved her more.

I thought about it for a few minutes. When I spoke, I said, "The best way I can explain it, Nem, is that the whole time I ever knew you, all those days and hours we spent side by side, working together for years, I never heard you speak about love or hate or despair or happiness or sadness or contentment or anything that would define you as a person. All I heard you talk about was finger nail polish or makeup or hairdos or clothes or your car or someone else's car or your pool or your house or your neighborhood. I never heard anything come out of your mouth that made me feel connected to you." She nodded and I said, "That's all I can think of."

Afterwards, I wish I'd told her that having the sheer courage to come ask me this was an act of humility. I would have liked to have told her that the tone she used while speaking of others was as if the human condition was not hers. In the guise of being helpful, I'd heard an element of cruelty in how she spoke. But I did not want to be critical. How can you tell someone you cannot feel love coming from her? What did she love? I never knew.

Somehow, just her asking me that was affirming of my life. All those stabs of pain I'd felt listening to her all those years validated I'd not been crazy.

Moving Ahead, Red Flags and All

Marijuana seemed to always lie on the fringes of our conversations, never quite in them. I knew Jack was smoking, I just did not know how much. But there was a constant theme that ran through my head. *Geez, I'll be glad when Jack finds friends who do not smoke pot.* After six months of virtually no work, Jack was working as a restaurant manager. Finally, we were saving for our upcoming wedding and honeymoon.

Three weeks before our wedding, Jack was fired from his job. The district manager caught him smoking pot behind the restaurant with his employees! He was fired on the spot. *Unbelievable! How does this happen? Surely a person could control himself enough to not smoke pot at work? And a manager with his employees?*

Two days later, stepping into her dress, my bridesmaid shook her head and said, "I can't believe you're marrying someone who smokes pot. That seems so weird."

I'd been frightened to - and frightened not to - ask Judy to be one of my bridesmaids. Mom wanted me to, so I did, even though I was afraid of Judy. More fear.

The invitations were sent. The bikes were ready and loaded. *We've been planning this for a year! What do I do?* I spoke to no one. I did nothing. I was a nervous wreck.

The day before the wedding one of Jack's college friends, who'd recently divorced, showed up. She stepped out of her car, walked up to Jack on the sidewalk, and gave him a *very* long kiss on the mouth. I felt ill.

That night I was alone with Jack's mother. Since she knew he'd been fired, I found myself telling her I felt apprehensive marrying a man who was fired for smoking pot. She agreed and said, "Yes, that is something to think about." *But it was the night before the wedding!* Then she said, "Do you want to go through with it? If not, we can cancel."

I barely slept at my girlfriend's house. Jack and the guys, plus his college friend, slept at our house. I did not like it, but it seemed suddenly I'd lost control of a great deal.

We married the next day.

Mechanically, I switched to another gear, ignoring every flag and my irritating feelings. We were married in the church across the street and the reception was in Mom's backyard. Jeff walked me down the aisle. I loved Jack and felt all of the love from the people there, but something was not right. Judy was fine and did not cause a scene the whole day. But someone else would the next day.

Arriving back from our honeymoon night, we found Jack's mother sitting on the porch smoking a cigarette. Frowning, she stared straight ahead. She did not speak to us, even though we spoke to her. She came into my Mom's house behind us, told everyone to pack up, and get in the car. They were leaving. "What?" Jack asked. They'd come all the way from California and we were all going to Nashville the next day.

No. She was leaving. She had everyone in the car within twenty minutes and she was gone. We never knew what caused this strange behavior, but it would not be the last of it.

The Bike Trip

We began our bicycle trip from Washington, D.C., in 99-degree heat. Both Jack and I were cyclists in pretty good shape. We planned to just take it easy, looked on the map for a red tent symbolizing a campsite, decided if we could make it that far by evening, and off we peddled.

Over a six-week period, we covered 2000 miles, to Maine and back, staying in some places several days. We generally rode thirty to eighty miles a day, but one day it was so hilly we only made it twelve! That's when we headed to the coast for flatter ground. We rode through Philadelphia, New York City, and Boston. We carried a cardboard sign marked "Through Tunnel" on one side and "Across Bridge" on the other, to catch rides. We kept to small country roads whenever we could, but sometimes we had to use main highways.

In all those miles, I got a lesson in porches. I never knew how fascinating it would be to ride past house after house. Faster than walking and slower than driving, a bike's speed must be just enough to get a glimpse of people's stories. I found out about the people I passed, by studying one porch at a time, at bike speed. The lawn mower stashed under the porch, the paint chipping from it, the screen doors slamming with the kids running in and out, chasing balls, folks waving from their steps or swings – giving the smallest clues of the lives we passed.

I have a list of the six hardest things I have ever done, and this bicycle trip is at the top of the list. It's the elements. A biker is always fighting the wind, rain, the sun's heat, the terrain, rocks, gravel, dirt, glass, twigs, animals – dead and alive - and the constant honking of horns that scare you to death. Semi trucks, and the fear of being sucked under them, were the worst. I also found water could alter everything inside the human body. To a dehydrated body, water was like a good drug, a miracle pill that changed the mind, the brain, and the muscles.

I got very fit on the trip and noticed my arms were getting just as much workout as my legs. I'd promised myself that I would not walk up hills, that I'd stay on my bike, no matter what. While I was on my bike for all those miles, a beautiful thing happened. I found myself saying over and over again: "You can do it, Lynnie." I was determined to go the distance, to last to the top of every hill. In two thousand miles, I only walked up one – a beastly climb leaving Mystic, Connecticut. The whole trip was a great time for meditating, filled with solitude, as Jack's bike was usually a little orange dot ahead of me.

We had no flat tires until one day when we had five. In a row. In the pouring rain. We did not stay in motels, but I told Jack I'd had it. I was stopping at the next motel I saw. He must not have believed me, because he passed one and did not find me until he peddled back an hour later when I was showered and tucked into my bed watching TV. I had my limits.

On the way home, I was wishing for hills and feeling bored on the flat roads. I became fit of mind. My new mantra, "You can do it, Lynnie," stayed with me for years.

Settling in D.C.

Jack and I decided to settle in Northern Virginia, near the home of my deceased grandparents. I immediately got two jobs and worked 60 hours a week as a bookkeeper and retail clerk.

Jack looked for work, but found nothing for months. An expensive place to live, and being low on money, I started sewing for people, making dresses and bridesmaid gowns. I was busy. By February we did not have enough money to make the car payment *and* buy groceries. Jack suggested we skip the $183 car payment that month. I thought about that for all of two seconds and decided I was never going to live that way. I paid the car payment, leaving $15 for food that month. We lived off frozen chicken, cans of mushroom soup, and peanut butter and jelly on crackers. I was not going to jeopardize my credit.

Jack was spending money playing Ms. Pac Man. Visiting me on my lunch breaks, he wanted me to watch him play to see just how good he was getting. I tried, but all I could see was quarter after quarter being squandered.

Jack had been a water polo player in high school and was hired at a local prominent university as the water polo coach, unpaid, but instead waiving his college tuition. So now I was working three jobs with a husband who was coaching what he loved, smoking pot, playing Ms. Pac

Man, and going to graduate school. I did not get angry. I didn't even know I was angry. I went back to using food as my drug. Resentment grew over time, but words failed me.

The Chicken

That May I took a job as a front office supervisor of a luxury hotel in Washington, D.C. Two weeks in, I was promoted to supervisor of the 3-11 shift. It was a fun place to work, as senators and celebrities came to the front desk.

A turning point in my life was about to happen at that desk.

The hotel had 99 rooms and booked up to 116 rooms on a busy night, overbooking by seventeen rooms. On those nights, my job as the supervisor was to tell guests, when they arrived, we did not have their room. The managers who'd authorized the overbooking had long since gone home, hoping those seventeen people would not show up and we'd fill to capacity. *What? What was I supposed to say?* I was given a number of reasons to recite, for example: "Tell them guests stayed over, and we just can't force them out of their rooms."

There I stood at 10:30 p.m. I watched through pouring rain as a man got out of his cab, struggling with his luggage. The bellman helped him and walked him to the front desk. I was to look him in the eye and tell him that we had "no room in the inn." This was my job. *This is horrible.*

Twice I told that lie. I was 24-years old and, seeing how hard this was for me, my co-worker, a retired military officer, volunteered to do it for me.

It soon became known to the upper managers, that Lynnie was a "chicken" and "not management material." This got me thinking. *I am not going to be promoted because I have a difficult time lying. I am not going to "make it" here. Wow.*

These thoughts played in my mind for weeks. We tell kids all their lives not to lie and here I was being punished for not being able to lie *well.* I could not see myself accepting this lifestyle. *Where could I go, where instead of being criticized for not being able to lie, I would be admired?* I had been a swim coach, a gymnastics instructor, and I loved kids. I also knew kids could smell a lie and, in fact, would not respect anyone who *did* lie to them. With this thought, I decided to become a teacher.

Enabling With No Words

Later I was promoted to reservations' manager, but Jack still did not have a job – one year after moving to the area. People kept asking me if he'd found a job yet. "Nope, not yet." Finally, Jack came home to tell me he'd gotten a job at a 7-11 convenience store, working the graveyard shift. Not the job I pictured for my husband with two degrees. It was hard to swallow. He explained that it was the best way for him to go to graduate school and become an Olympic water polo coach. I tried to be supportive.

With this night job began the period of time I stopped seeing my husband altogether. He worked through the night, coached morning and afternoon practices, and had graduate classes in the evening. My friends called him the "phantom" husband. I hung out with one guy from Pakistan so often, that Jack called him my "second husband"!

I knew Jack still smoked pot occasionally. He attracted friends who smoked pot, but he very rarely smoked when he was with me. The few times I did see Jack smoke pot, he'd take a freshly rolled joint, light it, close his eyes, and suck the entire thing down to his fingers - in one drag. I remember watching his face and thinking to myself, *Wow, I wish he loved me like he loves that joint.* I still believed his statement from years before: "When I'm with you, Lynnie, I don't need to do drugs."

Jack and his mother had a close relationship, too close. He'd talk to her for hours, ignoring the expense. Ever the martyr, I did not call my family much. Still, I did not know how to get angry. When our phone bills reached $250 a month, I asked him if he'd please not talk on the phone so long, angering his mother.

Jack had grand ideas of writing books and developing putt-putt golf courses for the handicapped. Forever describing his new inventions to have patented, he still wanted to be an Olympic coach. I listened and believed him, even as other thoughts crept into my head. *Well, if you're going to write a book, shouldn't you be writing something now?* And *Just do it! Stop talking about it! Do it! Do - something!* I heard a lot of dreams, but I was hurting inside, keeping us afloat, money-wise.

Jack's mother and younger brother visited, and I saved money to take us all on a camping trip. The trip was a disaster. It started when his mother raved about Jack's invention ideas and praised him for his wanting to help the handicapped. When she asked me what I thought, I said, "Yes, all of that will be wonderful, but we will have to make sure our children have good health and dental care." That moment, she stopped speaking to me. Later when new campers pulled up too closely, she screamed curse words about their proximity. I was mortified. I'd been a camper all my life, and only knew campers to be friendly. When we went to gather firewood later, mustering my courage I said, "Kitty, I feel really embarrassed when you curse like that - and everyone can hear you."

She snarled, "I'll yell anything at anyone I damn well please!"

The tension between us was thick but she still let me pay for everything. Jack watched how ugly his mother was to me. We returned home the day of their flight. I was shoving dirty laundry into the washing machine when Jack came in and whispered in my ear, "I will never put you through this again." His words made me feel like we were a team.

Just before his mom left, she stood up in the corner of the living room, "I have an announcement to make." She looked at me and said, "Lynnie, I have decided I just don't like you." Jack rolled his eyes and stomped around furiously, throwing their suitcases in the car, piling them into the car, and leaving for the airport early. That was the last thing she ever said to me – except for asking for Jack on the phone when she called. Jack continued to talk to his mom for hours on the phone and money continued to be drained from us. Our team was being sabotaged.

A Step for Me

As time went on, Jack began to take incompletes for almost all his graduate courses. I was discouraged because I'd thought when he finished his degree, it would be my turn. This seemed like a false hope. I decided to finagle a way for me to pursue a teaching certificate. The only sensible thing was to get a job at the university in the suburbs, which would allow me to take free classes. So I did.

Jack was getting more and more irritable. And depressed. One day when Jack and I were driving in the car, he said, "Wow. I haven't smoked pot for three days!" I just shrugged it off because that did not seem like such a feat. I did not understand what he was trying to tell me. This was a very big deal for him. He'd been trying to stop. He later told me he only ever made it those three days without smoking pot. He'd been smoking pot every day all those years. I had no idea. I later found out his friend went to the store where Jack worked almost every night, so they could smoke in the back room. Smoking pot. At work. Again. He ate constantly when he was home – large amounts of food. Almost every time I saw him, he was polishing off a half gallon of ice cream. This was fine, because I had started back into my overeating and over exercising again. Before, I had taken the subway into D.C. and walked the five miles home each day. Now during my breaks at the university, I walked six or eight miles. I was eating to cope with my pain. I was exercising to cope with my eating.

We were one dysfunctional mess.

Jack began a job as a lifeguard in the summer and found he could make a lot of money giving private lessons to kids and coaching the pool's swim team. He made three thousand dollars during the summers, which helped us tremendously. His schedule in the fall and winter was to work through the night, come home to take me to work since we only had one car, sleep three hours, go to water polo practice and then to classes, and back to his night-time job. We only saw each other during the 30 minutes when he took me to work.

Even on weekends, he was gone. Each weekend in the fall and winter, Jack drove his water polo team to a meet. All of them went together and had a great time. There was only one problem. Because the university did not have a women's team, one woman decided she'd play on the men's team. It became clear she had a huge crush on my husband. My husband loved me, so this young girl did not threaten me, but *she* hated me. She refused to look at, talk to, or even acknowledge me. Each weekend on these trips, she rode in the front of the van, next to Jack, the driver. I waved goodbye to them on Fridays. It was obvious - the sooner she could get him away from me, the better.

Once, I had the water polo team over to our apartment for a party. I was making scads of food, pulling goodies out of the oven, and putting them onto trays. The woman water polo player kept coming to get the trays and taking them into the living room to serve the guys, saying, "I'll do it! I'll do it!" It became apparent she did not even want me in my *own* living room! As soon as I realized that, I went into the living room and spent the rest of the night with the gang. The girl was extremely passive aggressive, but I did not know then what that meant. I had a lot to learn about manipulation and communication.

Her attitude toward me was particularly disconcerting because Jack's desire to have sex had decreased significantly. Even if we did not spend the nights together, I still wanted to *be* with my husband. He seemed very lethargic about the whole thing and this hurt me terribly. *Am I ugly? What has happened?* Every now and then I asked Jack if he remembered the last time we'd had sex. He'd take a guess. "A week?"

"Three weeks," I'd say. I felt terrible for saying anything, but worse if I didn't because I longed for closeness. I became increasingly lonely. I did not believe Jack would be unfaithful. I believed my sadness had more to do with the lethargic, depressed nature I saw in him more and more.

"Are you happy?"

An angel came back into my life, changing it once again. My beautiful sister Mary came home for a 10-month visit after spending three and a half years in Australia. She loved Australia so much that she overstayed her visa after six months and remained in the country illegally for three years. Originally, she'd planned to leave after six months, but before that time was up, she'd found a boomtown in the northwest corner of the country, a place to make good money.

I won't say Mary always wanted to be rich, but I know her mantra was she was *never* going to be poor. Her financial education began when she sat on the edge of Mom's bed sorting through the monthly bills, deciding which bills they could afford to pay. Our mother placed greater importance on giving to Catholic charities than paying off the bills. This infuriated Mary.

When my big sister reached the northwest town of Karratha, they were laying the pipes for the first offshore platform pipeline. Liquefied natural gas would be exported to Japan. Homes had to be built to house the workforce. There were no women on building sites. The town was growing so fast, Mary discovered the brickies didn't want to acid wash their own bricks. She started contracting to clean them.

Mary worked hard manual labor alongside men in remote areas of Australia. Did they harass her? Yes. But Mary had already, as a little girl, said "No!" to a shotgun pointed in her face. She found if she took two steps forward and swore at a bully, the man backed down. Every time. She said the two steps forward was key. I loved hearing her stories of the look on a man's face when she shook a screwdriver at his nose. No man there had *ever* seen the likes of Mary, I was later told.

Mary had come home to the states to travel. That fall, Mary stayed with us in our apartment for five weeks. During those weeks, she saw the schedules we kept, particularly Jack's. Going to polo matches, she witnessed the goings on with the girl athlete. Mary agreed with me that Jack was not interested in her, but she saw that the girl hated me. Mary also got to see Jack smoking pot and eating the way he did. Because of our budget, when I made a meal of stew or chicken and dumplings, I made a large pot of it, so that it would last all week for lunches. But when Jack got home, he'd finish off the entire pot. Then he'd eat a half-gallon of ice cream. This happened every time I cooked a meal. Mary saw him eat whole boxes of cereal out of a mixing bowl.

Mary noticed something that went over my head. Jack was constantly irritable. I, on the other extreme, was constantly happy. I was sickeningly sweet, smiling at everything. I was light and sunshine and lived by the motto "kill'em with kindness." I was a true victim, in every sense of the word.

Mary witnessed the whole shebang. One day, shortly before she was to leave, she came into my bedroom and sat down on the bed with me. She looked me straight in the eye and very gently said, "Lynnie, are you happy?"

My immediate reaction was "Yes, I'm happy! I'm so happy!" Blah, Blah, Blah. On and on I went, telling Mary how happy I was. And then I said, "Why do you ask?"

"I don't know. I was just wondering."

Brilliant. If ever a seed was planted, this was it. Those four words, "Lynnie, are you happy?" affected me deeply, but not as deeply as *my reaction* to her question.

I was repulsed by myself. I did not know why.

The Doorknob

Mary had not been judgmental or critical, but from the time she left, my whole world was magnified. It was actually her silence that allowed me to assess my life. Jack was gone. I came home each day to an empty house. When Jack was home, he was irritable, lethargic, and eating large amounts of food. He was not affectionate. Our finances were left to me to figure out. By now, he'd only finished two of the eight graduate courses he'd started. Worse to see, and glaringly apparent to me now, our lives had been like this the entire length of our marriage.

At the university where I worked people were always in and out. The guy who ran the facility came into the office every day. He was very kind and everyone loved him. We had become work friends. I stayed at my desk after hours to study while waiting for my class to begin. One night this fellow came back into the office and we had a short chat. Then he said, "Lynnie, are you lonely?"

I got huge tears in my eyes and just stared at him. That was all it took. He saw something I must have been trying to hide. I was embarrassed that we were having this intimate moment. He saw something in me that apparently my own husband had not seen.

It was true. My house was empty. Each night when I walked up the three flights of stairs, I began to shake. My hand reached out for the doorknob, to turn the key with the other, and as I lifted my hand to the knob, I watched my fingers shake. Something was not right.

What was happening? All I knew was I'd become terrified to open the door and once again find no one there. Every time I went to my apartment, it was empty. I began to call Jack where he was and ask him what time he was coming home. Sometimes I waited to come home ten minutes after that time, just so I could walk into a home when someone was there. When my husband was there.

Yes, I was very lonely.

At the office Christmas party, my work friend invited me over to his office for a drink. I didn't drink, but I went. As I was sitting there, I took off my shoes and put my feet up. As we talked, I realized I was starting to have feelings for this man. I was stunned. I quickly realized what could happen and left.

I told Jack that I'd had a feeling of attraction for another man. He just laughed and said it was normal to sometimes be attracted to someone else. None of this felt normal. I put in for a transfer the next day.

I was married, but did not spend time with my husband. With the words that I did have, I told him about my loneliness, in every possible way, but he did not hear me. Each time I sat Jack down to talk about this, he told me we were "working toward" something much better, that the early years of our marriage were going to be difficult like this, that we were making progress. But each time I walked away from these discussions unsatisfied. *How could we get ahead if six of his eight grades in his graduate courses were incompletes? Why did I have to be this lonely? What if we got ahead but lost each other on the way? Surely that is where we were headed!*

I was confused. I was scared. I felt crazy. I was speechless. I had no words. Not even words enough to say… I was frustrated. My level of emotional vocabulary was not even that high. And if I could not feel frustrated or annoyed, I certainly could not feel angry. I had shut her down. Remember? Anger was too scary. She was like a long-lost relative I never wanted to see again. The last visit with her had been so devastating, I did not care if she'd fallen off the face of the earth, never to be seen or heard from again.

But living with cousin Sickeningly Sweet was no fun, either.

I was a wreck. That fall, Mary had witnessed the damage. I was one dimensional in my communication skills and had no clue how to salvage myself.

Jack and I drove home to Kentucky to spend Christmas with Mom and Mary. We had a lovely time together. Mary would be going back to Australia soon. She was going to marry a man named Don in order to get back into the country to continue to work in the outback. Mom and I wanted to celebrate, but she told us not to make a "big deal" about it.

New Year's Eve day, Jack and I were getting into the car to leave. Mary came around to my side of the car and whispered in my ear, "If you ever want to get a divorce, Lynnie, I'll send you a ticket to Australia."

"Divorce? What do you mean divorce? I'm not getting divorced!" I was shocked she would even mention the word! It had never been spoken.

"Okay," was all she said.

Driving home that night, Jack got pulled over for speeding. There was pot in the glove compartment. Here I was, sitting in a car with someone who could get me in serious, serious trouble for life – arrested. Suddenly, I felt mad and sad, but mostly I felt like an idiot. *Why am I willing to let someone I hardly see ruin my life? I'm going to be a teacher!*

Ideas began turning in my head. I was still fighting the seeds that Mary had planted, pushing them from my mind, but I was restless, nonetheless. The first week of January, I began working in a new office at the university. It was a challenging and rewarding job. I thrived in the position, working so hard and fast, a large knot, the size of a golf ball formed in my neck and shoulders. There I worked with a woman who had words. Donna. Daily, someone came into the office angry. The person was escorted back to Donna. The way some people yelled, security surely would have been called had it not been for her. I got to listen to Donna, over and again, "soothe the savage beast." She was not afraid of these people. She stood there while they blasted her. She kept her composure, smiled, and began with the facts. She was able to bring calm to any situation - with words. I adored Donna and she became one of my finest mentors.

One day Jack told me he was very tired and needed to sleep more, and from now on, would I mind just taking the truck and letting him sleep? *Huh?* There went our thirty minutes a day together.

My restlessness led me to plan a trip to Greece. I had always wanted to go, looked into how much it cost, decided I could save enough money, and began to plan a trip for August. When I told Jack about my trip, he said, "I want to go, too."

"Okay, if you can save up enough money and get the time off." I was going, with or without him. I had to do something for myself. I did not know this consciously, but our separation was beginning.

That year our first day off together was May 18. We drove three hours to an amusement park and three hours back. It had been five months since New Year's and we'd had one day off together. My patience was thin. Jack did not even attempt to hide his pot smoking anymore. When I asked him to sit down so I could go over our finances with him, he'd go get his half-gallon of ice cream, come back with a spoon in his mouth, and lay on the bed. Looking up at me with puppy dog eyes, he'd say, "Okay, go ahead." By now, I wanted to scream. I was a faltering adult, alone with a child.

Whenever Jack and I were together, I found myself having imaginary conversations, ones I could not have out loud. When he told me something he planned to do, I was silent. *Prove it!* When he was supposed to take care of something for us and he did not, I was silent. *I knew you wouldn't do it. You never do. I have to do everything.* When he wanted to spend money, I was silent. *Then why don't you make some?* I was later to learn this was a very hazardous stage in a relationship – having nasty conversations in my head with my mate.

I was clearly living a lie. Somewhere, somehow, I'd built a cage around myself. I was trapped in a bubble of responses in my head. I'd met Resentment who wanted to introduce me to her sister Anger. Later we'd all meet up for tea with their friend Bitterness. No matter how unskilled I was at getting out my frustrations, I did not like meeting Resentment. She felt ugly. I was also not going to go anywhere near Anger. She was dangerous. I certainly did not do Bitter. I'd made it this far without her and I was determined she was not going to be part of my life. This was one tea party I was not going to have.

I'd spent my life up until now despising people who made rude comments about others. Now I was making them. In my head. Still, they were there. It would be only a matter of time before they started coming out of my mouth. I was trapped in silence again without options. Without words or communication skills, any options in front of me were equally repulsive.

Ready for a Sea Change

The trip to Greece was planned and we were going together. Then one day Jack walked in the door and told me he had accepted the assistant swim coach position at the university, which meant another job with no pay and now he'd be gone every weekend - of the entire year.

I was broken.

I was married to a man who did not want to spend time with me. I began to look at my life. *What was it that I wanted? What was I going to do with all those weekends alone? Why should I even be at home?*

I decided after Greece, I'd go visit my sister in Australia for three months. When I told Jack, he said, "Okay." What else could he say? Then a few weeks later, realizing I'd still just be coming home to an empty house, I told him that maybe I'd just spend six months in Australia. He said, "Okay." What else could he say? He was not going to be home during any of my time away.

I began to look closely at my schedule of classes for the following year and decided, if I was flying back to Greece from Australia, I might as well visit Europe while I was there – on the same plane ticket. I figured Jack could fly to Europe and visit me in the spring. In the spring! It was currently spring of one year and I was now planning to be gone nine months and see my husband the following spring! *What is wrong with this picture?* I reasoned I could get my boss to register me for classes and be back just in time for summer school. By then I would have received a ten-thousand dollar loan I was applying for, and I'd be able to finish my teaching degree full time.

I told Jack my plan. However outlandish this may have sounded to anyone else, it did not sound outlandish to me. I'd just spent the last three years on my own, not even sleeping most nights with my husband. I was ready for a sea change. The sad thing was, Jack said, "Okay." It was a reluctant and sheepish, "Okay." All the same, I would be going away during the same time he would be gone. In a strange way, it even made sense to him.

Now I would not be lonely.

With these plans and with this itinerary, I was on my way. Where? I did not know. I just had to get out of the dark place where I'd been. An adventure awaited me. When my girlfriend told her mother the biggest part of my week was watching "Dynasty" alone on Wednesday nights, her mother responded, "No woman in her twenties should be living such a boring life."

Maybe most husbands would not let their wives do this. Maybe most husbands would stand up and say "Hell, no! No wife of mine is going traipsing all over the world without me!" Maybe a husband might even say, "No way in hell I'm going to let you do that. If I have to change my schedule so we can be together and you won't be lonely anymore, that's exactly what I'm going to do!" But nothing like that was forthcoming. Jack knew full well that he was gone almost all the time. What could he say? I had been there waiting for him for three years, but he still had big dreams of an Olympic water polo team, of writing books, etc.... To listen to Jack talk, he loved me more than anything on this green earth. He told everyone this. I knew he felt like he loved me. I just did not feel it. *Saying* it was not enough anymore. I knew something even if he didn't. Our apartment had become just a place for him to sleep and eat.

Greece!

Greece is my favorite place in the world.

Jack and I spent three incredible weeks exploring the islands and mainland of Greece. In a nutshell, Greece was taking ships like taxis, watching black-scarved local women examine their food daily in the markets, riding mopeds all over islands, visiting the outside bars that sprang up out of nowhere just around the bends, picking green grapes from the vines on cliffs overhanging the sea, imagining the men whose hands two thousand years before had carved stone now in ruins, swimming in crystal clear green water, driving through the mountains with pine trees growing straight out of rock, hearing the music from the bells hanging from the roadside goats, passing mules and fruit stands and trucks of tomatoes, dodging wild drivers on mountainous winding roads, pushing in lines to get on buses I'd just thrown my luggage onto, sleeping away the afternoon on clean linen sheets with the windows open, eating watermelon and Greek salads in the breeze, taste testing octopus and the like, sitting on crowded verandas listening to music, reaching up and touching the stars at night, waiting on waiters who never came, but when they did, having six of them attending to our every need for hours.

I love Greece.

A great gift I got from visiting Greece was help with my body image. When we got to Athens, Jack and I had not seen any islands yet, so we decided to go for "a sampling." We took a ship loaded with European tourists to three different islands in one day. Once on the ship, we noticed everyone in "monokini," wearing only the bottoms of bathing suits. Everyone. Everywhere. Sitting around tables in the restaurants and bars. Breasts were everywhere. Beautiful bodies along with cellulite, stretch marks of all shapes and sizes, sagging breasts, big bellies of men, rolls and rolls of fat, scars galore. You name it, there it was, hanging out for all to see.

There I was – in a one-piece bathing suit, with shorts over top. Spending an entire day on a ship with families like this, watching them laughing, talking, and loving each other, affected me. While taking in the experience, perceiving how they felt about their bodies and how I felt about mine, I had a gradual awakening. Unashamed – felt right. Ashamed – felt wrong. On the beaches I looked for any trace of shame from the eighty year old women with rolls of fat hanging down from their stomachs, standing knee high in the waves and laughing with all of the children around them.

It was their joy that got me.

It became clear during my time in Greece that being an American, I had a lot to learn about loving a person's body. The answer in Greece was to love it any way it appeared. No one was examining bodies as closely as I. They were looking into each other's eyes and laughing – endlessly. No one was any better than anyone else, just because his or her body was thinner or had fewer stretch marks or rolls or scars or less cellulite or larger breasts or muscles.

This began to teach me that any embarrassment I had about my body, whatever I did not like about my body, I'd made up in my mind. Whatever criticism I feared, was what I imagined from the minds of others. Not real. What I began to see as real was the love among these people. I had been a fool to suspect I was ugly in any way. This was heaven. And that was the end of my one-piece bathing suit.

Kangaroo Landing

By the time Jack flew back to America we were more like friends. There had been little romance between us. That depressed me tremendously. We pretended this was natural, not at all strange for a wife to leave her husband for nine months of traveling while he stayed home to work and study.

I flew to Australia, but not without mishap.

There was no better way for me to enter Australia than to get stuck in an airport with 400 Greek Aussies. My fellow travelers and I waited at the gate for twelve hours for the flight to Melbourne. I got to witness what happens to four hundred people stranded at a gate in sweltering heat, with bad plumbing, low security, no communication, and little food. Major stress. Irritable, cranky, angry, nasty, mean people, and toward the end, ready to riot. When the twelve-hour delay was finally over and we had a plane, the same pilot who'd been waiting with us all day, welcomed us aboard. *Hmmm... this does not seem like a good day to fly.* While taxi-ing, the pilot struck the staircase attached to a semi truck that someone had forgotten to move from the tarmac. Fifteen feet of the wing of the plane – broke off! Mayhem times two began. We de-boarded and were sent to a hotel for the night. By the next morning, everyone was a different person. We all laughed when seeing a picture of our plane on the front page of the Athens newspaper. The attendants said they'd never seen such a happy group of people and left the lights on the entire flight to Singapore. It was one big party. People stood in the aisles chatting and playfully tossing babies above their heads. Watching this was a powerful experience. I made friends with ten Aussies on that flight. After

Broken wing in top, left corner

that I wished a 26-hour delay on everyone I knew.

In the hostel I found Heather's name on the bulletin board, request-ing a fellow traveler to hitchhike west. If, for a moment, you pretend that Australia is America, I landed in Miami and had to get to Seattle. Melbourne is in the Southeast and I had to get to the remote town of Karratha in the Northwest. Heather and I made it across the country to Perth in three rides. The Nullabor, the Aboriginal word for treeless plain, was fascinating. Mary had said, "Lynnie, you will never know distance until you come to Australia." She was right. The Nullabor was thousands of miles of blue sky, red dirt, and endless bush.

Since I was in Australia, people said I'd see scads of kangaroos. I was excited. While driving, I did see ten kangaroos – all dead. Australians loved their kangaroos, but motorists considered them a hassle. They caused fatal accidents, much like deer in America.

I spent nine days with Mary's friends in Perth. Heather and I went our separate ways while there, but teamed up again when it was time to head north. I sat in the front passenger seat of the car on the drive north. Heather sat in the back with the driver's son. It was an 18-hour drive on desolate road that ran north on the west coast.

Australia's population was only 18 million and the country was vast. Virtually one major highway circled the whole country. I traveled the *entire* length during my six-month stay. There were no fences because of the sheer distances and expense. Cattle grids were used to separate properties. In the dark of night, we traveled on. The headlights shone on the red dirt on each side and the highway stretched out before us. During the day we had seen all sorts of animals: sheep, cattle, lizards, and eagles. Now, I slept. Somewhere in the dead of night, the engine revving up and slowing down made me lift my head and say to the driver, "Why do you keep slowing down?"

"Ah, these damn kangaroos are driving me crazy!" he cursed.

"Kangaroos! Live ones? Wow! I'm staying awake for this!" Staring toward the windshield, I leaned my body forward, ready for the next one. Gradually, my eyes closed and my head drifted back to its dangling position as I slept again to the hum of the engine.

Then, in the deep crevasses of my mind, I heard the engine slow down again. I swung my head up as fast as I could, jutting my head toward the night. There it was – a gorgeous, big rusty-red kangaroo, thumping across the path of our headlights. I shrieked with glee, tickled at the sight of the massive creature. Then I saw the little joey bouncing along behind its mama. "Ping, ping, ping!" My excitement was even wilder than before! The second I took in the whole scene, there was a loud "Thump!"

I turned quickly to the driver, "Oh, no! We hit the baby!" I was devastated and began to cry. "We have to stop! We killed the baby!"

He waved his hand as if to say "Oh, bugger off, Lady!" and continued to drive. I could not stop crying at the thought of what had just happened – there had been the most beautiful joey, tagging closely along side its mother in the wild, and we had killed it. Apparently, this sort of thing happened often on the night roads. The driver was just glad the kangaroo had not hurt us. Now I'd seen dead kangaroos and a magnificent live one - and we had just killed her baby!

Heather and I parted ways in Karratha. I arrived with five hundred dollars in my pocket and needed to find work in order to continue my travels in Australia and Europe. I had been told in Perth the outback women were starved for someone to teach aerobics, so I secured a large room in the entertainment center and began teaching aerobics to adults five mornings a week. I also put up flyers to teach gymnastics to kids. I advertised on the local radio station, and within one week had collected over one thousand dollars in payments for gymnastics classes to be held over the next three months.

Mary, by then, was no longer cleaning bricks but managing the golf course. I applied for a job at the local tavern and was told I needed to know how to pour a good "middie" – a mug of beer. I went straight to the golf club's pub and had Mary's regulars teach me how to make drinks, particularly how to pour a beer with a good head of foam. I started working at the tavern on Friday night.

One week after my arrival, a low-bed pickup truck sat idling at the drive-thru window of the tavern. As I went to take the order, the driver said, "Hey, you know anyone who would want a baby kangaroo?"

Huh? What?

"Yeah, we killed the mother and didn't know she had a joey in her pocket," he said as he pointed to the back of the truck. There lay a huge, dead red adult kangaroo. The man next to the window was holding a cardboard box. Something little was moving inside.

"A baby kangaroo? A baby kangaroo?" They tilted the box to let me get a glimpse. "I'll take it!" That was it.

I had myself a baby kangaroo!

Quitting time was in thirty minutes, so I set the box on the back of the counter for the meantime. Excited, I peeked in. He looked like a Chihuahua! He was a beautiful little joey, with golden light brown hair and big brown eyes. Mine!

Uh, oh. Here I was, bringing a baby kangaroo into Mary's house at midnight. *She's going to kill me! But could she blame me? How could I pass it up?*

Mary was cool. She'd heard of other people raising kangaroos, so she went right to work. She got a syringe and filled it with skim milk. I was afraid of its jumpiness, so Mary fed him.

Mary got a pillowcase and hanger and hung the pillowcase on a dresser knob in front of my bed. She gently slid the baby kangaroo in so he could hang there naturally. Brilliant. The little joey chirped all night. In my mind, he was grieving his mother. I kept feeling like he was going to jump out, so I slept on the couch.

Next day, we let the joey out and he started to play with Mary's large dog. Guess what the baby kangaroo did? He began digging into the chest

Our joey

of the dog, searching - for a pouch! It was heart breaking to watch, and the baby did this for two days. Mary's dog licked him gently. On Monday we called the vet to ask what to do because the kangaroo would no longer drink milk. He said, "If you've been feeding that kangaroo cow's milk for two days, in about two days' time, he's going to have the worst diarrhea you ever saw – in fact, so bad you'll probably have to move out of your house." Being no dummies, we took the little guy to the vet that morning. He gave it to a woman who had already raised seven.

Working in the Outback
Within the first two weeks, I had five jobs that I juggled simultaneously. I taught aerobics in the mornings, gymnastics every Thursday, tended bar at the local airport for the few incoming and outgoing flights in the middle of the day, tended bar at the local pub at night and also at the golf course when Mary needed me. I walked all over town. Mary loaned me a little car, and I drove the Hertz rental cars to and from the airport to be cleaned at a neighbor's house. I never thought of myself as working because the Australians were so laid back. Walking home in the afternoons, I passed by house after house that had a grill fired up with folks cooking on the "barbie," offering me meals.

In the bar, my co-workers thought I was crazy when they saw me wiping down all the sinks and refrigerator doors and the like. They kept telling me to stop working so hard. But I'd been trained at McDonalds in high school, that had the motto, "If you've got time to lean, you've got time to clean."

I worked on new aerobic routines every day, and when I taught, I put my heart and soul into it. Sweat poured from my chin like water from a faucet. Many women in town loved the classes and became regulars. We often gathered at someone's house for coffee and cake afterwards. In Australia's northwest, the summers were extreme, stringing together weeks of temperatures well over a hundred degrees. Although the entertainment center was air-conditioned, our faces burned bright red. Fierce charley horses in my calves awakened me in the night, a pain so sharp, I could not make a sound. I set about making sure I had the minerals and water I needed to survive the outback.

I wore my wedding ring and kept busy. Internally I was moving, too. Since I'd left Jack I'd been wondering why everyone was being so nice to me. I was suspicious of everyone. Why were people laughing and starting conversations, helping me with my luggage, offering me food to take home, and helping me with whatever I needed? I was perplexed. It took me a long time to get used to this. There was a whole world of friendly people out there. Not everyone was irritable like my husband.

Men

There was also a dark side to living in the outback. This could have been any remote town in Alaska or Canada or Siberia. This was a mining town where men worked long days in the heat. They mined iron ore and salt, and drilled for liquid gas. There were ten men to every female. Many of the men lived in camps, some running from the law or family, all there to make big money.

There was a strange and confounding air to some men. Most were very nice, but among them often was a brute. I could see it in his eyes. His disregard for women was palpable. When I spoke to this type of man, he turned away, as if I'd said nothing. Ignoring I existed would be the norm. It seemed that man looked me up and down but would not talk. Or worse, did not want me to talk to him. In a remote area, this type of man was more concentrated. I had not experienced this. I was a tween in the early seventies when the women's lib movement was in full swing, so everything I'd ever heard about women was that we could do anything. For the first time in my life I was beginning to understand the vulnerabilities of women in the world. I had been hurt in my home, and thought of the outside world as safer. Now, in my mind, I journeyed back in time, thinking about the women who marched to get the right to vote, women who were being raped in wars around the world. I was in a place where people did not know me. Suddenly, I felt like an object. I tried to live in the skin of the women before me, wondering what toll being treated like this would have taken on their self-esteem. I could leave here, but what if I couldn't? *How would I have turned out?* I wondered how a woman broke out of this mold that had been poured for her. I could feel the drive women before me had to do this - break out.

There were no lights in the parking lot to the tavern. The night was pitch-black when I got off work. I made sure I never walked to my car – or anywhere – alone at night.

One night, while tending bar, a woman sat on a bar stool directly in front of me. She moaned, "Oh, I really need to go to the ladies room."

I pointed to the door twenty feet away. "There it is."

"Oh, no. I couldn't do that,"

"Do what?" I asked.

"He'll kill me if I get out of my seat." She was serious.

I watched as she sat on that stool for another hour until her man was ready to leave. All at once he nodded, she jumped off, and ran out the door with him.

The L-shaped bar of the tavern was divided into two sections. One was the workers' bar where men were allowed in, caked in mud, if need be, in order to have a beer and hang out with friends. The other side was the lounge where a person had to have had a shower to enter. One night, while working in the dinner lounge, I needed to get something in the bottle shop. As I was returning, there stood a man at the workers' bar looking at me with evil in his eye. "Get me three middies!" he snarled. I was so afraid, I complied. He was part of a large party at the pub. Each time I had to cut through, he stopped me. "Get me three middies!"

The third time I poured them, my boss said, "Hey, Lynnie. What are you doing over here? Get back to where you belong and stop pouring drinks for this guy." I said okay but shortly thereafter told my boss about the looks he'd given me and how afraid I was *not* to pour them. His stare paralyzed me.

"Oh," he said. "Yeah, they're in there celebrating his release from prison for beating up a bar maid."

Great.

While my victim was alive and well, Mary was not afraid of these men. She was there to make money, and she ran circles around them, saying, "They're thick as six bricks." Women tending bar were making $150 a week, but Mary planned to make a hundred dollars or more a day. She bided her time, and put up with a lot of gruff for six months while establishing herself in the man-world of building sites. She was respected as a hard worker, doing all her work on contract.

Mary was managing the golf club, but during the time I was there, she was transitioning into contract cleaning. In this boomtown, buildings went up like hot cakes, and Mary was ready to cash in. She meant to clean as many as she could, as fast as she could. She had a singular goal, and it was to never be poor.

Still Confused

My time in Karratha went quickly. Mary worked constantly; we even served dinner on Christmas Day to a hundred people at the golf course. Mary was working over 80-hour weeks, plus I was juggling all my jobs. We were not close at all during that time. In fact, I felt like I was a nuisance to Mary and that she really did not want to spend time with me. Her husband, Don, sat on the couch and complained constantly about how much she and I worked. I felt like he wanted us to sit home with him and hold his hand. Something about him gave me the creeps. It was not until my last full day that Mary and I sat down to have a real talk. She asked me if I was afraid to get a divorce because of the "stigma" attached to it. I was surprised, because we'd never had this talk – about my actually leaving my marriage. I thought I'd gone away to think about it. She assured me of her support should I choose to divorce Jack.

But I was not ready to divorce Jack. During my time there, I wrote him a 28-page letter, recounting our lives together, questioning what was going on that felt so wrong. Jack and I did not even fight. We had rarely said a cross word to each other in all those years. *Was it our work? Home? School? Money? Bills? Families?* My head continued to spin. *Why am I so fearful of my life back in Virginia?*

The Onion

Ready for a four-month adventure on my own, Mary took me to the bus stop. We said our goodbyes, not knowing when we'd see each other again.

This was to be a trip of a lifetime for a twenty-six year old woman. I was completely on my own on the other side of the world, able to make my own decisions. I chose to free myself. Of what, I did not know, but that first day on the bus, I tingled with possibility. I'd had a great four-month adventure of work that had put money in my pocket, and now I had four months of traveling sprawled out in front of me. Four months. One more in Australia and three traveling anywhere I wanted in Europe! Finally, I was free to think. For the first time in my life, I could sink into myself. I became the onion that I would peel, systematically, by doing nothing. There was nowhere I had to be, no one I had to talk to, no one I had to answer to. For the next four months, I leaned my head on the window glass of a bus, car, train, plane, or ship – whatever vehicle I was traveling – and down flowed the tears. Funny, when I was finally free, all I could do was cry. I never tried to stop it. I never tried to hide it. I just let my tears flow. My head was leaning on the bus window when the radio blared the news of the Challenger blowing up in the sky. I felt so alone, I wept for my countrymen.

I let my mind go wherever it wanted, not knowing I was experimenting with meditation. My thoughts went everywhere, a freedom of a kind I'd never known. Everyone traveling was still very nice to me and by now I was used to it. I met many people my age, all traveling this burnt country.

The landscape of Northern Australia was breathtaking. I was fascinated when watching a lightening storm over the ocean. We passed huge spear-shaped boulders sticking right out of the earth in a slant, as if warriors in the sky had flung them there. Once the bus driver stopped to show us that if we stepped off the bus, stood in one spot and made a complete circle, we could view about twelve different weather patterns forming in the distance. In one spot, dark clouds, further, dark rain falling, further, beautiful shades of orange and lavender, further, the sun setting, then, white puffy clouds, further, gray clouds, further rain falling lighter than before, turning further, a clear unclouded, bright blue sky, and further still, the sun reflecting off the clouds. It was magnificent. He also stopped twice to point out "willie, willies." These were little baby twisters that formed a narrow column of red dirt, gathering debris, but dropping it very shortly. I met workers in a hostel that taught me the words to a song I knew I had to memorize: "Give me a home among the gum trees / With lots of plum trees / A sheep or two and a ka-kangaroo / A clothesline out the back / Veranda out the front / And an old rocking chair!" I met an Aboriginal woman who candidly shared answers to questions I asked about her people. When we left each other, I missed her sweet, unassuming nature.

In Cairns I snorkeled The Great Barrier Reef. Then I went north to Cape Tribulation, a remote rain forest that had a hostel lodge where I met a group of girls. They were young women working in harsh conditions. We listened to tales of the poisonous animals and plants from the old timers, frolicked in a billabong, went horseback riding, and had parties in the lodge at night. I did not want to leave, but I loved to swim in the ocean. I heard tales of a jellyfish that lived on the coastline in the north. If it were to get its tentacles around your torso, its sting could be fatal. One girl had the creature wrap its tentacles around her calf. She'd spent five days in the hospital, and her wounds looked as if she'd be scarred for life. That was it. I headed south, away from the jellyfish.

Byron Bay

One of the best times of my life was the twelve days I spent in Byron Bay. It is the easternmost spot of Australia with a lighthouse marking the spot. The hostel's rooms were small, and we slept in bunk beds. There was a large communal setting with a pool, picnic tables and a separate kitchen area for all of us to prepare our own food. I spent $15 on food that first week.

Ten of us, each traveling on our own, gravitated toward each other and became friends. Each day was the same. I woke up, fixed, and ate breakfast. We sat around and talked for hours, and then, one by one, we were off to spend our days. I took a hike through a rainforest that led to a deserted beach where I spent five hours each day – all by myself. During these twelve days, I never saw another person on my private beach. After these hours, I took a long hike on a path past the lighthouse leading to my fellow travelers. They had been lying on blankets, and playing games in the sand for all those hours and were, like me, ready to go back to the hostel, but not before playing one last game of volleyball. We walked back to the hostel together, looking into the shop windows of this artist community. Every night was the same. When we arrived back at the hostel, we took showers and met back at the pool to play volleyball. We made our dinners together, ate together, and got ready to go out. Walking two doors down, we went to a restaurant with a live band. We danced and drank all night long. My drink, by then, was water.

Each of the twelve days was exactly the same. If I had to guess at the timing, I'd say we woke up at nine, sat at the tables until noon, I went to the beach until five, we were "home" and in the pool by six, fed and ready to go by eight, and danced until 1 a.m.

So much social time mixed with my daily five hours alone on a deserted beach was perfect medicine. It was as if a beautiful landscape of forest and sea had been laid out for me, a pallet, onto which I could purge anything that wanted to come out of me. For those hours I sat, not like a normal person lying in the sun on a towel. I did gymnastics in the sand and a variety of stretches. I put my head down on the warm, silky sand and let my thoughts flow.

I wept for what felt like the first time in my life. The tears that came out of me on this beach were unlike any I'd felt. Somehow, I intuitively created a place of safety for myself to release a valve that had held long-stored tears. Thousands came. I could feel myself going deeper. I went down into this place willingly and what I found there was a deep well of sadness. It took no shape or form. There were no pictures or words given to me for this sadness. It was just there. It seemed as vast as the ocean in front of me. I was not afraid of it. This was not depression sadness. These tears stood for something very real: a loss of great magnitude.

This did not surprise me. Now, alone on the beach, I let the rock in my stomach crack, and as I heaved my tears, my sadness crumbled, melting into liquid and draining into the sand, right there at the side of the sea. This sand became a sacred place. Each day when finally lifting my head to stare out onto the horizon, I felt accomplished. Every tear shed seemed to lighten me. I wasn't getting physically smaller, but it felt like I was, and so I peeled. I just let myself keep crying. Although, I came away with no new thoughts or grand words or solutions, this time changed me. So this became my project. I went off daily for more hours of peeling. On my last day, I turned my head for a last look and said goodbye to a piece of me.

The heaviest part of whoever I'd been melted away on that beach in my twelve days at Byron Bay. The combination of people, crying, fun-on-the-beach, eating good food, and dancing with friends, was unbeatable. Even though I never spoke to any of my peers about my five hours on the beach, I felt a deep closeness to them. We were lone travelers, searching for something. We each decided not to leave until one person had to, and on that day, we all left. But not until spending one farewell night dancing for hours at the bar and all of us buying the same T-shirt.

I left Byron Bay a different person. I still have that T-shirt.

Adventures Abroad

I had not seen an American in six months but on my last days in Australia, I heard the giggles and chatter of angels: three young women from North Carolina. All at once I was back in high school with my buddies. On my very last day in Australia, I ran into a Dutch man I'd seen five times in my travels. We'd traveled six thousand miles separately, but since Australia has few roads, everyone stops at the same roadhouses along the way. About the third time, we'd finally asked each other's name. Walking out the door to catch the plane, we hugged like old buddies. This would have been unheard of in the States, to run into the same person five times from Idaho to Maine to New York to Atlanta to New Orleans.

I flew back to Athens and took a bus to Corinth where I boarded a ship to cross the sea to Bari, Italy. On board, I met a group of kids my age from Australia and New Zealand. When we arrived in Italy, they were going to take the train, which I thought was too expensive. I had made five thousand Australian dollars during my four months in Karratha, but it only converted to $2,800 US. I had to be very conservative with my money and was planning to do Europe on a shoestring. Another fellow, Shep, also thought the train fare was too steep, so we agreed to hitchhike across Italy together. Lucky for me to have Shep. He was a shepherd from New Zealand who had studied all about Italy. He was a wealth of information. He had specific places he wanted to see. We went to Pompeii, which turned out to be one of my favorite places of all time. We went to the museums in big and little towns. He helped me chase down the gypsy who pick-pocketed me in Naples. The coolest thing about him was his whistling. He was on an extended holiday from his New Zealand farm for three years. Back home, he had seven dogs. Each dog had seven different whistles for seven different commands. On our hiking journeys by the side of the road, he described his dogs to me and practiced all 49 whistles.

A week later, Shep and I said goodbye in Rome, and I went to a small town on the east coast of Italy to live with a peasant family for three weeks. They were relatives of Mary's friends in Australia and wanted desperately to see pictures of and know about their family in Australia. I gave them that. What they gave me was more. Each day the whole family gathered at the breakfast table. They were joyous people and I watched them go off to work. I got to watch the women roll out the tablecloths, mix and roll the dough, and make pasta. Everyone came home for the noon meal, and then afterwards they rolled out the tablecloth again to make fresh noodles for the evening meal. I had my own Italian grand-mother, who, when she saw I did not eat much one evening, woke me up at four o'clock in the pitch dark morning shoving a sliced apple into my mouth saying "Mange, Mange!"

I caused quite a stir in this little town when I put my sweat pants on and went for a run every afternoon. Women in town gathered on their porch steps to watch me. I felt self-conscious and wondered if I was do-ing something wrong, but they waved and seemed to enjoy it. Still, I was an oddity.

The best part about living with my large Italian family was the looks on their faces in the morning. I had arrived in Italy knowing no Ital-ian. Shep and I studied it. When I got to this family, I sat in bed for three hours each night reading, writing, and studying Italian. I was de-termined to speak it. When I came to the breakfast table knowing more phrases than the day before, they looked at each other with amazement. How could this be? Their eyes wide, looking at each other as everyone shrugged their shoulders. What magic was being performed in front of them? How can this be the same girl? Yesterday, she could not speak like this! It did not occur to me at first that these people did not understand I was able to learn to speak Italian from reading a book. They did not read. As I understood this, I read to them in Italian from the language books. I was in love with these tender people.

The Italian language was beautiful, but the speed at which some people could speak made me feel I needed years to learn it. What did become clear to me is the loneliness a new immigrant could feel in his new country, not being able to express himself beyond nouns like fork and verbs such as sleeping. I could see how wanting to express one's feelings could be a driving factor in wanting to learn a new language in a new culture. I didn't want to forget this feeling when I went home to become a teacher to immigrants. By the time I left Italy, I could have an elementary conversation in Italian.

My next stop was to stay ten days with a family of ten children in Kussnault, Switzerland. This was the family of a friend I'd met at the Great Barrier Reef. Everyone was now speaking German, but I was exhausted from learning Italian. It took several days before I realized many people also spoke their neighbor's tongue. That helped, since my recently learned and unpolished Italian was similar to their known-but-rusty version. It was very exciting to be in and amongst a large family, here, too. The evening meal was very small, and I came to love this arrangement. Each day, the older children went off to work, and returned home to the large noon meal along with their married siblings, their spouses, and children.

Kussnault was a quaint and charming town. Small enough to walk through easily, shuttered windows with flower boxes on the window frames, church steeples, and a beautiful lake as its backdrop. I still got lonely in countries where I could not communicate easily. I'd heard Amsterdam was a cool place, and that was my next stop. Even in the damp spring, everything in that city was colorful. I spent the nights on a boat-turned-hostel docked on the water. I jogged the cobblestoned streets of Amsterdam and discovered real Belgian waffles!

Flashers

Women traveling alone get flashed. In the States, this happened to me several times. Once by a guy, pants at his ankles, standing on a railroad track, when I was riding my bike as a teenager. Once from a guy in a car on the side of the road whispering, "Pssst. Hey, Beautiful!" to me while I walked down the sidewalk at my college. Another time, by a psycho in the car next to me who would not leave my side, no matter how fast or slowly I drove on the expressway to get away from him. One man jumped out from behind trees with his pants at his knees, gyrating and flopping his belongings, flashing me as I rounded a corner riding on a bike path in Virginia.

Each time this sort of thing happened, I was jolted. It took quite a while for me to calm down. Then, I'd get angry. What upset me was I never got angry in the moment. *Why hadn't I done more? What gave these freaks the right to totally and completely disrupt my psyche and frighten me like this? And whom else are they doing this to? Little girls?*

After Amsterdam, I spent a week in Bruges, Belgium, just because the city was too beautiful to leave. While traveling, I had rules to keep myself safe and one rule was never be out alone after dark. One late afternoon I got lost in Bruges, and could not find my way back to my hostel. It was getting late, so I decided to cut across a park. There were people out walking still, but not enough for my liking.

In the twilight, from the bushes a man in a raincoat jumped out in front of me, opened his coat fully with both hands, and began gyrating his dangly bits. *Fully* naked, his tongue was out, and he was making indiscernible noises. I acted on my gut instinct. I did not skip a beat. I screamed at this guy, charging forward as I spewed at the top of my lungs, "You get your goddamn dick out of my face, you fucking pervert! Get the fuck away from me! Do you hear me? Get your goddamn dick out of my face!" Wide-eyed, he ran off in the other direction. I was impressed. I had words!

I hastily made my way back toward the hostel, satisfied I'd not reacted with fear as in previous times. I had one more bridge to cross and a long road to walk, to get back to the hostel, when I heard a sound coming from below the bridge. It was the pervert. He had gotten into a car, driven to a place below the bridge, and parked. He'd waited for me to cross the bridge! Doing the exact same thing, he opened his coat, gyrated his body, and made odd noises. I ran the entire way back to my hostel.

So riddled with fear growing up, I'd been cut off from my natural instincts to act. This is not something I could have articulated then in Europe, but I always wanted to react to someone who was attacking me. Ironically, spewing angry words such as this filled me with a sense of exhilaration. I'd defended myself. Funny, that was the last time I was flashed, as if the lesson I needed to learn in shoring up my anger to one of these guys was checked off my list.

European Experience

My time in Europe was priceless. Even though I rarely went to anything that cost money, I felt rich. Each hostel closed its doors to travelers between 10 a.m. and 6 p.m., so I had breakfast there, walked the city's streets, and went from coffee shop to coffee shop. I often met up with fellow travelers, learning much I never knew.

The faces, accents, people, countries, conversations, and laughter all blend together now, but as life was happening to me during all those conversations in all those cafes, I was changing. I was becoming a stronger, smarter, more confident person. Away from anyone who could define me, I got a clearer picture of whom I was when I sat among these people. I was listening, talking, debating, and discovering. I liked who I was. It felt like I spent a hundred hours sitting in cafes sipping black tea with cream, using the same tea bag as much as I could. I had read almost every Ernest Hemingway novel, and I often imagined the writer sitting in the same seats where I sat, gathering his thoughts. I still felt my onion of sadness peeling as I sat by myself, so I enjoyed my time alone as much as with others. I people-watched the days away. I bought one meal a day and ate sultanas and almonds the rest of the time. I got hungry, but I stuck to my budget. I was living a dream.

I'd sat in many a classroom, yet always hearing that traveling was the best education. I was in school twenty-four hours a day. At home, my world appeared much smaller and made me feel like I could control it. Traveling, I saw the vastness of the world and just how little control over it I had. Fascinating. I was letting go. I began to relax and absorb the tiniest details of my surroundings.

The Visit

Jack was to visit me in Europe for a week. He flew into Brussels, and we were very happy to see each other. I took him to a hotel. We lay in bed and talked for hours. Seven hours. Then we went to sleep. Sleep. I was confused. Awake, Jack wanted to see the red-light district of Amsterdam. I was more confused. We went to restaurant after restaurant that served marijuana. One was the Bluebird café, where one could order pot right off the menu. Jack was excited to try all kinds. So for one week, that's what we did. I smoked a little with him, but I was incredulous that this was how he wanted to spend his time in beautiful Europe, a place he'd never been. We ended each night by eating Belgian waffles at two o'clock in the morning. How utterly boring and useless - not to mention what it was doing to my body. I'd been exercising as much as I could because it was hard to stay fit while traveling. We could not get on the same page even while experiencing a new country together. The pot deadened him, so there was very little intimacy, something I was absolutely craving.

Since I was still in such a state of confusion, I wanted to hear from Jack what he was thinking. *Had he missed me? Did he want me to come home? Were we okay? Were things going to be better?* With these questions whirling around in my mind, I stopped cold on the sidewalk and asked, "Jack, do you want me to come home?"

"Sure."

Sure? Is that it? It's been eight months! Is anything going to be different? "You don't seem very excited about seeing me or my coming home," I said.

"I'm excited," he tried to reassure me, but his enthusiasm was not there. He noticed I saw this on his face. He grabbed me and twirled me around to tell me he was excited. It was a nice attempt, but it did not work. When he left, I was more confused than ever.

The Canadian Goes to Spain

Mom was going to be joining me in Europe in a month, so I decided to cover some ground and head to points south. A fellow traveler and I hitchhiked south to Lyon. Sleeping on the rough train station floor, along with others, the stationmaster kicked us out and directed us all to the shopping mall across the street. I was awakened at 4 a.m. by the noise of the buffing machines the custodians were pushing around us. Sweet. Soon I was in the French Riviera. How beautiful it was! In the hostel, I met a younger girl who had been turning tricks for money to travel. We agreed she didn't have to do that if she saved money by hitchhiking, so away we went to Barcelona and Valencia, Spain, eating oranges from the orchards along the roadways.

When my new friend got sick, we holed up in a room in a tiny town for days. Soon after, we separated and I went by train to Madrid, Spain. When I came down with that same bug, I lay in a hostel's bottom bunk for days. Getting my feet back on the ground, literally, people at the hostel told me I needed to go north. "Do not stop in France; go straight to England." The United States had just bombed Tripoli and, I was told as the planes were returning, one needed to stop and re-fuel in Spain. There was a *great* deal of anger toward Americans.

I'd already read reports of Kaddafi commanding his people to machine gun down any "lines" of Americans they'd seen. I was prepared for this. I was from Canada! When leaving Australia, I had purposefully sewn a large Canadian flag on the back of my backpack. Very visible. I knew the dangers lurking about. If asked where I was from by a complete stranger, I planned to say Toronto. I thought I could get away with that.

The first day I walked back onto the streets of Madrid, a dark-haired man with dark skin stood on the street corner with me, eight feet away. He looked daringly into my eyes. He walked closer, rolled up the magazine in his hands, dragged it across his throat, and said "Americana," while hissing a slashing sound with his tongue. *Yep. Time to go north.*

I called my friend in Madrid, a friend I'd made while working in the hotels in D.C. She said, "Nonsense! Come see me!" So I did, spending three days with her at a flamenco dancing fair. I felt safe with her and was glad I didn't pass it up.

I rode north with a trucker from England, heading to Brussels to meet Mom. In the middle of this three-day ride, I turned 27. The trucker bought me dinner for my birthday. We had very long talks. During that trip, I told him all about my marriage, and he told me all about his wife and kids. In the evenings, a red light from the dash reflected off our faces. Once while driving, he looked over at me and said, "You look very, very sad." I was. I still had not figured out what was wrong inside my marriage, in me, in the world I was returning to. I thought the visit with Jack would help solidify my feelings, but it had only muddied the water.

Mom in Europe

Since I was going to be in Europe, Mary thought it was the ideal time to send Mom over to finally meet her German relatives. She bought her a ticket and gave her funds for hotels, food, and a rental car. I'd be her chauffeur. It was the perfect scenario. Except for one thing. If you put a handicapped and extremely needy mother who is on twenty-plus different medications in the same car with a confused, and therefore irritable, twenty-seven year old woman who cannot figure out her life, even after having eight months to do so, fireworks are bound to happen.

This trip broke me.

The rage I'd carried all my life was about to come to the boiling point, but not quite - yet. During these two weeks, I did everything a human being can imagine doing to keep from screaming blue bloody blazes at my mother. I was so needy myself. How could I possibly help someone else with every tiny need she had? Even my mother?

I picked up Mom at the Amsterdam airport. There, someone drilled a hole into the keyhole of the passenger side. *Great*. I'd heard from fellow travelers that rental cars were vulnerable. I took this incident in stride and Mom and I went to have the "best" Belgian waffles. Holland had beautiful fields of flowers, and windmills. We stopped in a town to see the dikes where the ocean level was higher than land. I took Mom to a hostel in Antwerp, Belgium. I left her at a table with others, and when I returned I heard her saying, "Yes, my daughter is going to take care of everything for me, drive me all over Europe, and all I have to worry about is stirring my tea." She was simultaneously stirring her tea, tinkling the spoon on the side of the cup with each stir. I saw red.

I'd been in Europe changing cities, countries, money, people, languages and cultures. I was already worried about the current threats to Americans, and now I'd be navigating highways. Not to mention my anxiety about returning home to my marriage. This was too much for me. I know my mother was proud to have her daughter taking her through Europe, but I was going to need her to do *something* besides stir her tea. I'd called Mom a few weeks before to explain that being in Europe was dangerous for Americans. I was scared and said we should cancel the trip. "Everything will be fine," she'd said.

A while later, walking out of the post office, I blew up. I told her I could not possibly take care of her without major help from her. I *knew* my mother. She would let me do it all. I knew nothing about managing stress at this point. I barely had the words to tell her, but Mom listened, and I think she realized just how stressed I was. I knew, though, the bulk of the work would fall to me.

Anyone who has a mom understands just how frustrating, annoying, irritating, humiliating, obnoxious, nosy, in-your-face, manipulating, baffling, and guilt-producing a mother can be. My mom could be all that, but on the one hand, my mother was the sweetest, coolest, most open person in the world. When we were kids, she was exceptionally loving.

I'd felt accepted for who I was. My mother looked me in the eye, told me she loved me, and that I was a wonderful person every day. When she came home from working all day and not having seen us, she came to us in our beds and stroked our backs until we rolled over, so she could ask us about our day. My mother was a fighter, raising six children while being crippled, going back to college, finishing her degree so she could make more money, keeping us all together so we would not be orphans or adopted out to relatives. She was bright, well-read, well-educated, a walking dictionary. Everyone in town who knew Mom loved her. She'd helped countless people in her lifetime.

But the one grain of her that stood out now, the one that was piercing my soul, the thing she mirrored to me, and the thing I hated most in myself with a raging passion, was breathing down my throat like fire and suffocating me. My mother was a victim.

Yes, my father made her a victim in the truest sense of the word. He had shot her. But it was more than that. There was a part of my mother that was helpless when she was with her kids, and no matter how I try to explain it here, I don't think anyone will fully understand except her children. When Mom was on her own, she did much for herself, but the minute one of her children walked into the room, she relied on us for almost every move she made. How do I illustrate what this does to children so deeply hurting themselves? Somehow, it made us invisible. The focus continued to stay on Mom for the rest of our daily lives.

My mother was the one who had been shot. Everyone asked about our mother. Every question we ever got and every answer we ever gave about our family was about our mother. No one asked how we were doing. We had just "witnessed" the shooting. Even the newspaper article said we were "in another part of the house" during the incident. *Where did the reporter get that information?* The picture of our mother became so skewed, it felt as if only the six of us could have the vaguest idea of what it was like to be our mother's child. I suspect many people feel this complication in a family.

As an adult, I invited my mom's best friend, a nun and former classmate, to her birthday party. During our conversation, she said, "Your mom has had it quite hard in her life."

I replied, "We children have had a hard time, too."

"Oh, I never thought of that," she responded.

She was my mother's *best friend.* For me, that said it all. The amount of denial that existed and persisted among the community of adults around us, about the children being fine and strong, somehow was perpetuated by our mother. We were not fine. Now, almost twenty years after the shooting, I came to know just how not-fine I was. All those years of being silent about the shooting, all those years of people thinking we children were *so* strong, all seemed like a farce. It seemed my mother was bringing up any self-loathing I had, and of the cruelest kind. Almost everything she said sent me over the wall. I had no idea how to handle the anger bubbling inside me. When I was younger, I had fought. That did not work. Older, I had no words that I could say without hurting her. The words in my head were attacking and blaming. The last thing I wanted to do was hurt my mother. I did not know what to say, so I chose the next wrong way to communicate. I was silent.

I could barely open my mouth to speak to my mother for these two weeks. I have since learned it is highly abusive to do this to another person for an extended period, even for a couple hours. This was my method of controlling myself. My rage. One reason I did not speak was because almost anything I said made her begin talking endlessly, which was painful. When I did not answer and she continued to talk incessantly, just to fill the space, I felt more and more invisible. The only peace I seemed to find for myself was in the silence I created by not talking. So I opened my mouth only for necessities such as car keys, money, hotel keys, luggage, and what we were going to do next. I kept everything at a minimum. I was filled with utter hatred. I did not know why. I did not want to explode and take it out on my mom. What would I have taken out? There was nothing to articulate – it was a vast and empty hatred. Black. I knew it was not hatred of my mother. It was just black, throbbing hatred, coming up from somewhere inside me. It came out in the form of criticizing everything she did. In my head. I know she felt it, and the shame I felt during this time was powerful, but not enough to break me. Yet.

I held on, "white knuckled it," desperately trying to make it through the trip. *If I can just get her to Germany to be with my relatives, then I will be okay.* I could go out on my own and walk – escape. Somehow, being with my mom, I could no longer escape everything I had run away from. I was going home in two weeks, back to a marriage I had left and, as far as I could see, was exactly the same. The thought of going home was so terrifying, I was in complete denial of how terrified I was. During the trip, Mom wrote on a post card to a friend: "Lynnie's being a bitch." Something she'd never called me out loud, it hurt me to see, because as ashamed as I was at the way I was acting, I did not feel like I was being a bitch.

I was in pain.

Anyone who has a teenager or young adult knows how mean, nasty, gnarly, self-centered, selfish, irritable, silent, and impossible they can be. I'm sure my mother had no idea what to do with me, either.

The sweetest conflicts in my life - around this kind of pain - happened twice. The first was a time earlier in my teens, when I was, in fact, being a bitch and yelling at Mom. These outbursts were rare, so I could see her expression turn from anger to compassion at the contorted look on my face, the face of a cornered and caged animal. I saw in her eyes the realization that what was going on with me was so much bigger than any anger I could be feeling toward her. The louder and the more vicious I became, the calmer she became. The more I leaned toward her in anger, the closer she drew. Then a miracle happened. She opened her arms wide, cocked her head, and gave me a look that said, "I'm so sorry you are so hurt, Sweetie." In that moment I broke and fell into a heap into her arms. I cried out all of my anger and tears. It was the wisest way I'd seen to resolve a conflict. It was a present time shift in consciousness.

Completely removed from this incident with Mom, the same thing happened with Mary and me. Once I yelled at her so viciously that I saw an instant recognition that assured her this was not the sister she knew, something much bigger had to be wrong. She just gently opened her arms. I fell into them, crying that larger-than-life teenage cry.

On this trip with Mom, the same thing was happening, only I was internalizing it. *I have to shore myself up and get through Europe.* I wasn't exploding, I was imploding. It probably would have done me a lot of good to just crawl into her arms and cry like a wounded animal, but there was no time for that. I had things to do.

Mom wanted to go to Paris but I did not. I told her it was not safe. Mom persisted, so I told her I would take her into Paris on one condition: that she not speak to me around other people. They would know we were Americans. Mom agreed, so we boarded the train. My mom was

Mom and Lynnie in Paris, 1986

a talker. She began talking right away. I got up and moved to another seat. I was serious.

Our trip into Paris was early on in our travels, before my "not talking to her" thing had really started. When we arrived, I found Paris to be such a romantic place, that I was filled with love for Mom and walked with my arm around her. She wanted to go into the Louvre, and I chose to stay out and walk the streets. I found a crepe stand on the corner and got one filled with chocolate and coconut.

I had always heard the French were an arrogant lot. On the streets of Paris that day, I found out why. Everything about the city was superior to anything I'd seen in America, and by this time, I'd traveled to 39 states. Just one building with its massive size and exquisite architecture told me this right off the bat, but the endless rows of these ornately-decorated buildings was incomparable to anything in the states. Washington, D.C. looked like a "baby" town now. Even New York City was not like this. The artistry and craftsmanship of the clothes, pastries, food, and designs in all the shop windows were of a different league. I was beginning to wonder who the truly arrogant ones were.

Later, Mom and I strolled down the wide sidewalk next to the Champs-Elysees that led to the famous Arc de Triomphe. It was a beautiful spring day. Suddenly, a dark-haired, dark-skinned man with dark eyes jumped out in front of me and grabbed my right forearm forcefully. He shouted, "Do you need a tour guide? Do you need a tour guide?" This man was no tour guide. I immediately knew I was in trouble and had to get us away from him. Had I been on my own, I would have jerked my arm away, but there she was, my little, short mother, winding in closely and cocking her head up to us. Her expression said, "What does the nice man want, Lynnie?" Confused, she drew in more, trying to hear. Mom was too close for me to wrestle myself out of this man's grip.

"No, we do not need a tour guide," I said firmly. He pulled my arm closer to him and squeezed harder.

"Where are you from? Where are you from?" he shouted now, inches from my face.

I was trying to get Mom's attention, to have her step away, but she only came in closer, still unaware of the danger. *Oh, God. Mom's going to be hurt. How am I going to protect her? How am I going to get her away from this man?* I did nothing.

By now this man was gritting his teeth and *twisting* my arm. "Where are you from?" he yelled.

"Toronto," I said.

Mom could now see this was not a friendly situation. I wanted to motion to make sure she agreed to "go along" with Toronto, but I sensed I did not have to. She was with me. I had forewarned her and I felt her curiosity instantly change to concern. Seeing him twist my arm, she knew this was trouble.

"Toronto? You don't sound like you are from Toronto," he badgered.

"Well, we are," I said firmly. "We're from Canada."

He glared into my eyes. He wanted me to be from somewhere else.

"Let go of my arm! You're hurting me!" now my voice was raised. In this sea of people, a large circle of onlookers had formed.

"Where are you from?" he yelled again.

This time when I said Toronto, he glanced at Mom who was nodding her head. That did it. *Whew!* He flung my arm violently downward. "Fuck you, Lady! Suck my dick! Fuck you! Suck my dick!" he screamed baring his teeth, as he fell back into his fold of men.

Shaken, but relieved that we had tricked him, we continued on. I was ever so grateful for the crowd. I was a little irritated with my mom and wanted to say, "I told you so," but I dropped it immediately. I put my arm around her and was proud of her instead. She did not doubt we could be in danger anymore. We *had* to protect ourselves. Seven hours in Paris was enough. We headed south.

The next morning at the hotel, I went out to start the car to find the back window bashed in and some items stolen. I took the car into the rental shop and exchanged it. Mom wanted to go to Lourdes in the south of France to soak up some of its healing power, so we spent a night there. We crossed the French border and stopped at a pub just inside Italy. As we were ordering, we heard the TV news broadcaster saying "nuclear" again and again. *Huh? Oh, no. A nuclear bomb has been dropped somewhere!* When I went to inquire in English, I learned that the Chernobyl nuclear plant exploded that day. After that, we could eat no fresh vegetables during our trip because of the fear of radiation.

Next, I took Mom for a gondola ride in Venice, Italy, and then to beautiful Salzburg, Austria. In Vienna, Austria we left a restaurant to find our *whole* car stolen this time. We were at the police station until the wee hours of the morning.

Getting to our relatives in Germany was a real treat. I realized all the men had my brothers' foreheads. Foreheads! Not noses, eyes, or chins, but foreheads. I didn't even know genes could pass down a "forehead." We stayed in the home of Mom's cousin, her pen pal all her young life. This was their first meeting, and there was so much love between the two of them. They owned a slaughterhouse and a butcher shop. Another group of cousins ran a brewery and another owned a shoe store.

Mom was treated like royalty and, for this, I was elated. I'd finally gotten her to a place where she did not have to be abused by my silence. I was able to let go and watch her enjoy herself. I had a wonderful time myself. My grandfather had come to America from Bavaria in 1919. After the war, Granddaddy sent dollar bills, one at a time, to his relatives who were then able to buy land and property. They showed us pictures of the day in 1956 when he returned to Germany and they shut down the town and had a parade for him. One family bought a hotel that took up the whole side of the town square with the dollars he sent. We could still feel their gratitude all those years later.

I had always wondered why our family was so industrious, compared to so many I had seen in our neighborhood. I thought it was because we were poor and had to work that much harder, or because we had lost our father, or because our mother was handicapped, or because I had three older brothers and that's what men do – work hard. I thought all of this was situational. Not until I was in Germany did I come to think that maybe it was some sort of gene or at least a work ethic passed down by my German ancestors. In the three towns where we stayed with family, I was amazed to see the streets and sidewalks so clean, they were actually white. In a conversation I had with a male cousin, he told me he believed Germany was trying hard to clean away the shame they carried from allowing the Holocaust to happen. *Wow*.

I met my older uncle in Munich who told me the story, in very broken English, of his visit to my grandfather in America in 1939. My grandfather told him horrible things were happening in German politics, and pleaded with him to stay and live in America. My uncle said "No," that he had to get back to his mother. Years later, while serving in the German army under Hitler, he marched prisoners through the snow in Yugoslavia. While stopped, he sat down at the base of a tree and looked up at the moon. In my Uncle Fritz's broken English, he lifted his hand and stuttered, as if shouting, "My God, look at you! I could be watching you from America! You, this same moon!"

My mother was safe and sound with our relatives. We were supposed to leave together, but take different flights that would arrive at the same time. Jack would pick us up and Mom planned to stay two more days in Virginia. But four more days of traveling with Mom and then coming home to Jack on top of it, felt unbearable. My emotions were too pent up. I needed time on my own before facing what lay ahead. I decided to leave early and drive myself to Brussels. I arranged for my relatives to get Mom to the airport, and I left two days before her.

Little did I know the great awakenings about to take place in my life.

The Softening

202 | *To Soften the Blow*

Empty

When Jack picked me up from the airport, we were very happy, but before we left the parking lot, he said he wanted to stop at a friend's house. This was someone he'd met while I was away, and had mentioned several times. "Okay," I said, even though, I thought it a tad strange to be going right from the airport, when normally we might go home to shower, unpack, and re-settle.

This guy was nice. We talked about his upcoming wedding, and we left shortly thereafter. When we'd been home an hour, Jack said he needed to go to this same guy's house to pick up a table. "Okay," I said, but this time something struck me. *These two men are having an affair. Jack is trying to console him, because after spending so much time together while I was gone, this guy is worried that he will lose Jack. He needs to go there and reassure him that even though I am home, he is still important to him.* It was the strangest kind of feeling and my thoughts, logically, seemed farfetched, but in my gut, I knew. When the guys came back together high, it did not matter what was true. I had been home for two hours, after being away for nine months, and I'd seen this guy twice.

I was in my home now, with my husband. Mom thought being away from Jack was my problem and being back with him would make me happier. Wrong. My unhappiness came from bewilderment. My internal life was out of control.

My world was about to turn upside down. My anger had come boiling up with Mom in Europe. I was ashamed at its depth. In order to move forward, I was going to have to face hard truths. I had to admit my way had failed. I was to learn the true meaning of arrogance. You see, if two people are faced with something very scary such as a lion, a bad grade, or a romantic break up, Person One will say, "Oh, no, this is so scary," or "I'm so afraid of what my parents will say," or "Gosh, this hurts so much. I hate to lose you." This is the person who shows his feelings, the one demonstrating humility, showing human qualities. To many, Person One appears to be weak. Person Two will say, "No big deal, I can handle this lion," or "So what? Everyone gets a bad grade once in a while; my parents will just have to deal," or "Be that way; I didn't like you that much anyway, and besides you're ugly!" Person Two appears to be "together" or fine and able to move on – right past the thing he reports is not scary. In fact, it appears not to bother him in the slightest.

I had been Person Two. I needed to humble myself now and be Person One. On the inside, I was racked with the hurt, shame, and embarrassment I felt but could not say. For twenty years, I had learned how to be arrogant and aloof to my feelings and to others – on the outside. I was strong, I was tough, even intimidating. I was funny and popular and "together."

I was an actress.

I was to learn that there are many levels of humility, and my first lesson began on this trip to pick up Mom at the airport. I was caught. I was trapped. In many ways it was as if I was back on that fence again, soon to face Mr. Huggins. I'd been running from a fire-breathing dragon, only to be trapped on a short bridge, with another one on the other end. Which one was more dangerous? I think I knew. I picked up my mom and took her to the truck, shaking all the while, with the avalanche of me that was about to crack and fall.

In the front seat, I collapsed onto the steering wheel. I sobbed and begged Mom to forgive me for how I'd treated her, how I'd been silent, how I'd been gruff, how I'd been dreadfully hurtful. I told her things she could already see – what I'd been holding in, how confused I was, how I had no answers for my life, how I was broken into a hundred pieces, and how I needed help to put myself back together. How? I did not know. I was as empty as a person could be. Deeply ashamed. Although I had not screamed, yelled, called her names, or cussed at Mom, what I had done was just as deadly to her soul. I'd been silent, virtually for two weeks. Bookending my time being silent with my mom, and being with Jack, not knowing what to say, showed me I was floundering in a sea of ineptitude. For the two closest relationships in my life, I was blank.

All of the confusion, sadness, and hatred I'd felt over nine months wore me down. It was there in the seat of the truck I told her I was going to seek help, I was going to get therapy, I was going to sort out my life, and I would never treat her like that again. I vowed to myself I would never treat *anyone* like that again. The silent treatment was wrong. I learned in therapy that yes, being silent, withholding words and love, is emotionally abusive. As a teacher taking child abuse classes, it was eerie to learn that the same thing done to a child – withholding words - is just a different form of child abuse, and is placed in the "physical abuse" category.

Being a mother and the person that she was, Mom forgave me. Soon she was on her way back to Louisville. Brother David's poster "You don't have to know where you're going, as long as you're on your way," became very fitting for my jump-start into therapy.

From the readings of Deepak Chopra, I learned all a person needs to change is awareness, that awareness itself will change a person. It may take three weeks, three months, three years, or thirty, but once a person is awakened by a thought, change will come to that person. And, if the person is a willing and determined participant, change will come quickly. I, in my heap, was a willing and determined participant.

There's a Buddhist expression: "Be an empty bowl of rice." It means it's best to come into situations with an 'empty' mind, to hear and learn what another person has to say. An arrogant person enters situations with a "full bowl of rice." It is so filled with his own knowledge of the world that little new can be learned from someone else.

I was an empty bowl. This was not by choice, as if I were purposefully getting rid of my rice so that I could learn something new, willingly emptying my bowl. Everything I'd ever believed, from that point on, I was willing to question. Although ready to put together the pieces of my life, I forced myself to believe that my marriage would be a part of the picture when it was done.

I shored myself up and eagerly did what I could to be a wife and student. I immediately started my full-time graduate program, riding my bike thirty-three miles round-trip to the university. My schedule was set for fall. My loan arrived, which meant I could finish my degree full time. Jack had his summer job at the pool and all was going well. I was going to go to a therapist, but I had to get my life organized first. Well, I found out it works better the other way around. As I was going about my life, little "glitches" were thrown at me. Jack's polo players had moved into the apartment below ours, and Jack stopped in daily to smoke pot with them. Yes, he was still their coach at the university. He was smoking pot with his student players - in their home. The months of teaching aerobics and freedom from stress had changed me. Initially, all the guys wanted to know whom the cute new girl was that had just moved in. Jack never mentioned my changes. I was leaner, fitter, my hair longer, and blonder from the Australian sun. But the real difference was that I was a happier person with a skip in my step.

While I was away, Jack had been paying the monthly rent on my credit card. He "could not keep up" with the bills. I learned that Jack had been going to nightclubs, dancing wildly on the dance floor – by himself. He'd begun to drink liquor heavily, something he'd done little of before. He admitted he had thrown up in the front seat of our truck more than once.

The biggest difference of all was that Jack was irritable all the time. Or was that a difference? After having people be so nice to me for so long, it had become normal that people treated me with patience and respect. Remembering back to my earlier suspicions of people being nice to me, I realized it was Jack who was different.

A word about irritability – everyone is irritable every once in a while and everyone has the right to be. Every once in a while. Not all of the time. When it becomes all the time, it is simply abusive to anyone who has to listen to it or "sit in it" or be impacted by it. "Prolonged exposure" was a phrase that became meaningful to me. Jack was irritable constantly before I left and doubly so when I returned. All those months I spent trying to figure out what was wrong with my marriage, I was really trying to figure out how to make Jack not so irritable.

Still, my insides were in utter turmoil. I decided to keep my promise to myself and looked into seeing a therapist. The university offered sessions for free, so I signed up.

The Second One-hour

Aside from sitting in a dollhouse for an hour to be observed by a social worker, I'd had no therapy. I walked into the small, twelve foot by twelve foot room of the therapist. Her first words, after a few preliminaries, were, "Tell me about your marriage." I began to speak. For one hour, I told story after story about my life with Jack. She did not speak, and let me talk the entire hour. As I listened to my words bounce off the walls, they came back and hit me squarely in the face. Being in a small room, there was neither a big ceiling for them to dance about on, nor a wide space for them to get lost in and disappear. It seemed this room made my words travel back to me far too quickly. There it was, the constant barrage of my life coming at me. Could she see me cringe at the stinging sensations landed with each blow? I tried to hide it.

I realized that everything I'd just told her about my marriage, each and every story, had to do with drugs and alcohol. In the end, she saw me make this discovery. I looked at her, "My life is filled with drugs and alcohol." With dumbfounded disbelief in myself, my whole life up until this point, I added, "I'm terrified of drugs and alcohol." My words made me realize I'd created a life of the very thing I feared. Having said it, there was nothing to hide from anymore. It was something I could face. This took one hour of my life.

A Ton of Bricks

One night shortly thereafter, I took a friend with me to pick up Jack and his friend who'd biked twenty miles out, but they'd realized it'd be too dark to cycle back. When we got to them, there was also a small, young gay man in the parking lot in the same predicament. He asked us for a ride. Three of us rode up front in the truck while Jack and the gay man rode with the bikes in the bed. We communicated through the open window that connected the bed to the cab. The gay man was from Jamaica and he was hysterically funny. We were in stitches laughing with him. But Jack began to boil and made comments to this man that bordered on cruel. When we got to the place to drop him off, Jack heaved his bike into a bush.

Arriving home, Jack was livid. I'd never seen this part of him. I'd never seen him violently angry. I stood at the top of the stairs as our two friends went in to get their gear. I headed back downstairs, passing Jack in the stairwell. He was carrying his bike into the apartment and, when I asked him a question, he screamed, "Fuck you!" This was something he'd never even come close to saying before.

I was dismayed, but as he whisked past me on the landing again, something hit me like a ton of bricks. *This man is an alcoholic.* All at once, seven years into our relationship, I was one hundred percent certain. Before that moment, I'd never carried a vague notion about this. It was the key I'd been searching for to unlock the door I could not find.

That moment, that realization, was the turning point in my adult life.

I see it all the time on television – someone asking someone on a talk show, "How did you not know?" Meaning, "How did you not know your husband was a drug addict?" or "How did you not know your wife was an alcoholic?" or "How did you not know your husband was gay?" or "How did you not know your wife was having an affair?" or "How did you not know your husband was molesting your children?" People ask this of others all the time and, in the asking of the question, the accusation is clear. You knew all along. Not only that, you allowed it to happen right before your eyes. You just weren't admitting it to yourself.

I heard Ted Koppel say on "Nightline" years ago, "To those who understand, no explanation is necessary. To those who do not understand, no explanation is possible." I did not know that my husband was an alcoholic. I did not know that my husband was a drug addict. I did not know.

I believe this is true for most people when asked this question about another person's addiction. Think about it. If the addict's denial is so tremendous, doesn't it make sense that the person closest to him would have the same - or close to the same - amount of denial? Otherwise, as soon as they entered into the relationship, one would say, "Hey, by the way, I'm an addict," or "Oh, my, I see that you are an addict so I'm out of here." The relationship would not be able to exist long if both people knew the exact secret to each other's misery. Years would not be racked up in the relationship – only hours.

The flickers and the flashes and the glimpses and the glances and the flags come in tiny flashes of light, shut out as quickly as they are let in. I came to see my mind shut out very quickly the things it did not want to see.

The big thing I learned about addictive, abusive behavior is that whatever behavior you used in your family to survive, you'd seek out someone who'd allow you to continue that same behavior, so you could move seamlessly into the relationship with them. "Geez, I feel so comfortable with you," and "Being with you makes me feel so at home," and "Wow, I feel like I've known you all my life," takes on a whole new meaning when viewed from that perspective.

It took a long time for me to see that initially feeling uncomfortable with healthier people was normal. I did need to change many things about my behavior and personality if I was going to be around them. Being with Jack, I'd continued the same behavior I'd grown up using in my family, getting away with not being fully honest.

The First Step

I started with priests. "What should I do?" One priest after another led me to Al-Anon, a 12-step group. I tried other therapists, trying to find someone who might say something that would make it all better. Each one recommended I go to Al-Anon.

My first Al-Anon meeting was held in the upstairs of a church in Arlington, Virginia. We sat in a circle with a large round table in the center of the room. There were two layers of chairs for people. I sat on the back row of the circle. I listened. A woman said, "I thought it was the furniture, so I changed the furniture. I thought I wasn't smart enough, so I got another degree. I thought I didn't make enough money, so I got a new job." She was explaining it took "forever" for her to realize she was living with an alcoholic. It had been the underlying problem all along, one she totally missed until she'd exhausted all other possibilities. I related to every word. In the 28-page letter I'd written to Jack from Australia, I listed everything in our lives that could possibly be part of my confusion. But it hadn't been until I, too, had landed on alcoholism that every part of me screamed, "Bingo!"

Many people spoke that night, but it wasn't until a woman sitting directly across the circle began to speak, that I was moved out of my skin. I do not even remember what she said, but I do know it was the first time I'd heard it, or the possibility of it. She was talking about herself and how she manipulated situations to create the struggles in her life. She was admitting that fifty percent of the problems she had in her marriage were her fault. She did not say that exactly, but that was what sent the eerie feelings pulsing through my body. I was tingling as she spoke, wanting her to stop, but knowing all the while that the words she was speaking were some of the truest I'd ever heard. When she finished, I immediately blocked out all she'd said, forced the feeling of recognition away. But it had pierced me thoroughly on that first night, and now that it had introduced itself, I could not ignore it when it repeatedly came to tap me on the shoulder. I could no longer get fully away from the idea that I was at fault for many of the situations I found myself in. *That's the opposite of a victim!* I had made every decision that led me to that point.

I must have spoken in the meeting, questioning if I was to stay or leave my marriage, because a woman said to me afterwards, "You don't have to make a decision today." It was the first good news that gave me peace. I hung onto those words in the hard days ahead.

Another woman I spoke with that night after the meeting listened as I went on and on about what a wonderful guy Jack was. "But he's so smart and sensitive and creative and imaginative and loveable…"

"Honey," she said, "they all are."

It hit me. All those women were there because they loved a man who was a delightful person in most respects. It took years before I got the full impact of that statement.

Moving Toward the End

I went to a meeting every night. I met a friend and confidant, Geenie, whose mother had been chronically ill all her life. She had been her mother's caretaker and, in fact, had become a professional nurse. Her sadness at the hardship of tending to her mother daily reminded me of Mary's. Geenie and I were newbies at this recovery game and called each other several times a day.

I realized right off the bat I'd never dealt with the shooting in my life. I was shocked to know I'd married an alcoholic because of my own denial of the disease of alcoholism. When Mom had always said, "Alcoholism is a disease, and this is what it can do to a family," I did not know I, too, had this "disease." I was to learn that I did. There was actually a term called the "family disease of alcoholism." I was told hearing uncomfortable stories would make me want to push away and say, "Oh, this is not about me. I'm not that bad." Denial. Instead, what I was supposed to do was listen intently to the parts where I could relate. I immediately began to listen to every word said, to see what might fit. I soon learned that it would speed my recovery if I kept an open mind to an idea that I initially felt did not fit. If I tried it on, walked around in it for a while, I might discover I was in more denial than I'd previously thought. I began to say, "I know I am in a lot of denial, I just don't know what it is yet!"

Jack did not want to get help for himself. He was more irritable and angry than ever. Along with the "ton of bricks" that had hit me, I realized Jack had never given up drugs when he met me. He'd smoked pot almost every day I'd known him. He had not wanted me to know it was an everyday habit. Years before when he'd told me how proud he was of himself that he'd "not smoked pot in three days," I had not realized what a big deal that was. He had tried to stop on his own. Many times. His overeating, gorging himself on sugar, his unrealistic views of our phone bills, and irresponsibility with money were signs of being out of control. He'd been depressed, lethargic, irresponsible, irritable, and nonsexual. All of this was due to drugs. Taking incompletes in eighty percent of his graduate classes showed his inability to follow through. Smoking pot with his employees and then his student players was an indication that his thinking was askew. The risks were too high. Moving to hard liquor and, I'd later learn, pornography, was a sign of his escalation. His life was in just as much turmoil as mine. He was keeping that turmoil at bay, just as I'd been.

It was clear. I had married an addict. But my father had been a raging alcoholic, a violent man. I thought I'd been so careful. All who knew him perceived Jack as a gentle man, and although he was often irritable, he was not unkind to me. He was a depressed person with an addictive personality. I called my mother and told her what I'd learned about my marriage. She was compassionate and loving. I called my brother Jeff and told him to sit down. I wanted to tell him what my life had been like for the last seven years. He was very supportive, as well.

We'd come from dysfunction, and we communicated dysfunctionally. This is largely what drew and held Jack and me together. But I'd traveled to fifteen countries in nine months on my own. I'd come home a different person, more confident, separated from Jack in my thinking. I no longer believed everything he said. I compared him to the hundreds of people I'd met. I now had a measuring stick by which to judge what went on in my home. I did not like it. I was alive and energetic and bursting at the seams to tackle the year in front of me after which I would have my teaching degree. There would be no incompletes for me. After traveling and walking through the doors of Al-Anon, I felt as if I'd moved light years. I knew I deserved more from a person than this. The people I'd sat with and discussed topics with for hours had liked me. I deserved to be liked in my own home.

To listen to Jack talk to others, he loved me more than anything on this green earth. But the reality was that we had not spent time together in years. Forget quality time, just time. Our future had turned into nothing.

Then, sometime during the first five weeks I was home from Europe, I thought I was pregnant. As much as I wanted a baby, as much as I wanted to be a mother, it was crystal clear to me that I did not want to have a baby with Jack. And worse, I did not want my baby to have Jack, an alcoholic, as a father. I could only see a life of misery ahead. I prayed that I was not pregnant, and for a short time one afternoon, contemplated abortion.

Oh, my God! Here I am married to a man whose baby I would want to abort! I've always wanted a precious child, and here I am, killing it in my mind. That was the defining thought that turned my mind toward divorce.

Just to Prove It

Thinking about leaving my marriage, a strange phenomenon came over me. I became scared to death to mention my thoughts to Jack. For days I was possessed with a fear I hadn't known until my friend, Geenie, pointed out that when my mother announced she was leaving my father, he'd shot her. *Ah, I see. Yes.* It became easier, knowing where the fear stemmed from. When someone tells another person his fears and the listener says, "Oh, that could never happen," about situations like this - my fear of being shot - my mind says, *Yes, it could happen, it does happen, and it happened to my family.* How can we really know what is in the mind of another person? I began to honor that fear inside me, while mustering the courage to speak to Jack.

After visiting several therapists and priests, I found a therapist and asked my husband to go with me. He said he'd go alone. When he came home, he said, "The guy thinks I'm an alcoholic." He asked me point blank, "Do you think I'm an alcoholic?"

"Yes," I responded. I'd decided this from everything I knew about Jack's past and present. He had all the signs. He immediately got up from the table, went to the sink, turned and said, "Well, I'm not a loser. I'm a winner. I'm not an alcoholic." He had thought of an alcoholic as I had: someone who was nothing like either of us.

That night he went out and came home very late, very drunk. He lay down in the bed. He began to gurgle, then projectile vomit a massive amount - straight up – splattering the ceiling with brown dots that came raining down all over our bed and me. I got up without saying a word, went to the bathroom to wash, and made my bed on the living room floor. Although sad, I could not escape the irony of the situation. It was as if he was proving to me he wasn't an alcoholic by going out to get drunk and coming home to vomit all over me. Just to prove it.

I did nothing to clean the sheets and two days later when I was getting ready to sleep on the living room floor for the third night, he said, "Lynnie, why don't you come to bed?"

I said, "Because there is vomit in our bed." He'd been sleeping in it each night and did not realize it. He'd not remembered vomiting, and apparently had not even noticed it in the sheets.

31 Times

The situation looked bleak. I decided I had to leave. My friend Sally called. When I told her my situation, she told me her mother was looking for someone to live in her house and clean it, in exchange for room and board. I went to talk to her mom and prepared to move the next day.

In the morning, I went to Jack's swimming pool. I sat in a lounge chair, watching him teach his swimming classes. I was there to tell him I was leaving. He'd already told me several times that there was nothing wrong with him, and if I needed to leave, that was what I'd have to do. That did not make it easier. In fact, it made it harder. It was going to have to be done by me alone. I wanted desperately for him to say, "No, Lynnie. Don't go. Your being gone for nine months was bad enough. I will do whatever it takes to get well and keep us together. I will get help." The pain of pulling myself away from him was so great that I sat in that chair for three hours. I realized if I made this move, there would be no turning back. I sat there watching and grieving the man I loved. Jack walked over to the lounge chair several times and said, "You'll have to do whatever you have to do."

Finally, I dragged myself off the chair and drove home. As I was packing, I called my friend, Debbie, 31 times. We counted them. When I got to our sleeping bags, I called her crying and to tell her they were bought to zip together, so we could snuggle. When I got to a certain T-shirt, I called her to tell her about the place we'd been together when we bought it. That's how each call went. Each time, Debbie listened intently and then said, "Okay, call me back when you hit another hurdle." That's how I got and kept the strength to leave.

It is ironic that the day I left was June 17, the exact same day it had been seven years before when I met this man, the guy on the sidewalk with a towel wrapped around his head.

My Drug of Choice

I arrived at Sally's mom's house and settled in. When I got the urge to call and say how much I missed Jack, I restrained myself. Each night I lay in bed and forced myself not to call.

Three weeks later, Jack called. I listened as he told me he was the only person who truly knew me. I'd never find anyone else like him. More importantly, he explained, I'd never find anyone who'd understand me like he did. I held the phone out and looked at the receiver. *If this is the person who knows me best in the world, I must be terrible at intimate relationships.* When I hung up, I drove to the store to buy a half-gallon of ice cream. A Mack truck could not have stopped me. I purposely took out a very small bowl and fixed myself a bowl of ice cream, thinking the small bowl would keep me from eating too much. I sat in the same spot on the couch where I'd taken the call. I finished and got up to get another helping of ice cream. In this very small bowl. Then I went to get another. And then another.

When I finished the fourth bowl, I was numb. *I'm going to be a baby whale if I keep doing this.* I knew that I was eating sugar to push down pain. I knew something else. The amount of pain that needed to come out of my body was enormous. I would never get the job done if I kept stuffing down my feelings with sugar.

On the couch that night, I decided to give up sugar. For the next five years, I did not eat anything that blatantly contained sugar such as cookies, candy, pies, or cakes –desserts. I did find myself having extra helpings of ketchup or barbeque sauce sometimes. *Geez! This is so good!* As soon as I realized what I was doing, I caught myself. Giving up sugar was the best decision I could have made to facilitate my own healing.

My Chair

I began my journey in "12-step" rooms. The meetings began with a "pre-amble," the reading of the steps, and someone leading the group in a topic. People in the room spoke at random. The first three months that I sat in these rooms, I cried the entire hour. When I spoke, I said whatever was on my mind, whatever I needed to say. Out of my mouth came the vilest words. For the first time in my life, I forced myself to talk about the shooting, the violence in my family, and the mental illness all around me. In public. Each sentence was agonizing to say.

Once, leaving a meeting, I heard someone say, "I can't stand it when people don't stick to the topic."

I turned to Geenie and said, "Topic? What topic? Are there topics?" She explained that yes, there were topics given at the start of meetings and, basically the meeting was meant to follow the topic. I had no idea. I'd been so wrapped up in my own misery, I hadn't noticed. In three months! I sat so low in my seat and cried so hard when I was in those meetings, I'd been aware of little else. I'd kiddingly said I was "on the floor," by the time the meetings were over. After that, when I had something to say, I still said whatever I needed to, only now I made sure I also mentioned the topic!

Geenie and I met Fred and we became fast friends, a package, like the three musketeers. We were each other's security blankets. So much was surfacing from our pasts that we sat for hours around tables in homes or restaurants night after night, listening to each other.

Those first days showed me the great denial I'd been in about the mental illness present in my family. My grandmother was catatonic, my father was obviously psychotic, and Judy was now being diagnosed as schizophrenic. Stammering to say this out loud to others, I had no idea that I was carrying so much shame. I learned, though, shame went away more quickly, if talked about. I made sure talking and admitting my shame to safe people became a part of my life.

In those early days I learned to stop starting sentences with the word "You," and begin them instead with the word "I," especially when communicating a problem with someone. I was shocked at how often I started a sentence with the word "You."

One of the greatest gifts I was to learn early and be forced to continue to learn was the art of listening.

I had no idea.

I had no idea how to listen.

I had no idea I had no idea how to listen.

I had no idea that most people have no idea how to listen.

I had no idea how valuable listening was to healing.

I had no idea of the miracles that could happen through listening.

I had no idea that the bulk of my healing would come through my learning how to listen and then finding people who could listen to me.

I had no idea one simple word could be so hard to actually do.

I had no idea that it was the key to unlock my stress.

There is a beautiful rule in support groups called "no cross talk," which means that no matter what someone else is saying, no one in the room can speak or shout across the room, "Why'd you do that?" or "Well, that's dumb!" or "Are you crazy?" or "Why would you say that/ feel that/do that?" or even "Can you repeat that?" No comment may be made. And, just as valuable, a person speaking cannot refer back to or speak to the person who has just spoken such as "I really relate to what you're saying, Matt, because..." or "You reminded me of something..." or "When Lisa was talking it reminded me why I never..." or "Well, if I were you, I'd..."

Listening sounds like the simplest thing to do, but for one and a half years, I sat in rooms with my stomach in knots, constantly wanting to "say something," but because of this rule, I had to hold back what I - repeat I - was thinking.

In order to learn how to listen, I had to be *forced*. There had to be a *rule* to get me to do this. My stomach churned and gurgled because of it. Even in the communications world, advice giving and comments were called roadblocks. *Roadblocks to what?* Most people sitting in these rooms had never had anyone really listen to them. Most had never been taught to listen. *Oh, roadblocks to recovery!*

Ever so wonderful, along with listening came eye contact. Giving and receiving.

The lessons just kept coming. Another beauty of the "No cross talk" rule was that I could speak and, because no one could say anything – until after the meeting – I got to sit in my own space and believe that whatever I said was okay. For one hour, I could believe that whatever I was thinking - and then saying - was okay. No one was interrupting me and, in fact, people were actually listening to me. They were being tolerant and respectful of the feelings that poured out of me. Even if they were judging me harshly on the inside, I would not know that. Everyone sat very still and just listened to everyone else. It was a wonderful way to imagine being accepted for who I was.

One friend often repeated a quote she'd found in the book *Inside Alcoholics Anonymous*. "My sponsor told me this was a spiritual program so I joined EST and Catholicism, but the only place I ever found God was looking into your eyes and listening to the words that you say." I remembered this quote, because that, too, is where I found God – sitting in these circles looking into others' eyes, listening and speaking.

Over the course of many years of this, I came to believe that I could heal from anything as long as I had someone's eye contact and someone's ear. All I needed was a witness to my pain. If someone listened to me, and could not comment back, I was forced to go inside myself and listen to my inner voice. Remember that thing? The voice that Mr. Huggins had "matched"? It was something I'd not done in years. I'd piled so many layers onto it that I did not even hear it during my time on Byron Bay's beach. There had been this huge, empty hole of black. Black sadness.

Gandhi said, "There are people in the world so hungry that they will only know God in the form of bread." Reading this, I imagined a person, so weak, so cold, so hungry, all huddled up in rags on the ground, not being able to budge. He could not think beyond his hunger, and out of "nowhere" someone handed him bread, the very thing he needed to survive, to be happy just for a time.

I found what I had needed all my life in those 12-step rooms. My bread was people's eye contact and their listening. It seemed that what had harmed me so much in my life – the witnessing of violence on the night of the shooting - was also going to be healed by the miracles I encountered that same night: the power of eye contact and words.

I tried "Al-Anon" and "Women Who Love Too Much" and even "Overeaters Anonymous" meetings, but where I found my home was in "Adult Children of Alcoholics," ACOA for short. The first night there, I listened to everyone speak, and when we stood to say the "Our Father" together at the end of the meeting, I felt more safe and happy than I'd ever felt. It was home. It became my chair.

There is a Buddhist saying, "Find a chair and sit down." This saying refers to the fact that in spiritual teachings, there are many vehicles that can lead us to the same place. But a person can only fully come to understand herself and her place in the universe, by "sitting down" and studying *fully* a particular avenue. Many people find their spiritual path through reading the Bible, or Torah, or Koran, or Course in Miracles, or through a certain type of therapy. Some find their path with 12-step programs. This is the chair I picked to sit down in for the following two decades.

Softening

To anyone who knew me before, I'm sure I appeared the same. All the things I did not like about myself - my insecurities, faults, lacks, excesses, all my failings - they were still there. Whatever issues I had were still in full view to others. It would be years before significant changes would take place in my outer world. But my inner world was a different story. If my life script had once been written in a chaotic confusion of baffled bewilderment, it was now being re-written in words. I heard others' words. I spoke words to others. I was using words. I could hear words now. I could place each one in a row, create sentences, lining up the pictures of my life. All of the validation I was receiving in these groups was affecting my insides. Finally, I could make sense of the little flickers of wisdom I'd had but never knew what to do with.

If while traveling my tears had peeled the onion of my sadness, letting the layers drop off my shoulders, I could see now that was the easy part. This crusty rock inside me was going to take work. But my chisel was out. I'd never known excitement like this. I carved with each deliberate tear shed, each deep breath taken, each kind word given or received, and with each truth heard or spoken. I was calmer now. I was softening. I felt like I had a kind friend inside me. I could feel her in my breath. I was melting. I was slowing down. I was relaxing into my skin.

Unlike the sadness I allowed to fall off me in whole clumps, I was aware of the parts of my rock I wanted to keep. My rock had formed to protect me when others hadn't. I would still need some of it, like a tree needs a trunk, but I felt joyful knowing I could let go of my hardness. I chiseled happily but carefully, realizing a new person was going to be formed. This time, I would have a hand in creating her.

There is a term called universal intelligence, which, to me, means we know truth without being taught it. We humans know so much more than we can articulate. The best way I can describe it is when, while reading a profound statement in a book, we say, "Oh, yes. This is so true. This is exactly how I feel!" It is not that the person who wrote it is smarter. The writer may have just spent time studying deeply in that area, allowing him to better articulate his findings. It may be something that we already knew, but did not have words for. That's what made it "profound." Once, we, too, are able to articulate it, we add it to our knowledge base and demonstrate it through our emotional intelligence, our common sense, and how we treat others.

Our bodies are very smart, very intelligent. When I sat in meetings listening to others making sense of their lives, they were making sense of mine. When I heard true words I said to myself, *Yes! Yes! Yes!* Their words were my words. Finally, all the things I knew to be wrong were validated. And all the things I knew to be right were validated. Lucky are the people who don't need this validation. Lucky are the ones who were given words at the start of their lives, who had parents who said, "Use your words." I started to trust that smiling, kind friend inside me. There is an American Indian saying: "When the truth is spoken, everyone in the room knows it." From where I now stood, I used every truth told to me to fill my empty bowl.

Feelings

Having given up sugar, I had nothing with which to stuff in my now constant, oozing emotions. The soup had been stirred and my feelings were coming out in every direction. After a meal, I wanted something else, something sugary, but wouldn't let myself have it. I watched myself shake. I called Geenie and, with my elbow on the table and my hand splayed out in front of me, I described to her my shaking hand. I had not been eating tons of sugar, just enough, to "keep the edge off" my feelings. The tiniest bit of sugar, I learned, was enough to stuff them down. But up they were, so I told all my feelings to Geenie and Fred.

As I went with them to support groups and dinner several times a week, it was with these two I practiced my new words. Every alcoholic, when he enters AA is given a list of feelings. You've seen the list – with faces drawn above the feeling words, such as nervous, surly, disappointed, etc.… I was not an alcoholic, but AA was the father of all 12-step programs, so what was used to spiritually heal the alcoholic, could be used to heal others with compulsive problems.

It may sound like a joke to some, but it was a valuable tool for a person recovering: a list of feelings. It was on this list that the power of recovery lay. I came to see I did not use feeling words in my vocabulary. If I had any conflicts in my life, I had no idea how I felt. How can a person know how she really feels if she has been told to shut up all her life? How can a person know how she feels if she has been hit? How can a person know how she feels if everyone acts like a huge act of violence she witnessed never happened? How can a person know how she feels if no one asks her how she feels, no one appears to care how she feels? How can a person know how she feels if she has adults around her who don't know how they feel? I had shut down feelings for so long, I didn't know I had any in particular.

That is the premise of AA. When a person comes out of a dysfunctional home and goes out into the real world where some people are functioning effectively, it is probably because they can use "feeling" words, to a certain extent, or at least they know how they feel and can act on their feelings.

As an adult in the real world, you get lonely, hungry, tired, angry, sad, depressed, irritated, frustrated, confused, delighted, and a whole host of feelings rain down on you daily, hourly. If you cannot find anyone to share these feelings with because you may feel too embarrassed, ashamed, guilty, or fearful, you still have them. Just because you do not have someone to *tell* them to, doesn't mean they don't exist. It is these lingering, unspoken, unable-to-be-said feelings that lead people to "medicate" their feelings.

Another premise of AA aside from *having* our feelings is to *share* them - with someone. Have them. Share them. So there is a culture of safety that is created for people to say their seemingly ugliest feelings. If this human feel-good need or feel-whole need cannot be filled, an addict will turn to something to feel - good or whole - another way. Drink. Use. Twelve-Step programs are called spiritual programs. *Looking into the eyes of another human being and saying how you really feel is spiritual? Hmmm... Interesting. Eye contact and words.*

I practiced my new words on Geenie and Fred. One night at a restaurant, when the waiter put a plate in front of me with a large burrito on it, Fred said, "Wow! You're going to eat all that? That's enormous!"

His saying that made me feel horrible. I had a million thoughts wash over me, but the main feeling was embarrassed. I did not say anything. Driving home, I sat in the back seat, with Geenie and Fred up front. I asked Fred if I could tell him something. He said, "Of course." I leaned forward, mustered my courage, and said, "When you said what you did tonight when my food came, I felt really uncomfortable."

I was shaking like a leaf. Uncomfortable. That is the word I'd been taught to say when I could not pinpoint another word. It was the "feeling" word that was the least threatening to say to someone. I was filled with fear just to say that sentence. But there it was. It was out. B throughY in practice. Fred accepted what I said easily, but getting my words out that first time, you'd have thought I was facing a dire consequence.

Tying Up Pieces

Jack and I got in touch and decided to meet at our old apartment. When I got there, I sat in a chair while he lay on the floor. He made no attempt to clean the apartment, which was now in shambles. Aluminum foil, used for drugs, and pornographic magazines, never there before, were spread on the tables. Jack asked me if I wanted a divorce. I said, "Yes." He told me he could not believe I was "leaving so soon." Ironically, later when I gradually told people what my life had been like, many declared they could not believe I'd "stayed so long."

At one point during our conversation, Jack asked me, "Were you embarrassed that I worked at 7-11?"

"Not for the first year and a half."

I told him I'd married him without doing any work on myself, and I knew the work ahead in uncovering the darkness of the shooting was going to be a full-time job. Since he did not want to get help and I did, that was the only road I could see for myself.

I also said, "And you know, Jack, I can't help thinking that there is some form of latent homosexuality being played out here."

He turned to look away and softly said, "Yeah, you may have something there." It was the only confirmation I got about this topic, but it was enough to feel resolved. I was happy he acknowledged something I'd felt in my gut. Still, I had a lot of guilt about leaving my marriage. *I have vowed to love this person. Should I stay and help him through his problem? Can we learn together?* Everyone had seen us so happy. Certainly there was still love there. *Wouldn't a good wife stay and help her husband? Have I abandoned a human being?* Whenever I ran into anyone around town who'd known Jack and me together, I never spoke about his drug problem. To many it looked as if I was dumping him after he'd waited patiently for my return from gallivanting around the world.

Many people loved Jack. He often wore a shirt and tie, his water polo and swim team members admired him. He was fun and friendly at his night-shift job. He'd worked beautifully with children at the pool. Parents adored him, sought private lessons, and tipped him well. All this could be achieved while he smoked pot daily. No one knew the inside workings of our marriage. I came to see that it was the person who had the intimate relationship with a person who knew him best. I'd watched Jack's brain change over the course of time. His reasoning was different. He was more suspicious, paranoid, negative, and judgmental than he'd been seven years before. In the end, I felt I got a first-hand lesson on the power of how a drug can debilitate a life.

One line in Robin Norwood's book *Women Who Love Too Much* summed up my feelings. It gave me the confidence to move forward with less guilt. "Being miserable is reason enough to leave."

My close girlfriend in Louisville, one I'd had since first grade, stopped talking to me after I left Jack. When she'd asked me why we were splitting, I told her I could not take the drugs anymore; I was going to get help with my own illness around my family's disease of alcoholism. She said that someone doing drugs was not reason enough to leave him. She was furious. Her husband and Jack often smoked pot together.

Later I realized that she had to get mad at me and leave our friendship. Otherwise, she might have had to look at her own relationship with drugs, her husband, and her family of origin. And, if I'd learned anything at that time, it was that people do not go into counseling or seek change unless they are driven to do so.

I was driven.

The Bad Rap

I blamed Jack for nothing. Something was made abundantly clear to me at the onset of my recovery process. Alcoholics get a bad rap in our society. It is because their disease is biologically fatal. It has been researched, studied, and proven to be deadly. We know exactly how to label a person who is addicted to alcohol: alcoholic.

People generally get addicted to alcohol because they are medicating pain. But what about all the other addictions or compulsive behaviors that people use to medicate pain? Those are not scientifically *proven* to be biologically fatal, but can be just as harmful. Other compulsions can lead to systematic suicide or the spiritual death of relationships. They are just not labeled.

This label is the main difference between an alcoholic and any other person using a compulsion to medicate pain. In a sense we are all alcoholics without the label. We *all* medicate our pain, but not all of us use alcohol. Most of us use something. I used sugar, which has a chemical make-up close to alcohol. I learned to use the alcoholic's healing path as my way out. I learned to be vulnerable with my feelings, Person One. I never wanted to be arrogant again, Person Two.

In the beginning, the soon-to-be alcoholic has a painful feeling. If he is too embarrassed to tell anyone, the uncomfortable feeling persists. Soon, not finding any constructive way to get out the feeling, he reaches for something to push it back down, to make himself feel better. This time it is a drink. This pushing down is successful for a short time, but the feeling will eventually resurface. When it does, he reaches for what helped him feel better the first time – a drink. If he happens to be pre-disposed to being addicted to alcohol, it becomes his drug of choice. He will have many painful incidents in life come his way, and having no one to talk to, he can pretend he is okay. He *is* okay because he has a drink keeping all his feelings at bay. In fact, he does not even have to say these feelings - at all. That is the arrogant part. Trouble is, these ugly feelings that have been squashed, creep out in destructive ways. He may always be in a rush, or say mean things to loved ones, be late, be careless, or become irresponsible. High-functioning alcoholics hide their destructive habits best. Our work places are filled with them. A person cannot die from being arrogant, but enough alcohol in the human body can cause the liver to deteriorate. The person can die from this consumption.

How does a person heal this addiction? By getting in touch with the feelings that come up in the body, that need and want to be expressed. He finds other safe humans to tell those feelings to, gets them out of his system. They are gone. Relief is here. No more pressure.

What is generally needed to do this? Courage, eye contact, and words. That is why most people in the business of recovery will tell you the only way to heal alcohol addiction is through spiritual means. This involves having to be humble around other humans. Icky. This is the vulnerable part. If each of us turns to something as our drug of choice in order to medicate feelings, it is important to know what our *something* is.

The *family disease* of alcoholism means that when one person is not saying his true feelings, others – out of fear - stop saying theirs. While they may not be alcoholics, you can bet they, too, will need to turn to something to stuff down the feelings they are not allowed to say. These other addictions or compulsive behaviors do not get labeled as easily. Sure, it is easier to see if a person overeats, and obesity is now being looked at as a fatal disease. But what about the people whose compulsions cannot readily be seen, but they are using them to shut down feelings, all the same? Harmful compulsions could be using drugs, legal or illegal, work, television, computers, video games, shopping, spending too much money, sex, masturbation, fingernail biting, chewing gum, gambling, cutting, rushing, over-scheduling, being late all the time, making excuses, interrupting, complaining, arguing, hobbies, sleeping, reading, exercising, talking, being alone, being with people all the time, and _____ (fill in the blank).

The same concept of healing alcoholism works with any of these compulsions used to medicate pain. When I'm having a feeling, I need to label it and tell someone. Otherwise, I may want to use food as a way of keeping those feelings at bay. The trouble is it takes enormous courage to open our mouths in front of someone and reveal feelings such as shame, fear, hurt, loneliness, exhaustion, anger, and sadness. Many of us are not close enough to someone to "just start talking" about these feelings. Who is safe to do that with? How will they react? Will he laugh? Will she think I'm weak? Will they think I'm crazy?

When a person steps into a 12-step meeting room, everyone knows he is not crazy. Prolonged exposure to silencing our feelings affects our mental state. Newcomers are given the piece of paper with feelings words because our vocabulary growth for 'feelings' words has been stunted. Once we begin to find groups of people where we can speak freely, we become more and more free *everywhere* we go.

Believing and Speaking

I had the good fortune of landing in a US History 101 course my first class back from my nine months of travel. I'd been asking a question in my head while traveling, *Why are we so different?* In teaching, there is no better way to get students interested in an upcoming topic than to give them a special prompt. My "prompt" had lasted for nine months. My quest for an answer about America was so intense that when I got the textbook, I read it cover to cover. I was an older student taking the course for my teacher certification.

I got my answer. After reading the nitty-gritty details of how America got its start, I realized the desire to believe what a person wanted was great. So great that generation after generation of people risked their lives settling in a new land where they thought they could do just that. Scores of people died so they could believe what they wanted to believe. Not only that, but after thinking it, they could say it out loud.

I began to understand freedom on a whole different level. Freedom of religion, for me, meant the freedom to believe. Freedom of speech meant being able to say that belief out loud. Those two simple thoughts formed our nation. People, like my grandfather, who endured whatever it took to come here simply did not want to live without saying what they thought. Two simple ideas. But from them stem the ability to think far beyond any limits placed on us. New ideas stem from having that freedom to believe, speak, and do. Anyone who has ever been oppressed can well understand how almost *all* creative thoughts are suppressed while a person is fearful. *Really* learning this simultaneously with my new life of saying what I'd been thinking for years was true happiness for me.

Overlapping that class, I took American Literature and learned about the transcendentalist movement. Earlier in history, God had been seen as an entity outside us. If lightning struck a farmer, others believed he'd done something bad, and God had willed it upon him in condemnation. But the early American freethinkers began to write about the possibility of God being inside us, about being able to hear the voice of God from within.

The valve had been turned and my energy released. In my support groups, I began to talk endlessly. Everyone else wanted to talk, as they, too, had just awakened from deep denial. I talked on the phone, had coffee, dinner, and walks with all sorts of people for *hours* over many *years*, learning and growing from every word said. I came to believe that just as the healing power of words, both spoken and heard, could not be understated, the abusive oppression of not being able to speak a person's mind could not be overstated.

"I will be back."

I drove to Louisville to meet with a group to plan for the following year's ten-year high school reunion. I spent a few days with Mom and explained to her that I was about to undergo an intense and vital search into my past, into my rage. I could already tell it was not going to be pretty and, since I did not want to hurt her more than I already had, I would be "going away." "I'll still be here, but I won't be getting in touch with you that often. I want you to know I need to do this for myself. But I promise you, when I am finished, I will be back."

My mother turned out to be my biggest supporter in this endeavor. She, too, had gotten into Al-Anon. During the same seven years that I was with Jack, my mother struggled with Judy's mental illness. She could no longer control or deny Judy's mental illness, and I could no longer do the same with Jack's addiction.

It was now time to work on my emotional illness of control and manipulation. I knew when I went in to look, I'd find my mother's victim stance. The victim stance I'd taken in my life was the thing I hated most about myself. I'd learned it from her, and I had to un-learn it on my own. I knew this journey inward was going to bring up fierce anger toward my mom. Now that I was aware of this, there would be no one to blame for my troubles. It was time to grow up.

I also wanted to do the work on my own, without the influence of any family members. It was clear that my family members were not the support I needed to get well. I had felt like a tennis ball, bouncing from one wall to the next, trying to keep up with what my siblings "should-ed" on me. Mary thought I should work more, Aaron thought I should travel more, Carl thought I should make more money, and Jeff thought I should save more money. Judy thought I needed to spend more time on my looks – wearing make up to fix myself up, to look "better." I just wanted peace. I knew where I had to go to find it. I wanted to embrace my inner voice.

It would be three-years before I'd come back. My mom had her own support groups. She told me many times she clung to my words. She believed I would be back when I felt more well and able to deal with our family. It was a motivator for her to get well, too, and she used her time wisely.

Ten Fingers

I met my former classmates and reunion planners for a meeting. We left a restaurant parking lot at 3:00 a.m. I went straight back to Mom's house and to bed. Soon I was sound asleep. Somewhere in my mind, I must have heard the slightest creak, because I questioned softly, "Mom?" tilting my head to listen, eyes closed. Nothing. In my grogginess, I moved my head on the pillow again, my eyes still closed, "Mom?" Nothing.

"Mom?" I opened my eyes. One foot from my face were two hands, ten fingers splayed. A man leaning over me. In the pitch dark, I could only make out his spread fingers and a white hat. "Mom! Mom! Mom!" Now I leapt up, screaming bloody murder.

The man scurried out fast. My mother heard me and turned on her light just in time to get a look at a man tottering out of my room, shoulders bouncing off the walls as he rounded the U-shaped hallway and ran from the house. Mom ran to me. I was screaming, clawing her nightgown. She called the police. In no time they were there with dogs, fingerprinting the house, asking us questions, and roaming the house.

The dogs followed the scent to an empty space in between two parallel-parked cars in the alley behind our house. Gone. Turns out, a man had been following women home from that restaurant, raping them in their homes. Mom assumed Judy had left the back door unlocked when she'd visited that day. Thank goodness for my mind becoming aware of someone in the room. It was like a scene from a movie, but it had happened to me.

Beginning with Dave

That summer, I met Dave, a man who would be instrumental in my life. We met at the Sunday night 12-step meeting, my home group. He came with us to the restaurant where we gathered afterwards.

On my return from Louisville, Dave and I drove to the Shenandoah Mountains to camp with friends. As we were driving, I told him the story of the man coming into my bedroom. I was giggling. He reached over and squeezed my forearm tightly as I told the details. I stopped giggling. He listened to me while he drove. I could feel in his grip and sense in his eyes, as he looked straight into the highway, he took this very seriously. I was struck by this protective quality.

By this time in my life, I was used to danger and took it in stride. I had not given much thought past my initial fear, what could have happened had this intruder gotten his hands on me. I did think it ironic, though, that I had traveled around the world for nine months all by myself, keeping myself relatively safe, only to be attacked by yet another man in my mother's home.

I found in Dave a man who loved nature. That became the constant grounding force of our relationship. When we sat together in nature, it was as if whatever else was happening on earth stood still. Only the ants moved about, while the leaves blew in the trees, and the cows swished their tails and snorted. I felt this way in nature on my own, but this man had such a deep appreciation for the earth that I felt it all the way through him and out the other side. There was no part of him that did not feel grounded in the earth, and the attraction he held for me in that one simple fact held us together through all else.

We walked and held hands. Often we didn't say a word, just drank in every tiny yet marvelous site. When I stopped to see a stem that had twined itself around a branch, I stared at it, holding hands with him next to me, both of us drinking it in. We took drives in the country every weekend. He'd grown up on a farm and loved cows, so we stopped and talked to cows every chance we got. In my mind, anyone would have fallen in love with a man who loved cows like this farm boy did. To listen to him talk was comical and profound all at once. He had a wicked good sense of humor.

Dave had lost himself in books all his life and the knowledge he gained from reading could be heard in the way he formed his sentences. It was like he was an author sitting and writing a book, but speaking slowly, finding the right word, so as not to waste one. I felt special experiencing him all to myself.

How else do I describe Dave? He was, like me, a tortured soul. The universe had big plans for us. Plans that would only be revealed to us after each test we passed. Those tests we gave to each other.

I can only describe Dave now by looking backwards, as we never could have imagined the mountains we'd move together. To this day, he and I have more respect for each other than most people we've encountered. I know I can speak for him in this regard, as he has told me this, and I've told him, but in the telling of our story together, it will not be initially apparent – even most of the way through. But I can say this as a fact: no human being has helped me more to unearth and heal the demons locked away in my physical, mental, and emotional self.

Dave has the clearest channel to God I have found in a human. I have searched and found healers to help me in my personal growth endeavors. Dave was my boyfriend, but he was more than that. He was a fellow warrior on the path of spiritual healing. Our relationship was my spiritual practice. You have heard the saying, "He doesn't practice what he preaches." Well, Dave practiced every spiritual law he learned. He practiced it on me, and everything I learned, I practiced on him. When we "walked the walk" we took a direct path right through each other's lives. We tackled this recovery business like it was a college course, and we were determined to graduate with honors. Oh, if that were possible!

The stories I will lay out will look nothing like a spiritual journey, but keep in mind that we were both products of violent households, desperate to heal from them, and if my writing does any one thing, I hope it will ultimately reveal the spiritual implications on the *other side* of violence.

Once a friend who also knew my brother, Aaron, said that people from backgrounds like ours either turned out to be angels or demons. Aaron, she said, was an angel. Dave and I were angels, too, but we were definitely carrying demons around with us. Another way to put this is that Dave and I came out of our homes as "A's" and everyone around us told us that was the wrong way to be. We should both strive to be "Z's." I have said this before: the road from B through Y is ugly. The road of Lynnie and Dave is ugly. But, each time, on the other side of ugly was a sliver of light that kept us moving toward something we'd never known but only felt in our hearts. We wanted to be well.

When I met Dave he told me that in his previous relationships he'd systematically demolished the women with his logic, that they had not stood a chance. When he found out his former wife was pregnant, he forced her to have an abortion. His last girlfriend had finally left him to marry someone else, and when he was living on the cot in the backroom of the store he owned, he spent each night imagining how the blood would look splattered on the wall after he'd shot himself in the head. He hated his mother with a passion that was alive in him every day, a sure sign of not-dating material. She was manipulative, yet loving, and although the whole town revered her, she had vile words to say to her husband, his father. To make matters worse, he was tall and blonde like her. He had been reared on a farm by his stout, alcoholic father who repeatedly became violent toward the machinery on the farm. Witnessing that anger had been enough to make Dave stay out of the way of his father's blows. Dave was left with tremendous guilt after watching his father berate his younger brother and then telling Dave to "Come on!" The two of them walked away and left the young boy. Being torn between fearing his father's wrath and harming his younger brother beyond repair had left a life-long scar on his manhood. He thought himself to be a coward among men. It did not help, either, that he looked almost exactly like the woman he despised most in life.

Sounds like a real catch, eh?

I admired Dave for telling me this. I was in listening school, and believed in the healing that took place after someone revealed his sins and set out to create his life anew. He felt remorse for who he'd been and wanted to change. I knew I wanted to change my life badly. I believed I could. I wanted desperately to believe he could, too.

I felt I was no gem, either. I had a past I was not proud of. He was dating me, a newly separated woman who was just beginning to look at the shooting that had occurred between her mom and dad. We accepted each other. Until we didn't.

When Dave was upset, his tone was harsh and his words the cruelest I'd ever had spoken to me. But Mary was the one who'd said "No!" on the night of the shooting. I assumed a victim's stance, a frozen position under threat. My life's work was now laid out in front of me: learn to say "No" to abuse and learn to protect myself. I had not been protected by my mother, my father, my siblings, my grandparents, my church, and countless adults in my life. I would have to begin from scratch.

Dave was the scariest person the universe could have brought me. I would learn to protect myself and practice saying "No!" to him either literally or figuratively. Sweet arrangement, but what did Dave get out of the bargain? Plenty.

The sickeningly sweet, kill 'em with kindness, manipulative and seductive parts of my personality were still in full swing, so I was the perfect person for Dave to learn to protect himself from. I hadn't the vaguest notion how to deal with the rage I'd carried for so long. I was a sugar-coated-doormat, a volcano, dying to explode, if only I could just be taught how to do so without hurting anyone in my path. Alas, I hurt him with my inability to express my emotions in a healthy way.

When Dave was harsh with me, I moved into protecting myself by speaking up. Words. I needed words. When I was manipulative with him, he moved into protecting himself from me by speaking up. Words. He needed words. Sounds so easy, but we're talking about two people paralyzed in the face of each other's most despicable characteristics. Usually, my speaking up to him turned into my crying and his speaking up to me turned into his shutting down. Fancy that, a true male/female relationship, albeit, lived in the extremes.

Although my story is of an extreme nature, I learned early, while listening to stories far more extreme, to look for glimmers of myself inside others' stories and drop the attitude of "this could not possibly pertain to me." It helped me tremendously to do that. I'd never been raped, but I listened to people who had been. I'd never been a victim of incest, but I listened anyway. I'd never been stabbed, but I listened to a person who had been. What I learned was that pain cannot be compared or measured. If I listened closely, I would find my story in every person's story.

Dave was already seeing an expensive psychiatrist who was the only doctor in the area specializing in the treatment of "adult children of alcoholics." In the next few years, I watched the doctor publish several books and appear on television. I thought it remarkable that Dave invested so much money in himself, and us, because he wanted me to attend these sessions with him. Dr. Will was excellent, but often the sessions were extremely painful because Dave was still working out issues from a past relationship. That woman was mentioned many times.

Dr. Will pointed out to Dave that he had a difficult time loving and tried to get him to just "let go" and love me. He said he could see that Dave loved me, but he just did not know how to show it. He tried to show it, but that was not something Dave was ever able to sustain during our time together as a couple. Painful.

Dave's radar helped me zero in on some of my most unhealthy characteristics. When Dave was uncomfortable about something I did, he began to shut down. The thing was, often what I was doing *was* wrong, and he had good cause to shut down. Usually, I was not being completely truthful about my emotions and he sensed it. But no matter how fast I learned something new about myself and worked to change it, he'd have already shut down, which lasted a long time. It was the "long time" thing that was the killer.

I was needy, and Dave was harsh. Then I'd get mad at his harshness and he'd go away for two weeks. I'd be crushed, but as the two weeks moved on, I learned to live without him and ended up loving it. Those same two weeks when he felt relieved to be away from me at first, he'd end up missing me and coming back just as I was getting over him. But not quite.

Our relationship started out passionately but after two months it was never the same and, in fact, was always a struggle for both of us to get our needs met. Dave told me that women he'd dated before me ended up staying with him for long periods of time because the first two months had been so wonderful. There I was, still in the game well after two months, and would be for many years.

The greatest thing I learned in those early days from Dr. Will was to notice if a person's words or actions took my self-esteem down a notch. If so, I needed to say whatever I needed, to bring myself back up to the state where I was before the person said or did it. I needed to say my feelings. He taught me I was only to say my feelings for myself. I was not to say them to alter the other person in any way. And, in fact, if I could let go of changing the other person and just focus on saying the feelings in me – the ones that relieved me – I'd know I'd grown tremendously. I got it.

In the fall, I became a full-time student at the university, working on my teaching certification, and a part-time waitress at a local steak house. I also worked at the university for the next many years when I was needed. I was getting "on my feet" in my new surroundings at my friend's mother's house, cleaning the house from top to bottom one day a week and cooking four meals a week for the family. I was also going to support group meetings at night. I was busy.

Fortunately, giving up sugar allowed things to come up for me, but unfortunately, I was constantly struggling with what was coming up!

The floodgates of my life had opened. Now, not only was I continuing to have my daily visual pictures of the night of the shooting, other painful pictures were coming up. These were of beatings I'd experienced or witnessed or words I'd heard. Each one brought up feelings I must have felt long ago but had suppressed. I was doing nothing to suppress them now and, in fact, was willing them to come up. But I had no control over how many or how fast they came.

Imagine you are beating cake batter in a mixing bowl. You do not want to lift the beaters, lest the batter splatters all over everyone and the walls. My job was to keep my beaters tucked in the mixing bowl.

Not Proud

Growing up in our house, it was a given that no one was to look through anyone's private things. I felt confident that my privacy was honored, so I knew how to reciprocate this respect. But I broke this rule as an adult, invaded someone's privacy, and hurt myself deeply in the process.

The fall after we met, Dave shut down. Confused, I wondered why and asked, but he would not talk about it. He kept a log beside his bed each night, and one day I looked in it. I was devastated to find he was writing about his previous girlfriend and how despondent he was that he'd lost her. He lamented losing this beautiful country girl who was a skilled horsewoman, the daughter of wealthy parents. If that were not devastating enough, he wrote that he felt so low about it that he had actually put an unloaded gun in his mouth and pulled the trigger. Just to see how it felt.

I was frightened on many different levels. *What am I doing with a man who loves someone else? What am I doing with a man who gave up 'beauty' and 'wealth' to be with me? How demeaning! Why is he still thinking about this? He is with me and he is imagining killing himself? Over someone from his past? It has been years since he was with her. What in God's name is going on? How can he be this unhappy? He is with me. I am a country girl! I am a horsewoman!*

Because I knew how wrong it was that I'd invaded his privacy, I could not tell him what I'd done, what I knew. Anyone else would have run for the hills, right? Not me. Apparently, I was not miserable enough. I did not tell Dave for three years. When I did tell him, he easily forgave me and was more concerned about the fact that I'd held in my natural feelings that the information brought up. I'd like to say this cured me from ever looking at someone else's things, but it would happen one more time years later.

Learning to Nap

Pictures of my childhood flashed rapidly in my head now. I found myself being so restless and shaky that my eyes darted around in my head when I tried to sleep.

In order to preserve the sanity I had, I had to come up with a way to keep sleep deprivation at bay. I had to figure out how to nap. I began to lie down on my pillow and, when the pictures ran through my head, I pretended the hand of God was rubbing my head, from my forehead, across my hair, to the crown of my head. With each stroke, I imagined God saying, "I love you, Lynnie. I love you, Lynnie." And if there was anything from that day I was criticizing myself for, I mixed in, "I forgive you, Lynnie. I forgive you."

Before long, if I stuck to it, kept my mind on course, I fell into a beautiful sleep. If I woke up in fifteen minutes or two hours, it did not matter. When I awoke, I had a brand new day.

I still, all these years later, take naps in this manner as a way to heal my soul. I consider a nap a spiritual experience, because when I wake up, I feel healed. The first thing out of my mouth is, "Thank you, God!" I also began to look at naps as getting two days for the price of one. If my mind was drained from the restlessness I'd felt, my nap let me wake up feeling refreshed. I was able to accomplish in the second part of the day what I hadn't been able to in the first.

Over the years I read that getting lots of sleep was one of the most important factors in good health. This was especially true when dealing with emotional issues such as grief or trauma.

Living Right

Once while working in my office at the university, I got a call from the Director of Financial Aid. "Lynnie, can you come over to the office for a few minutes?"

I walked across campus, thinking she had something to give me for my boss. When I arrived in the outer office, I was shown back to the director's large office where she sat at her desk. When she saw me, she rose and walked around her desk to greet me. Then she directed my attention to the left, to a table where five older women were seated.

She said, "Lynnie, this particular sorority is in search of someone to give their scholarship to, someone who we think will make a fine teacher some day. The woman who has had this scholarship for several years has just graduated with her teaching degree. The sorority has selected you as the next recipient of their scholarship. You may continue receiving it until you have earned your teaching certification and masters degree."

I stood there, dumbfounded. Speechless. They were tickled that I was surprised and obviously happy. As each woman got up to congratulate me, I thanked her. We stood chatting for a few minutes, they gathered their coats, and left. I still stood in disbelief. Someone was giving me money.

The director saw the look on my face. Smiling, she walked around her desk, opened the drawer, and pulled out an envelope with the check in it. She licked the envelope, and as she handed it to me, she winked. "That's what you get for living right."

Well, blow me over with a feather. In all of ten minutes, I'd been given a scholarship! And the people who gave it to me were already gone. Who would I have to thank when I came out of shock? I was to get a check each semester until I could call myself a teacher! It would be years before I could tell this story without crying my eyes out.

Being Early is on Time

Before going to Australia, I had a golf-ball sized knot on the right side of my neck and shoulder. I called it my "golf ball." It was created by stress from frantically working a mile-a-minute at my university job. It was also from living on the edge with time. I was never early anywhere I went, squeaked into work just on the button, and when I could get away with it, I was late to meet friends. I had the whole "social butterfly" thing going on. I booked meetings with friends too close together. When I was with one, I did not want to leave "so soon," and so I apologized to the next person when I arrived late. This was a terrible cycle.

Being in Australia, relaxed as I was, teaching aerobics, then travel-ing, my golf ball had disappeared completely. When I arrived back in Virginia, I immediately felt the buzz of society moving much faster than in Australia or Europe. I promised myself I would not fall into the same trap. I did.

Two things happened to change me.

I was driving to a college course, planning to arrive in the nick of time. I sat at a traffic light, nervously waiting and "Ping!" I felt the long-lost golf ball return in my neck. I decided in that moment, instead of chancing being late, I was going to leave thirty minutes earlier to every place I went. What made this a big deal was, in my mind, it had never, ever been cool to get some place early and simply wait around with other people. I had been "above" that. Arrogant. Not anymore. My health was too important. I was willing to do things differently. The wonderful result of arriving early to places was that I began to help out where I could and soon began to feel much more like I belonged wherever I was. Amazing.

The next thing that changed me happened when I was traveling between meeting friends, only the friend on the later end was Dave. When I arrived 45 minutes late to his house, he met me at the half-opened door. When I tried to come in, he said, "No, I'll see you another time." He said he'd been excited to see me, but now he was just not excited anymore. The sharp jab inside my chest could only be tempered by the fact that this made sense. I knew that feeling! I apologized because I knew he was right and henceforth I worked very hard to show respect to everyone by being on time, or at least calling when I was going to be late. That half-opened door proved to be a very powerful wake-up call about my disregard of others. What I have learned over time is that being on time is a sign of respect. Being late is a sign of disrespect. It is as simple as that.

Starting Anew

I set out to find a new place to live and met Harry, a 70-year old man who was a retired naval officer and a Virginia gentleman. He lived in the full basement of his house and rented out the top three-bedroom ranch, complete with furniture, lamps, linens, and even small appliances that had remained after his wife's death, just two years prior. A large brick wall with a barbeque pit surrounded the house. Right smack dab in the middle of the yard, and just off the deck, was a huge built-in swimming pool. The two-car garage was a renovated cabana. Harry rented the house to me and I invited two fellow waiters to move in. We moved in after Christmas, just in time to settle in before starting my internship as a teacher.

It was after New Year's when I got a call from Jack in Las Vegas. "Lynnie, I want to tell you that I am so, so sorry. I see now what you lived with. I had no idea how painful it was for you. I understand now why you left. This is unbearable. My dad is acting towards me the exact same way I acted towards you. He is just so irritable at everything. I am so, so sorry." Hearing this, my heart softened. By living with his dad for just a few months, Jack felt his dad's irritability in the same way I'd felt his. He was not calling to get back together, yet what was reassuring about his phone call was that it made me feel that yes, I had loved him all along. It had just been unbearable living with him.

Growing Professionally and Personally

Good or bad, I don't think any teacher forgets her internship. Mine was awesome. I began my student teaching with the best person I could possibly have had: Sue. She was dynamic, smart, a go-getter, funny, and caring. In our three and a half months together, we did not have one bad day. She was incredibly direct, which I was learning to be. I practiced all my new communication techniques with her, and she heard every word I said.

One day she sat in the back of the room and watched me teach. When the kids left, she walked up and said, "Lynnie, you're too indecisive. I was the same way and my co-operating teacher told me to wake up one day and say, 'No' to everything the kids asked of me on that day. Then, the next day, wake up and say, 'Yes' to everything the kids asked of me. It got me in the habit of knowing exactly what to say. I want you to try it."

It was true. The kids walked up and asked if they could go to the bathroom. To one I'd say, "No, the bell is going to ring." To the next one who had puppy-dog eyes, I'd waver back and forth. That's it. I tried the advice she'd received from her teacher twenty years before. It may sound like a funny way to get someone to be decisive, but it worked!

Each day Sue asked me, "What are your fears?" I listed them aloud. She helped me tackle each, one by one. She knew I knew my content, so I was really impressed when she went straight to helping me with the difficulties of teaching. She constantly shared techniques that developed my emotional intelligence for *managing* students.

Sue was a writer and a born teacher. With every assignment she gave the kids, she wrote along side them and read her work out loud. Sometimes it was awful and she laughed at herself, but most times it was wonderful. The point is, she was teaching writing to the kids as she wrote *with* the kids. All day long.

No matter what kind of agony I had going on internally, I never spoke of it to Sue. She was cheerful and quick and an expert at what she did. Principals always sent her new teachers to mentor. I was number thirteen on her list. I thrived in her presence. At the end of our three months together she wrote, "She was the best student teacher I've ever had, and I've had many." She said I was the only one who could keep up with her, move with her, stay by her side. I took initiative, and worked until I finished a task. With all of my inner turmoil coming up, I still felt guilt while working with her because I knew inside I was not able to give one hundred percent. She is a retired writer now, but more than twenty years later, Sue lives on in my classroom.

If Sue's professionalism sustained me at work, Harry's love did so at home. He had a twinkle in his eye, a wide smile, and a zest for life. I loved him from the start. When I got home at night, I fixed my dinner, opened the door at the top of the stairs, and yelled down, "Heeeeeeeeeey!"

When Harry yelled back, "Heeeeeey!" that was my cue. I took my full dinner plate down where he sat with his, on a tray. We watched the evening news and "Wheel of Fortune" together. I had a ball sitting on that couch with him. He was so funny, and he thought I was so smart! Words were my thing. "Say, we've got to get you to California, so we can get you on this show!"

Living there was perfect. The pool house was a great place to have parties and Dave and I had potluck dinners every two months, like clockwork. By now, we were meeting scads of people in our meetings, and it was a wonderful house to create a large community of people around us.

In May I received my teaching certification but continued taking graduate courses that summer so I could secure my master's degree within the year. The county where I lived paid higher, but they hired later. I was so nervous about becoming a teacher, I wanted all my books early to read, study, and prepare. Trying to waylay the stress of a new job, I applied to outlying counties.

I went for an interview at a high school 35 miles west of my town in

Northern Virginia. I interviewed with the English department's chairperson, and with the two principals. During the interview, the department chair said, "I have never seen anyone with so much empathy for kids." When the decision was to be made, the principals asked the department chairperson, Millie, who she wanted and she picked me.

Well, they liked me, too, but explained they had others in mind. Another woman they interviewed for that position had a husband they wanted to hire to teach history and be the wrestling coach. Each would only say yes if the other got a job. Millie told them, "You did not ask me who I wanted to be the wrestling coach. You asked me whom I wanted to have as my English teacher. I pick Lynnie."

This later was a joke among the principals and me. Another joke was on them, only I did not do it on purpose. They passed over the couple and called to say I had the job. I said, "I would like to visit your school for a day before I say yes."

Uh, oh. Now the principal said to Millie, "You'd better do something darn special to make this girl want this because I just lost a wrestling coach because of you!"

On the morning I arrived at school, my department chair walked into the principal's office in full Dolly Parton gear – the wig, the dress with fringe, the boobs complete with protruding nipples, and scores of plastered-on makeup. "Do you think this will impress her?" When they came walking out of his office, there I was. These were the people for me. I spent the day at this school, loved it, and accepted the job.

I'd been hired into an English department of 22 teachers who had been named the number one English department in the state of Virginia that year. I could not have found a group of higher caliber people.

Quaking

I still took graduate courses and I attended four support group meetings a week on average for those first four years of my recovery. In each meeting, I spoke. I always waited until I had something to say, which generally happened about 45 minutes into the meeting. I'd had nothing to say when I entered the room, but after listening to people talk, I soon wanted to speak so badly, I would have been disappointed if my time had not come. I was to later learn that was called "quaking." The Quakers sat in their meetinghouses for quite some time, with no one speaking, and then all of a sudden someone stood, moved to say something that was churning powerfully inside him.

That's what 12-step meetings were for me. Each time, I had something churned up from inside, I said it, looking into the eyes of my fellows. Each time, I felt the presence of God. There it was again, in eye contact and words.

Dr. Will

I stopped going with Dave to sessions with his psychiatrist after nine months, and was hearing people in my support groups raving about a bodyworks therapist. I decided I would try him. But first, I went back to Dave's doctor and asked him for a synopsis of me. I told him, "I came here for several months, and that was for Dave, but you got to know me, too, and you saw how I interacted with him. I need you to tell me what you see in me, where I need help with my behavior, my past."

Dr. Will said, "Lynnie, I never saw your needs as voracious. I see in you one of the most remarkable things a person needs in order to be mentally healthy. You have the ability to see your side in a problem. That is very rare and must often be taught. If it comes naturally, it is the highest level of mental health one can achieve. If a person has that ability, she can move forward in relating well with others."

I was stunned. I went there thinking he was going to tell me just how incredibly messed up I was. I was ready to take notes. But when he said this, it did match what I thought to be me, deep down. His words built my confidence in relationships. I wrote them down and tried to remember exactly what he'd told me.

Ten-year High School Reunion

I was going to give a speech at our ten-year reunion. In that speech I saw myself thanking Jim Huggins. Without telling them why, I asked Phyllis and Jim Huggins to come.

For the first time in my life, I bought a dress. It cost $44. I was twenty-eight years old, and aside from blue jeans and inexpensive tops, I was buying my first piece of clothing.

That night, I went to the podium feeling pretty honest. I'd now been in "recovery" from my past for one year. I opened my mouth to speak of Mr. Huggins. I did not speak of the shooting, but I did say, "Many of you know I came from a family of violence…." The side conversations of folks standing in the back ceased. I knew I had my classmates' attention. I did not speak long, but when I talked about what an inspiration Jim Huggins had been to me, I saw his reaction. He shifted in his seat and smiled a big smile. I asked him to say a few words and walked away from the podium. When I turned back, Mr. Huggins was leaning over the microphone with tears in his eyes saying, "If you know a teacher to thank, please do, because this feels more wonderful than I can express." He's come to all of our reunions since.

I had several guys tell me I could have been telling their stories, that Jim Huggins was instrumental in turning their lives around. I was surprised. I had not known he belonged to so many. He *was* a hero. I came to see that a teacher had the ability to move countless people toward a more positive position.

Driving to my reunion, I'd been feeling nervous and scared, similar to how anyone might feel before a reunion. *Oh geez, I'm going to see all these people and what have I done in ten years? Here I am divorced… How embarrassing… People will be married and have kids and what do I have?* I realized this was wrong thinking, so I spent my 12-hour drive to Kentucky thinking about my accomplishments. After the reunion, at a restaurant with two cool guy friends, one said, "So, Lynnie, what have you been doing in the last ten years?"

I rattled off a few things like going to college and spending my holidays traveling to Massachusetts, California, England, and Ireland, getting married and our 2000-mile bicycle honeymoon trip, working in D.C., my nine months journey to fifteen different countries, coming home to get my teaching degree, and beginning my teaching career in a month. They looked at each other. One guy said with a chuckle, "Uh, well, uh, let's see… I have the whole 'TV Guide' memorized!" I was not trying to brag, and they were just poking fun. We were great friends and had a good laugh, but it did make me feel better driving back to Virginia, knowing that even though I was getting divorced, I still had something to show for the ten years I'd been away.

Closing My Door
I was constantly at odds with the other students in my graduate courses. The negative talk about students was overwhelming. Many of them were

jaded, long-term teachers. Not all of them. I could see in the eyes of the more positive teachers a desire to influence kids. I continually gave my colleagues a different perspective of dealing with negative situations with kids. "Yeah, wait 'til she gets in the classroom," I think many thought.

One point I made about the impatience of kids today was how they were a product of us, the society we'd created. When they were little ones and carried into 7-11 on their mother's hip, if there were more than three people in line, the mother became annoyed. The kids picked up on this. It was not their fault that we wanted our lives to be easier and our gadgets faster. How could we blame them that they wanted life the same way – easier and faster? And this was even before computers!

I did wonder and worry how I'd be as a teacher, not with kids, but how adults would accept me. I could not imagine acting the way they told me to act – be stern here, strict there, don't smile until November, etc.… All the advice I got seemed counter to how I naturally interacted with kids. I remained confused.

That summer in graduate school I read *Teacher Effectiveness Training* by Thomas Gordon. *Ahhh! Now this is the advice I need!* Thomas Gordon worked with troubled kids and came up with communication techniques in the classroom that positively impacted the troubled kids, as well as the not-so-troubled kids. Everything I read, page after page, matched how I believed kids should be handled, talked to, disciplined, etc.… The techniques that Mr. Huggins used with me were on every page. At once, I was calm. Nothing could stop me. I knew I could handle kids in the classroom easily. I would just have to keep my door closed so no adults could see me!

Sue called the night before school started. "Do you have your teacher face ready? Now, remember, don't smile at them. Show 'em who's boss!"

"Okay," I said, deciding not to tell her the truth. I was just going to be myself.

The Teacher I Was Not

I knew I was in the right place when the head principal, a huge guy and former Philadelphia Eagles football player, stood at the first faculty meeting and said, "I do not want to hear one negative word said about a kid. It is our job to create citizens of them and that is what we are going to do." The implication was we couldn't create good citizens with negative criticism.

I loved this guy. If he never opened his mouth again, that one rule could run a more effective school than ones I'd seen. He turned out to be more extraordinary every time he spoke and proved to be one of the best administrators I ever knew. He had an assistant principal who stood by his side. The two were strong, solid, and wise men. And, that's from someone who has pretty good taste in principals!

I began teaching tenth grade English under an umbrella of loving, supportive, and intelligent administrators and colleagues. The "clientele" was diverse. We had kids of senators who grew up on horse farms, as well as others who wanted nothing more than to go back to their farms and become welders or plumbers and drive tractors. It was a great mix.

My first days of school went smoothly, except for one thing. There was no air conditioning. In the afternoon I stood in front of my students with sweat literally dripping off my elbows. I saw furrowed brows with wet hair matted to the sides of foreheads. On the third day, one boy, in particular, wore a striking scowl. Had I been Michael Jordan or the Queen of England, it wouldn't have mattered. The heat made the ones who already did not want to be there, *really* not want to be there. With his image in my mind I stood with a large circle of teachers gathered at the end of the front hall.

"How are things going, Lynnie?" Everyone wanted to know, as we watched the buses pull away.

"Great! Except, what do you do with negative students in this heat?"

Several teachers chimed in with advice, but another English teacher pulled me aside.

Meet Ms. Hadway. Charming Ms. Hadway. Squinting, she glared into my eyes pointing her fingers around to demonstrate what she meant. "Negative students, Lynnie? Here's what you do: you put them in the back of the class and don't look at them for the rest of the year. That's what you do. You don't give them any eye contact. None. In fact, never look at them again. That will fix them. You'll never have a problem after that. Never, ever look them in the eye."

I was so stunned I did not know what to say. This woman later played an important part in unlocking my voice, but at that moment, I was flabbergasted. Her idea was so fundamentally different from what I believed. She gave me a few other tidbits, but this was my first clue to stay clear of Ms. Hadway.

The next morning I could not lift my head off the pillow. I had a bug. I got sick three times before winter break. I missed three days in a row each time it happened. *Ugh!* New teacher syndrome. My immune system was not used to being crammed into hallways with coughing, sneezing, pushing, shoving, sweating, spitting, smelling, slobbering, yelling, screaming, blabbering teenagers.

Ms. Hadway made gestures of friendship toward me that fall, but I was pleasant to her and kept moving. Most of her negative comments I heard came when I walked through the teachers' lounge as she and a small group of ladies sat smoking between classes. For me, she was classic literature: the stereotypical spinster, the mean school marm, the villain. Once she must have heard me in a department meeting discussing the distribution of grades in the classroom. She walked into my classroom that afternoon. "This is how you do it, Lynnie: you read off all the kids' grades. That will save you a lot of time."

"But, then all of the other kids will hear everyone's grades, won't they?"

"Sure, but what does that matter to you? It's faster and it is easier. You'll never hear one of them laughing; but if one does, you just look up and give the kid a dirty look. That will get him to shut up. Then move on."

"But still," I replied, "won't that be humiliating to kids who have D's and F's, to hear their grades read aloud to the whole class?"

"So, what? If it saves you time, so what? I'm telling you, this is the way to go," she pushed.

Ms. Hadway did something else I thought peculiar. Before I began to teach, Dave gave me some valuable information. He'd said, "Lynnie, you need to know that every tenth grade boy is thinking about sex one-hundred percent of the time." *Wow!* It made me aware of my clothing and how I sat or moved in the classroom. I found it odd that Ms. Hadway, who was large breasted, came to school braless every day. And you could tell. Every day. On back-to-school night, parents lined up at her door twenty deep in order to talk. Their teenagers complained about the way they were being treated.

Once, when I entered the teacher's lounge, Ms. Hadway called out to her friends, "Now, everyone, stop talking! Lynnie is here, and she only wants to hear positive talk, so everyone stop talking." Seeing she was trying to undermine my relationships with my new colleagues, pegging me as a Pollyanna, I said nothing. These comments went on all year. I knew she was angry that she had offered herself as a mentor, and I had not crawled under her wing.

A small miracle happened at year's end, which marked a new me. I had been working on past issues for almost two years, and one of the clearest issues I had was learning how to get angry properly. Although I knew it was still inside me, any danger of my rage spewing out had long since passed. Now my job was to *not* smile and be nice when someone was being mean to me. Words. I needed words. I had prayed for words. "Please, dear God, give me words in the moment I need them." This little end-of-the-year miracle brought them.

I did not know the last English department meeting's procedures, so I just sat and watched as the department chair's room filled with not only the English teachers, but also all of the principals, counselors, and librarians. Apparently, we were picking recipients for English academic scholarships, along with other leadership roles for the school, for the following year. It was a big-deal meeting.

More than thirty of us sat in desks arranged in a large half-moon shape around the classroom. I sat in the front row at the middle of the half moon. Ms Hadway was sitting to my left, at the end of the half-moon shape. Many selections had been made. The meeting was winding down when the topic came up of whom would chair next year's Sunshine Committee. Evidently, that chairperson went around the school, spreading cheer and sending flowers and cards to people sick at home or who'd had a death in the family.

No sooner than this had been announced, Miss Hadway leapt from her chair, her tall body towering over everyone as she literally flapped her arms up and down, "I know! I know! Lynnie should be Miss Sunshine! She's perfect! Lynnie should be Miss Sunshine. She's so positive. She'd be perfect! Let Lynnie be Miss Sunshine! Lynnie is sooooooooooo positive!" Both of her arms, now motioning toward me.

From the moment I'd seen her body make a slight move from her chair, before this extravagant leaping scene, I felt her energy and knew what she was up to. Without skipping a beat, I turned my head abruptly to the left with my face scowled, my teeth gritted, and said, in a stern, hard voice, "Stop it!"

She floundered. Startled, she said. "Uh, what?"

"Stop it!" I said again, in the same even, forceful tone, my eyes not wavering from hers, my head still positioned directly toward her.

"Uh, uh, why, you'd be perfect... you're the perfect Miss Sunshine!" she said in a sputtering tone, clearly knocked off her perch.

"I do not accept!" my voice was slow, deep, and measured.

"But, but, you'd be perfect!" her arms out, motioning to me.

Again, ever so slowly and forcefully, "I do not accept!"

Defeated, shoulders drooping, she sat. Not once had my head moved or my tone changed. I had stood my ground. My body had flushed red with anger, burned hot, but was now cooling. I turned my head back calmly to look straight ahead. I heard a voice in my head, say confidently, "If everyone in this room hates my guts right now, that is okay."

It was a moment of drama not to be forgotten. After the dead silence passed, the meeting was quickly wrapped up. I decided to stay seated, as I did not want to meet this woman on the way out. In an even voice, I turned to my friend. "So, what are you wearing to the prom?"

In all her wisdom, having absorbed the situation in full, she very calmly and coyly said, "Now what do you think?" My friend's favorite color was red, so the answer about her dress was obvious. Her eyes projected her strength, and I was back to my center. For the first time in my life, when someone was being so clearly disrespectful to me, I had words. Appropriate words. I had them in public. In front of my bosses.

I walked back to my room, sat down at my desk, and was completely done with the whole matter. About ten minutes later, my department chair, Millie, cracked open my classroom door, stuck her head in slightly, and said, "You okay?"

"Yeah, I'm fine."

"Well, I think you should come out into the hall for a minute."

When I walked into the hallway, about fifteen English teachers gathered 'round me to pat me on the back, laugh, hoot, holler – the whole nine yards – giving me the reception of a champion. I heard things like, "Lynnie, we had no idea she was after you!" and "No one ever knew!" and "Oh, my goodness, she has made my job so miserable!" and "I almost quit the first year I came here because she was so mean to me," and "I cannot tell you how many nights I have cried myself to sleep over something she said to me." Most of all, I heard, "We thought she had completely left you alone, because you never said anything." Apparently, some had been waiting, observing.

The chatter from my colleagues continued, but I felt strange and said, "I do not want to gloat. I said what I needed to say, and I would like to be done with it." Everyone agreed, and we dispersed. That night I got a phone call from someone telling me Ms. Hadway was on suicide watch. I did nothing.

The next day when I arrived at school, there was a bouquet of yellow roses on my desk, given to me by the woman who told me she'd almost quit her job when she came to the school because Ms. Hadway had been so mean to her.

Ms. Hadway did not come to school. I did nothing. A friend of hers asked me to call her to tell her I was sorry. That felt creepy, yet familiar. I did not. The following day, when I was standing outside the door to my classroom talking to a student, Ms. Hadway came and asked the student to step away. She turned to me and said, "I'm sorry that *you* were offended by what I said."

I looked her in the eye and said, "I accept your apology," even though I realized it was a backhanded one – she was sorry *I* was offended. The funny thing was she did not hear me accept her apology because she was so nervous and distracted by the students in the hallway that she had immediately turned her head as I said it. So, when she turned back, she said it again, as if she'd not gotten a response from me. "I'm sorry that *you* were offended by what I said." This time I looked her in the eye and nodded my head.

We did not speak again, yet were civil to each other. I felt no ill will toward her. I later learned she was an alcoholic. Active alcoholics do not like me.

The Teacher I Was

I took to teaching like a bird just out of the nest. I flapped and up I flew. It was the most natural job I could have. Once I watched a video of myself teaching. I was dumbstruck by one overwhelming observation: the love I had for the teenagers.

I did just what I said I was going to do. I kept my door closed and acted like myself. There was no anger in me and there was no lack of words.

I just followed my instincts. I treated students exactly how I wanted to be treated. Each class, first thing, I asked my students to pair up with someone and talk about a topic.

I'll never forget a young fellow standing up. "Hey, this teacher wants us to get up and walk around! This teacher wants us to talk!" I did. After about two minutes, I'd ask the students to sit down and Voila! They were all ears. It was the simplest technique, and yet it made the kids ready to learn. I intuitively knew they needed to move, and since their social needs were great, they needed to talk. I later heard a friend and long-time principal say, "Kids are needs-fulfillment machines. Fulfill their needs, and they will do what you ask of them."

At any other point when I needed to get the students' attention and couldn't, I asked myself, what needs of theirs, as a whole, are not being met? On the Maslow's Hierarchy of Needs chart, achievement was higher on the list. I asked myself which one of the needs below it was not being met? It was usually social. I'd give them a content-oriented assignment that enabled them to move and talk – for another two minutes. Then they were all mine. It worked every time. I just had to respect their needs.

I was enthusiastic. I was energetic. I was positive. I saw myself in every kid. I remembered well not knowing how to do things when I was their age, so I didn't call out one particular student. I didn't say, "Susan, don't do that." If Susan wasn't doing something I wanted, I'd say, "Everyone has three sheets of paper on his or her desk," or "Everyone is on page 372," or "Everyone has eyes forward."

I'd heard "Don't" all my life, so I could "Don't" very well. For about three minutes. When someone said this to me when I was young, I placed my hands at my sides. *Don't do that, Lynnie. You're not supposed to do that. Hold your hands tighter, so you don't forget. Oops, you almost did that again. But don't. Be good; don't do that again. Try, try hard not to do it, oh, please try hard, Lynnie. Don't get yelled at again.* I was always trying hard not to do the wrong thing that I had just done minutes before. It was exhausting. Had someone told me what "to do," I could have at least exhausted myself with that.

For much of my life, I wondered what "to do." I did not know. I was willing to do what I was supposed to do, yet I sat wondering. I'd look around and think, *How do those kids know what to do?* Even though I could see them doing things, I did not seem to be able to get the "order" down. I do not think I had ADHD. I believe I just needed instruction. I did not have or even know the tools to use. I taught students in my classroom under the assumption that at least one was a little Lynnie. I decided I was going to teach all the kids what "to do."

It worked. It did not matter if these were first graders or college students. Any student, who may not have wanted to do what I asked, now saw the whole class being given specific instructions, and followed along by peer pressure. Students who came from high functioning homes did it anyway and, I sensed, felt very comfortable with my instructing the entire class.

When I told harmless little stories about my life, interspersed in lessons, students perked up. I'd always wanted to hear these myself when I was a student. It made me feel connected to the teacher. I had needed more connection. I was going to give it to my students.

I already knew that a person's name was music to his ears. I learned every single student's name on the first day. I made it my job. I went over and over their names with them. I called it "The Name Game" and told students they had to learn them, too. There would be a test. I made it a point to use every student's name every class, every day of the year. I did not want one student to go unnoticed. I also wanted each one's attention, and calling their names achieved that.

I required every student to say "please" and "thank you" and to preface a question or statement with the person's name. Instead of saying "Will you give me a worksheet?" I required each student to say, "Ms. Vessels, will you please give me a worksheet?" These were fifteen-year olds. They knew how to do this. All I had to do was require it of them from the onset.

The most powerful tool I had with my students was my use of words. Now, I was an English teacher with a fairly good vocabulary, but words from the dictionary were not the words I mean, not the words I needed as a teen. Intuitively, I knew they needed real words, coming from a real person. The same words I'd longed to hear from an adult but rarely had. Words that modeled a person. I needed a model.

When a student rolled her eyes at me, I said, "I'm uncomfortable with your rolling your eyes at me. It makes me feel disrespected. Please do not do that."

If kids were talking too much, I'd say, "I'm really annoyed with your talking and I cannot seem to get my thoughts out right when you're having a conversation."

If a student was angry, "I'm sad that you think it is okay to talk to me in that tone of voice. I would not speak to you that way."

I began to realize that students respected a teacher under stress if she told them how she was feeling. Under stress, many people "act" a certain way but do not take the time to "say" a certain – simple – line. Students explained this. Once a student said, "Ms. Vessels, you never get angry."

"What do you mean? I get angry all the time. I'm always telling you I'm irritated or annoyed or bothered by something someone is doing."

"Oh, that's not angry."

They described angry teachers as coming into a classroom, slamming cabinet doors, pacing around, huffing, puffing, and saying, "Everyone turn to page 53 and read. Now!" They acted as if they were mad at the kids. The kids were too smart for this. I was. I knew I was not responsible for most of the adults' anger I saw around me. Still, it had been directed at me. Even if I had done something wrong, I believed I deserved to have it shown to me the right way. After a while, I think kids get tired of adults pretending that they are the problem. I learned to say to my students, "I'm feeling really irritated right now, but it has nothing to do with you. If you give me a few minutes on my own, I will be okay."

I got a memorable lesson on how to handle stress in the classroom. On the Sunday night before we returned to school on Monday after Thanksgiving break, my principal called to prepare me for the next day. One of my students had shot herself in the head that weekend. The next morning, I had car trouble. I had to get my car into the auto body shop and talk with the mechanics on the phone throughout the day. During the first class my deceased student's chair sat empty. By my afternoon class, I was ready to explode with built-up anxiety. I realized that as my class came in. Several kids came up to talk, needing something from me, and I realized in those moments, I was not able to cope. I said to the class, "One of my students has died and I am feeling very, very sad right now. It is just hitting me. I just need three minutes on my own. If you guys just give me some time on my own, I will be okay."

Most students were aware of the student's death. The classroom was still. The students sat quietly. I sat at my table in front of the room, quietly working, wiping tears from my eyes. It really did just take three minutes to regroup. When I stood up, I was ready to teach a lesson. There was an unspoken respect among us. It took that event for me to see how important it was for adults to communicate stress with students. I was modeling how to act truthfully under great stress.

Many times bad things happen and students see adults just moving right along. When I was young, I always wondered how this could be. *How come no one is talking about this? Not just about the shooting, but about other bad things that happen? Why am I having these feelings, when no one else is? What is wrong with me?* There was nothing wrong with me. I was human. But I was not seeing human emotion modeled. I needed to *hear* it.

I decided as a teacher I was going to model how to be a human. When I was young, if ever I heard a person use a "feeling" word in reference to herself, I practically glued myself to her. If not actually touching the person, I wanted to be close. I wanted to know that person, be around that person. *Ah, ha, a real person!* I wanted to know *how* to be a person. I decided to continue to work to humble myself in front of students and help them see how a human moved through obstacles *with words.*

I woke up one morning feeling depressed. By the time I got to school, I felt much better. I just casually mentioned in class, "Geez, I woke up feeling so depressed this morning!" Almost every eye in the room darted toward me. Not the bodies, just the eyes. Those sudden glances of many pairs of eyes all at once spoke volumes. These were teenagers. Teenagers get depressed every other day of their lives. An exaggeration, yes, but girls certainly feel the ebbs and flows of life frequently. Had they ever heard an adult say she was depressed before? In public? In that moment I "got" teenagers' simultaneous fear to reveal, yet hunger to reveal, their feelings that drive them. I knew from their writings what their feelings were, if they had the courage to write them.

I was a public speaking major. I knew how to organize my thoughts. Now I knew I'd continue to teach writing at a whole different level, using speaking and storytelling as prompts. I told little stories of my travels, like my having a baby kangaroo. I did not tell them sad stories, but I think it was the tone and the honesty within the stories that made them want to write honest stories about themselves. As a graduate student, my writing instructor said good writing was an act of courage. I knew courage required safety.

One day while my students were writing personal narratives, I moved from desk to desk, sidling up to students to edit their papers. One boy wrote a story of his mother leaning down to him at five years old, looking him in the eye, and saying, "I'm going to the dentist." She never came home. He was now 15-years old. The story ended with him seeing her at a party at a relative's house a few years later. He saw his mother laughing and talking in the next room. He just stared at her. I looked at him and quietly asked, "Did you ever talk to her?"

"No. We just went home. I never saw her again after that." My respect for him went through the roof. This simple, country boy was carrying this story while trying to make it in the world.

My big gigantic principal came into my room on a regular basis, walked directly across the room, sat in a chair, leaned down with his elbows on his knees, and, with a wide smile on his face, watched me teach. He generally sat for ten minutes. He was warm and kind. The assistant principal was my official mentor. One day while reading some of the papers of the lower level students hanging on the back wall, he said, "I cannot believe you got this out of these kids. I would never have imagined this level of student producing this work. I have never seen a teacher be so vulnerable with kids and be so effective." Another time he came in, walked around the room, ran his hands over the essays, and said, "We have got to find a way to get you out of the classroom to show people what it is you do to impact kids on this level. I've never seen anything like it."

I was proud to see teenagers respond to my honesty. I was living the life I wanted to live. I was learning the words to say in order to resolve conflicts, the words I had always wanted to hear in my own life. I was practicing them with my students. I was being the kind of teacher I would have responded to. I had been called a "chicken" because I could not lie to clients in the hotel industry. But I often giggled at the irony, thinking lying to adults would have been much easier than mustering courage every day to live an honest life in front of teenagers.

I had my hard times with a student here and there and, like every new and dedicated teacher, spent almost every waking moment trying to figure out what to do next with him. Each day, I went back into the classroom and tried another technique on this unsuspecting soul, trying to get him on my side. In the teaching world, this is known as trial and error. You will hear teachers say that the personalities of students stay the same, only the name changes. In general, it's not really the personality, but the distraction that type of personality creates. It is true, and some personality types push buttons more than others but, by the grace of God, it is usually only one or two a year.

That year mine was Frank. Frank and I butted heads. I could not get him to settle down. Day after day, I went to school using my techniques on Frank. Finally, I was exasperated and wanted administrative intervention. It was March and I'd had it. I wanted Frank removed from my class.

It seemed simple to me. All cut and dried. I'd explain it to them. *Just remove him from my class and all will be well. I can get this thorn out of my side, and everyone, including Frank, will be happy. We will be rid of each other. Surely, they will see I'm at the end of my rope.* As naive as I was, I thought once I explained to these two very smart principals all the techniques I'd used on Frank, only to see each one fail, they would surely realize there was nothing else to do but move him to another class. Fat chance.

My face was numb as they talked about making a citizen of Frank. I could not believe it. I had thought tomorrow was going to be bright and beautiful! No Frank in my room! I could once more soar as a teacher!

That is the moment I learned there is no discarding a student. I wondered just how many of my teachers had wished to be rid of me. These principals had already talked with me about paradigm shifts. I had one that day. It's the process not the product, and that goes for relationships, too. There is a saying: "Nothing's changed. My attitude's changed. Everything's changed." With the few words my principals said that day, my attitude changed. When my attitude changed, Frank changed. I now saw him as a person who, like it or not, was not going away. I'd better find something to like about him. Not just like, enjoy. I came to see myself as a person he could articulate his angst toward, someone he felt safe confronting.

That one change of thought turned me into a true leader in my classroom. Find something positive about him – to enjoy! I was going to find out the things I liked about each and every student, no matter how hard it seemed at first. I knew I had a lot of good in me as a kid, but so few saw it through the masks I wore. I was going to dig.

While leaving school one day, I saw my student jump into a car with her parent. As I passed their car, the daughter rolled down her window while the mother leaned over and introduced herself. "You are the talk of our dinner table every night."

Hmmm… Not a bad goal to aspire to, I thought.

Conscious Teaching

There was a saying among teachers: "You will never really know the good you do. You just have to trust that your efforts will help someone, some-day." To me, this was nuts. I knew the good I was doing for these kids in the moment I was doing it. I knew I was changing lives every day. I was conscious of everything I said and everything I did. There was not a mis-step in the words I used. I knew the love I had in my heart and I was extremely cautious not to hurt anyone. *If a person does not know what she is doing, she should not be working with kids.*

Soaking It All Up

Sometimes when people talk about self-help books, they seem to do it in a smirking way, as if they are bogus and a waste of time. During this time in my life, if I read only one line in a book that helped me, that was enough. I was desperate to be set straight.

I drove an hour and a half each day. I spent many of those drives riding in silence, but when I wasn't, I listened to books on tape. I had no time for fiction; these were self-help books. I listened to one book about conflict resolution written by a married couple, both counselors. They convinced me that in every conflict I have, I am fifty percent of the problem. I am not zero: *It's all his fault.* I am not one percent: *Well, maybe I did do a little something wrong here.* I am not one-hundred per-cent, playing the victim. *You're right. It's all my fault.* I am fifty percent. That information made me a smarter, wiser, more responsible person. That one line – I am fifty percent of every problem – played out in countless helpful ways in my life. I saw it play out in countless hurtful ways in other people's lives. It was the piece I was always trying to block out when I blamed someone, the same thing the woman across the table in my first Al-Anon meeting was trying to say. I was fully responsible for creating the life I had. I was fifty percent responsible for creating any conflict I had in my life.

Funny, *Teacher Effectiveness Training* taught win-win problem solving, and when these two thoughts merged, I saw the ease with which solutions could be had if both parties accepted fifty percent of the blame, and neither party walked away from a problem until both sides were equally satisfied. Watch any bitter divorce playing out and you will see what I mean.

Another book that had a profound impact on my life, one I listened to almost twenty times, was Norman Vincent Peale's *The Power of Positive Thinking*. I listened intently for ways in which I could use his simple wisdom in my life.

From Shaki Gawain's book, *Living in the Light*, I learned I'd had an intuition that I often listened to, but other times readily ignored. I looked at the times I'd ignored my intuition and examined the outcomes. From Janet Woititz's *Adult Children of Alcoholics*, I learned what felt "normal" to me living in an alcoholic home was not normal at all to others. From Sharon Wegscheider-Cruse's *Choicemaking*, I learned that one's alcoholic home could be filled with love, wonder, excitement, and happiness. The same home could be filled with horror, dismay, misery and dread. The two could exist simultaneously. This was the very reason people from alcoholic homes felt messed up. Ms. Wegscheider-Cruse also taught me that as I became healthier, my choices would become harder. I would no longer be choosing between good and bad. I would be choosing between good and good. Better. I would have to pick out the often-subtle differences.

Life with Dave

My relationship with Dave was my practice ground for communicating with a human being. Even though there were many parts of our relationship that were unhealthy, there were parts of it that were the healthiest relationship I'd had with anyone. Anyone.

I think it is very difficult to understand why two people are together. When someone obviously does not treat someone well, others wonder why the other person does not leave. I am not able to explain this for anyone but myself, and I don't know if I can do a decent job, but I will make an attempt.

This man was working so hard on himself. I knew he did not like certain parts of himself that were difficult to acknowledge. But he did. I respected that. I was trying hard to change, too. I wanted desperately to feel comfortable in my own skin. I wanted to handle myself capably in stressful situations. I wanted my words. My faith in myself, I lent to him.

People can talk all day long and never say a thing, but the words I am talking about are the ones where you make yourself known to another human being. My first attempt at telling Dave how I felt about something, we sat sideways on his bed. I looked at the wall and tried to open my mouth. He sat with me. I do not remember what it was, but I was probably trying to tell him about something he did that hurt my feelings. The point was he sat there with me. He sat with me while I quivered, quaked, and shook. He watched each tear ball up and trickle down my cheek. He did not move. He wanted to know. He did not break eye contact with me. His patience became the proof of his commitment.

When my words finally came, the earth had not moved and we were not destroyed. We were closer. I do not think that either one of us had a clue that the key to the changes we made would come in the words we were able to say. I do know it was these moments, over the years we knew each other, that were the most spiritually elevating of my life.

Often when one of us needed to say something, there was no announcement to be made. The other just sensed it and became still. That stillness cleared the path to allow it to be said. We sat looking into each other's eyes and talked. Our words came out very slowly, I think, because of how humiliating they sounded in our heads before we said them. The fear inside us was real. The desire of one to hear what the other person needed to say was irrefutable.

It was the moment with Mrs. Warren and the electric toothbrush over and over. The moment we both realized that somewhere in each one of us there had been so much harm done, so much damage. Being able to speak honestly to another human being was immensely difficult. We knew that fear and we respected that fear, but, more importantly, we respected the courage it took for the other to face that fear. These were blessed moments. So we looked into each other's eyes, opened our mouths to speak, with huge tears welling, each one dropping off the ledge when the puddle had reached its capacity.

We were having confrontations. We never yelled at each other, we never called each other names, we never spoke in ways most people think of as harsh, but sometimes the honesty was harsh. Part of the ugly of B through Y. We did not know how much truth to say, so we hurt each other going overboard. That was rare, because we sensed when to pull back. Still, what had been said added to our pain. Mostly, these confrontations were getting out our feelings. We learned where to have boundaries – in how much we could say and in how much we could hear.

When I wanted to tell him (or anyone) my feelings, in my head I heard a negative voice. "Who in the hell do you think you are? Who cares how you feel? Who gives two shits about you?" It caused me to wonder. *Why would anyone want to know my feelings? Why would anyone care?* I had to lean on another belief. *My feelings matter. I am somebody and I do count. This person wants to hear how I feel.*

I suppose there are people who naturally do conflict well and would not have any idea what I am talking about. And there are probably some people out there who shy away from conflict entirely, and under all circumstances try to avoid it. I suspect they, too, would not know what I am talking about. But to anyone who knows what I'm talking about, anyone who has attempted it, in the face of great fear, knows the greatest feeling of all comes at "the peak."

I think that when there is a conflict, initially, people quickly react in their minds, "Uh, oh, here goes…" or "I must be in trouble," or "We are breaking up now," or "I must be getting fired now," or "This person does not like me anymore," or "This person hates me," or "I've done something terribly wrong. I'm about to get blasted."

I have had all those thoughts, but the beauty of being able to shore up the courage to face those fears in present time, connect eyes, and listen carefully to what another person is really trying to say, is it's the only way to better the relationship. How else would we get to the other side? In that moment of confrontation, in the place where the fear is so great that I sometimes want to zone out, the tension is thick, my body is tingling, the hairs on my neck are standing up, my body is flushing, changing temperature, even sweating, my heart is racing. The peak. When all those things happen in the "face" of someone's words, as the words actually come out – fully – and I have not interrupted or been interrupted - then the tension dissipates, my body is not tingling, the hairs on my neck are lying flat, my body is cooling, my heart is slowing down.

When all has been said, my body returns to normal. I regain my equilibrium. There has not been an angry word said, no objects or body parts thrown, no racing over to hurt me, no spitting, no shooting, no death. I am still alive. In my life, that peak is the pinnacle of spiritual connection. It is the words of truth, the peak of fear, and the dissipating of tension. A conflict has been resolved.

A confrontation, when done respectfully and properly, only shines a flashlight on the truth. I was able to find my truth, hear Dave's truth, and connect to something outside myself at the same time. Once Dave visited a nun for counseling and he told her, "Sometimes I am drawn to do or say something that seems to go against everything that is being done or said, but there is a strong feeling in me that I am right. I can't explain it. I need to speak up."

He told me her response. "Well, Honey," she said, "that is when you are walking hand in hand with the Holy Spirit."

Years ago, there was a commercial on television about the insurance broker E.F. Hutton: "When E.F. Hutton speaks, people listen." The joke about Dave among our friends was "When Dave speaks, people listen." He did not speak in meetings all the time, but when he did, he did not waste a word. He usually went right to the nitty-gritty point. I was attracted to the truth that Dave told. But in the reality of every day, it did not make him any less distant and me any less needy. It brought us close for a time. Then we reverted back to our ingrained behavior.

We knew we were acting out unhealthy behaviors we learned in our families. Although we were repulsed by each other's behavior, we were not trying to control it, as much as we were trying to control our own. We each desperately wanted out of a cycle we'd perpetuated. We were trying to practice new ways of living. No matter how many times we failed, by my being too needy or his being too distant, the one time we succeeded drew us closer. We knew what we were doing took grit and it could only be realized with a partner who had the same determination. No matter how ugly things got, our gratitude toward, and respect for, each other stood at the core of our relationship.

Change takes time. A long time. We had no idea about all this at the time; we did not know how long we'd be emotionally inept. It would still take time to know this was a lifelong process. We wanted our lives *now*, and we continued to be disappointed with each other that we could not give or be what the other needed. I wanted to feel loved and be close to him while he wanted to be independent and have space.

If someone says something to you that is harsh and you already do not feel good about yourself, then you wonder if what he is saying is true. *Is everyone else just being nice and is this person telling me the real truth about myself?* If few people seem to speak their true feelings and you find yourself in an intimate moment with a person telling you his true feelings, you feel you are getting what you have hungered for all your life. Even if Dave's views of me were mixed with negative views he had of himself or of his mother, at least he was talking. There was no black and white to us. There were only myriad shades of gray. I was not able to cut and run. I had much to learn.

It is a very difficult chore to find out what is real, if you have never been taught to identify, trust, and act on your feelings. All of this takes time. I have enormous compassion for people who find themselves in controlling relationships. I was not yet able to let go and let my inner voice, over my outer voice, control my actions.

Dave and I muddled through, each of us willing to lose the relationship in order to tell our own and separate truths. We shared much together - his work, my teaching, nature walks, camping, all the parties we gave, and all the friends we'd accumulated. Most importantly, we knew and understood quiet suffering on a deep level and the powerful effects on a person growing up in a violent and alcoholic family. We knew the spiritual implications of violence and the determination it took to transcend it.

Going Diving

That winter I started bodyworks therapy with a well-known counselor named Patrick and his co-counselor Carrie. I eventually spent fifteen months in a room with seven women and these two therapists, learning how to listen to what my body was telling me.

My support groups had brought me to a place where so much emotional gunk was coming up, I needed a place to put it, to make sense of it. I was ready to work in a new way. Among the seven women, two of us, Tess and myself, were warriors, determined to heal at all costs.

In bodyworks therapy, you do a little talking, and then the therapist asks you to stick with feelings and, when you can pinpoint one, he asks you, "Where do you feel that in your body?" It's amazing. When asked that question, a person can actually point to it. On the first night of bodyworks therapy, I walked in and sat down in the circle with eight others. A woman said she wanted to "go first." I do not remember her saying more than one sentence. She'd had an encounter with her boss that day, and said she felt terror when dealing with him. The lead therapist asked her to lie down on the mat in the center. She was to lay her hand on the part of her where she felt the terror. She felt her stomach. In a series of breaths, "work," she was able to find the actual place where this underlying fear was stored - in the heat of her stomach. When she was able to get to it, she would be able to release it – with work. She worked hard to take herself back to times in her life when she had felt this same terror. The point was to get to the underlying belief system she may have locked in place during that time, such as "I'm not good enough" or "No one notices me," etc.... When a person gets to that hidden belief system and realizes it, she can change it. The work will let it go. Two hours later, she released it, and we left. Very few words were spoken that first night, and nothing else was accomplished for anyone else, except for witnessing what it took to release that kind of feeling. I was disappointed that I didn't get to "work," but I had much to learn before I'd "get" the process.

This bodyworks business was one of the most remarkable experiences of my life. It taught me to trust my body's feelings when I was in situations that brought them up – to never ignore a body sign – and to later go into the feeling as deeply as possible. I was supposed to find the sentence that was lurking there, trying to make me believe it. They were usually ugly ones such as "I am nothing" or "I am stupid" or "I am not enough." We were to search our bodies and find these built-in sentences so we could take control of them and later change them into positive statements such as "I am quite something" or "I am very bright" or "I am enough."

This may sound all too simple for some and it may even sound like rubbish to others. It was the basis for unlocking every bad thing that happened to me, that I'd witnessed, and that I'd somehow held onto, if only subconsciously. I knew I was a good and kind person, but I also knew there was rage inside me. I had no words to attach it to. I wanted to get it out in the most responsible way. In this room, it showed itself. I was happy to finally meet it. At first, when the therapist tried to coax out my anger, I could not feel it. It was weak. It was limp. It was unenthusiastic. I watched others get in touch with their anger, and gradually came out of denial about my own.

When someone got deeply angry, Patrick brought out the yellow pages, gave her a four-foot garden hose and leather gloves. "Have at it." The person hit and hit the open phone books. The papers ripped from the bindings and flew about the room. Patrick stood in front of the person saying the ugly core belief sentences that he believed might be hidden inside her. He was only guessing, but when he hit on the right one, boy, you knew it. The person went wild with anger – to dispel that belief. I got to see rage unleashed.

It was not scary. It was easy to watch. It was easy to see how the rage still inside the body had nothing to do with today. The reason for the rage had long since passed, but it was still real, just obviously contained – in a body. I experienced pulling up my rage with the phone book pages, lazily at first, then with gusto. The therapist encouraged us to put words with the feelings we were having. *Ah, words. Yes, that is what I need. Words.*

I began to realize long-carried pain came in the form of sentences. The way to heal that pain also came in the form of sentences. Fancy that. An English teacher being asked to put together sentences. Easy, eh? Not when the sentences were buried inside. Buried over years, it would be a process to unearth them. Each one of them. Separately.

And so began my journey of picking up the dirty, mucky, filthy, algae-filled rocks at the bottom of my well. With each one representing an incident of abuse from my past, I took a scrub brush to it. I scrubbed it clean, talking about it, meditating about it for months. When I was finally finished, I laid it down clean. Then I picked up another dirty, mucky, filthy, algae-filled rock at the bottom of my well. I took a scrub brush to that one. With each lifting of another rock, the scrub brush unleashed a barrage of cloudy, tumultuous filth, swirling around the water of my well. The way out never seemed clear. So with a humility I had never known, I picked up each rock, one by one, believing one day I would come to the end. Nothing this painful could last forever. It would not be until many years later that the metaphor of cleaning the stones at the bottom of my well came to me, but there is no better metaphor for what I was doing.

Patrick said if a person looked deeply at a painful situation from the past and felt it all the way through, she could be rid of it forever. He trained us how to feel the worst possible feelings that might come up. He wanted us to discover if we let a feeling come all the way up, did not push it back down with drugs, sex, or other compulsive behaviors, did not fight it, and felt it all the way through, it would eventually leave. It would be gone. For good.

He did not want to keep anyone in his therapy group longer than two years. He only wanted us there long enough to help us discover we would not die if we let the feelings of our past come up and move through us - out of our bodies.

It took me a long time to realize that a huge reason people act out compulsive behaviors is they believe the feelings they are trying to stuff down are so formidable they might die if they feel them all the way through. This is not a conscious thought, but the psyche will have us convinced that we are going to die. Why else would we panic so over a feeling? It was true. A painful feeling could not really kill us, but to sit with it at length, for months even, without medicating, took dedicated skill. It was a good thing I'd given up sugar. It helped my feelings come up more quickly. I could not use sugar to stuff them down, so I was able to move through the process more quickly each time, if you call months quickly.

For most of this whole discovery process, I felt like my back was up against a brick wall. There was no going back. Going back only meant living a spiritual death. I'd witnessed people comfortable enough to lie each day on the job at the hotel in D.C. I'd lived with Jack who did not tell the truth. I'd often pretended to be nice when I was angry. I'd said yes when I meant no. I giggled when something wasn't funny. I ignored a comment when I really needed to confront the person. And worse than any other sin, I excluded or avoided someone by talking about him behind his back, not having the courage to face him. Going back was not an option. With all this knowledge, I proceeded to do the dirty work of therapy. As scared as I was, I moved forward, away from the brick wall. I was committed.

A strange thing I did not expect happened during this process. Because this process was so painful, I came to have enormous compassion for people who did not work through their issues. I saw the time, the sacrifice, the dedication, the focus, the will, the energy it took from me to continue, and the true unhappiness it brought me at times. Many times I wanted to quit, and it was in these times I respected the fact that some people just may not want to do this.

I realized then many people would live and die addicts of some kind. I had to face that. My dad had been one of them. It made me think of a saying I'd run across: The ferryboat to nirvana is very small. I began to look at active alcoholics - and overeaters and drug addicts, etc... – differently. Instead of judgment, I had a gentle voice inside me. *Wow, I understand how painful it would be to give up that drink and do this work, because all of these feelings would come gushing out. And it hurts.*

Containment

I had been carrying anger for years. I was somewhat conscious of it and careful not to hurt anyone with it. I found out, though, anger that is not dealt with will generally come out sideways. It will seep out in a conversation, or in an act of disrespect. Therapy and support groups now gave me a container for my anger, a place to put it. When something happened that made me angry, but I did not yet have the words for, I learned to contain it. This container was not a place; it was more of a promise I made myself. *Okay, this makes me very angry. Right now I will put it aside. I promise myself I will deal with it. I will not allow it to seep into this situation.*

I no longer had to mask my anger. I did not have to carry it with me wherever I went. I put it away and brought it out when I had time to look at it, to delve into my past and find the place from which it stemmed. I was not going to fly off the handle, and I was not going to be a victim. I might say to someone, "I feel really uncomfortable about that, but I'm not sure why." I gave myself time to look at what was real and what was not real. Later I might return to the person and say, "Yes, I am more than uncomfortable about what you said, and now I need to tell you what bothered me." This process worked. I was able to buy time, to find my true self in the middle of this pendulum swing of emotions. I did not want to hurt anyone, but I was not going to be a doormat anymore. This was B through Y. It worked. I try to keep the promises I make to myself.

Walking Through Fire

Confrontation. Many say they hate that word. It had not been part of my vocabulary because telling someone I was mad or hurt had never been an option. Besides, a person needs words to confront. Just the thought of confronting made my psyche content to blow me up. I was not going to let her have her way.

Tess, from my therapy group, called to ask if Dave and I wanted to join her and her husband at a live concert. I was thrilled and arranged it. I spoke to Dave on the phone just before he came to pick me up. He made a cruel comment that I cannot remember. I was well aware that I could not remember it two minutes after he'd said it. In those two minutes, I told myself to write it down. *I should write this down because no one will ever believe me that he said something so vile.* So vile, in fact, any other woman would have broken up with him right then and there, never seen him again. But by the time I got to a pen and paper, I had forgotten it completely.

How can I go on a date with him now? How can I keep seeing him? How can I? But I cannot even remember what he said. What proof do I have? A woman can't just walk away, not knowing why, can she? I have to have a reason, don't I? I did not believe I could leave without proof. My feelings of shock were not proof enough. *I must keep my ears open and if he says it again, I will have cause to leave him.* All I knew was it was the most cutting remark I'd ever heard.

This happened many times in my life. Not to that extent, exactly, but I found myself still with someone, man or woman, who'd just said something very disrespectful to me. It was not name-calling. It was words put together in sentences and said in such a tone no respectable person would have stood for it. Most would walk out and never look back. Why could I not walk out? There was something paralyzing me. I did not know how to judge my feelings or the person. *Was this normal? Is this acceptable?* This was a pattern of mine. I stayed when all evidence said, *Leave!* I later came to see one reason I stayed was because leaving abruptly would have traumatized me in another way. I'd be alone and would have to grieve the person I'd left. I could only deal with so much trauma at once. I came to know this about myself.

To the concert we went. What happened next was directly related to the comment Dave made, the one I'd forgotten. The concert was beautiful, but I was a zombie. When I had to use the restroom, I went by myself, with no one else around. When I opened the restroom door, there was a large mirror directly in front of me. Boom! As quick as a flash, my whole chest was blown apart with a shotgun blast. My blood and guts splattered in all directions. Then the vision was gone.

It was the first time that happened, and it was the most dramatic in detail, full-spectrum color, and size. The mirror took up a large part of the wall. That blast would happen many more times in the course of my recovery from this stress disorder.

Many say they hate confrontation, they fear it, and avoid it at all costs. It became clear the quality of my life was going to depend upon my ability to get through conflict. I had been the physically aggressive person. I had been the sickeningly sweet, kill-'em-with-kindness, wimpy person. I had been the silent person. All these roles I abhorred. I had to learn how to confront.

I promised myself I would not let people abuse me anymore. I would stick up for myself. I'd speak up. To fulfill that promise would become the most humiliating of my tasks. It took me solidly into the middle of B through Y, the murkiest and thickest parts of my journey. Picture, for a minute, reaching the deepest part of a cave and turning to realize the way out has been blocked. The lights are out, but you vaguely remember, or, was it just sensed, another way? On your knees you crawl, groping, praying your senses will guide you, your memory will be restored. Possibly by sheer luck, you will get it right. You are willing to take any way, as long as it will get you out. Pride is not a luxury you can afford.

While delving into my past experiences, I also had to live and deal with present-time conflicts. I could not allow any more to build up. That required words. Courage. I sensed mine was not the ordinary, everyday, run-of-the-mill kind of courage needed. Leaving all drama at the door, my task to confront even the littlest problem was going to require risking my life. The gun blast was real to me. But again, no one could see it. I saw the vision of myself being blown up in the chest probably forty times, with separate conflicts in those years. It was one thing to sit alone and work through the ickiness. It was another to have people witness the obvious fear it took for me to say the simplest of sentences. This gun blast did not happen when someone *said* something unkind to me. It occurred when I began to *think about saying something back* to the person, to tell the person how I felt. It was the *thought* of my confronting someone that caused the explosion in my chest.

When the explosion happened, I tempered it. *Yes, this person could become very angry with me and he could very well shoot me in the chest. I could very well die if I choose to say this.* Then I realized that my life was nothing if it were not my own. It would never be mine if I continued to be a doormat. Having died a spiritual death, I already knew what the inside of that coffin looked like.

I have some theories about why this happened. There seemed to be a force that was determined to scare me to death – to keep me from confronting. At the same time, it seemed my psyche's way of telling me I had to deal with this conflict, because if I didn't, I knew where it could eventually lead. But why being blown up in the chest, instead of the middle of my body and arm, like my mother? I think because that is where the gun had been pointed, where the initial blow would have hit and killed my mother, at my place at the dining room table, had she not stood and turned to run. Pretty tricky, that psyche, eh?

Before a confrontation, and while seeing the visual explosion in my chest, I had a mantra. *If today is my day to die, then I have had a good life.* I made whatever arrangements I needed in order to create the opportunity for me to resolve a conflict. Then I opened my mouth. There was quivering, there was quaking, there were tears, the racing heart, and becoming drenched with sweat. There can be a contorting of the face when a person cries that causes a person's looks to change and be quite scary. I knew my face went to those eerie places sometimes. It was incredibly shameful. Each time I imagined saying my feelings, I heard a voice say, "Who in the hell do you think you are?" and "Who cares how you feel!"

Some people think it negative to imagine beforehand the possible bad results of a planned confrontation, but in my case it worked. I could name what I was afraid of: being laughed at, spit at, hit, kicked, stabbed, shot, or killed. Why not imagine a great result? I was not there yet. Before I could move forward, I had to sit and visualize the person hurting me, and my either making it through alive, or being okay with dying. If I was going to be traumatized by someone, I was going to prepare myself mentally. *Then* I was able to visualize the positive results.

I had disastrous confrontational moments, but many triumphant ones. Some people thought I was a nutcase, but no one hurt me. The beautiful part was most people sat there with me while I quaked. They let me take my time. God bless those people because they helped me become well. My spirit, my confidence, my self-love, all lifted after walking through what I called fire. I had made it to the other side of a confrontation. The blast did not thwart my efforts.

It is easy for me to sit through conflicts today. I am not afraid. I do not run from them. I welcome a conflict because I see going through it is often the only way to get to the other side of a situation, to improve it tremendously. Having ineffective communication due to a lack of a necessary confrontation is something I fear more.

Leaving the Bathtub

If I was to practice the therapy I received, I needed a peaceful place, to lie down and feel. The most natural choice for me was the bathtub. I'd lie there for an hour or three with my hand on my stomach, asking for guidance. As if on cue, just when I thought it had been a huge waste of time, a great rumbling churned in my stomach. This is when my sentence, the code I was to crack, was given to me. In the moment I got it, the great knot in my stomach broke in two and out poured the essence of what it carried. It was indeed a sentence. It was as if I was sitting again in Mr. Huggins' office convulsively crying, feeling the glass shatter, the twigs break, a hundred stabs, shooting every which way. Anything hard became soft. Draining the water, I curled into a fetal position. I heaved and cried, keeping my hand on the spot where the sentence had emerged. I held it there until it dissolved into nothing. I lay there conscious of the drops of water, ever so slowly, evaporating from my skin. Sometimes I allowed myself to sleep the good sleep right there in the tub.

There was a safety for me in the bathtub I could not explain. One day it occurred to me: that is where I'd been before all the turmoil in my life began. I think there was a part of me that wanted to pretend none of this ever happened, a part of me that wanted a simpler life, wanted a family like others. I wanted to be in the tub. For years I used it as my haven to explore beneath my surface. Long ago I had left the bathtub beginning a horrific journey. Now, leaving it was as if the water carried my pain and all its debris down the drain. I stepped out of my porcelain chamber a newer, softer person.

July 28, 1988

I was always ready for anything when I walked into my bodyworks therapy room. July 28, 1988, was no different. I was ready to "work." Tess was also always ready to work. On that day, one person talked and went through the process. It took quite a while and I realized I might not get any time that day. Then Tess went. She was always really intense and stirred a lot of stuff up for the rest of us. She worked for a while and, when there was about twenty minutes left, the therapist asked her to continue if she wanted. She glanced over at me and said, "I think Lynnie has something she needs time for. I'll give my time to her." Bless her.

The therapists asked me if I wanted to speak. I wanted to draw. They gave me markers and poster paper. I began to draw out the shooting – the actual pictures, where I was standing, where everyone was in the house. I told the story. I described every detail, opening the door, stepping into the blood…. A curious and beautiful thing happened. I was telling this in the voice of a seven-year-old girl.

Wow! Where'd that come from? I heard myself continuing on, looking up at everyone as I drew. Reaching for different colored markers, big splats of my tears dropped around me. My eyes filled with a steady and continual volume of tears. Everyone sat still. "My little girl" told it in far fewer details than I would have as an adult. She was certainly not as articulate. I saw myself draw a big eye with a black dot in it for my mother who was crouched down on the hearth. I heard myself describe Mom as a "scared little bunny rabbit." I can still hear that little-girl voice coming out of me. Wonder upon wonder. I was telling the story as if to someone who'd asked me about it the day after it happened. Twenty-one years had passed and I was still that little girl.

When my story was finished I looked up at everyone and something just as remarkable happened. I looked into each of their eyes, one at a time, and asked, "Was this bad?"

"Yes," the first person said.

I turned to the next person, "Was this bad?"

"Yes," that person said.

I went around the entire circle. I looked into each person's eyes and asked the question, "Was this bad?" I studied faces carefully and drank in their answers as each one of them affirmed that it was indeed very, very bad.

Patrick, the lead therapist, said, "Yes, Lynnie, it was bad. It was horrible. It was never supposed to happen to you. You did not deserve something so bad to happen to you. It should never have happened. And yes, it was a very, very bad thing to have happened."

Several things happened for me on that day. First, I got to meet a little child inside me, a part of my soul that somehow lives. I've not seen or heard her since, but I know now she exists in my psyche. Everyone who was there that day got to meet her, too, and more importantly for me, to witness her. Next, I could never have predicted the question I directed to everyone afterward. I did not know it burned inside me. Since no one really talked about the shooting, I must have believed people thought it was not as bad as *I* thought it was. Everyone went on with his or her life while I remained haunted. I'd thought something was terribly wrong with me. That, itself, affected me tremendously. *Why could I not deal with this, get over it, and move on? Why was I so trapped by this scene from so long ago? Why did I still see it, hear it, feel it?* On that day, I learned it was indeed a very bad thing that had happened and I had every right to pursue healing it. With this session, the full meaning of validation hit me.

But the greatest thing of all and the reason the date was burned in my head, was from that day forward, I no longer had the flashing pictures. For over twenty-one years at that point, I had any one of these images flash in my head at least three times a day: my father with the gun, Mary standing there yelling "No!" while my mother crouched behind her, my Mom's lifeless body leaning against the refrigerator, her dead hand on the floor, our legs sticking out over the couch, my Uncle George's head rolling back with laughter, or my father's black silhouette coming through the door. I heard the sounds of my bare feet as I lifted them from the sticky floor. When I tried to make myself feel better, I saw the sparkling punch bowl or my Mom's lips reaching up to kiss me from her hospital bed. No matter where I was, who I was with, there had been no rhyme or reason for these images to appear. It was not like something in my everyday life prompted it. But the next day, on July 29, after telling the story to my group, the images didn't come – and they never came again. I had told the story, just the way it had been, out loud to people, looking into their eyes, them looking into mine – for the first time. Eye contact and words worked to heal me once again. I was 29 years old. Free.

My healing was in the details. By then, I'd said many times in groups, "My father shot my mom." But that sentence did not include the details.

That day with the group, I told exactly what happened, step by step. Had I not told the details, I believe those images might still be with me. If anyone reading is looking for a better plug for therapy, I don't have one.

Mary's Home!

Mary came to visit me for eleven days. We had a ball. We spent 24 hours a day together, gallivanting all over the place. I took her to meetings with me. She loved them. She drank in the words people said. When she tried to give me sisterly advice, I asked her not to and told her if I found enough people to listen to me, I would be guided to my inner voice. I'd figure out on my own what I needed. She was ecstatic! "You mean I never have to give you advice again? I'm free? I don't have to worry about you? I don't have to tell you what to do? How wonderful!" Her burdens in taking care of her little sister were lifted.

It had been over two years since we'd left each other in Karratha. We had not been close there. When Mary got to Virginia, she told me of her divorce from Don. He'd been an alcoholic and a liar. She'd found garbage cans of whiskey bottles in the shed out back. He became foul with her, and she'd had enough. All this happened after I'd left. She had been working long hours, managing a golf club, managing their finances and dealing with an active alcoholic – all while I was there. I thought she did not want to spend time with me, but she had been under great stress.

Mary and I went to outdoor concerts, amusements parks to ride roller coasters, and visited friends. One morning, when she picked up a blanket to fold, I took it out of her hands, flung it over my shoulder, and said, "Come on! We're not doing an ounce of housework while you're here!" She laughed, and we ran out the door to play.

One night while sitting in a restaurant, the subject of money came up. Mary said in a hard tone, "Well, you know, Lynnie, you never have been good with money."

I put my hand up and told her to stop. "Mary, I'm not comfortable with you talking to me like that. That puts me in a box. Whatever way I have been before, I do not want to stay in the box you have made for me. I feel scared when you talk to me like that. I cannot have you talk to me like that again."

That was the only boundary I ever had to set with Mary. She is a smart gal and got the point. Instead of her seeing me as she always had, she now saw a different person. We were equals.

While visiting, Mary saw the kindling box that I had from our family's belongings. Our dog Laddie had chewed on it and the marks were still there. She became sentimental and asked me if she could have it. "Yes!"

She broke down and cried, "Lynnie you are such a generous person. You are so easy to love!" *Easy to love? I'm easy to love? How nice that sounds.* I had another sentence to carry with me. Mary also told me I did not have a mean bone in my body. I found that amazing. I knew I had loving thoughts toward people, but I had still not forgiven myself for hurting people when I was young. *Mary knows me better than anyone, so I'll believe her.* I began to wonder about kind words. *How can kind words lift me so fully? Why am I so needy for them? Is everyone? Why are kind words said so rarely? Why are they not said on purpose and out of the blue more often? Why does it take so long for people to say them? Why? What holds us back? They seem so easy to say. So powerful to hear!*

Our family had the tradition of standing and waving to a person who was leaving, until the last possible second, just in case, the person leaving took one last look back. When it came time for Mary to leave, we cried for three days. When I put her on the bus, our faces were bright red from crying. Seeing her sad made me want to do anything I could to help her. There was nothing I could do. We had to leave each other. I walked back down the aisle and got off the bus. We stood there looking at each other through the window, crying. I waved to her until the bus drove out of the garage. Then I noticed through the bus station window, that her bus would still be in view from the glass front of the station. I ran as fast as I could and burst out the front doors just as Mary, still looking back, was taking in what had been the last vanishing moments of me. The second she saw me pop through the door waving my arms wildly, she burst into a surprised and joyful smile, bouncing up and down in her seat, clapping. It was beautiful.

Dave had gone to a weeklong graduate course for personal growth and called me to say, "It will be years before I will be able to have a good relationship with a woman." He broke up with me – after two years. It was hard to hear, but Mary had just left and I felt strong. I always gain strength from my visits with Mary.

Harry

My landlord, Harry, needed to sell his house and move to San Diego to live in the "Grannie flat" his daughter built for him. I helped him. I told my friend about the sale of Harry's house and he bought it, allowing me to move into the cabana in the back. I had a yard sale with Harry's stuff, we packed his belongings onto a 15-foot rental truck, attached his Mazda to the back, and I drove him and his mangy cat to Coronado. We had a blast!

I was to visit Harry and his daughter and grandkids a few times over the next few years. He and I sat and talked and watched TV like always. I stayed in his granddaughter's room, took walks, went to the beach, and had a California vacation. I remember once overhearing his son-in-law question our relationship. Why would a thirty-something-year-old woman want to spend time with a seventy-something-year-old man? I felt sad to hear our relationship through his perspective. My answer was why would I not? Harry was my friend. I loved him and he loved me. We enjoyed our friendship. He was probably the grandfather I never really had, so polite and kind. Being with him was constantly a this-is-how-men-are-supposed-to-treat-you lesson.

Why was that so hard for his son-in-law to understand? Did he not place value on quality relationships? Did he not respect Harry enough to believe that someone would want to be his friend? Harry is gone now, but I would not trade my time with him for money.

Being Still

When I moved into the cabana, I had a beautiful little place to myself. It had a huge fireplace that took up a whole wall. In my self-discovery, one thing continued to disturb me. I was still a social butterfly. I was moving too fast. My life was spinning.

One day I noticed if I wasn't getting my usual barrage of phone calls from friends, I panicked. This was not healthy. I allowed many things to interfere with my inner voice. I had one, but how could I hear it if my life was so fragmented by the constant interruption of phone calls? Why was I afraid to listen? I decided to conquer that fear.

I placed a blanket in front of the fireplace to remind me to lie down whenever I walked past it. Not sit down. I knew sitting would be too easy for the butterfly in me to flutter away. I'd be up as soon as I got uncomfortable. I was learning that in order for me to be well, almost everything I did to get there was going to make me feel uncomfortable.

Whenever I found myself going too fast, I laid my body down on that blanket. Not my bed. My bed symbolized sleep. I wanted this to symbolize that I'd caught myself – my body or mind – moving too fast. It worked. I did this for over a year.

I realized I was accepting far too many offers to go out with friends. I had no real reason to say no. I decided my mental health was reason enough. I put an "X" on two days of the week, and when someone asked me to do something, I said, "I can't Thursday. I'm busy." It was not a lie. I was busy with myself.

I forced myself to stay home alone with no plans. I made a no television rule and decided to see what I was made of. I walked around my apartment, bored at first, then sat down and read. I walked around, sat down and wrote. Then I got up and cooked. Later, I pulled out photographs and started putting them into albums, played soft music, built a fire in the fireplace, went to bed early, and woke up in the morning well rested. I'd had a date with myself. I saw how much I needed this time. I put a third "X" on my calendar for each week.

I was happier. Calmer. Later whenever I found myself buzzing – having too many thoughts running through my head – I sat in a chair by the window. If I found myself vacuuming and trying frantically to get things cleaned up, I stopped and sat down. Whenever my mind or body was moving too fast, that was the perfect time to stop. Overwhelmed with stress? Stop. Everything. The stillness made me well. Big discovery.

I sat and looked out the window. I watched the sky, the birds, and the waving of the tree branches. I waited until I came to a place where everything felt right with the world. Sometimes I sat in that chair for hours. Then I got up and moved along. I often heard people saying sitting for hours, or meditating, or even exercise - took too much time. I had a singular goal: to be well. It did take time. Time I was willing to invest.

Funny, while running around fast, feeling fragmented, I got little done. When I stopped running and dug my heels into the ground to rest, later when I got up, I was more productive than ever.

Depression

If there has been one theme of depression in my life that overrides all others, it is that I have been sad not to find many people who experience joy like I do. Another theme is being shocked and befuddled by people who say mean things.

Because depression goes hand in hand with posttraumatic stress, I learned to look at it totally differently. First, realizing that depression is part of the grief process and a natural phenomenon and function of the body, I decided to accept it. When I got overwhelmed and too many things physically, mentally, and emotionally were piling up, I *let* myself be depressed. For three days. I decided not to fight it. Instead, I wallowed in it. Wallow. Wallow. Wallow. Three days.

Secondly, I used my time wisely. When I was depressed, I saw that was the time I needed to pray and meditate the most. *God just wants to spend more time with me. He wants me all to himself. I am to be with him now. In prayer.* I said the same thing to myself when I got sick. *God just wants to spend more time with me. I need to slow down and be with him.* Amazingly, this was the time I heard my inner voice most clearly.

When I changed my thinking around this, it helped me when I saw "it" coming - the overwhelming feeling of depression or the "coming down with something," an illness. I began to be able to slow down and fend off depression or sickness. If and when it did set in, I began to notice what brought it on. How could I be so capable, so strong, and so productive on many days, being able to accomplish a series of tasks, far more than expected of me? On other days, I woke up barely able to accomplish one? I was heavy, lethargic, dull, and weepy. What was this? What caused this?

On the days I felt depressed, I realized I had a *lingering conflict* that had not yet been resolved, generally with a person. I used the time to visualize the conflict being resolved. I was back untying the knots from my youth again, only now I was using words in my head. "I feel very uncomfortable with what you said to me." I watched how the person responded. I saw the worst scenarios played out in my head. I saw my words fail. "Too bad for you!" There was still too much angst and blame in what I imagined saying. No matter how much I tried to conceal my blame in my "I" messages, no one believed me. I remembered how difficult it was for me to hear the tone of someone blaming me in anger. The overwhelming message was I was not a good person. I blocked the person out and shut down. I clung to my inner voice that was nice to me.

If I was going to get my point across, to resolve this conflict, I wondered how I would be believed. I turned to what *I* believed. I took myself into the place I found in Judy's eyes and listened to the tone of Mary's voice. I had seen a huge conflict resolved by words. Words from a little girl to a maniac. I knew it could be done. But I also discovered they could not be my words. They had to be words the other person could hear. I had to trust what I knew. I had to pray for love.

What I found was I was being asked to do something outrageously difficult. *No way! I cannot!* I was shown I had to humble myself before the person and say how I felt. Not just the feeling words I was practicing, but how I *really* felt, bringing myself into present time, into Judy's eyes, where everything was real. Loving. As I saw this in my mind's eye, I heard the words come. When the words came, the chemistry in my body changed, the knots in my stomach released, the tightness in my shoulders slackened. I was relieved of pressure. The confrontation now held no fear. There was only one answer to clear my path to good health. I had to go in peace to this person, holding him or her in love and the highest regard. Having visualized this resolution, I was certain the right time and place would present itself to resolve this conflict. I popped out of bed and was on my merry way, depressed no more.

Being Spotted

That summer I had an Interpersonal Relationship course with a large group of graduate students. I'd heard there was a bigwig from my home county's main office in the class, but I never knew who he was. Our delightful professor led us in many full-class discussions. Like everyone else, I gave a presentation on the last day and, while we were having refreshments afterwards, the man walked up to me. He looked me in the eye, pointed his finger, and said, "Any time you want to work in my county, you just give me a call and the job is yours. I want you working with our kids."

The Whiteness in the Mirror

Although my break up with Dave initially hurt, by the time he came to our Sunday meeting a month later, I was fine. After the meeting he followed me to my car and asked me out. I replied "No." We had broken up. I knew I loved him and did not want to be tempted to do the back and forth thing like some couples do. It was best we not see each other.

He was surprised. He'd previously had a lot of control in our relationship, and now he did not. He stood there as I began to back away. No, he wanted to see me. No, I told him. He asked me three times. I told him "No" each time. I was firm but kind, and drove away.

I had a beautiful little experience at home that night. I was singing at the top of my lungs. As I waltzed around my cabana, uplifted and strong, I passed a mirror. My face was as light-colored as I'd ever seen it. Glowing. Angelic. There she was, an angel, looking back at me. It was not the face of an angel superimposed over my face. It was my face, just very, very white. I had just said "No" to Dave in a powerful way. I had walked away guilt free. That was a first for me. Growth. Apparently, I had not done this alone - or at least, was not celebrating it alone. Looking into the mirror, crying and singing, mascara ran down my face. Even that didn't block out the overpowering whiteness. Not glowing like a light, just really, really white skin - my complexion had never looked this way. My happiness went on for hours and whenever I thought about this later, I figured that was the night I met my angel. She was awesome.

Two Reactions

I had no idea what I would find beginning therapy. I soon realized I had guilt because all I'd done on the night of the shooting was stand and scream. Mary had been the one who took action to save Mom. She stood in front of the gun and, most importantly, she had words. I did nothing. I did not know I carried these feelings of guilt.

It helped when people explained that I needed to forgive myself for doing exactly what a seven-year-old girl would do. Mary had acted inordinately brave. I loathed the victim stance I still assumed when threatened. My paralysis repulsed me. I wanted desperately to protect myself, to repair the part of me that was broken. The more I longed for those skills, the more I realized I hated myself for being so inept. I learned that before I could go forward, I had to go back and love that little girl who froze twice that night. *Love her? I can do that.* Loving her the way she was meant to be loved, with patience, changed my whole perspective. I began to be kinder to her than I'd been with anyone. Compassion oozed from me like a loving parent. Soon there was no room for repulsiveness and self-loathing in my forgiveness toward this little girl.

Master's Presentation

That fall, I took my last courses to finish my master's degree. In one course, I took a hugely detailed exam. I studied and prepared for weeks. When I sat down to take the test, I wrote 23 pages of essay answers. I aced it. In the other course, I gave my master's presentation on what I do during the first month of school to assure that I have the students' attention and, hopefully, respect until the last day of school. I had only completed two "first months" of school at that time, but I was convinced there were specific steps to build safety, trust, and a loving atmosphere in a classroom where kids could thrive. I had that belief then and I have that belief now. I see many teachers engaging in power struggles for an entire year. My presentation was about investing time in the beginning of the year to build rapport. My students continually tell me through the years that I treat them "like people." Speaking my beliefs in public about how to treat kids respectfully was the most natural part of who I was. This was not stressful for me. It was exhilarating.

Ingrained in me was the decision I'd made on the night of the shooting. Looking at that piece of furniture that night, I decided I was not going to respect an adult just because he or she was an adult. I was going to give students in my class something to respect. I had needed time, attention, comfort, and a feeling of safety. If there was one kid in my classroom looking for that, I was going to give it. The beauty was I discovered all of them were looking for that. There is a saying "Kids don't care how much you know until they know how much you care." No matter how much curriculum and technology have changed, slowing down and taking time to get to know kids is a teacher's best discipline tool.

My First Roll of Butcher Paper

My bodyworks therapy was nearing a close. I had gotten in there and wrestled my beast. Wearing leather gloves, going into the ring, I'd had a crowd cheering me on. The warrior in me "worked" at finding my rotten demons. I found many of the sentences they had carved in stone. I was now convinced that if I explored my rage, or any feelings I had, I would not die. I could do this. Patrick had taught me well.

One day I began a fascinating technique. I'm not sure what led me to it. Maybe because I like to write, draw, and color. Maybe because I'm a visual learner and want to "see it." Maybe because I had butcher paper available to me. Maybe because of the initial drawing of the shooting I'd done with my group. For whatever reason, one day at home, I was feeling particularly pent up, my feelings bubbling over. I did not know where to turn. I was filled with anger and rage and had a hundred pictures running through my head. I decided to get them on paper. I rolled out butcher paper. I picked up a black marker. I began to draw the images in my head. Not of the shooting now, but of the images and words I could see and hear from my youth. The countless acts of violence I'd experienced or witnessed - cruelty of words, the angry faces, the shoving, the pushing, the hair pulling, the slapping, the punching, the rug burns on my back from being dragged around by my hair or feet, the seemingly-permanent overlapping and multi-colored bruises on my arms, the constant cowering, the wincing in fear, throwing my arms in front of my face, the waiting to come out when it was safe. I wrote all the words I could remember hearing. I wrote all the angry words I now had to say back to these people who still filled my head so many years later. I cursed and cursed some more. I wrote and I drew and I wrote and I drew. I screamed and cried. Twenty feet and an hour later, I was spent. My strength drained, I had purged this round from my soul. I drooped. Then I dropped into a pile at the end of the drawings that were still attached to the giant roll of butcher paper. I was weak and my body had moved from feeling heavy to light. I curled into a fetal position on the paper. Becoming utterly silent, I lay still for a long time. In the stillness, I "got" the sentences that all of this anger had brought up. The feeling I had from way down deep in the pit-knot-ball-rock of my stomach was, "You are worthless. You are filth. You are the stupidest person alive. You do not deserve to live. You should be dead right now. You do not deserve to be on the face of the planet." It was a small miracle. There it was now. I could hear it. From inside the rock in my stomach, it was hissing.

Upon the realization of what I'd carried all along and had not known, I wept. I lay in this pile of myself, weeping convulsively. Heaving and crying, screaming, and gasping for breath, I sobbed until my mouth was dry and all the fluids from my saliva, tears, and sweat had soaked onto the paper. I cried until there were no more tears, until my heavy breathing finished and there was only silence. In this second round of silence I lay – too weak to lift myself again. The rock in my stomach had broken up and disintegrated from my convulsive crying. Every heave had been like a sledgehammer to stone. Beaten, weak, and empty again, I lay there still. And in that period of silence, another miracle: a voice! It was not someone else's voice using the word "you." It was my voice. I heard, "I am full of worth." Startled by this, I perked up and immediately grabbed the black marker. I drew a vertical line just after the terrible wretched stuff I'd written and drawn – the stuff that had given me the messages that I was worthless. I drew a thick black line, a wall to separate the two. Now, in neat handwriting at the top of the page, I wrote the opposite of the ugly sentences I'd found: "I am full of worth." I gave it its own line. I continued. I still have that poster from that very day and here is what it said in its entirety:

"I am full of worth.

Many people love me.

Many people believe I have a lot to say.

'You have been my teacher, Lynnie.'

'I have learned the most from you.'

I love you, Lynnie.

I have a right to say how I feel about

anything, regardless of how others

will react.

Dave may leave me but he will not shoot me.

If he leaves me, I will be okay.

I am a loveable person.

I am a miracle.

I am a miracle of God.

God loves me and he will move

me to speak when he is ready for me to.

God, please remove my defect of becoming

a victim and thinking I am worthless.

I am full of worth."

Affirmations

I always read that if you use an affirmation daily, it can change your life in 21 days. Well, I guess that is for fairly well people, because changing my life, coming to believe I was a good person, took years.

I know some people will laugh at this and dismiss every bit of the "affirmation" business. Al Franken on "Saturday Night Live" did a won-

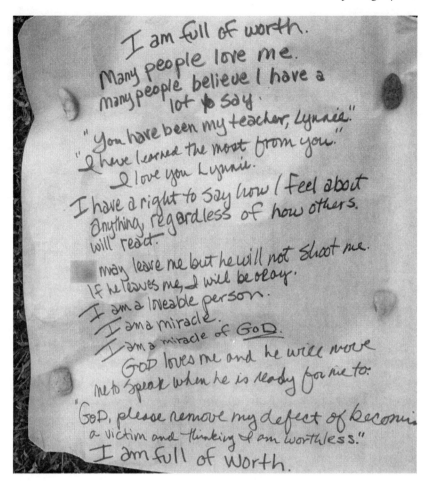

I am full of worth.

Many people love me.

many people believe I have a

lot to say.

"You have been my teacher, Lynnie."

"I have learned the most from you."

I love you Lynnie.

I have a right to say how I feel about

anything, regardless of how others.

will react.

___ may leave me but he will not shoot me.

If he leaves me, I will be okay.

I am a loveable person.

I am a miracle.

I am a miracle of GoD.

GOD loves me and he will move

me to speak when he is ready for me to:

"GoD, please remove my defect of becoming

a victim and thinking I am worthless."

I am full of Worth.

My first end piece

derful job with making great jokes looking into the mirror saying, "I am....... and people like me........." That skit alone did a powerful job in helping people dismiss affirmations. But sarcasm comes from a Greek word, which means "the cutting of flesh." If there is a major tool that healed my life, aside from having other peoples' eye contact, while they listened to me, it is affirmations. Finding the negative sentences about myself that I did not know I was carrying, and turning them around and into positive sentences, ones I could begin to believe, worked. Period.

The Silence of Violence

Physical violence comes with a multitude of words, and it comes with no

Long rolls of anger...

words at all, simultaneously.

For example, when I was picked up by my triceps, I saw an angry person coming at me, huffing and puffing, twirling me around, grabbing and pinching my arm, getting just the right hold on me so he would not drop me. I was lifted, and carried, sometimes for good distances, while my legs dangled in mid air. I was silent out of fear or screaming out of pain. When he got to our destination, I was thrown forcefully several feet away from my carrier, onto whatever was there – a floor, a carpet, the ground. No words. But plenty of them.

It is the "no words - but plenty of them" that have to later be "found" somewhere deep inside the body and then re-worded. The scenario of my being picked up, carried and thrown had many unspoken words: "You are not worth my taking the time to tell you what I want you to do. You are not worth my taking the time to walk you over there myself. You are not worth my looking you in the eye. You are not worth an explanation. You are not worth my giving you instructions. You are a nuisance and a nobody and I need to get you here to this spot, no matter how you feel, what you think, or who you are. I do not care who you are. I only care that I get you over to this spot so that you can do this chore. That is all you are good for. I can do anything to you I want. I can hurt you and no one will hurt me. I can hurt you and you cannot hurt me back. I can hurt you and no one will stop me. You mean nothing to me. Nothing.

...to get to the end pieces

Nothing."

I could go on, but you get the picture. I'm sure if given the chance the person would not have actually said or even meant these words, but what matters is the unspoken quality of violence. The person receiving the violence gets to make up any words available in her psyche. The point is that violence is anything but silent.

As an adult, I learned in a psychology class, in order for a child to feel like he has a sense of control over his life, it is important to tell him where you are taking him. Brilliant! The advice was even if the child is still too young to comprehend your words, tell him you are moving him to another place. Apparently, even garbled words are better than no words!

Behind Glass

I wrote on that first strip of butcher paper the week before my last body-works therapy session. They knew it was my last night and asked me if I wanted to say anything or "work" on anything special. On top of our laps, I rolled out my first butcher paper product. It went clear across the room. I showed them what I'd done. I let them look at it and read parts of it. I told them about the process by which I came to write and what had happened in the end. I showed them the separate affirmation part at the end – after the dark line had been drawn. This part I had detached.

"Now, I want you all to help me tear it up, sort of like a ritual – to get rid of it. Let's rip it to shreds!"

That did not go over well. Each person stared, one opened mouthed, and that woman spoke. "I could never tear this up. This needs to go under glass in a museum." They could not participate in tearing up something of such value. *Value?* It took me a moment to get it. This was a record of my abuse. And my healing.

Somewhat disappointed, I took it home with me. The ending affirmation part, I hung in my bedroom to see and read each day. I wanted it there to remember the awesome feeling of the voice inside that had fed me the *new* lines. Knowing this loving voice was there, deep down in me somewhere, was fascinating. Equally fascinating was knowing there were very negative voices I'd been carrying with me all along. I had them stored inside my rock. Something told me this was a valuable process, so, as I left this very comfortable group, it was with this butcher paper tool. I believed it was a very similar process to that of the group's. Only now I'd be doing it alone.

Whenever feelings came up and needed some other place to go, I lugged out the butcher paper and markers and went at it. The process was always the same. What was different now was that I began switching colors every time I changed topics. All of the acts I recorded were presently perceived hurts mixed with past events. I could see how my victimhood had been a magnet for abuse. I began with whatever I was mad at that day, realizing my anger was far greater than warranted. Slowly, as I wrote, I was able to pinpoint abuse from the past that gave me similar feelings to those I was currently having. The fourth step in a 12-step program asks the person to go back and find a place in the past that also brought up similar feelings. Whatever needed to come up, I let it flow – curse word after curse word.

Whenever a person's anger is greater than the situation warrants, I think of my rolling out the butcher paper and going at it. I trained myself not to attack anyone in present time, to go back into my past, get words to use, and later confront the situation when I knew I was on an even keel. No one deserved rage. I kept that battle private. The warrior in me battled the demons inside. One of my favorite lines from Mahatma Gandhi is "The only demons in this world are those running around in our own minds, and that is where all our battles must be fought."

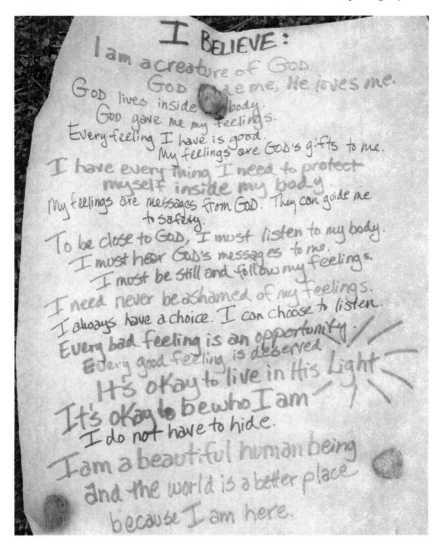

Various end pieces I hung on my bedroom wall...

Each time I wrote at least fifteen feet worth of garbage. Each time I gritted my teeth as I cursed and wrote. Each time I was fierce in my revenge toward whoever hurt me. I crawled along breathing heavily enough to get it all out, sweating, clenching my jaw, being unbelievably angry. Each time, I hung my head in defeat and despair. Each time I wilted into a fetal position and felt the pain. Each time in that silence, the rotten sentence I carried cracked the concrete knot in my stomach. As it surfaced, it was like a drowning sea creature sucking in the open air

End piece

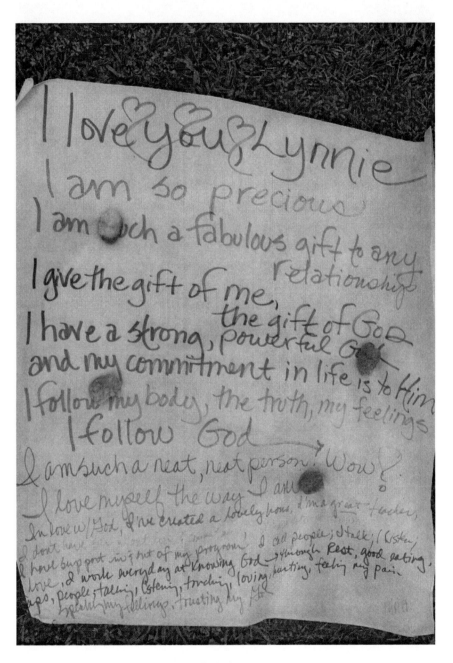

End piece

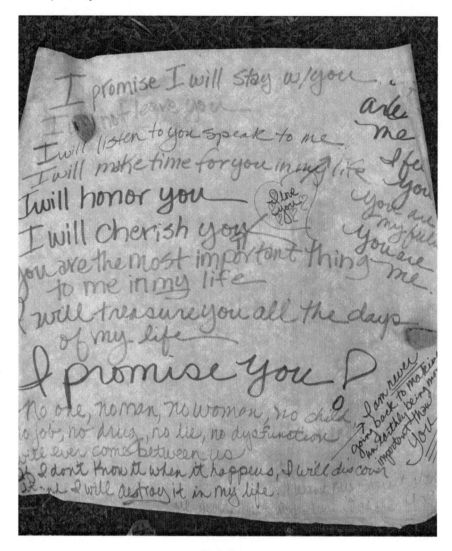

End piece

that was its doom. Upon reading it, my convulsive crying and sobbing started. Getting the sentence, I wrote it down, wanting to be exactly clear about what unconscious, but now unearthed, thought had haunted me. I wanted to know the slippery, slimy beast. The sight of it spilling out of my handwriting broke me. There it lay in living color in front of me. I met it. I could no longer deny it. I did not want to deny it. I wanted it out in the shining light of day. When I saw these words staring back at me, the sadness of a hundred broken hearts melted me into

Rolling out the butcher paper after twenty years

my fetal position. The heaving started and broke up the rock inside me. When I was soaked, exhausted, and spent, the silence came again. I lay in my sweat until I dried. If I could see it, I was free of it. I had beaten it. But beating it wasn't winning.

Winning came as I lay there in the quiet. Like the sun peeking up over the sea, tiptoeing in as soft as a whisper, came the new sentences – always positive and always the exact opposite of the negative ones I had literally just cried out. The truth of who I really was came pouring out of this new channel I had opened and cleared. Slowly and powerfully, I lifted myself back to my knees, picked up a marker, and defiantly drew the line. I began to write the new words I heard. Every line was a different color. Every sentence replaced the slain and silent beast that emerged after twenty feet of paper. "I am a beautiful child of God. I deserve to be here. I am full of love. I am the essence of beauty and love. God is all around me, wanting the best for me. I am willing and grateful and free. I am free to love everyone and all parts of me. I am happy to be alive. I deserve to be here."

This beast was dead. Days or weeks later, when the next one came along, I went back to my knees, rolled out the paper, coaxed it up and out, met it, and replaced it in the same way.

The "affirmation" ends of the "battlefield" posters, measured approximately three feet by four feet. I hung them on my bedroom wall. Six posters of that size fit. As new ones came, I replaced the old. I used this method to purge, to understand to re-work, and re-write my negative thoughts. *My script. I was rewriting my script!*

In keeping with what I was told in my group that day, I kept each one. I did not look at the long pieces again. I kept them rolled up and boxed away. During several moves I was tempted to throw them out, but out of respect for how far I'd come, I did not. I unrolled the long posters and matched them with their short counterparts for the first time in over twenty years, to take pictures of them for this writing. I did not need to unroll them for myself. They were a part of me and, like I'd seen them yesterday, I knew exactly what they said.

The Bug

That Christmas I was alone and single. Dave called me out of the blue asking me to drive to Michigan to have Christmas with his family. I told him no, that I was in a lot of pain. I would stay home and feel it through. He was perturbed and told me it sounded like I was addicted to pain. I was just committed to getting through some "stuff." I wanted to make it through the holidays by not reaching out to him. There was no sense in our getting back together. He'd made it clear he was unavailable.

In January he called again to ask if I'd accompany him to help him pick out a suit. I agreed. Once there, he took me by the hand and told me we weren't really there for him, but rather to buy me some nice hiking boots. It was a sweet surprise. He made it clear he wanted to be with me. Soon enough we were dating again, but I was uneasy. Then something happened that ingrained in me a new way of thinking.

My commute to work was through the beautiful countryside. There was very little traffic and few lights, a smooth-flowing ride. On one of these morning drives in late January, a fierce debate roared in my head. Thoughts were stirring, buzzing in me, and there were two different sides.

The side on the right was a fast, buzzing and mean-spirited tone. "He's using you. He only wants you for sex. He hates you. He's using you. You're a fool. You're a fool! He's using you!" This voice was mean, and negative. But the side on the left - and seeming to come from somewhere out there in the green countryside, said in a very loving and kind voice, "No, that is not true. Dave is a wonderful man. He loves you. He is a good man. He is everything beautiful that you think he is. Everything is okay." This voice was gentle and positive.

The buzzing sound on the right began anew. "No, no, he hates you. He's using you. He only wants you for sex. You are such a fool. He is using you!" Mean and negative. Again the voice on the left tried to soothe me with "Dave is a wonderful man. He is full of love and that is what you are attracted to. He is a precious child of God. He is warm and loving and funny. That is what you are attracted to. All is good. He loves you." Gentle and positive.

This went back and forth in my mind several times. All of a sudden, I glanced up and to my right. Between my rear-view mirror and face appeared a gigantic bug, hovering ever so slightly, in an up and down movement. Its large wings flapped in the same vibrating rhythm as the negative voice. The bug had large black eyes, the size of apricots. Its body was light brown and hairy with strips of black running through the hairs. Its claws were curled around with shreds of hair hanging over them; its tentacles flopped downward. Its wings flapped violently as it repeated everything I'd just heard. Only this time, I could see the negative words in the form of this bug.

I glanced away. When I glanced back, it was gone. In that flashing second or so, that bug taught me the world.

For some reason, even though it was the bug that appeared real, I came to see whatever that creature said as false. If ever I was to hear a mean-spirited voice inside me or from someone else, I knew immediately it was false and I could ignore it as the pest it was.

The voice I could hear but not see, the one coming from the left, from the beautiful green countryside, I decided was real. The calmness, the love in the voice convinced me it was the truth. I saw given any situation, a person could hear two voices and so had two choices. I knew then that I never had to make a choice again. I knew which one of those voices was real. Anything good, kind, and loving was the voice that was real, and therefore the one to choose.

I knew I had made this choice before. Seeing my choices between the bug and the countryside took me back. All of a sudden, I was standing on the blood-splattered floor, screaming. I was looking back and forth at my dad's vicious attempt to murder my mother and then into the loving eyes of Judy. I was being given the message again unmistakably and powerfully. A gross and gruesome bug versus a flowing and peaceful landscape. This was a clear sign to make a clear choice. Choose love.

In no way did I take this as an indication that I was supposed to stay with Dave. It just meant that stay or go, I could choose to see the best part of a person. This one true thought was my lesson. The bug had shown me this. I did not have to be tempted by ugliness or negative talk. Anything negative I heard about another person, I knew instantly not to be true. I made a decision to approach that person from a standpoint of love and generosity. I even began doing this with myself. Any of the things that had been said to me in the past that I still carried, I looked at as untruths, made-up fiction. The thing I could see – my father with the gun in Mary's face – although it happened, I was shown it was not real, not the truth. The gentle, loving peace I saw in the floating space of Judy's eyes was real. It was as if I was being shown that the negativity playing out on earth was an illusion and only the loving feelings we have are concrete. It seemed incongruent. What was intangible was real; what was tangible was not real. It was a choice. Choose the love in Judy's eyes or violence. Choose loving thoughts or the bug.

New Year's Resolution

In the Washington Post I found someone's one-line New Year's resolution: "This year I am going to systematically eliminate any relationships that are not good for me." *Really? You can do that? Wow! I did not know that.* That got me thinking about all my relationships.

I was not ignorant, but to demonstrate how little control I thought I'd had, I once thought I had to stay with Jack my whole life. I had known he smoked pot when I met him, and how was this any surprise? People said, "Well, didn't you know he smoked pot before you married him?" This question implied that since I was so stupid for going ahead with the wedding, I was stuck with him. I had to buck up. What was really skewed is that it never occurred to me I could ask another human being *not* to do something. I thought I had to accept whatever anyone else did, that it was his life, and I just had to deal with it the best I could. I had seen my mother move on with her life, not being angry at my father, just accepting what had been done to her, dealing with it the best she could. I had *no* idea in those seven years being with Jack I could have actually said, "Jack, I do not want you to smoke pot anymore."

Making the Call

That spring I called the school supervisor I'd met in class the summer before. I told him I would like to be hired as a teacher in his county. He said, "Okay, Lynnie. You have to do this and this and this and this and this and..." rattling off about nine steps I had to take in order to apply.

I said, "It is all done. I have completed every step." Before I'd made the call to him, I spent about two months gathering the paper work and completing the task of applying to his county.

"Oh," he said. "Well, then, you just sit tight. I don't know when it will be, but I will find a position for you here." I was thrilled. Although I'd be leaving my wonderful first school, this would be a smart move for me, both professionally and financially.

Party

For five years, I'd gritted my teeth studying and working for my master's degree. Four of those years I kept saying, "When I get this degree, I'm going to have the biggest party I've ever had – and I'm going to invite everyone I know." But by the time the last year came around, therapy had changed me. I decided I was not going to invite everyone I knew, just everyone I loved and everyone I knew loved me. This was different for me. I was still being nice to people who did not treat me well. I used this party as a way of helping me separate those folks. I sent out invitations without a shred of guilt.

Dave asked me if I wanted to use his large house for the party. My administrator from the university put on his cap and gown and presented me with my degree. Eighty people were there. There was no alcohol, but a lot of food, laughter, and love. In fact, even years later I'd run across friends who'd been there that night. They'd say something to the effect, "There was something wonderfully different about that party. I don't know... it was just the feeling in the house. I don't know what it was, but..." They could not put their finger on it, but I could. That house was filled with love.

The Reason for Using a Shotgun

I was in the library with my tenth graders. They were hunters and look-ing up information on different types of guns. I asked them to tell me about shotguns. What did they know about them? I learned from them that a shotgun was meant to scatter pellets. It was meant to shoot a bird out of the sky, to wound it, not necessarily kill it, just get it down. It had a large range. *Wow, a shotgun is meant to wound a bird flying in the sky and from a far-off range? Not meant to shoot a woman at a three-foot range across a dining room table? Wow.*

Shortly after that I saw a movie in which a man was standing in front of a white van. Another man shot him with a shotgun at close range. In a second, the bloody shreds of who he'd been splattered all over the white van. In living color, there was the effect of a shotgun blast to a body. For months, I struggled with the idea. *What kind of man shoots someone with a shotgun?* I could not figure it out. A shotgun shatters a person, anything in front of it. *Why not a bullet? One hole? Or two bullet wounds? Had it been a bullet, maybe it would have missed. And if it did hit, it would only be once, perhaps not doing serious damage to an arm or to someone turned sideways. Why obliterate the person? Why rip the person to shreds?*

Later I was camping with some friends, one of whom was a former soldier. When we were alone at the campfire, I asked him about guns. "Why would a man use a shotgun to kill his wife at the dining room table?"

"It was probably the only thing he had."

Yes, that was true. Mom had cleared out all the guns in the house, afraid my father could be violent. She remembered seeing the shotgun under the wrapping paper on the floor, but left it, thinking it was only a BB gun. *The only thing he had. Interesting.* This is how I began to piece together the puzzle. *Why had this happened? How had this happened?* I needed answers. Of my siblings who stood with me in the aftermath of the gun blast, I was the one who remembered the devastation so clearly. The details of color, flesh, words, screams, lights, sounds, steps taken. Even with the clearness in my mind, there were holes. I was curious to fill in the holes. I wanted a complete picture. I set about interviewing the people who'd walked across my childhood.

Angel

All my readings about healing trauma, coached me to be very loving to myself. One piece advised me to stand in front of a mirror, light candles, and put lotion on, while telling myself nice things. This became a ritual. I had worked with a mirror many times, so I knew the mirror was a powerful tool for healing. I was to learn it was the most useful of all.

Standing in front of the mirror, I became very conscious of the muscles in my body – my neck, arms, stomach, and legs. And as always, very conscious of my eyes.

That year I had a troubled teenager in my classroom that became very disruptive in class during the spring. I later learned her parents had informed her in March that they were getting a divorce. Her anxiety was coming out in her treatment of me. She was abusing me in front of the students. *Why was I allowing her to do this?* I could not figure it out. I did not know how to handle this student, so she was, essentially, walking all over me. *What was happening here? Why was I letting this happen?*

As irony would have it, the student's name was Angel. Angel had bleached blond hair with dark black roots and wore dark black mascara and eyeliner every day. She wore a spiked dog collar around her neck, spikes around her wrists, and black clothes. She was not necessarily dressed in Goth, more like a rough biker babe. She chewed her gum like a cow and was loud and obnoxious. She happened to be in my honors class, so she was no dummy. She had been this way all year, but her behavior in the spring became abnormally abusive and directed straight at me. I was afraid of her. On one particular Friday afternoon, Angel walked out of my classroom, and in the loudest voice possible, she screamed, "Ms. Vessels is a fucking bitch!" I told the principal, which felt like a weak attempt at solving this problem, but I could not figure out what else to do. I was confused about why I was afraid of this girl. My fear of her was apparent in my inability to discipline her. She got away with much more than others. Then a thought that had been only a glimmer came to me in full view. *I am teaching my students how to be abused by a person. By not stopping this, I am showing them that this is okay.* THAT was simply not acceptable. I determined I'd take myself through the bodyworks process that weekend. Hoping to get to the bottom of why Angel had such a hold on me, I began my work that night.

I rolled out the butcher paper. I sat and thought and thought and

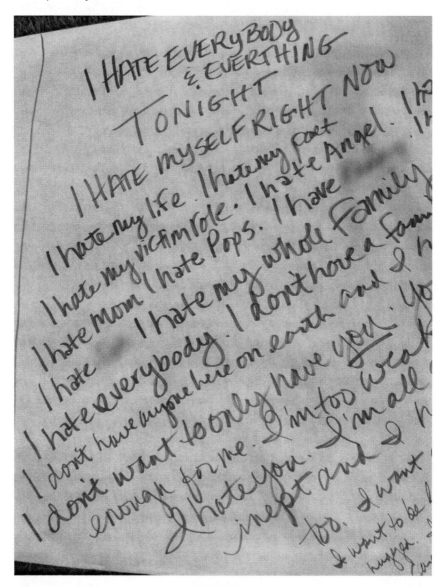

I HATE EVERYBODY & EVERTHING TONIGHT I HATE MYSELF RIGHT NOW I hate my life. I hate my past. I hate my victim role. I hate Angel. I h... I hate Mom I hate Pops. I have... I hate ___ I hate my whole family I hate everybody. I don't have a fam... I don't have anyone here on earth and I h... I don't want to only have you. Yo... enough for me. I'm too wea... I hate you. I'm all... too. I want... inept and I h... I want to be ... bigger.

Ugly hate

when feelings came, I began to write. But this time, I found myself going over to the mirror, too, and saying the angry words I'd been writing. An interesting thing happened. As I came closer to the mirror, in my angry eyes I recognized people in there I'd never seen before. People who'd hurt me flashed through my eyes. The anger in my eyes, reminded me of theirs, especially family members. As I got closer and was saying the angry words they'd said, I noticed it was my way of fighting the person. I saw this person reflected back to me. I met him, eye to eye. I cursed him down, ranting. I gritted my teeth. I snarled. I flexed the muscles in my body and watched them flex in the mirror. I was a warrior, ready to kill, but now I was standing strong, no longer on my knees at the butcher paper.

Each time I went from the butcher paper to the mirror, I saw a person and screamed that person down. Then the next person showed up. Any person who'd ever criticized me or hurt me physically, mentally, or emotionally, I now saw in my eyes. I cursed each of them. As I screamed, these people of my life passed through my eyes. Then I saw her: the little redneck girl *I'd* been. It was Angel. I had been Angel. Not exactly her, but the feeling she brought up in me was the same. I hated her. I had hated myself. Then and there, I faced her. I hated the bitch that I had been. I'd been mean, nasty, and surly during my teenage years. I had never forgiven myself. I pushed her so far back, I'd not even remembered her – until she showed her face to me. Seeing her clearly now, I was flooded with memories of all the people I, too, had hurt. Oh, this little girl in my classroom was a gift! I'd been so angry *at* others, I'd blocked off all the hurt I had *caused* others. Now, I had a more realistic view of where to direct my anger.

I went back to my compilation of tangled and enmeshed hurts. Then to the mirror. Standing there, I began to untie the knots. Again. I went through the list of each hurt. Each brother, each sister, myself now, then to my mom, and finally to my dad, and there I was staring down the gun myself, just like Mary. I found the courage to stand there and grit my teeth and snarl at him. Then something even more amazing happened. All of a sudden, those people at whom I'd been screaming, including my dad, were no more. What was left was a demon. Only a demon. Like a dragon, a monster, not a family member, and certainly not me. I could only see this demon in my eyes, as if there to block out the realizations that would make me well, blocking out the love I'd once been shown. Now the real fight began. It was and is the most gruesome I have ever been, a state in which you never really want to see yourself, unless of course, there is no way out other than to bring up this demon. Nothing else had worked like this to bring up what I desperately wanted out of me. *The only way out is through.* I knew this and continued.

When I felt the feelings come up, I made sure my windows were closed, my curtains were drawn, and the music turned up loud. Most times, when I got to the demon, I stripped off my clothes and flexed my muscles at "it" and roared, growled, and snarled. I became as fierce as any demon that might try to hurt me. With this demon, I was the rage I had always feared. Here, my rage was warranted. I knew this was the true - and only - entity that deserved my anger. I was protecting myself in the most primitive way. This fight did not belong to anyone I ever knew. It belonged to a demon, some evil thing out there that lurks in all of us, possibly. Again, I thought of Gandhi's quote: "The only demons running around are those in our own minds and that is where our battles must be fought." And here was my demon – in my eyes – made to look like everyone who'd passed before me in my life who had hurt me with a cruel comment or some demeaning gesture - and then looking like no one I'd ever known.

It was comforting to finally learn with whom I was angry. It was nothing real. This demon was like the bug in my car – buzzing, mean, negative and fierce, but not real. But, at the same time, it was the very real demon that had consumed my father, and possibly a force that consumes others who commit acts of heinous violence.

Exhausted, I went back to the butcher paper or slept or ate or rested. Then I went back for another round. It was draining, but I had a mission. I wrote a tremendous amount. Answers had come. There was another thing about Angel that scared me, aside from how she looked, acted, and reminded me of me. It was something more tangible. One day I'd seen her at a gas station sitting in her boyfriend's truck. He had a shotgun in the rack, just behind his head. It was these rednecks *and their gun* I was afraid of.

Each time I went to the mirror with anger, the anger became less and less, the swearing became less and less. Power came in the form of words – words that were acceptable in public. It was a long process, but the rage moved toward anger, and the anger moved toward stern but acceptable, confronting words. Little by little, I came to know the words to say back to someone disrespecting me. Little by little, I met this demon, not with fear, but with dignity. Dignity with a snarl. This method taught me not to blame the mean *person* but his *demon*. It would be to this demon I addressed my words.

By Sunday evening, the glare in my eye was the look that defines the expression "if looks could kill." I was determined to kill this demon in this little pipsqueak of a teenage girl. She was not going to get away with abusing me any longer. With that, I would no longer be teaching my students it was okay for someone to treat them the way she'd been treating me.

The next morning, I looked into the mirror one last time and said aloud, "If today is my day to die, then I've had a good life." Gun or no gun in her boyfriend's truck, I was no longer afraid if it meant that I could stop this permanently. I was as calm as I'd been in a month. Armed with words.

I'd used a standard prayer: "Dear God, I know the time has passed now for me to have had the courage I needed, but please, when the opportunity comes for me again where I can use that courage, please give it to me in that moment. Please let the words be yours. Please let me not hesitate to tackle the problem at hand in the moment it needs tackling." My prayers worked. When I got to school and went about my day, I had truly forgotten about this girl.

Then it was time for her class. Students filed in and Angel took her seat with the rest of them. I sensed her anger and heard her making comments under her breath. At the start of class, I handed back previously taken tests, which now revealed grades. Wearing a dress and high heels, I walked around giving a paper to each student. I handed Angel her paper and turned to continue. She gasped at the sight of her grade and began to badmouth me to others. In one fell swoop, I turned around, leaned my face toward hers, and gave her a glare to stop traffic. "I have had it! I have had it with you! That's it! Talking trash about me? Those days are over. That's it. I've had it. That's it! You can trash yourself, trash your life all you want, but you - *will* - *not* – *trash* - *mine*! I have had it. Over. It is over. Over! That's it!"

I felt comfortable with what I'd said, however much I surprised myself with those words. (Words like "trash" I had never heard myself say.) I turned around quietly, walked to my stool, sat down, crossed my legs, cleared my throat, and began to go over the test I'd just passed back. Angel, in the far right corner of the room, sheepishly raised her hand half way and, with a quivering lip and shaky voice, she stammered, "May, may I go to my counselor?"

With the same snarl and glare I'd used moments before, I spat out each word slowly, "You - may - sit - right - there." Her hand went down. I took a deep breath and looked around the room. In that moment I took in a feeling I would come to experience often in my teaching career, although I've never had to resort to such harsh words again. In that moment, I knew, beyond a shadow of a doubt, every student in the room felt safe. I had put a stop to Miss Nasty and I'd just proved to my students it was okay to protect themselves. Best of all, I was not a wimp, a doormat, or a victim! There was lightness and ease about the room from that moment on. I began to go over the test with the students. I'd gained my students' respect. I never once had a problem with Angel again. And I was still alive.

When I had seen myself in Angel in the mirror, I had to face several things about myself. I had been an abuser. As an angry teenager, I had hurt people with my attitude. I spoke to Angel in the tone I intuitively believed I needed, when I'd been acting like a bitch back then. She had been testing me. She continued to test me, until I set a very clear boundary.

I had learned that each person from a dysfunctional home might eventually play out all three roles – the victim, the rescuer, and the perpetrator. It had been easier for me to think of myself as a victim, even a rescuer. It took this jarring for me to remember myself as a perpetrator. That was the last thing I wanted to look at. But it became crystal clear that I would *never* be truly well until I looked at that side of me. Seeing the side of me that had hurt people with my anger, my manipulation, and my frustration of not having words, knowledge, or understanding, turned out to be the largest component in my becoming a healthier person. It is often called looking at one's shadow side.

Walking through the Angel experience was key. I had no idea I needed to forgive myself for the anger I'd carried and the harm I'd caused – to others and myself - *just* for being angry for so long. I began to forgive myself for all of it.

It became one of my core beliefs that every abuser wants to be stopped. This made it easier to confront people. Instead of feeling fear of the abuser, I began to feel compassion for the person, because he'd not yet met enough people who confronted him for being such a jerk. Or, in other words, confronted him with the pain he was carrying. I wished more people had confronted me. Being an angry teenager can take many forms. Dave could not believe his parents did not get help for him. They did not think it odd enough to seek counseling for a teenage boy who barely said a word in the home.

With more insight into the teenage mind, I began telling my teenagers that it was very normal and natural to be angry. If they were not angry with adults, they would live with them their whole lives. They would not go out and get married and have kids and the whole human race would die out in a generation. I told them it was my job to teach them how to communicate their anger effectively, to get results. I began to see troubled students, teenagers, and adults not as mean jerks as I'd often heard them called, but as people carrying a great deal of pain. As a teacher, I considered it my job to find out what the student's pain was, or at least acknowledge it was pain. I knew the anger was not a reflection of who the person was.

To a student who was angry with me, I took in the hallway and said, "I do not know why you are angry, but my guess is you have a very good reason to be. Someone has hurt you. You don't have to tell me what it is, but it is my job to help you separate the pain someone else has caused you and what you want to communicate to me right now." It became my experience that if I acknowledged this much to most teenagers, I got them on my side. I would have loved for someone to tell me point blank that my anger was from being hurt, and I probably had a very good reason to be angry, because I did.

To Cry is to Soften

My anger was lifting. This process was working for me. Each time I got angry, I trained myself to ask where I'd felt this feeling before. I allowed myself to be irrational, to let it take on a life of its own. I continued to do the writing on the butcher paper, falling into a heap, standing in front of a mirror, glaring down anyone I found in my eyes. I grew strong. I learned these demons were not real. No one could really hurt me if I was strong enough to know they did not exist. I was a good person who occasionally got things wrong, messed up, or made mistakes. I was not worthless, and I did deserve to exist on this planet.

In this training, I learned there was indeed evil, which lived in me in the form of hatred. This hatred built up when I saw someone do something I knew to be unjust. I saw this hatred in my eyes, and I chased it out. "Get the hell out of me and don't come back! I will kill you if you come back! I am stronger than you! Don't even think that you can live here anymore! Get out! Get out!" Always, always, my eyes came back into a calm, clear state. I lightened my load. This demon was going to have to find another home. It was not welcome in me anymore, and it knew it. It was giving up. My negative thoughts about myself decreased. I was becoming too confident for this demon to infiltrate my thinking.

I did not want anyone to have to witness my dramatic struggles. Not that I was ashamed of it, but I think it would have been confusing. I now knew my rage was separate from who I was, and I treated it like that. I knew that no little girls on earth should have had to witness what we witnessed and then have their father come sleep in their bed. That was wrong, and I had every right to be angry. Unfortunately, I had a lifetime's worth of anger that needed to be dealt with. I did not know if anyone else, aside from those in the group I'd left, was smart enough to be able to understand that this anger was not really who I was. I did not want to hurt anyone in the process.

When I drew the line at the end of the butcher paper rolls and wrote the affirmations, those were the words I was beginning to believe: "I am a beautiful person. I am a precious child of God. I am meant to be here. I have a place in this world. I have so much to offer the world. I am here. I am me. I am a good person, through and through." The end part of the purge, I was willing to share.

Mary had instinctively stared down the mouth of the lion and could say "No" to almost anyone after that. Her channel to her natural instincts was clear. Whenever anyone made Mary mad, she gritted her teeth, scowled, and spit out words for about ten to twenty seconds. Not curse words, just true, clear words of anger. Then it was over. When Mary yelled at me like this, I thought she hated my guts in that moment. But in a jiffy, she was finished and all was fine. My instincts had been thwarted. I was an adult before I realized how dysfunctional I was at saying "No" or displaying anger. But gratefully, I had a model for it. My father had been transformed by Mary's fierce never-wavering anger, then her gentle words. I wanted to be strong enough that the meanest, nastiest person attacking me could not take me off my center.

In a favorite book, I found a story about a woman who wanted to help heal her angry husband who'd just come back from war. She went to the local medicine woman who told her she could make her loved one well, but the woman would have to obtain an important ingredient. The medicine woman needed a hair from the throat of the crescent moon bear. The woman set out on a treacherous journey through the brutal elements, miles and miles up a rocky mountain. She placed food out for the bear for days, a little bit at a time. When she finally came face to face with the crescent moon bear, it opened its mouth to devour her. Although its great roar made the woman's bones hum with fear, she stood firm. She loved and she was determined. In the bear's mouth, she saw the world. All of the seas and the valleys and the mountains and the oceans of the world glistened before her. She saw in the bear's throat, all of the peacefulness on earth. The bear was impressed with her courage and did not eat her. It allowed her to pluck one little hair from its throat and be on her way. When she got down the mountain and handed over the hair, the medicine woman turned and threw it into the fire. In an instant, the hair disappeared in the rising flames. The woman was aghast! She had gone through all of that torturous work to get the hair, so how could the woman destroy it like this? The medicine woman told her to review all that she had learned from her journey of retrieving the hair from the angry bear. Now, she was to take this knowledge and apply it to the man she loved.

I froze when I read this, the part about the woman seeing all of the peacefulness of the world. That is what I'd seen in Judy's crystal clear green, little-girl eyes on the night of the shooting. I'd been in this state, my bones, too, humming with fear at the scene before me. But beyond my fear and in Judy's screaming eyes, I saw that peace. I had seen the seas and the valleys and the mountains and the oceans of the world. That's what grounded me.

I was never entirely the woman who stared down the throat of the bear – until now, when I did this work in the mirror. This demon in the mirror was my bear, my gun. My dispersing it from my eyes, my screaming it down, gave me back a part of myself I'd lost. This made way for the peace that belonged there. I longed for the balance of being able to protect myself while being able to love fully. All the fierceness coming out of me made me incredibly sad. I was a woman and I did not want to be a warrior. So the softening came with every tear.

Crying had a very real place in my life.

As I grew stronger, whenever I felt the urge to cry, I never tried to stop. In fact, I became a cheerleader for tears. If I was in pain, it was as if I could step out of myself and become a cheerleader, one who knew wellness came with the purging of stress. "Go for it, Lynnie. Cry it out. Get it out of your system. Don't hold anything back."

Often times you see someone cry and a person nearby says, "Don't cry; don't cry… Shhh…." When that was said to me, it made me stop crying, alright, but I knew something important had been stopped mid stream. I knew it was my job to find a wiser person who was not afraid of tears. I learned to be that wiser person, to say to someone crying, "Go ahead, and cry it out. Get out every tear. And when you get home, cry until your tears are gone." I have always found this soothes the person. Sometimes people need permission to cry. There are few things more intimate than listening quietly but with pierced attention while someone cries, not interrupting him, and waiting until the last drop is out.

Later when I told my story to audiences, people wondered how I spoke so clearly about such a difficult topic, even adding humor to my presentations. "The reason I can tell you these details without crying is because I have already cried a zillion tears. You do not have to feel sad for me. The sadness has lifted."

When I have a crying teenager on my hands, I may say, "Why don't you just go home today, throw yourself down on the bed, and bawl your eyes out?" Through her tears, the child will look up at me and smile. It is against our norm to say this in our society, but I think a teenager's intuition hears the wisdom in this. Stress comes in blows to the psyche. Tears release stress. They soften the blow.

Words to Stories
Out of my tears came words. I was getting the words I needed for situations in which I found myself. There were fallback words I could rely on like "uncomfortable," if I found myself mute. Better to say something than nothing.

I thought deeply about words. What were the words that I, in my younger fragile state, could have heard from someone? When someone confronted me, I felt under attack. I blocked out every word the person said! Not because I wanted to. My fear level was so high around conflict I became a statue. No resolution would have been possible. I began to meditate and picture the fragile person I was. What words could have possibly been said to me that would have caused me to stay in my body and listen, rather than jump out and become numb?

I learned that when confronting a person, he might feel threatened if I used the word "You" instead of "I." I practiced using the word "I." Then I had to attach a feeling word to it. If I had to attach a feeling word, I had to figure out how I felt! Ugh! This was difficult. I worked at it. I attempted. I mustered courage to "stay in" a situation and deal with it, to not walk away. I meant to stay grounded.

Learning to pray for things in advance became helpful. I prayed to stay in present time and to have words if a conflict came up. I made it my occupation. I challenged myself to not let moments of opportunity pass. I determined that my feeling infantile around words would not arrest me forever. B through Y was ugly, but I got a sense it would not always be.

Through *Teacher Effectiveness Training*, I learned that before a person learns a new communication skill, she is unconsciously unskilled, not knowing what she does not know. When she learns about it, she is now consciously unskilled; she knows now what she does not know. As she begins to practice it, she becomes consciously skilled at it, thinking about it each time she uses it. She then moves into the area of being unconsciously skilled. She does it without thinking. This happened to me. All the skills I was learning from day one in support groups were overlapping each other. I continued to become conscious of the areas I needed to work on and I gradually became unconscious about the not-so-new skills I had learned to incorporate in my everyday life.

I told stories in my meetings of the exciting, and sometimes unusual results I had resolving conflicts with my new words. One day at a faculty meeting, a librarian stood and told all of us NOT to put toner in the copy machine ourselves, but to leave and she would do it the next morning. None of us had been trained to change toner and we were all making a mess of things. One night, I was at the copy machine and "out of toner" flashed. Without thinking, I immediately opened it and pulled out the toner, some of it spilling around me. As soon as I did this, I knew exactly what I'd done. I cleaned it up and wrote the librarian a note of apology. The next morning, I could not find her. The copy machine was fixed, so I sat and waited in line to use the machine. At one point the librarian walked in, marched up, leaned over me, and yelled, "I told you not to do that! Didn't you listen? I told you!" Her veins popped out in her neck. I listened to her yell, but then she turned and shuffled away.

Before she got to the door, I said, "Wait. Will you please come back here?" She was surprised, but turned around and walked back. I said, "I understand you are mad at me. I know I did something wrong and I am very sorry. I knew exactly what I'd done when I did it. You have every reason to be mad at me. But please don't walk away from me. I'm okay with your anger, but I'm not okay with your walking away. Will you just sit here for a few moments, so we can finish this and be done with it?"

Surprised, she sat down quietly, stared at me, and said, "I guess I did overreact. I was just so angry. I'm not angry anymore."

"I'm not angry anymore either. Thank you for sitting down with me so we could finish." When she left, I felt completely whole. There was no avoiding each other or talking about each other behind our backs. We'd finished what we'd started.

These were the stories I told my groups. It seemed each day I had a new one. People said they had no idea what to expect next. I loved this conflict resolution thing! The visions of being shot were becoming fewer, the fires were dying down, and I was walking through them with tools. That was the difference. I was happy I had words. I was getting better at resolving conflicts.

My school counselors told me they liked when I was at a parent conference because angry parents did not intimidate me. I got to the heart of the student's problem right away. The truth came out without having to go around the barn sixteen times. My department chair said I reduced her predicted five meetings to one because I was so forthright. I said things others were thinking but no one had the courage to say.

I had a secret. My courage was nothing without the right words. I was building a vocabulary I could live a life on. Everyday I had hundreds of opportunities to use my new words in my classroom. I was always experimenting. *What words can students hear best? What is the most nonthreatening way to say this? How can I get them more fully on board with me? What words do they need from me right now?* Every time I reached out to kids with kind words, a little part of the kid in me healed. I was starting to really love who I was. To my friends I told the stories of the words I'd strung together to get results from students, colleagues, friends, acquaintances, store clerks - whoever crossed my path. I now saw conflicts,

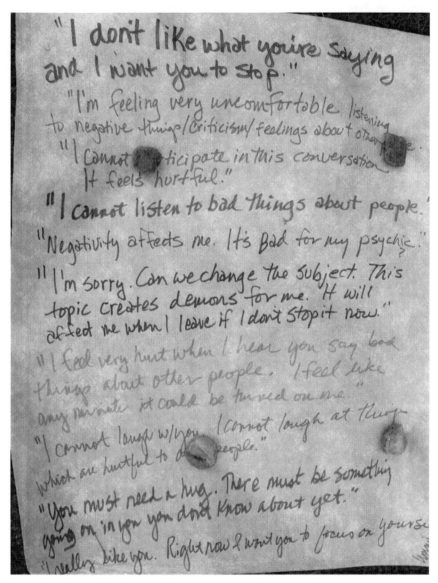

Finding words

big or small, as adventures. Some were hysterical, some terrifying, but to my friends, all were entertaining.

I once heard that you can gain as much insight about yourself as possible in therapy, but if you do not go out and use that information to "do things differently in the world," therapy has not done its job. I was doing things differently in the world.

A Powerful Guide

Along with the stories I told, I added my revelations during my experiences. After meetings, people said, "I read that here..." and "I read that there..." and "That is a quote from..." and "That is a line of scripture in the Bible." I had not read what they pointed out. I discovered it through meditation and prayer, and walking through difficult emotional problems. I began to believe that if everyone worked through terrifying situations, we would all come up with similar revelations, insights, and epiphanies.

These comments gave me confidence I was on the right track. I believed more than ever we were all taking slightly different vehicles, trying to get to the same place. My world began to open up to the major religions of the world. I saw people guided by different faiths. I listened intently to other people's spiritual and religious beliefs. I was open to what anyone said, although I felt closed off to people who claimed their faith was the only way. My favorite bumper sticker became: "God is too big to fit inside one religion."

For many who first entered 12-step meetings, the word "God" made them cringe, myself included. It was obvious to us newcomers that the God we'd learned about growing up had failed us. We'd been relying on ourselves, yet were disgusted with the pickle we found ourselves in. Why else would we be sitting in a meeting with strangers - unless our lives were a mess? I skipped over the word God as quickly as I could while reading the 12-steps. I could not even say the word. For the first year and a half I felt put off and removed from any talk of God.

Learning about feelings made sense to me. The one firm belief I began to rely on was that I came into this world naked and I would leave this world naked. Whoever made me, whoever created me, he or she gave me everything I needed to survive right inside me. When I was nervous or in danger, my heart raced, my glands perspired, my pulse increased, and the hair on the back of my neck stood up. When I was content, my mind was calm. I felt joy.

I had my feelings. I began to think if I were in Outer Mongolia, I could communicate to someone with my facial expressions, my gestures, my body language. We had the same feelings. We were both humans. I could use my feelings to guide me. I saw the danger in that, too. I'd followed my feelings and had gotten myself into all sorts of trouble. Many people were not emotionally well and had either misused their emotions by manipulating people or had been harmed by the emotions of others. I saw that some people got the creeps by talk of feelings or too many feelings, using the words "touchy feely" as a label to show their disdain for such talk. I, too, had been victimized by people who didn't know how to address their feelings properly.

But there was one unmistakable truth I could not deny. If feelings were so creepy and touchy feely, why were leadership roles all about managing people's feelings? Who does the angry customer want to talk to? The manager. Who does the angry parent want to talk to? The principal. Who do angry workers want to talk to before going on strike? The boss. How a person manages his own emotions will determine how he manages the emotions of others. Some managers are wise while others are inept. Some managers are tyrants. If we look at some of the best-run organizations, we find leaders who are looking out for and planning their reactions to others' feelings. I did not buy it when people shrugged off feelings as nonsense.

I became very in touch with my body and the messages it was giving me. This was something I was denied as a child, but could change as an adult. The importance of taking care of my body came to me with resounding clarity. I had to "feel" what it was trying to tell me. I'd heard, "Your body is your temple." I came to understand my body was the place from which I prayed, and it was the place where I would receive my answers. I decided I'd pray to the loving force I felt inside me. I knew taking immaculate care of my body was the only way I'd hear my answers.

I knew one thing for certain. There was a powerful, positive force in the world and there was a cruel, evil force. I tried hard to believe the former was the strongest and won out in the end. I knew to put myself around strong believers and followers of that powerful loving force. I did not care what they called it, or even if they had no name for it. I watched how they lived their lives. I listened for the words that came out of their mouths. I hoped against hope that Gandhi was right when he said, "When I despair, I remember that all through history the ways of truth and love have always won. There have been tyrants, and murderers, and for a time they can seem invincible, but in the end they always fall. Think of it—always."

What I Did Not Know Consciously

I periodically talked about Judy in support meetings. One day a woman said, "You're afraid you will become sick too, like your sister, aren't you?"

I did not understand what she meant. "You mean schizophrenic?" That had never occurred to me.

"You think it is going to happen to you, don't you, Lynnie?"

"What do you mean?" I asked. She told me that she, too, had a schizophrenic sister and for years she thought the same affliction would strike her. She was to learn that the disease hit people when they were generally between the ages of eighteen to twenty. Judy had been eighteen. Standing there with this woman, I was 30 years old.

"You are well past that, Lynnie. It is not going to happen to you."

"Is there something I am saying that makes you think *I think* one day I will become sick like Judy?"

"No. I just thought it was information you needed to have. I spent a lot of years believing down deep that some day it was just going to "hit" me. I just thought I would tell you that it is not going to hit you, just in case you ever needed that information. You are well and you will stay that way."

I thanked her and felt grateful that she felt comfortable enough to tell me. The full impact of what she said did not hit me until later. I did not know consciously that I had that thought. I would never have said it out loud. It was not even on my radar. But the more I thought about it, the more I realized she was right. I did think that since so many people in my family were mentally ill that, yes, someday it could happen to me. This woman had acted on her intuition and it did, indeed, restore something in me I did not know was in need of repair. It made me see how important it was to share information I had with others who might not have it.

What she told me made me relax in my own skin. Mary and I talked about our mental health a great deal, and we knew how important it was to talk. Once while Mary and I talked of our own struggles, she mentioned Judy. "It's a whole lot easier to go crazy." It hit me what she meant. It *was* much easier to go crazy than to work at being sane. We saw the state taking care of Judy. "Three hots and a cot" it is called in the military or prison. It was true. Institutionalized, Judy no longer had to struggle for food and shelter.

Coming Back to Mom

Three years had passed since I'd told Mom, "I'm leaving, but I will come back." It was time to go back. I knew enough of my anger had passed that if I spent time with Mom, I would not attack her verbally. I did not. But our entire relationship had, indeed, changed. I could never have predicted all that was in store for me on this visit home.

Parents say things that set off their children, and vice versa. Comments between a parent and child that go unnoticed by others can cut like a knife through the hearts of two people in this special bond. I'd heard, "Your mother is a mirror of yourself." If that was true, I'd seen my face in my mother's and hers was the face of a victim. I was no longer a victim. I no longer saw myself in her image.

During my visit, my mother said things that crushed me to the bone. She had me in a box. She treated me like I was the angry, moody person I'd been with my family, or when traveling together. I had been that, but now I could feel feelings I couldn't before. I could put words to them. It was time to push the lid off the box before I suffocated in my mother's presence. Every time my mother said something that caused me to feel fear, anger, guilt, embarrassment, humiliation, sadness, shame, hurt or happy, I said one sentence. It was either, "Mom when you say that, I feel terrified," or "Mom, when you say that, I feel angry," or "Mom, when you say that, I feel guilty," or "Mom, when you say that, I feel embarrassed," or "Mom, when you say that, I feel humiliated," or "Mom, when you say that, I feel sad," or "Mom, when you say that, I feel ashamed," or "Mom, when you say that, I feel hurt," or "Mom, when you say that, I feel really happy."

Her initial responses to any of these statements were "What!!!!!!!!! Why?????" She was completely horrified that anything she said to me would hurt. She was being who she'd always been. I had learned to put a period on a feeling statement. I had learned that anything after that period would become criticism and start an argument of "Well, you said…" or "And Furthermore…" so I restated the line I'd just said. I left it at one sentence.

When my mother pushed, I said, "Mom, I never want to have to explain my feelings again to anyone. I just have them."

When I'd first come home, I'd made it clear to Mom that I loved her and I wanted to have a relationship with her. It would be years before I learned these special words formally in a communication class. I'd said this to her intuitively. I meant it. I did not need her to change in any way, but I'd always remembered what Doctor Will said. All I needed to do was bring myself back to a calm level, a place where I'd been before a hurtful statement was said. And stay in present time.

My Mom had a lot of mental illness in her own life: her mother, her husband, and her daughter. Mom had no therapy around the shooting, something that had harmed her life on every level. She was still taking care of other people when it was time to take care of herself. In the worst way, I wanted my mother to focus on her own mental health.

Whenever I got truly angry with Mom, I went out into the back yard, sat down and wrote in my notebook all the ugly thoughts I had. I already knew these ugly thoughts about my mother were not real, but they needed a container. I wanted them up and out of me. There were hundreds of reasons to be angry, but not one reason to be mean.

I did not attack her once. I did hurt her by telling her my true feelings. After her initial reactions, she realized I was not going to berate her, so she calmed down and was able to listen to my "feelings" statements. She found she did not have to do anything about them. She just had to hear them. She did.

I was different from the person who had driven her through Europe. I did not have all the words I needed, but this was a start. I knew what to say now when she did something that set me off. The rest of the time we were able to talk, go to dinner and plays, and have a nice time.

This ten-day visit was hard on Mom. She had to do some looking at herself and said she'd felt she'd been through an intense therapy session. But a wonderful result was that we were calm and peaceful with each other. She had her daughter back.

Finding Pieces to the Puzzle

Delving into my past, I still had unanswered questions. In Louisville, I tried to get some answers. I asked Mom to give me names of my father's friends and co-workers. I went downtown, searching. I told each person I was Ed Vessels' daughter and wanted to know more about my father. Everyone was welcoming. One lady from his former workplace told me my father had pictures of his wife and kids on the desk and talked about us incessantly.

Did she ever have any indication that he went home and beat his children at night? "None whatsoever." She said she would not have dreamed it in a million years. She said my father was bright, intelligent, and friendly. She, along with many others, called him charming.

One thing stuck in my mind. "Whenever I saw your father, he looked like he'd just stepped out of the shower."

"Why, was he soaking wet or something?"

"Oh, no, no. His hair was always neatly combed. His shirts were crisp and he always had the most beautifully ironed pleats, running down his pants. He was an impeccable dresser. Like he stepped out of a magazine."

My mom would have been the one who ironed those pleats.

I spoke with his best friend. I was sure it was he who posted bail for my father. "No, I was in Florida that night." I believed him. He did not know who might have. *Who was it then?* It was the one burning question I would never get answered.

I asked my Aunt Betty, my father's older and closest sister, "What might have made my dad so brutal? Had he been beaten by his own father?" Her answers left me exasperated. She told me she had never seen her father be harsh with his son, her brother. I wasn't so sure. If my grandparents had such an aversion to touch or soothe us on the night we grandchildren needed them most, what might they have been like under normal stress, raising their own children?

Mary told me our father had told her that a neighbor's dogs had chased his sisters home from school. His father, my grandfather, went to get a gun. Although my father did not know what his father did, no one ever saw those dogs again. He may have just been protecting his kids, but Mary said she took from that story that our grandfather was a brutal man. I had never seen him that way. I'd always been on his knee laughing as he hid toothpicks in his mouth. I thought he was warm and funny, and in fact, he was kind, generous, and giving to my older brother, Jeff, who had a close relationship with him.

I do remember being at another aunt's house when my grandparents were there. On several occasions we three girls were told to go play in a room. We were guided in, and the door was shut. After several minutes, someone returned and we heard the door lock click. All of a sudden, playing had an eerie feeling. Maybe as younger children we had cried to come out when the door was locked, but as older children, no one had a word of complaint. We just waited until there was another click, which meant the door was now open and we were free to come out. No one ran to the door right away. We waited. By waiting, we conveyed we were not eager to come out, that this was not a difficult experience. But we *were* eager to come out and it *had been* a difficult experience. We knew to act the exact opposite of how we felt. From the first click to the second, all I could think about was getting out of that room.

I went back to our grandparents' house. When I drove up, the house seemed bleak and empty. It looked like no one was home, but there was a truck parked way out back. I knocked on the back door. A man, about my age, answered. I told him the truth. "Hey, I don't mean to bother you, but my grandparents lived in this house when I was a little girl. Something very bad happened to me one night in this house, and I have been trying to heal it. I thought maybe coming here would help me do that. I'm just wondering if maybe you might let me come inside."

He could not have been sweeter. He was immediately friendly and said he understood because bad things had happened to him when he was a kid. He said I could come in and take all the time I needed. He walked me around a bit, and then we went into the living room. He told me he'd leave me to it. Yep, there it was. The living room where the couch was, the dining room where the buffet was, the kitchen where the table was. The archway door had been remodeled.

I entered the bathroom that stood between the guest bedroom and my grandparents' bedroom. I was amazed to see how close they were. My grandparents. The two of them had been so close that night.

When I walked into the bedroom where we three girls had been lying in the bed, I immediately smelled whiskey. I knew in that moment the night my father walked into the bedroom, he had whiskey on this breath. This was not a memory that came back to me. I had never known it. My psyche remembered it. She is a tricky little one. I had come to trust her. Funny, though, because my father's drink of choice was scotch. Maybe he couldn't be choosey just out of jail.

Mom filled in holes for me. From her I connected getting her new hairdo and picking us up from Brownies happening on the same day. The reason she was at the hearth when we came out of the bathroom was because the crucifix she had always worn was on the mantel of the fireplace, waiting to be taken to the jeweler for repair. When she thought she was going to die, she raced to it. She recalled, too, leaning against the refrigerator "letting" herself die, believing her blood loss was too great. Then she suddenly remembered the boys needed two number-two pencils the next day.

Aaron said he first hid in a bedroom closet before he fled the house, something I did not know. Mary remembered being up on the ceiling and floating from the living room, around the corner and into the back of the kitchen, looking down onto the linoleum floor. She saw her feet floating above the linoleum and intermittently touching the carpet in the living room. She remembered being in front of the gun, but only had "snapshots" of it. She remembered clearly saying to our father, "Now I don't love you anymore." She later said about the incident, "In that moment, anything I had with him, I just wiped the slate clean; anything he had banked, was gone. That is how I felt and he heard that." If my mom had come back to life for the love of her children, my father had stopped trying to kill his wife because of the *loss* of love from one child.

I stopped at another aunt's house at a family get together. When my aunt and I and a few others sat in the kitchen talking, I mentioned the therapy I was doing around the shooting. Everyone seemed surprised at how comfortable I was about this taboo topic. Other family members began trickling in, first at the doorway, and then into seats. My aunt sat steadily. It was the first time she'd heard one of us speak of the crime her brother had committed. She started to ask questions. Her stillness showed me she was aghast at what I remembered. As far as she'd known, all had been forgotten.

I loved this aunt. She had in the past few years lost her only son, my cousin, to cancer. Her depth of pain at losing a child made her the only one of my father's sisters who could venture into this murky territory. I watched as she realized how devastated we children had been. I admired her for allowing herself to "get it."

To a room full of fifteen relatives, some who'd sat at the kitchen table on the night of the shooting, I shared my experience. I spoke without anger, without fear, without tears, without stammering and, in fact, with ease. Self-knowledge and good mental health were coming together for me.

Near Death

I was fascinated by accounts of near-death experiences. I felt I could relate, but I had no reason. These people had died and come back to life. They had often seen themselves lying in their hospital beds, had seen a white light and followed it, maybe gotten a message about love. I'd never even broken a bone, never been in the hospital. But to these stories, like a magnet, I was drawn. I couldn't figure out why.

One day I landed on it. Standing there with Judy on the night of the shooting, screaming, I must have thought I was going to die – at some point, that it was coming, that I'd be next. It made sense. I had never left my body, seen visions, or wandered into the light, but I had wandered somewhere. Into Judy's eyes. The loving feeling that people said they felt when they moved toward the light in their near-death experiences, was the same feeling I felt when I finally let go and allowed myself to be pulled into Judy's eyes.

I realized it was the length of time of this ordeal that had the biggest effect on me. I've often wondered in what situations someone else might have this vantage point, to stand and scream in terror for *so long*, without being dragged away or actually killed eventually. I began to think of scenarios.

I imagined it could have happened in trench warfare. When a battle was in full swing, men were in the trenches, getting shot at, and dying one at a time. There could have been a man there, loading his gun and firing, watching his buddies fall and die. What feelings of terror he must have felt! Then he may have seen another man, just feet away, wounded but not direly. That man would have looked at him with his sparkling green eyes. The two of them would have locked eyes and just stared. No words were said, but each of them was saying with his eyes, "Yes, this is really happening, and yes, our buddies are dying, and yes, we might, too, and you may be the last person I ever see. Let's look into each other's eyes because right now, you are the only thing that is real in my life. The rest of this – the blasting, the screaming, the dust flying, the cries for help, are not what is real. What is real is the love, the understanding I see in your eyes." If one or both survived, I do not believe either man would forget the moments that sustained him when he believed he was going to die.

Standing there naked in our mother's blood, I had believed I was going to die.

Smokey

The one person I could always rely on to tell me about our father was Smokey Bolt, our next-door neighbor growing up. He and his wife Janice were about fifteen years older than my parents and my parents relied on them. Mom asked Janice for child-rearing techniques, recipes, and, of course, cups of sugar. Smokey was a "man's man" and he and my father got on like wildfire.

Smokey had no illusions about who my father was, but he chose to talk about his positive qualities. He told how my father could hold a conversation about anything, laugh heartily, tell jokes, and charm the socks off a president. He always described how incredibly intelligent my father was. Smokey loved Pops.

Whenever he discussed the shooting with me in my later years, Smokey dropped his eyes to the table and shook his head. It was like my father had been his little brother, one who had done something so wrong that he desperately wanted to forgive, but could not allow himself to. I wondered if it seemed to him that he would be betraying all of us, if he did. To watch him go from talking about my father in the jolliest way to his somber thoughts about what the man he loved had done was beyond sad. So very sweet and so very bitter. My father had disappointed him in the worst way.

I was grateful to have Smokey, as he was a wealth of information about my family when I needed a question answered. Janice provided the same, although she remembered more of the ruthless acts she witnessed. She told the story of how my dad did not want anyone eating anything when they crossed the line from the dining room into the living room. She'd seen "little Judy," at about two years old, wearing only a shirt, walk "over the line" while eating a peanut butter and jelly sandwich. My father swung his hand and hit her so hard on the bottom, she went flying down the length of the hallway, spinning like a top, peeing all over herself. If Smokey remembered him most for his charming personality, Janice remembered him for his brutality. Both views were equally helpful, as it gave me a full picture of my father.

These two people were loving guides for me in my life and we were able to talk about many issues when I got older. They were my surrogate grandparents, just as they'd been surrogate parents for my mom and dad. It was never lost on me for a moment that it was Smokey and Janice Bolt that Mom wanted when she was in the hallway bleeding to death.

The Two-faced Monster

After her many episodes of bizarre behavior, Judy was in Central State Hospital, a secured facility for mentally ill patients. Whenever my siblings came home, they visited Judy. I thought I could, too.

To visit Judy on her ward, one had to be let in by an orderly with keys. There was a long, wide hallway that led down to the nurses' station on the left and a doorway to the common area for patients on the right. When I entered, I was asked to sit near the door, and I waited while someone brought Judy to me.

Judy arrived all giggles, oozing love and happiness. She had a high-pitched tone in her voice. I could tell she was straining to appear "happy," as if trying to be normal, to hide her dismal existence. It seemed she would have liked, in those moments, for just the two of us to be on a park bench somewhere. Judy told me she was very happy to see me and asked me many questions about my life in Virginia. She was happy, happy, happy. Too happy. After about five minutes, she announced, "Looneybird, would you please excuse me for a minute?"

"Sure."

I waited for her to return. And waited. After sitting there for over twenty minutes, I thought I'd go see what had happened to Judy. I walked down the long, wide hall to the nurses' station and said I was there to see Judy. Just as I said that, I heard Judy's voice. I stepped over to the lounge room doorway and saw Judy sitting with her back to me, smoking and talking with a group of people.

In a tone of total arrogance, with a deep hatred, Judy said, "My sister is the biggest bitch. She thinks she is so wonderful because she is a teacher in Virginia. But she is a fucking bitch. She's a whore and a slut and a goddamn mother fucking bitch. She thinks she is so great. I hate that fucking bitch!"

The tone of her voice and the words spewing from her mouth shook my core. I had never heard her speak this way about me. Just then, one of the people in the group looked up at me. Judy turned around quickly to see me standing in the doorway. She knew I'd heard what she'd said. Her eyes were fierce. I knew I was in trouble.

I turned quickly and said to the nurses, "Please open the door for me.

Quickly!" Perceiving the situation to be urgent, a couple of nurses came out of the station area to me. By then, Judy had leaped into the middle of all of us, grabbing and tearing like a wild animal. Within seconds orderlies from every direction came to help.

Judy was kicking, cursing, grabbing, and spitting ugly words as she dragged all of them with her while lunging at me. I thought for sure she'd get me, but just like in a movie where a person gets out at the last possible moment, I was let out in a crack of the opening door. The door was being pushed by the scurrying mass that was Judy and the staff. As I wrangled myself out of the crack, I saw the orderlies letting Judy go. There were eight of them.

As I was walking down the hallway to leave, I walked by a large glassed-in area. It was a mezzanine that led out from the lounge area where I'd seen Judy talking. Judy had run back down the hallway, through the lounge room, and out into this lighted, glassed-in mezzanine. Large palm plants draped the courtyard that made it look like an outdoor patio. She came to me and plastered her body to the glass. Her demeanor was now completely changed. "Looneybird, I'm so sorry. Please come back! Please come back and see me. I won't hurt you. I'm sorry. I won't hurt you. Please come back! I didn't mean all those things I said. Please come back. I want to see you!"

She was saying this so loudly I could hear every word through the glass. I shook my head and said, "No, Judy. I can't come see you anymore." She stood there looking sad, realizing the gravity of "anymore." She repeated her plea. I stood there sad, shaking my head. She stopped talking now and just looked at me with an equally sad face. I told her, "I'm very sorry you are in here, Judy. I love you. But you cannot hurt me. I cannot see you because you try to hurt me."

She nodded her head as if to say, "I know," and her face twitched with the realization of what she'd done. It was that pure and pitiful look that could have made me go back in that door. I loved her so much. I resisted. This was my education in mental illness; a course I'd never enrolled in. I stood there with her for another minute or two and said, "I'm going to go now."

And turning away, dragging six dead elephants through a foot of mud, I did. If there is any pain greater in life than having to walk away from someone you love so much, because they are truly not good for you, I have yet to find it.

I was scheduled to pick up a high school pal, so I went straight there. Soon we were sitting in a Burger King. I told her I had just visited Judy and that Judy had tried to attack me. "It makes me so sad."

"Oh, my gosh! Don't give me that! Judy is sick. You should be over this by now. I don't want to hear that this makes you sad. Take me home!" She threw down her uneaten burger. "Take me home!"

I did not argue. I said nothing. I was unaffected by the insanity of it. I stood up and went to my car. We got in. I drove her home. Neither of us said a word. I did not see her again for several years when she told me that, at that time in her life, she was living with a man with a violent temper. She had to be rescued from the situation by her family. She had not wanted to hear anything about *my* feelings.

By now I had faced the fact that as I changed, my former relationships would, too.

Mary, Lynnie, and Judy

It had always been "the three little girls" or "the three of us" or "Mary, Lynnie, and Judy" in that order. We shared the same bedroom. When the boys were separate from us, we were rarely separated from each other.

Before Judy got sick, we three girls were very supportive of each other. I do not remember any of us ever being jealous. Even in present time, when it was happening, I felt I always knew why. Each one of us knew the pain it took for the other to be standing there, walking through a day. Whenever anything bad happened to one, the other two were there to console, to hug, and to encourage. Never did we want anything else bad to happen to each other. When one of us had a special occasion coming up, the other two helped to prepare, to sew, to "fix up" the one going to a dance or a prom or just on a date.

We knew the good, the bad, and the ugly of each other. Mary's ugly was being incessantly irritable, mine was being angry and moody, and Judy's was being impulsively violent. We knew these things about each other, but forgave them. It was the good we focused on. We wanted each of us to make it. It took Mary and me the better part of fifteen years to face the fact that Judy was not going to make it. It was as if our silent prayer was, "Just make it. Please make it. If you can, I can. And if you can't, I'm afraid for myself."

Mary, Lynnie, and Judy

Watching Judy fall apart was exhausting. Shoring up the other's sadness about it was an exercise in rebuilding the life Mary and I had always known with her. What would life be like? What would our lives be without her? Judy was ours. For all of the years after we realized Judy was ill, Mary and I grieved the loss of her so fully, that today it is the miracle of grief work that we can talk about her without crying. We did it best when we were with each other, either on the phone or in person. You never heard such sadness pour from the hearts of two women when we talked about Judy.

Judy had been the light in both our lives, so bubbly, loving, joyful, and so, so honest. She was wise beyond her years. Judy was a truth teller. She told it like she saw it, and was often right. I have heard it said the youngest kids within dysfunctional families are often the healthiest mentally. Is it because they look around at all they see as they are growing up, and judge what appears to them to be right or wrong, no matter what else others are saying? I think it goes back to having a universal intelligence. Judy had a keen wit about such things. Her words were disarming at best and humiliating at worst. She had a way of getting you to admit truths about yourself that you would have loved kept hidden. Not with Judy around. She was too smart.

She was also blonde and beautiful and had a figure to die for. She had no idea. Nothing like that registered with her. She was that innocent.

My whole life people have asked me where I got my energy, how I stayed so happy. I knew I could look at a weed and see the wonders of the universe in it. My joy was no secret to me. But Judy's joy was a sight to behold. Everyone loved her. Everyone gravitated to her. She loved animals and misfits and was a natural teacher to the young.

Although Judy and I were best friends when we were young, Judy and Mary became very close in their late teenage and college years. Judy went to Mary's college during Mary's last semester. They had a separate and special bond all their own.

When Judy started displaying signs of illness, it was frightening because she'd instantly revert back to the beautiful person she'd always been. It was as if she lost that person slowly and the ill person overlapped, eventually taking her over completely. She became unpredictable in a devastating way.

To say it was difficult to watch would be the understatement of my life. When a friend called me to tell me she'd seen Judy squat down and pee in the middle of the main street in downtown Louisville, I was numb. When I heard how she spoke to a boy who was supposed to be her boyfriend, I wondered what on earth pained him so that he would stand for such belittlement. When she followed a migrant apple-picking Hispanic man across the country to be with him even though he was abusive to her, I wanted to go get her. When Mom called to tell me Judy told her she had been raped yet again, but this time, when in the morning there was blood in the sheets where she'd slept, it was difficult to ignore. Thirty minutes after that call, a policeman pulled me over for speeding. I had a meltdown with the officer on the side of the road. Poor guy. When Judy called me at my brother's house having one of her psychotic episodes, I handed the receiver to my brother so he, too, could

hear the extent of Judy's illness. In these calls she carried on about how I was not really where I thought I was, but instead, I was being raped or stabbed in the room next to her. When she accused me of having sex with her boyfriend, Mick Jagger, I just told her simply, "That's not true, Judy." When she had wars in her head with peas and carrots, my brothers humored her. My brothers coped with many things by laughing at them. Carl laughed the most, but he also loved Judy the most. He visited her often and bestowed many kindnesses on her.

When Mary first moved to Australia, talking on the phone cost $3 a minute. In those early days, the high costs coincided with the beginnings of Judy's illness. There was no time to waste. We got right to the heart of the matter. When one of us was feeling something about Judy, we called and cried to the only person who could truly understand. One heart aching on the other side of the world brought up so much in the other sister, she would have to take her turn. We listened intently, because in between the tears something important could be said... a word or a sentence the other person could cling to in the separation. We were hoping to make sense of a situation that made not one bit of sense to either of us. It was heart wrenching to hear Mary's sadness on the other end of the phone, but comforting to know there was someone out there whose pain about Judy partnered mine on every level.

Losing Judy is the greatest sorrow of my life. Mary's too.

Colorado

I was happy to leave Louisville and set out on a vacation adventure of camping in Colorado. Almost there and at a roadside rest stop, a fellow walked up to my car, pointed to my license plate and said, "Did you drive here all the way from Virginia by yourself?"

"Yep."

"Why, you must be very good company!"

It took me a second, but I got it, and in fact, I thought it was a very good pick-up line!

These fellows, Jim and Ron, invited me over to their site for spaghetti. While sitting around the picnic table eating, I found out these guys and the three others – another Jim and his 15-year-old son from Denver plus Bo from New Mexico - were planning to hike a 14,000-foot mountain the next day. After talking with me, they realized I was pretty fit, and asked me if I wanted to climb. They were a great group of guys and I felt comfortable, although one guy, Bo, seemed very negative. I hated some of the negative thoughts that came out of his mouth. *There's always one in a group, I guess.* I was eager to climb.

I learned there are 54 mountains in the Rockies that are over 14,000 feet. Ron, a retired geologist with Exxon, had hiked all 54 mountains twice and he was on his thirty-fourth hike of the third round. Yes, he was a fanatic; I called him a Billy goat! They shook my tent the next morning, and we all set out for the trailhead at 4 a.m., reaching it by daybreak. At the base of the mountain, there was a massive red sign warning hikers to give themselves at least 12 hours of daylight for the return hike.

We started out on a switchback. It was not too long before I began to question what I'd gotten myself into. I was hiking with five strong men. After that first hour of exerting myself fully, I had fierce cottonmouth. *I need to stop!* I imagined the guys regretting they brought me. *"Oh, brother! Whose idea was it to bring a girl?"*

I battled with that until I could take it no longer. "I need to stop." Everyone stopped and we sat and drank water. Far too soon, we were back at it, hiking at a fast pace. When I began to struggle again, I said, "I need to stop." Everyone stopped again. Pretty soon we were out of the switchback and now each step we took after that was literally a step "up." Like a staircase, we stepped onto boulders or the path ahead for the rest of the journey. Realizing this, I wondered if I could walk a staircase that high. *You can do this, Lynnie.* Again and again I had to say, "I need to stop." I had to fight back the feeling of being a burden to the group, especially in Bo's eyes. No one said anything, but I was self-conscious. Probably at the halfway point, Bo from New Mexico and Jim and his son from Denver decided to move ahead. That felt fine to me. Jim and Ron and I sat and had wonderful chats along the way. We also were able to stop more often.

The climb became very difficult for me. When I took a step onto a boulder, sometimes I did not gauge the height of it well and stumbled. I began to take every step very carefully. My thighs were stinging. Jim stayed behind me to make sure I was in good stead. But the climb went on. At one point, it snowed! At another point, it was brutally hot! And steep! At one point, we had to walk along a very skinny ledge; I was out of breath and feeling light headed. Hikers generally say hello to each other when passing, but when a group rounded the edge of the cliff, moving downward, I stayed to the inside as a woman passed me. She must have seen my face and my inability to speak. As she rounded, very close, she whispered into my ear, "It's okay, Honey. This is the hardest one I've ever climbed and I've climbed a lot of them!"

Oh, great. My first mountain has to be the hardest!

I continued to climb, and I continued to say the mantra I had counted on. *You can do this, Lynnie.*

Once, feeling weak and tired, I looked up and I saw the top! Great! A minute later the three of us stood facing what looked like a bridge, twenty feet long, but it was actually a four-foot wide rocky ledge, with two hundred foot drops on either side. We had to cross this to get to the top!

I will surely fall off this cliff if I try. I knew I was wiped out and I didn't feel I had the strength to make the crossing. But I could see the peak! We sat and pondered the situation. Ron went first. He got down on his hands and knees and waddled across, creeping slowly, low to the ground, clinging to the top edges. I was terrified, just watching him, but Jim told me I could do it. After five hours of hiking, I really wanted to get to the top, so I mustered every ounce of energy and courage I had left. I began my trek across the steep, rocky bridge. Like Spiderman, I was plastered to the rocks, inching my way across. *You can do this, Lynnie. Think great thoughts!* Like an inchworm, I wiggled slowly, my hands clinging to the ledges that dropped down on either side. I was scared. Terrified, in fact!

The other three had apparently reached the top already and had hiked back down now to walk the last bit with us. I could hear Bo laughing. *Ugh!* I looked up to see him coming. I just knew he was going to say something negative. I wanted to yell. *No! No! Do not come out here! You might say something that will make me fall off! Stay away!* I did not know if I had the strength to keep going if my mental strength got zapped. *He's going to say something negative! Oh, no, Lynnie. Don't listen to him. Do not fall off, Lynnie. Whatever he says, do not fall off this mountain!*

Bo inched his way out to me on a side ledge as I inched my way in his direction. I got closer and closer. Out there in the wind, I could only hear my heavy breathing. I clung to each boulder and pulled myself along. I kept saying to myself, *Whatever he says Lynnie, hold on. Hold on. Do not fall. Stay steady.* Shortly, I was right along side Bo. Standing on a small ledge below, his mouth was literally five inches from my ear. Into it, he whispered mightily, "You're doing a wonderful job, Lynnie!"

I was stunned. It was the exact opposite of what I thought he was thinking. He surprised me with this paradigm shift. I felt strength grow in me that had not been there before. All of a sudden I was Wonder Woman. I was strong. I was happily wrong about Bo and that filled me with power.

When I finally made it to the other side, the guys cheered, Jim came along after me, and the five of us headed to the top. We fell into a joyful heap and relished in our success. We pulled out a Ziplock bag from underneath rocks, opened it, unfurled a scroll and each of us added our names to the list of fellow hikers. How rewarding!

Going down was very painful because my toes banged into the front of my hiking boots. We stopped and we each had to cut corn pads to stick to our blistered feet in order to make it bearable to continue our descent. It was evening when we made it down. Each of us took off our shoes and socks and soaked our feet in the ice-cold creek. *Ah!*

Soon we were at a Mexican Restaurant. The guys lifted their beers to congratulate me, but just in the middle of it, one of them yelled, "Hey, wait a minute! Didn't you just come from sea level yesterday?"

Climbing Mt. Shavano

"Yeah, Kansas."

"Yesterday?"

"Oh, no!" they chimed.

"What?" I asked.

"No wonder it was so hard on you! We would never have asked you to do that if we'd remembered that!" *Wow!* There had been a reason it was extra difficult on me. A valid reason: my lungs had not been acclimated to the altitude. I was proud of myself. Climbing Mount Shavano that day was hard, second only to the physical difficulty of the bicycle trip.

Afterwards I learned that Jim and Ron were not going to stop until *the girl* wanted to, so they liked it when I said, "I need to stop." That would have been great information to have!

An added gift I got that day was watching a man stay behind me. Not for a moment did Jim get in front of me. He knew how physically demanding and how emotionally and mentally draining climbing this mountain could be for anyone. He knew how a newbie could easily become filled with feelings of doubt and inadequacy if left to the rear. I was never the last person on the trail, all the way up and all the way down. He showed me who he was by this simple act of respectful kindness. I will remember him as a gentleman as long as I live.

Summer Camp for Adults

That summer of 1989, I went to Massachusetts to the same personal growth class that Dave had taken the year before, taught by a husband and wife team, Sam and Sarah Stevens. It was a wonderful week filled with a startling amount of strategies to heal past wounds.

Sam was a university professor who had written several books on the topic of values and healing, but it was Sarah I was drawn to instantly. Her gentle and calm voice led us through exercise after exercise of getting together and listening to others. On Tuesday, the second night of the week, she told her own story of growth and the healing of her ten-year incestuous relationship with her father. I admired her and drank in every word. Never before had I seen such a powerful woman telling such a disturbing story, yet one from which she had spent many years healing, enabling her to freely share with others her newfound recovery.

We slept in dorms, ate our three meals together, and had classes from 8-12 and 1-3 then 7-10, every day. Sam and Sarah led us in creative lessons and took turns facilitating activities, which involved pairing up, talking, listening, reading, writing, and even singing. Many volunteered to read their writings at the microphone. We started with exploring our parental relationships and then other relationships. It was the first time in my life I'd heard the expression, "Are you getting uninterrupted eye contact on a daily basis?" *Is that what I am supposed to be getting?* I was getting it from my support groups but many people in the class agreed it was a rarity elsewhere. The key word was uninterrupted. I'd not heard people talking about the enormous benefits of eye contact. I was intrigued.

One day during the course, I had an experience that again softened me. One afternoon after playing tennis, I stepped into a shower stall for a quick rinse. I glanced down to see that someone had left her shower caddy on the floor of the stall. *Oh, brother! How could anyone forget her stuff? That's dumb!* I had been such a meticulous and precise person that it confounded me that someone could be so careless. When I glanced back at the caddy, I saw that it was *mine*. In that moment, my critical voice about my own and others' misgivings went up in smoke. While there at the class, I'd been so relaxed and happy learning so many wonderful things, my anal-retentive self "forgot" something! After that, I began to laugh at myself for not catching all the details - and would actually congratulate myself. I realized that if I was forgetting things that were inconsequential, it was because my energy was focused on the big picture. I was no longer perfect. My becoming consciously forgiving of myself and others blossomed from the moment I saw my shower caddy.

The most beautiful activity that the Stevens taught us was about giving each other affirmations. I'd been giving myself affirmations, after rising up from my heap on the butcher paper, but I'd never really been given affirmations. I could probably count on two hands the good things people had said about me. Mr. Huggins saying, "You have so much energy," was the first. This was a whole new experience for me in class and I drank it in like a thirsty child. It quenched a part of me that had lain dry and dusty most of my life. These affirmations from others matched my inner voice.

People can say some of the nicest things in the world to you, but if one person gives you criticism, that is what sticks. This seems to be a universal experience. I took a lot of criticism growing up and had to admit that I was more sensitive to it than most. I realized I did not have the cushion of affirmations around me to fall into when I got knocked down, criticized. There had been no soft landing, only what felt like hard concrete.

I was with a group of people now who were being trained to say nice things to people – and they practiced on me! Whatever good qualities they saw in me, they told me or wrote them down and I received them in a mailbox everyday. I did the same for them. I was in hog heaven. No longer was I lying on my floor at home in despair, waiting for a voice to come to me to replace an ugly sentence with a wonderful one. I was among people who knew and believed in turning negative thoughts into positive ones, and instilling that concept.

I learned an affirmation could have a powerful effect if someone said something wonderful that I had a hard time believing. A sharp pain arose. It was then I realized that the good thing the person was saying about me was the direct opposite of the harsh thing I must have believed about myself - one of those ugly sentences that lay somewhere in my core. The strikingly nice words brought up the ugly sentence – faster.

So, in essence, the affirmations given to me by others were therapy, healing something very specific and deep inside. This was profound, as I had often heard someone say that by marrying a certain person, she had "healed her life." *This must be how that was done. To hear nice things about yourself over and over, must really change you.* Affirmations would become the cornerstone of my teaching.

When I returned home from my first week with the Stevens, I took my phone off the hook and curled up in my bed for three days. I did not want anyone or anything to disturb, change, modify, intrude upon, or break the spell of the beautiful feeling I had about myself. I wanted it to last forever.

By placing myself in the company of good, solid people who saw the best things in me, supported me with what I needed to change about myself, and trusted that I could do it, I was able to heal by leaps and bounds. I learned from Robin Norwood in her book *Women Who Love Too Much* that when I got around healthy people, I was going to be very bored at first. She was right. I'd been too cool to arrive early to meetings. I'd been too busy to stay home and be with myself. I'd been too unwell, too disbelieving, to appreciate healthy, calm people. Being cool, busy, and unwell were becoming ways of my past.

When I returned home, many of my friends noticed I'd clearly changed, so much so, that four of them took the same course the following summer. I even went back and took my mother! We had a wonderful week of discovery and healing together. I ended up spending a total of five weeks studying with the Stevens in the summers from 1989 to 1992. The amount of personal growth from these courses was immeasurable. It brought me to a whole new understanding of what it meant to share my personal experiences with people. I learned countless strategies for facilitating regular activities in my own classroom and workshops, with students and teachers.

My New Digs

While in Massachusetts, I got a call from the supervisor of my county telling me he had a job for me. Even though I was sad to be leaving my colleagues at my first school, I celebrated.

I had taught tenth grade English my first two years. Now I was teaching seventh graders. I got a seven thousand dollar raise, it was a beautiful new school, and I was working with wonderful people again. But something peculiar struck me that took two months to figure out.

I was angry.

I could not believe how needy the kids were. I was irritated by how much they needed from me, how many questions they had, how much attention they wanted, how slowly they picked up information. I'd gone from teaching fifteen-year-olds to teaching eleven and twelve-year-olds. I was not used to having to slow down. So much! I was frustrated. Each afternoon, while stopped at a stoplight, I found myself banging the steering wheel. I had enormous anger coming out of me. But why? I loved these kids.

A good student of my emotions now, I'd learned enough to know my anger had nothing to do with anyone outside of me. It had everything to do with me, and that is where I had to deal with it.

One day I gave instructions to the seventh graders such as, "Okay, write your name in the top right corner of your paper, draw three columns going sideways like this, label each of the columns with the three titles you'll find on page 254 of your literature book, and turn to the person on your right to…. Blah, blah, blah…"

I was rocking and rolling, students were following, and I was ready to teach. Then a student in the back half-heartedly raised his hand and said, "Uh, uh, wh… where did you say to write our names?"

I was dumbfounded. I was waaaaaay past that instruction. I repeated the instructions slowly. As I turned to look up into the corner of my room, a tear trickled down my face. I missed my tenth graders.

I had to slow down for these kids. I had to answer more questions. I had to explain things further. Some of the questions they asked were so bizarre, I could barely believe anyone would ask such questions. Questions, questions, questions. My tenth graders had not asked so many. Ugh! It was driving me batty. These kids were needy. But patiently, I answered their questions, and I made it part of my routine to slow down and listen more. I began to watch out for them, nurture them more.

Still, I was angry. So I did what I do. I talked about it. I searched my brain. I tried to feel it through. Where was this anger coming from? I continued to go inside to find the place. One day it came to me like a thunderbolt. *I must have been that needy.* But there had been no one to answer my questions. I had to figure out so much on my own. I watched and failed and watched and failed and finally I'd figure it out. Myself. When I took myself back to this age, everything felt hard. No one had been around to give instructions to me.

I resented the fact that I had to give instructions to kids when no one had given them to me. Part of me thought of these kids as spoiled. The angry parts of me wanted to tell them to figure it out for themselves. But then I realized, kids asking questions was normal. That's what they do. This was natural. They trusted me. They came to me and expected their questions answered. They expected help from me. They were not spoiled. They had been nurtured and loved by adults around them and they were used to going to adults for help. They were asking the questions I *would have* asked, had my life not been disrupted, had the adults in my life had time. Discovering this, my anger lifted.

My administrator was a good mentor. I had a few glitches. Because I was still a harder grader and had not yet adjusted to the seventh graders' abilities, many received F's for the first interim. She had a fellow come in to talk to me. One sentence he said struck me. "You know, Lynnie, when you grade homework, you are really grading whether or not a child has parental support." That was all he had to say. He was absolutely right. We had done homework faithfully every night around our dining room table, even while our mother was at work. But education was well respected in our home. What about the kids who did not have this? There were many things I had not gotten at home. Had this been one of them, I might have been a poor student. I had a lot to learn as a young teacher.

Present Time

I was going out and meeting new people all the time. Having a ball, I was leading a new life, spending time with healthier people who said positive things to me. But still, inside me lived a force that believed I was bad. I thought I must have done something terribly wrong for people to treat me so poorly when I was young. Deep down, I still had this hidden voice inside me, one I could not coax out.

Dave and I saw each other only occasionally now. He had a hold on me that I did not like. It scared me. He was very nice to me, and then at some point, he'd say something mean. It was that something mean that drew me to him as much as the something nice. *Maybe he sees something in me I do not see. Maybe he can show me this thing that I do not like about myself. Maybe he sees it better than I do. Maybe he'll show me. If I can see it, I can change it. What is it? He must know. He sees how bad I really am.* This was the pull. No matter how wonderfully my life was going, if he was uncomfortable with something I said or did, I thought he must be right. His words matched my inner voice, too, only the ugly inner voice of "I am not good enough" or "I am too much."

Men's group meetings were popping up all over the place. Dave and his guy friends read a widely received and popular book. I read it, too, and was very attracted to the author - in print. I was fascinated by his beliefs after studying the major religions of the world. In the end, he believed that each could be summed up in two words: let go. When I heard he was coming to town to speak, I went to meet him and we began dating.

After two months, I realized something was not right. He'd written the book several years before and had since been traveling around the country giving motivational speeches, workshops, and interviews on TV and radio. The spiritual practices in his book, he was no longer living. *What had happened?* He had become famous, sought after. He barely spent any time at home where he could be himself. He liked me and asked me if I'd move to his town. I sat with him at his kitchen table one night and said, "When I look into your eyes, I do not see anyone there. I think you are a good man, but you are not at home." I did not mean literally. His eyes were vacant. He was not living in present time. This fellow thanked me for being honest with him, and my friends could not believe that I broke up with someone so well known.

The shooting was a horrible thing, but I took from it many spiritual lessons. I am fortunate that I had Judy's eye contact to keep me connected. I stayed grounded in that moment and have worked to stay present since. My decisions have not always been the best ones, but I was in present time when I made them.

Blood Scene vs. Bed Scene

The night of the shooting was separated into two parts for me. I knew these parts needed separate and equal attention. I had just spent four years purging my rage over the "blood scene." I had not a clue how to unlock the "bed scene." Still, I did not feel altogether safe in an intimate relationship with a man. There was nothing concrete that I could bring up. Acknowledging that was all I was capable of, but at least I was conscious of it. I formed a prayer in my mind about the "bed scene": "Please help me unlock this fear."

If the "blood scene" had slapped me in the face like a bucket of water being thrown, the "bed scene" had entered into me like a gas. It permeated me. I was in present time with both events, but it took sitting down with eight other people to describe for them the shooting - the "blood scene" - before I could have validated, "Was this bad?" And that was with my mother's mangled arm out in plain sight for everyone to see my whole life. *Hell yes, it was bad.*

The "bed scene" had a much more subtle effect on my life. When a man did or said something I did not feel right about, it took me forever to trust that feeling and do something about it. Even then I second-guessed myself. In those times of having to make a decision about something I felt uncomfortable about, I felt the same paralysis I'd felt when lying in bed that night with my father. *This should not be happening, but he is acting like it is okay. So it must be. Who am I to say?*

I was still looking for someone to protect me. No one was coming. Of all the other areas I felt I could conquer, this was the area where I wasn't well. I was willing to be shown.

At least I had male friends and had had several boyfriends. I was amazed at the overall feelings of respect I had toward men. I blessed my mom for that. Not talking poorly about my father was a sign of her high character and civility toward humanity. In spite of all that happened in our household, I came away with the utmost respect for each of my brothers. They were good men who, like me, were trying to make their way in the world.

My only hope to unlock the bed scene seemed to be prayer, so I continued to pray for it to be unlocked.

Johnny

I got a call from my mom telling me that my cousin Johnny had hanged himself. My little sister Judy got on the phone and begged me to come home for the funeral. "Please, please, please, Looneybird. Please come home!"

"I can't afford a plane ticket, Judy."

"I will pay for the ticket," she said. "Please, just come home!" My little sister wanted me to come home so badly she was going to pay my airfare. I agreed to go. Even though Judy tried to hurt me, I still wanted our relationship to be well. The scary thing about mental illness is that it is predictable that it will be unpredictable. That is also what is comforting about it. *Maybe this time it will be different. Maybe it will be okay this time. She wants me to come so badly. Surely she will not attack me. Listen to how badly she wants me to come. Everything will be good this time.*

I picked up Judy at Central State Hospital and drove her to the funeral home. I walked up to Johnny's casket and stood over his body. My Uncle George, the same man who'd thrown his head back in laughter on the night of the shooting, walked over and stood, also looking into the casket at Johnny. After a moment or two, my Uncle George, who was also Johnny's uncle, shook his head and said, "Tsk, Tsk, it's a darn shame. But I want to know how she did it. How did she do it?"

"Do what? Who? Who are you talking about?" I asked.

"I want to know how that little woman got a rope around a 225-pound man in his sleep," he responded, "and got him up there."

Perplexed but a little tingly, I asked, "Up where?"

"Up into the hallway, where she hung him," he said flatly.

We are talking Alfred Hitchcock family here. "What? Are you kidding? His wife? Are you kidding?" I was scowling.

He continued to shake his head and said, "I don't know how she did it."

"Are you kidding, Uncle George?" I asked, annoyed. "Johnny hanged himself."

"Nah, I don't believe he would do that." He was still shaking his head. "He couldn't have done that to himself."

"Why not? Johnny was abused all of his life," I said.

"Abused?" his voice high-pitched. "What do you mean?"

"Johnny was called 'Stupid' every day of his life. All day. Whenever I was around, he was always being called Stupid."

He could not believe this. "Nah, really?"

"Yes, really. Every day of his life. He committed suicide. It makes perfect sense to me," I replied, dismissing his comments as idiotic.

"You really think so?" I could see he was truly bewildered by this. "Nah, I don't think Johnny could have done that to himself."

"Believe me. I was there," as had been my Uncle George during family get-togethers, but I did not mention that. "I saw how Johnny was treated. He committed suicide," I walked away, rolling my eyes.

What? Johnny's wife? Getting a rope around his neck? While he slept? Dragging him down the hallway? Hoisting him up to the ceiling? On her own? In the middle of the night? His wife? The woman who loved him? Are you kidding me? More rolling of the eyes.

Johnny was slow, and his now deceased father had called him 'Stupid' at least ten times when we visited. I'm sure he said it when we weren't there. On top of being slow, Johnny was sad and depressed and compulsive. He was also a beautiful person.

After the funeral, we all went over to the apartment where Johnny's mom lived. I had never met Johnny's wife and eight-year-old stepson because they lived in Florida. Both were sitting on the couch in the living room. Immediately, something drew me to them. I stooped down to talk to the stepson, his legs dangling over the couch. I smiled at his wife as we chatted. I turned to the little boy and chatted with him. While we chatted, they both looked up at all the people walking by – a bunch of legs milling about in front of them. I could tell by their faces they were in shock. They had the kind of look that showed they wanted to smile, but somehow could not sustain it. They were very sad over the loss of Johnny.

Something did not feel right. I did not know what it was. People had gathered to chat. Having heard what my uncle had said, I wondered if others were thinking the same thing. *Had he talked to them, too? Had he told them he thought Johnny's wife was the one who hanged him? Had they believed him? How sick were these people? What were all of these side conversations about? Why was not more attention being paid to these two outsiders from Florida?* They were the most affected. They lived with Johnny every day – and loved him. Most of these people had not seen Johnny in years.

Something wasn't right. *What was it?* I did not know. I left the experience feeling drained. Then slowly, like a dripping faucet, I filled with rage. The faucet was just a drip, not flowing, so my rage just gradually seeped over the edges, sliding down the insides of me. *What was this rage? Where had it come from? Out of nowhere? What was it?*

I was not afraid of my rage now. We had made friends. I did not shun it when it came creeping around this corner. It had become my teacher.

I smiled at it and asked it to come closer. I was curious. *Why at this moment, have you shown up? What are you trying to tell me? Teach me?*

I took Judy home without incident. The next day, Mom and I had dinner at a steak house with my Uncle George and his wife, my father's youngest sister. I sat down at the table ready to complete my task. I was to figure out the all-important message my rage was trying to tell me. I'd heard a person needed anger long enough to know that something was wrong. Once anger ignited in me, I knew something was wrong; I could let it go and begin to handle a situation. I had trained myself to do that. But rage? Something was definitely more than wrong. Maybe rage brewed longer, to give me enough time to understand something deeper. I had to follow my newly awakened instincts.

The topic of Johnny's "murder" came up. I listened intently to what was said. I sat there in their words. These people refused to believe that Johnny had anything to do with his own death. It was plain to see. Then it hit me. Right smack-dab in the middle of my forehead in the middle of dinner in the middle of a restaurant in the middle of my hometown. *I* was that little boy on the couch. *I* had my legs dangling off the couch. *I* had been looking around at everyone talking. *I* had been wondering what the heck was going on. But the permeating feeling floating around in the room, that I had not gotten the night I sat on the sofa, came to me now. "What had Frannie done to make Ed shoot her?"

This had been everyone's thought. I never had to confirm it. I was certain. The denial in this family was so thick that if they had to look at the horrible behavior of one of their own, they would have to look at themselves. That was not going to happen.

The author, Scott Peck, wrote a wonderfully spiritual book, *The Road Less Traveled,* but he also wrote another book called *People of the Lie.* In that book he explained that some people are so unconscious, it borders on evil. The story that stuck out the most was about the parents who wrapped up a shotgun and gave it to their son for Christmas, the same gun his older brother had killed himself with one year earlier.

The unconsciousness of my grandparents was to tell us to stop crying, to leave us in a dark room, not come to us, not touch us, not talk to us, but sit around and tell stories and laugh, wondering what my mother must have done to provoke my father into such a hideous act. "It must have been a horrible thing she'd done. What was it?" It was unconscious

336 | *To Soften the Blow*

of them not tucking us in, not locking the door, not waking up when my father came home, not saying something to us, not telling us it was wrong, what had happened to us the night we slept in their guest room. With him.

Now my uncle was making this woman on the couch not just responsible for Johnny's death, but guilty of his murder. This woman loved Johnny and the little boy loved Johnny. They were sitting there on the couch that day, terribly crushed and in shock. Little did they know, as I had not known, the words being whispered around the room were words to incriminate them.

Freedom

Had it not been for the confidentiality of support groups, I don't know how much I would've shared about myself. I told bits and pieces of my story to many people in support groups over the years. Whether real or imagined, I felt loved and accepted. I got comfortable with talking. I'd come a long way since college. I was not giving speeches now; I was just talking to large groups.

I listened to others and whenever a shameful thought or revelation washed over me, I imagined, *Oh, I could never say that.* Then I took a deep breath and replaced it. *Yes, it will make me well.* I opened my mouth and said what I never thought I could. Pretty soon, that was behind me. I'd said it. It became part of my story. Another day when, again, a shameful thought washed over me, I took a deep breath. *If everyone in this room hates me after this, it has to be okay.* I opened my mouth to speak. I did. Then that was behind me. Little by little, I came to be able to verbalize my story, each time at the expense of allowing myself to be judged harshly.

The no cross talk rule was awesome. If anyone in the room had disdain for me, he could not say it. This gave me the illusion of being accepted. Even as an illusion, I was willing to believe it. I was determined to change my mind and think good thoughts about myself.

It is hard to explain the experience of being in a room with a group of people of all faiths who are devoted to and talking about being physically, mentally, emotionally, and spiritually well. You never knew what a person's religion was, or if he had one. The guy next to me could have worshiped a paper clip, for all I knew. The point was, no one cared. The only thing that was important was how we practiced our faith, how we treated people, how our faith played out in our daily, practical lives. I often felt a higher presence among these people. *One* higher presence. It was as though there was a "lifting" of the room. I craved this feeling and being among diverse people who spoke simple truths. I believed what Gandhi said. "There is no God higher than truth."

I found an unshakable connection to high mental health and the ability to speak what a person believes. On a very small scale, measuring my own life and my mental health, I felt a divine closeness to our founders who came before me, who knew real freedom depended on the freedom of speech and the freedom of religion. Freedom of religion, in my mind, meant the freedom to believe what a person wanted. Freedom of speech meant freedom to say what a person *needed.* Creating concrete documents to secure these two ideas was nothing short of intuitive genius.

Deciding to Leave Virginia

I made the decision that spring to move near my favorite camping spot in Colorado. I wanted to live in the mountains. I wanted to live where I could afford a house on a teacher's salary. I wanted to leave a congested area. I wanted a new adventure. These were all my reasons I gave for leaving Virginia and moving to Colorado. What I told no one, even myself, was the real reason: I wanted to leave Dave and the hold he continued to have on me. That's called a geographic cure.

Of all of the therapy work I did, I could not count another person with whom I shared so much in common. Dave and I met at the same "home" 12-step meeting and attended countless other meetings over the years. He joined a men's group led by my therapist, Patrick. He was learning the same techniques. We read the same books on recovery and admired the same authors. We both attended, but not together, the Stevens' personal growth courses. We joined separate workshops that used the same workbooks and that lasted months and sometimes years. Both leaders, we spoke in public often. We knew many of the same people, as our lives intertwined on varying levels. Lastly, we attended the same church, a place that was very special to each of us in our own personal way. We had a very strong connection that distance proved not able to break. But at the time, I felt I needed to get away and begin anew. Somewhere Dave wasn't.

Forgiving Pops

I applied to different school districts and flew to Colorado Springs to interview. I had several glowing letters of recommendation. I was hired by a school to teach one class of drama. Other English classes, they told me, would open up. I was moving west.

Remembering at Sunset

In all the years of my anger, I was not consciously angry with my father. He just seemed like a person mixed in with the batch. I did not realize what deep anger I felt toward him until it lifted.

One evening, I sat and watched a beautiful orange sunset, thinking nothing in particular. Boom! With a burst of energy, it came to me. My father loved me. In all my anger, I had forgotten that simple fact. At once I heard his laugh, saw his smile, and the twinkle in his eye. Remembering this seemed to give back a gift I'd not known I'd lost. I did have a father. And he had loved me. It was worth remembering. This moment marked something special. My rage was gone. I had purged the "blood scene."

You Don't Hit a Kid

One afternoon I stepped out of my cabana, just in front of the pool, to take in the beautiful day. I heard a ruckus and turned to my left. I saw Billy, my landlord's brother, chasing his three-year-old son, Henry, across the grass. Henry curved to the right. So did Billy. As Billy jogged along the left side of his son, he took his right fist and boxed the child's left ear. Henry flew six feet, landing in the grass. I witnessed this. A grown man hitting a tiny child. Very hard. I stood there. Leaving the child, Billy marched up the sidewalk to pass me, pointed his finger in my face, and threatened, "Don't you say a word!"

My body started to quiver, then to shake. The child scurried past and ran whimpering to his mother. In seconds I was shaking vigorously and uncontrollably. Billy walked up the steps to the pool and picked up a garden hose. He could see me shaking. He looked straight into my eyes and snarled. And then, I began. I leaned my body forward and out it came: words! Sweet glorious words! I yelled and yelled. And I yelled. And he yelled and yelled. And he yelled.

I gritted my teeth and snarled back at him. He was shaking, too, and kept pulling the hose to him while wiping the sweat from his forehead. He was above me. He could have flung the hose at me at any time.

The words we yelled went something like this:

"Who do you think you are?"

Hissing, "Keep out of this lady. It's none of your business."

"It *is* my business. You don't hit a kid," I said forcefully.

Smirking, "He's my son; I'll do whatever I want."

"You will not! You will not do whatever you want! Not while I'm here! You do not hit a kid. You get therapy if you have to."

"Leave me alone, Lady. Mind your own business," he complained.

I didn't stop. "This *is* my business. You don't hit a kid!"

"What do you know? You don't have any kids!"

"I have 130 kids a day. You do not hit a kid!" I screamed.

"There's something seriously wrong with you, Lady. You need therapy."

I was the 'crazy' woman coming after him, making a scene. *Okay. I'll go there.* "When I need therapy, I get therapy. You do not hit a kid!"

"Leave me alone."

"I will not leave you alone. You cannot do whatever you want! You don't hit a kid!"

"I'm tired of you, Lady. Leave me alone."

"No. I will not leave you alone. You do not hit a kid."

Billy took huge breaths to yell at me. I took huge breaths to yell at him. I did not stop pressing him. He did not stop defending himself. We were, the two of us, raging dragons. His brother came out to see what the commotion was. Billy's wife was standing behind me with a baby in her arms, three-year-old Henry clutching her leg, and their ten-year-old hugging her while she cried. I had been loud. He had been equally loud. We had gathered a crowd of neighbors. Then I realized my shaking had stopped. I took deep breaths and stood there, letting myself become calm. I turned and walked back into the cabana.

The phone rang. It was my mother to tell me about my cousin's baby shower. I told her I could not talk. I'd call her back. I sat down and rested from the physically and emotionally exhausting ordeal. In ten minutes, it was as if this screaming match had not happened. My body was completely calm. I walked outside.

Billy had loaded his wife and kids into the car. I walked over to the rolled-up window on the driver's side where he sat, starting the car. I knocked on it. Frustrated, breathing heavily, and in obvious angst, he rolled down the window. I looked into his eyes and, with no ill will, calmly said, "Well, I guess I know now what I do when I see someone hit a kid."

"Leave me alone, Lady. If I never see you again, it will be too soon!"

Billy and I had had good rapport, and I sincerely meant it when I said again, "You know, I've never seen someone hit a kid, and I had no idea what I would do, how I would react. Now I guess I know what I do when I see someone hit a kid." He grumbled and backed the car out of the driveway.

The next-door neighbor walked up with her arms high and wide open. She gave me a big hug. When I walked back inside and thought about this situation, I realized not a single cuss word had been said between us. I'd not said anything I did not mean, and I did not waste a word.

Ah, sweet words!

I knew Billy used cocaine but had no idea how much. I also knew he could be rough, but when I ran into his wife in the future, I learned he went to NA and got sober. *Awesome.* I often wonder how that experience affected the children who watched me yell at their father that day. It made me try to imagine the thing I'd never seen: someone bark down my father after he hurt one or all of us. What a sight to behold that would have been! When I put myself in the position of those children, I'd like to think it was a positive one.

Now I knew exactly how I'd react if I ever saw someone hit a kid.

Right Question, Wrong Time

My brother Jeff came to visit me that summer with his wife and small child. I was in the midst of packing to move to Colorado. Jeff had always had a habit of telling me what to do without ever asking me what I thought first. "Lynnie, don't do this..." and "Lynnie, don't do that..." and "Lynnie, you should do this...." When he came to visit me this time, he continued this habit. But I'd had some therapy under my belt, and was "feeling." This time, I could feel how rotten I felt when he snapped orders at me. *I should do this, I should do that...* It was hard to listen to him. I loved my brother and I was glad he visited me. Then one afternoon, Jeff said flat out, "Lynnie, don't buy a house in Colorado." *That's exactly why I'm moving to Colorado!* My dream was to have my own home. He did not know that about me, because he'd never *asked* anything about me. He went on, talking about taxes and about what I should do and why. I became angry. I said, very emotionally, "You don't even know anything about me!"

Immediately his wife came to the defense of her husband, got very agitated with me, leaned forward and coaxed me in a sarcastic tone, "Well, tell us about you. What don't we know? Who are you, Lynnie? Who are you?" Her face was red, her voice lifted. Jeff sat very still. The way she said that last "Who are you?" felt as if things had escalated into a yelling match and I did not know how to respond. Had the conversation been only with my brother, I may have been able to continue, but his wife was visibly upset. I wanted to tell them all about me, how much I wanted my very own house, but I was too afraid they'd laugh at me, so I said nothing.

Finally, *someone* - a family member, at that - had just asked me point blank: "Who are you?" and I froze.

After that incident, my brother and sister-in-law considered me "too emotional." Our mother had been "too emotional" for Jeff, and I think he saw my mother in me. After that, even though we visited each other once a year, he distanced himself from me.

This was a great example of how my B through Y was awkward. I did not have the right words, the right tone. I would have given anything to be close to the two of them if they could have sat through the awkwardness of me.

Moving West

I attended another one of the Stevens' personal growth courses that summer before heading to Colorado, but not before my friends gave me a big going-away party. It was a wonderful night. People from all my "lives" came. One woman said, "I cannot believe you are leaving all of these good friends."

I told her something I truly believed but didn't realize then how hard it would be to achieve: "I believe I will be able to build these kinds of friends wherever I go."

Dave had not come. He did not want to see me go, but called during the party and asked me to come out onto the street. When I met him there to talk, I was in a completely different emotional state than he. I was thrilled to be leaving. He was sad and lonely to see me go. He could not believe I did not feel sad. He and I had not been a couple for more than a year, and I was trying hard to be over him.

A friend and I drove across the country in a moving van, dragging my new Volkswagen behind us. Another friend had arranged to go to a conference at a five-star hotel that week, just so I would have a place to stay while I looked for an apartment. He was a guy friend, and we were very close. We spent so much time together that many people wondered why we weren't a couple. One night sitting around the pool, he told me he was gay. He was thirty and I was the first person he'd told, he said. He was terrified of telling his family members. I told him of the talk my mother had with me when I was about twenty years old. She'd said, "You know, Lynnie, now is the time in your life when you should probably know 'which way you go.'"

"Huh?" I did not understand. After a little more discussion, I realized that my mother was telling me that if I did, indeed, have feelings of being gay, it would be okay with her. I did not have to hide it. Of course, I was stunned, having only learned my freshman year in college that there was such a thing as homosexuality. But again, it gave me great insight into the person my mother was and how very fortunate I was to have her as my mother. She'd been a psychiatric nurse and had obviously seen many people destroyed by having to hold in the secret of being gay because they were too ashamed to disclose. Mom did not want me to waste years of my life going through that, if it happened to be the case. She did not want me to suffer in the way I was watching this man suffer now. Hearing my story, tears streamed down his face. Had my story been his, he would have been spared all those years fearing the rejection of his family.

Too Casual for Me

Before I arrived in Colorado, my hiking buddies, Jim and Ron, and I had big plans for hiking fourteeners, but Ron fell off Kit Carson Mountain and died two weeks before I got there. It took rescuers a week to find his body. When they did, his watch read 3:30, the time of his fall. The helicopter carrying his body flew through a double rainbow as his whole family stood on the mountainside. My billy goat friend died doing what he loved best. Of my two friends in Colorado, one was gone.

I found a very cute apartment right away. I had a car, a place to live, and one class to teach at the high school. I also got a job as a waiter at the five-star restaurant in town. Each day I walked out my door and greeted the Rocky Mountains. I began teaching drama to the neatest kids in the world. They were a mixture of 9-12 graders and I used my newfound skills and life experiences to teach the course. Many of them were "drama" queens and kings and many were seniors, so we were all very creative together. It was a brilliant experience with lovely kids.

But there was something odd going on at the school. I did not feel safe in the hallways. I'd never felt this way before, even when substitute teaching years before in very diverse areas in Northern Virginia. This was an affluent area, mostly Caucasians. Kids were bullying each other and disrespectful to teachers. Teachers were expected to stand outside their doorways between classes but many said they could not take the abuse they suffered, so stayed inside their classrooms. Since I only had one class, I was not expected to be at the school all day, but I did substitute for teachers. On those days, I saw how incredibly disrespectful kids were. A disproportionate number of students wore black clothing.

Five weeks into school, I was asked to take on two more classes of ninth grade English. This was a double-edged sword. I could use the money, and it would take me closer to becoming a full-time teacher for

344 | To Soften the Blow

the following year, but as any experienced teacher can tell you, taking on

the following year, but as any experienced teacher can tell you, taking on students after the school year has commenced can be extremely difficult. I was going to get two classes of the students pulled out of other classes. Most of the time, this pulling out would be random, but I got all the troublemaking kids I'd seen as a substitute teacher. One woman sent me a sympathy card referring to a kid she'd had and failed the year before.

It was a disaster. For me. Although, I tried every technique I possibly could, I did not have the support of the administration. I talked to teachers who said, "I have eleven more years before retirement, and I'm just trying to make it until then," and "Never go to the administration; you will not get help," and "I do everything on my own. I never ask for help from the administration because I know I am not going to get it."

Thank goodness for one widely respected teacher. She was the epitome of sanity. All of the teachers gravitated toward her, she ran a great classroom, and helped teachers who were having problems. She regularly had parties at her huge, beautiful house below the mountain range where we teachers gathered to gain support from one another. She saw the anxiety in me and reached out to help, warning me not to involve administrators. Her kindness caused me to feel validated. Having worked under these conditions for many years, she was far wiser than I when it came to maneuvering around the bosses.

But I'd not yet experienced administrators who were ineffective and incompetent.

The student government for the senior class did not have a sponsor, because the principal wanted to "empower" the kids. Not a good thing. My classroom had a large glass window that led into the audiovisual room the students used for making announcements. Students were in there, lighting one person on fire while the other one was trying to keep composed, speaking over the microphone. Yes, these seventeen-year olds without a sponsor were being empowered all right, empowered to light each other on fire.

The tones used over the announcements were sarcastic, mean, and cruel. One teacher told me he went to the principal and warned he would sue the school board if the kids said his name on the announcements again. Each day the schedule stopped for twenty-five minutes for the kids to have a "break." Loud, rock music was piped into the hallways and into every teacher's room. There was no way to limit it only to hallways. I never saw so many completely miserable teachers.

Throwing popcorn at teachers and students in the hallways was commonplace. My classes were staggered, so I had breaks in between. Once I walked through the cafeteria where the kids gathered for their twenty-five minute break. Here was the most beautiful new school in the state, all glass windows looking out onto the Rocky Mountains, a beautifully carpeted dining hall – and the carpet could barely be seen for the French fries strewn across the floor. One custodian was vacuuming as I came by that day. He saw my wide-open mouth. He shook his head and said, "Don't blame the kids; it's the administration. They let them do this." He, too, had resigned himself to the current state of affairs.

When I voiced my opinions to my colleagues, they felt validated by a new person experiencing what they'd felt for some time. I listened to their warnings about going to the administration. I could see these were sensible people operating under far too permissive administrators.

That fall I experienced "fuck-you" letters, "fuck-you" phone calls, "fuck-you" posters left outdoors, and even in-person "fuck-you's." When a student said, "Fuck you" to me in class, I sent him to the principal only to see him return ten minutes later tossing the pink return-to-class note on my desk. Students stood outside my classroom and broke glass bottles on the brick wall while yelling curse words. Yes, that was scary. I pulled every single trick out of my hat to try to get these kids under control, and for the most part, they were, until they weren't. That would depend on whether or not they wanted to be.

One day standing at the copy machine, a woman asked me how I liked teaching in Colorado. I told her I liked it well enough but there was something distinctly different that I noticed between there and teaching back East. I had been reared in the South where people said "Yes, Ma'am" and "No, sir." I had lowered my expectations about that in teaching altogether, but I told her I was floored that most of the students did not say "please" and "thank you." *I thought everyone alive said those words!* "Oh, that's because we're casual here!" *Very interesting observation.*

The wild boy, who had failed the year before, truly was wild, but I got support from his father, even to the point of his father saying, "I will do anything you want me to do."

"Okay, tomorrow when he comes back from lunch, I want you to be sitting in the desk next to his and I want you to sit there quietly for the whole period."

The father did, the boy was shocked, and it did help the situation for a few weeks. The real problem was the ringleader: the assistant principal's daughter. A slew of girls followed her every sarcastic remark and obscene gesture. The best way to describe Monica is through her parents. One afternoon, I was going to a teachers' party after school. Her mother was a teacher at another school and was arriving at the party at the same time. She ran up to me in the middle of the street and said, "So, how do you like Monica? She's a real bitch, isn't she? Go ahead, you can say it. She's a bitch, isn't she?"

I was taken aback. I looked at her, cocked my head, crinkled my nose and said, "Well, she is a handful."

"Oh, go ahead! You can say it. She's a bitch. I know it and everyone knows it." She was egging me on to call her daughter a bitch. The truth was, I was still working with Monica to find out just what her problem was. *I think I just discovered it!* These parents had made a deal. Since the father was an assistant principal at the school, the mother handled all problems that went down with Monica. No help there. Basically, the father was useless. Great. I couldn't go to the principals for anything. Or could I?

I saw no other teacher voicing a word. *Surely anyone in his right mind will see how crazy this is. All I have to do is present them with the facts.* They saw crazy, all right. They just saw it in me. I involved an administrator in a problem with a disrespectful student who was angry with me for moving his seat away from his friends. *Duh!* The assistant principal sat between us and asked him what he did not like about me! She let him go on and on, something another principal would never have let happen. I was mortified that she did not stop him or defend me. I sat there "in it." To my disbelief, when he finished his rant, she said to him, "Well, Matt, what would you like to see happen?" I knew then, I was sitting with a mad woman.

But it all came down when I had had it with Monica and gave her detention for back talking me. In December. Three months into school, and after trying every which way to handle her, I finally gave her detention. She went ballistic and called for a meeting with another assistant principal who asked her to recount the words we'd said to each other. Monica had said something out of line, and I told her I felt irritated with her.

"Who gives a shit how you feel?" she responded.

The assistant principal listened to Monica tell her story, then drew closer to her and said in an understanding tone, "So you felt set up?" As if the words I'd said to her *caused* her to say that back to me! The one detention I'd given to the most disrespectful girl in the ninth grade had been revoked. I was done for.

I was new in town and although I went to many support groups and had work friends, I still did not have a good foundation under me - not enough to deal with the constant stress I was under. My mom came out to visit me in Colorado, finding me at my wits end, groping for what to do next. Teachers around told me of the many who'd resigned from the school. The thought of it was a kick in the stomach. That had never been an option. Teaching was my life. Mom said, "You can come home, Lynnie, until you decide what you want to do next." *Ah!! Yes, I could go home! To Kentucky.* If I needed to. I would not resign yet. I would think about it during the winter holiday.

Eight Pancakes

On the last day of school before our winter break on December 14, I walked out to find all four of my tires flat as pancakes. I walked back into the school and into the head principal's office. I stood at his door and said, "Someone has slashed my tires in the parking lot."

He met me at the door, guided me to the desk of the secretary who'd already gone home for the holidays, reached down and grabbed a yellow pages book, and placed it in front of me. He said, "We don't deal with that here." He walked back into his office door three feet away, leaving it open. By now, a fellow male teacher, who'd been standing there, had taken it all in. He knew what kind of administration he was working under. He immediately took over, calling the service station to tow my car, and helping me organize a way to get my mom to the Denver train station that afternoon.

I was told this principal's behavior was incredulous, but when a person is in shock from one big jolt, the smaller ones don't register as powerfully. All I could think was it had to be a very large knife to get those kinds of gashes in my tires. *And who carries a knife that big? And why my car? No one else's tires had been slashed.* I called Dave to tell him what happened. He tried to talk me through my shock.

For the Christmas holiday, I visited family and friends in Kentucky, Virginia, and Ohio. I returned to school on January second, parking on the other side of the school. On January third, I walked out to find all four of my tires sliced. Again. Large gashes in each of my four tires. Now all I could think was whoever was carrying a knife that big had tracked down my car until he found it. Again. Big trigger. This time, I was angry. I marched into the principal's office, opened his door, sat down and said forcefully, "Someone has slashed my tires again, and you are going to deal with it here and now. I want you to find this person. I am not working in your school until you take this seriously. Do something now." I thought he took me seriously and he began making calls. As the gravity of the situation set in, I cried. Big mistake. Only crazy people cry. People with "psychological problems."

I called Dave that night, "Well, you told me how to handle it when someone slashed my tires once, but you never told me how to handle it if he did it twice." Dave was alarmed. He offered to fly out there that night. He assumed I was in danger. But Dave was not my boyfriend anymore. I told him how much I appreciated his offer. During that conversation he found out I'd been to Virginia but had not come to see him. I had to tell him that my relationship with him had been so on again, off again, I had not wanted to confuse him. I also told him that I now planned to resign and move back to Kentucky. I was not going back to that school except for exams. He asked me if he could fly out to help me move back. I did not think that was such a great idea, but I could not deny the fact that I had strong feelings for this man who seemed to care so much.

Once when I was in the building after the second incident, the same custodian said facetiously, "Obviously they do not know who slashed your tires because no one has confessed to it." He had seen it time and again, the kids getting away with no consequences. When I asked the principal what he'd done to find the person, he told me it was virtually impossible to question every student in my classes, even though I'd seen this done at other schools. A police report had not been made on either of the slashings.

I remembered back to my first administrators in Virginia. Some school board members did not like the way they ran things. Too public. If drugs were suspected in our school and the police wanted to come in to search the lockers, the head principal opened our doors and said, "Bring in the dogs." Pictures of the searchings were on the front page of the county's paper. The whole town knew what was happening, and with that came different opinions about the quality of our school. The district and the particular school in Colorado had the best reputation of all schools in town. It was a farce. The difference with that administration was they did not let the media know the bad things that happened.

I thought I was leaving Colorado on good terms and my principal told me he'd put a letter of recommendation in the mail to me. At my last faculty meeting, one teacher boldly stood and announced I was leaving and asked for a donation for the $800 it had cost me to replace eight tires. Her voice quivered and everyone knew why. It had never been announced publicly that my tires had been slashed. She was taking a risk. In the midst of an incompetent administration, the teachers collected $803 for me in five minutes. I was touched.

Ironically, the drama class I had that year in Colorado remains one of the most fulfilling of my life. On exam day, I walked into an empty classroom. From the doorway, a hand reached inside to dim the lights and music began. A single student walked in with a long-stemmed red rose and handed it to me with a big smile. Then another student walked in. And another and then the next, and so on until all twenty-five students were in the room and my arms were filled with red roses. A lovely student named Juli walked in last with a large glass vase engraved with the comedy/tragedy drama masks and the words "You gave us everything." Nothing that happened there could lessen the love I had for those kids.

As years passed and people knew of my departure from this school, they said, "Wow, those must have been horrible kids." My response was, "No, kids are pretty much the same everywhere you go. It is how leaders manage them that makes all the difference."

Psycho Kid
Through contacts, I found out who slashed my tires. It was a strange boy in one of my English classes who sat and stared at me with a smile on his face the entire period. He was weird. He did not read when I asked him to; he did not write when I asked him to. He just sat and stared at me wide-eyed and smiling. I told people I didn't know if he was madly in love with me, or if he hated me. I guess the latter was true.

I remembered back to the day of the second slashing. When I walked through the cafeteria during lunch, I passed this boy. His coat sleeve brushed my arm and I thought, *Why is he wearing a heavy jacket in school?* I got my answer: to conceal a knife and to be able to leave the building in the middle of the day in the cold of winter.

Heading East

News of the Persian Gulf War was breaking as I drove my moving van home through a blizzard. I arrived home sick and when I lay down in bed, I did not get up for two weeks. I later learned from Dave, that he, too, had lain in bed those same two weeks, very ill. We talked and realized how important we still were to each other. He talked about traveling to do business in Kuwait and I told him I would go with him. He asked me, "Could you come with me without getting romantically involved?"

"No."

There was quiet. Dave thought we might go to Kuwait as friends but, at this point, I was not able to be just his friend. The idea dropped off a cliff. After that, I thought nothing else about the two of us being together. I would later learn it was this conversation that made Dave start thinking we might be together again.

By the beginning of March, I still did not have my letter of recommendation from the head principal, so I called the school. I got a letter – but not a letter of recommendation. In this letter the principal told me that an angry parent of a student who had been suspended and later failed, came in to blast him about the other principal's daughter not getting detention because of whose daughter she was. The principal accused me of informing the parent. I had not. Any ninny could see that she was given detention by me, and later bragged she did not serve it. He expected a response.

Devastated, I spent my waking moments composing a letter to the principal, describing my time in his school and denying that I had given the parent information about another student. To my horror, I received a letter of recommendation with two sentences describing that I had worked there and that he could be called by phone for further comment. In a second letter, he stated that he did not believe me.

The six letters of recommendation I already had were glowing. *Was this last letter of recommendation going to ruin my career as a teacher?* After my illness, I walked around in a state of shock. I had no idea what I was going to do with my life. *Would I ever teach again? Could I ever teach again? Why in the world would this man not give me a good recommendation? What on earth would this man say to anyone who called him? Certainly, it would be bad. How would anyone ever believe me over him? What had I done that was so bad?* It was March now and school would not be starting again for six months. I needed a job. *But what? Substituting? Waitressing? A whole new career? I love teaching! I worked so hard for my degree!* This whole non-letter-of-recommendation thing threw me for a loop. It messed with my head. *Maybe I wasn't a good teacher after all. Maybe these people knew best. Maybe it was all in my head, those first three years. Maybe I just thought I was respected. But they'd written good letters of recommendation. Were they making it up? I was the same person. How could these views of me be so different? There were scores of other teachers having problems with these kids in their classes. I was not the only one. Besides, these kids were vulgar, wild, and abusive. I had only tried my best. Surely the administrators saw all this. What had I done wrong?*

I had gone to the administrators for help when I had been *warned* not to.

Hawaii

My brother Aaron called and asked me to come visit him in Hawaii. "The tickets are only five hundred dollars right now, Lynnie." I was not even tempted. He called the next night and asked the same thing. Again, I said no. He called again on the third night and I said, "Why not?" I figured this was a great deal – a cheap ticket to Hawaii, and getting to see my brother, his wife and new baby, neither of whom I'd met.

One of the most beautiful sights I ever see is people greeting each other in the airport. They run up to each other and kiss and giggle and hug. You miss having this greeting when you travel alone. I arrived in Maui, all excited, got off the plane, and looked for Aaron. He wasn't there, so I gathered my luggage at baggage claim and stood, looking around. I'd been standing there for a while as a group of people moved, and there sat Aaron with his son, looking at me. He'd been sitting there all along. He said, "Oh, hi, Lynnie." He did not move or stand up to greet me, so I moved over to him and sat down on the bench. It felt weird. He said, "I just thought I'd sit here and see how you acted when you got off the plane." A sadness washed over me that Aaron had no idea how his sitting there on a bench watching me, as if I were an experiment, made me feel. He even thought it was funny. When I sat down, he immediately put his hands up to the corners of my eyes and rubbed along the sides, "Wow, you're really getting crow's feet!" I was all of 31.

If anyone ever wanted to imagine a full-fledged hippie, in thoughts, attitude, and spirit, Aaron was everything rolled into one. The freest spirit, by this time, he had traveled all over the world. Sometimes he had a shaved head; sometimes he had three long ponytails. Once he'd bought a little sailboat, taught himself to sail for two years, and sailed through the Panama Canal and across the Pacific Ocean to New Zealand. Everyone agreed it was a certifiably crazy thing to do in a 23-foot sailboat. I asked him why he did it. He told me it was something his father and two brothers would never attempt. He believed the other three did not have the courage to take such risks. This made him feel good. He had lived on the edge so often that he regularly said he'd probably be dead by 35.

Aaron was indeed a risk taker and encouraged me to be. Since he and I were the two paired up when we were young, he was my hero, my friend, and inspiration. I did follow his ideas. In my late teens, he encouraged me to hitchhike everywhere I could, and to wherever he was, so we could visit. He was proud of me. But I will say this, hitchhiking is a very dangerous and lonely activity, especially if you are alone and a female. It is dangerous, because you truly do not know when a totally crazy and murderous person is going to pick you up. It is lonely because when you have the good fortune of feeling comfortable with a nice person or group, you find yourself not wanting to leave them, not knowing what your next ride will be. It is the unknown that both ignites fear and emphasizes the feeling of being alone. I once read that a person with posttraumatic stress is left with the inability to assess risks. Aaron held up hitchhiking to be an adventure. I ignored my fears and thought I needed to be brave and walk through them. Everything in me that screamed "No!" was doused by what I convinced myself was an exhilarating experience. Once I overheard Aaron's women housemates at college complaining that he should never encourage me to hitchhike, and what was he thinking, etc... They were incredulous. It was years before I understood exactly what they meant about his encouraging me to do something so perilous.

I got to meet Aaron's 18-month-old baby boy and his new wife. We all lived in a large house with lots of people, high up the mountain of Haleakala Crater on Maui. It was beautiful. Hawaii was green and blue: green grass in front of me, moving down the mountain of green trees giving way to more green until it met the blue ocean, the blue-lined horizon, and the blue sky.

One night Aaron took us to a party. I walked up to a man and woman, stuck out my hand to introduce myself, and they both just stared at my hand. It was odd, but I was not offended, just appalled by their arrogance. *Oh, well. I'll just sit and enjoy my family and the friends I've come with.* There was dancing and we had fun, but I watched Aaron do something all night that broke my heart. He went to person after person, being friendly. Each person rejected him, as the pair had done to me, only he continued to be friendly with the next group. If someone did give him attention, it was strained, yet I felt he did not notice.

The next day I told him how hard it was to watch him go after people who were clearly rebuffing him. I saw the same little boy in him reaching out to our father. It was as if this rejection was natural, as if he believed if he just tried harder, they'd see how friendly he was and like him. I told him the things I'd learned about myself in therapy, and he told me what he'd been learning in his own therapies. Later I was standing at the sink doing dishes and Aaron's housemate who had also been with us at the party asked how I enjoyed the previous night. I told him I'd never seen so many arrogant people in my life. He came closer and, with great sincerity, said, "Well, it's true. I guess you would find a lot of spiritual arrogance among those people."

I wiped the soap from my hands, turned to him, and said, "Think about what you just said. Spiritual arrogance? That is an oxymoron if I ever heard one."

The Importance of "No!"

One of my clearest first memories is one when I was about four years old. I was lying on my back on the kitchen floor with my feet and hands raised in the air, kicking and screaming at the top of my lungs. My mom was stepping gingerly over me as she attended to her stove and her conversation with a friend. The long telephone cord bounced and dangled over me. My mother had just told me "No." I lay there screaming for some time. The moment I realized that my mother was not going to back down and that I, indeed, was going to have to live with this "No," I had an excruciating pain in my chest. Focused on the extent of this sharp pain, I was horrified to know that my mother's "No" meant "No." This was the day I learned "No."

Rarely did my mother have to say this more than once. We all learned "No" well. She was a good teacher of children. Now Aaron was an adult teaching his son. On the first night I arrived on Maui, Aaron laid out a large map on the floor to show me the volcano on Maui that he and a large group would be hiking through the next day. He wanted to show me the extent of it, and let me decide if I wanted to join them. As he was pointing at the map, his eighteen-month-old son came running across the floor, ripping a line straight through the map. Aaron immediately stopped him, looked him in the eye, and said, "No!" The boy sat there crying. Aaron continued to look at him while he cried. "You cannot do things like that." I supported Aaron, remembering how we had learned "No."

Aaron and I had stopped what we were doing and were looking into the eyes of the little boy, being fully present with him, but not giving in. Aaron's wife, watching us and holding herself back from rescuing her child, swooped in, finally, and grabbed the boy. Off she ran. I felt disgusted. Aaron had not hurt the boy and his crying was not hurting him. "No" was appropriate for what he'd done, and crying about being told "No" was natural.

Several minutes later, I walked down the hallway where his wife was holding her still whimpering child. She looked up and said, "I don't think you can spoil a child with love." I wanted to throw up. Aaron had married a very emotional woman who did not know how to say "No," This childrearing difference was a factor in their later divorce.

Ironically, two years later, his wife and I picked up Mary at the Auckland airport and the three of us women and this same child, now three, walked out to the van to look at a map. Aaron's wife took the large map and laid it out on the asphalt parking lot. The three of us squatted to our knees to check out the route we were going to take to the Bay of Islands. As we were looking at the map, the three-year-old boy came running up as fast as he could, running right through the center of the map, tearing it, almost in half. The exact same thing - two years later. The child had still not learned "No." As soon as we were in the car, the child reached into Mary's shirt and grabbed her breast. His mother was still breast-feeding. We sat in the van for an hour and a half waiting for the mother "to be able" to buckle the child's car seat. He screamed and hit her each time she tried, and each time she backed down and allowed him to win, round after round. She did not want to "force" the seat buckle around him. Again, I wanted to be sick.

I felt very sad for Aaron because I could see he loved being a father and wanted the best for his child. In my mind, he was loving and kind and could firmly say "No," but his wife would not allow it. His authority was usurped and the child was suffering because of it.

Choosing Paradise

Aaron took me to meet his friends. These were massage therapists, reiki masters, people who knew all about channeling, crystals, aromatherapy, and other therapies. It was all there on Maui.

Food could be picked off trees. Aaron, as did many men in Hawaii, carried a machete in his trunk and was constantly breaking open food for us to eat. He was resourceful. Aaron was a wheeler and dealer and could talk the socks off a homeless person. He could talk to anyone, any-time, anywhere. He was a delight to be around, but I was uncomfortable with the things I saw in him that I did not like in myself. Aaron was still manipulating and seducing people into doing things they initially did not want to do. He was wonderful at it. As I watched him, I saw myself doing some things I had worked to change. I was using my mind now to discern what behaviors felt real and right. I could see how much I'd grown and I slowly realized Aaron no longer had a hold on me. This excited me not because I thought Aaron's way of life was wrong, but because what was right for me was becoming clearer. I felt myself becoming an individual. I was a late bloomer.

One day, I went down to the beach by myself. I swam, and then sat on the beach. I looked out into the beautiful blue water and listened to the waves. At one point, I turned to look behind me. Not far away was a wall of trees, mostly pines. All of a sudden, I was back on Byron Bay, at *my* beach, the one where I'd peeled so much of me away. *Hey, this is Hawaii. This is America. My teaching certificate is good here. I could teach here. I could move here. I could treat myself to living in paradise, living in my own Byron Bay!* Decision made. I was going to heal what ailed me – in paradise.

I Had a Plan

Back in Kentucky, I'd had a nice break from the angst of the whole Colorado business. I would not be able to rid myself fully of the humiliation of that experience for years, but I felt better. I decided I'd wait tables for three months to make money before moving to Hawaii.

Those three months spending time with my mother are ones I will cherish. I continued to go to support groups and I was glad to have a plan. But the nights I'd come home and sit with Mom were beautiful. She sat in her blue recliner reading and watching television. As I sat with her, we talked and I came to feel like I had my own personal audience with a wise professor.

My mother made many poor choices in her life, but I forgave her shortcomings. Whenever her behavior disappointed me, I thought of the little girl she'd been, standing on the screened-in porch in the rain, holding onto and eventually losing her mother. That immediately took me back to seeing *her* breathless body leaning on the refrigerator. The moment she "came back to life" had been one of the most profound of my life. Having come so close to losing her only heightened my sense of *her* pain of being motherless. Whatever her faults, my mom was highly intelligent. She'd been a nurse for forty years and had taken what seemed like a seminar each weekend. She was well read and kept up with politics. She had a wealth of understanding about people and the way things worked. She was bright and I drank in her wisdom. I often sat on the floor in the midst of all the papers she'd read, milling through them with her.

Mom's friends came over and we all sat around the living room and laughed. We watched comedy shows and the monologues of Jay Leno. Mom attracted younger people, many from her support groups. Her older friends, I loaded up in the car and drove all over town to free events. They clipped coupons for senior discounts, called each other, and ordered their taxi. Me. They were hysterical and I loved them.

One thing stood between my getting close to her friends in support groups. I did not like that they did not have a strict "no cross talk" rule in meetings. I had come to understand the full value of healing with the rule and the destructive nature without it. It would have been like Mr. Huggins stuffing tissues in my face, rubbing my knee, and *talking* while I cried to him. Some friends were living as victims and could not see the value of *not* "helping someone."

In Virginia, there were "cross talk" police who had an open avenue of pointing out cross talk when it was done because it was part of the groups' rules. I had even been abruptly stopped while cross talking. It usually only took stopping a person once, to have the point well taken. Basically, it was about being able to listen to a person without interruption, to help him get out what he needed to get out. Why it pained me so badly was because I wanted to have a healthy relationship with my mom. I worried this would not happen unless she "got this" thing about therapy under her belt. But people she knew continued to "Eew" and "Ah," comment about, and defend her circumstances and she with theirs.

For me, cross talk, road blocking, or unwanted comments about my truths were the one defining thing that kept me a victim. It was the true listeners who transformed me by making me look inside myself for my own voice, made me take responsibility for myself. They did not agree with me when I made negative comments about my situation or someone else. When someone truly listened to me without giving comments or advice, I was guided back to my inner voice, and I *had* to listen. This was crucial to my becoming emotionally well.

One of my favorite lines came regularly from my 84-year-old lady friend in Colorado who, after listening to me, said, "So, are you happy with the life you've created for yourself?" Nothing used to eat me alive more. The answer in my head was a resounding *"No!"* and I was left to sort out what I'd done to create the messes I'd found myself in. I loved her for saying it to me so many times - and it was always after she'd listened to every word I'd said.

The Best Television Show I Ever Saw

I saw a television show one night that made me believe it would be worth enduring fifty years of horrible TV in order to see this most valuable one of all. It was an hour-long news program about a French woman in Canada who ran a rehabilitation house for girls who suffered from anorexia. She had a 98% success rate in healing anorexia in very severe cases. Her solution, as they say in healing circles, was simple, but it was not easy. And nothing I have ever seen has made any more sense than this.

When entering the center, each new girl was assigned a partner who rotated with others on a three-hour schedule. Essentially, the new girl was NEVER left alone. The partner working on the three-hour schedule had once been the new girl, now healed of the disease of anorexia. Her job was to whisper loving words into the new girl's ear.

What the partner knew about this horrible disease was that the new girl had ferocious and horrendous thoughts running through her head on a moment-by-moment basis. Demonic thoughts. "You are so ugly. You are so fat. Everyone is looking at you. I hate you. You are a terrible person. Everyone hates you. You are a nightmare. No one wants to be around you. You should just die. Why don't you just kill yourself? Look how fat you are. You are disgusting. You're a fat pig! You disgust me. I hate you."

The girl who was healed stayed next to the new girl, cupped her hands and spoke non-stop into her ear. She spoke wonderful lines. "I love you. I think you are beautiful. You have the most beautiful body I've ever seen. You are a child of God and I love you. You deserve to be here. You have a beautiful body. I love you. We love you. We all want you to be here. I think you are beautiful. Stay here with us. We love you. We want you alive. We are so happy you are here."

To this day, it is the most brilliant piece of healing I have ever seen. I was dumbfounded. Stunned.

I would venture to say that I, along with almost every girl I knew, suffered from some sort of eating disorder. Anorexia or bulimia are just extreme cases. I once told a doctor I was concerned that I was on a roller coaster, overeating and then over exercising, and he said, "Don't worry about it. It does not show. You look fine." *Duh, that's not the point!* The point was my *mind* was crazy!

As I sat there in my mother's living room, I thought of the hours and the reams of paper I filled with all my ugly thoughts and visions in my head. I thought of my butcher paper and how I struggled and cried, searching for the horrible sentence that plagued me. When finally getting to it, I fell into a heap. And if I lay there long enough, quiet enough, and felt deeply into my core enough, that ugly feeling would be replaced with the truth of who I was. Out poured all those beautiful thoughts -

from my marker to the paper. There they were - the words I truly was, staring at me. Those are the words I tore off and taped to my bedroom walls, so I could read them and feel them. It took me years to re-word my insides.

What this leader of this house was doing with these girls was what I'd done on my butcher paper. She was having them do it verbally and in person. These girls got love, touch, comfort, devotion, time, affection, attention and, most of all, words. New words to replace the old ones. Affirmations! I could tell her work was going to take an enormous amount of time and effort to achieve, but this *was going* to work. It was going to stick. She was going after the core issues of a false belief system — false sentences - and changing them one word at a time — with new sentences. If I'd been a millionaire, I would have sent money to fund her project.

One thing saddened me. I knew if anything were going to heal Judy of schizophrenia, it would be medication and some kind of therapy like this. Judy needed someone with her around the clock, pouring sweet words into her ears.

My Barometer

I waited tables in a popular restaurant down the street from Mom's. Two important things happened for me while working there. One day I sat on the veranda with another waiter, and said, "You know, I think I'm going to start eating sugar today." I ordered a piece of pie. I'd decided I was ready to eat sugar again.

It was one month shy of five years since I'd given it up. I found that was enough time for me to realize what sugar did to me on the occasions I did eat it. I could feel how it changed the chemistry in my body, raised my heart rate, clogged my insides, sped me up and slowed me down. Being without it for so long, I could feel it enter my bloodstream, which gave me a guide of how much was too much. I knew sugar would no longer have the attraction it once had. I did not need it to stuff down feelings. I was learning to listen to, trust, and say them. My life was better now with real feelings. It was a simple choice. Did I want to be clear or clogged?

Another thing happened. I got to see how well I was when I visited with Nem and her crew. Each one of these girls and I had been friends before and separate from my relationship with Nem, so they knew me well. One girl I'd known since we were six, the others I'd known since we were twelve. By now, these girls had been hanging out for the fourteen years since we'd left high school. All lived in or around our hometown. We agreed to meet at the restaurant where I worked and have dinner and drinks when I got off. In my work attire, I sat down to eat with them. We talked about varying topics and were having a great time. Then, at one point, Nem said, "I have an announcement to make. Quiet everybody! I have an announcement to make!"

Everyone stopped talking. Nem, sitting to my right, turned to me. "Now, Lynnie. We know you have not been in town with the rest of us. We have all been together all of these years and we have celebrated each person's wedding showers and baby showers and births and deaths of family members and most of us have been in each others weddings. We know everything about each other. We have been doing everything together, and you've missed out on all of that. And now that you are back in town, we want you to join our group. We want you to do everything with us. We want you to feel comfortable coming to all our parties that we have in each other's homes, you know like Christmas parties. We want to invite you to do things with us. We want you to know you are welcome to be in our group."

I could feel the mood of our table drop. I looked to my left as the girl looked into her drink, rolling her eyes, sucking on her straw. I looked cross the table. Another girl looked into her lap, while yet another rolled her eyes. They were shaking their heads as if to say, "Just shake it off, Lynnie. It's just Nem." But I could see that Nem was proud of herself. She was smiling from ear to ear. When she finished talking, she said, "Well, that's it," and went back to talking to the group. There. It was all said and done. Lynnie's part of the group now. Her announcement was over and now we could move on.

This is classic literature. She is a famous character from... somewhere. She is a villain from one novel, or several. She has made the decision that I can now be in their group... because without it, I was... what? Not going to be invited to anything? If not to everything, then nothing? It was all too complicated. I'd never participated in anything like this and now I knew why. I felt fine knowing I never could. I was not moved in any way. I was calm and peaceful. But I did want to respond, so I interrupted the chatter and said, "Do I get to make an acceptance speech?"

Nem turned to me, startled, and said, "Sure, go ahead."

I turned to her and to all the girls at the table and said, "I love you guys very much. You are part of my history. Whatever you do, I want to join in and celebrate with you whenever I am in town. But I have never belonged to a group and I will not be joining yours. If you ever have events you want to invite me to, I will be glad to come."

They listened and Nem said, "Oh, okay." The others wanted to laugh off the whole thing. One girl had a look of "You go, Girl!" But I was fine, unaffected. That's when I began to say I used Nem as a barometer for my recovery process. The things she said used to irk me, sure, but that was before I had words. It helped, too, to put her controlling behavior in perspective when I noticed each time I saw her she drank heavily.

Sadly, when "You, go, Girl!" got up to go to the restroom, another girl said, "Oh, Kelly gets more and more like her mother every day." She had a very emotionally despondent, negative mother. She'd been in this group all those years, too, but lived on the fringes, always trying to break away, always trying to come up with comebacks to ugly things said, with little result. These things she told me herself years later when she was able to eventually cut loose from the group. As she'd been in the restroom, something unkind had been said about her. Her fears had been valid. It was true; she was not hanging out with girls who respected her. When I got home that night, I told my mom about the comment made about the girl. I was proud to say, "If someone said I got more and more like you every day, I'd take it as a compliment."

May 10, 1991

All my life I've figured out problems using my dreams. Often they'd mirror what was going on in my life, such as being in a car that was going up a hill so steep, I thought it might flip backwards. The next day I'd wake up and realize I was in the midst of a stressful challenge that overwhelmed me. I was grateful for these clear messages from my psyche. It seemed "she" could sort out what was going on in my world, better than I.

Never was a dream more clear, more vivid, and more detailed than the one I had on May 10, 1991. In the dream, I was teaching at a private school up the mountain on Haleakala Crater in Hawaii. I had passed this school coming up and down the mountain where Aaron lived, although I'd never entered its gates. As the dream started, I was lying on a cot with my hands behind my head, just relaxing with other teachers who were lying on their cots, too. We were in a white building, the teachers' sleeping quarters. My overwhelming feeling while lying there was of being respected as a teacher, again, as I'd felt my first three years teaching. All at once, the earth began to shake. Violently. We all ran out the door into the courtyard that faced down the mountain and to the sea. Other people were running out of their white buildings around us. From the moment we ran out, the earth was cracking into long lines, running all the way down the mountain. People in front of me and behind me, ran screaming ahead, with their arms straight out in front of them. Many were falling into cracks. We were in the midst of a tremendous earthquake. I robotically ran along with the frantic crowd, but suddenly stopped at the top of the hill. *Why am I running? I'm not afraid to die.* I sat down on a very large, brown rock. The earth continued to rumble, people continued to run, their arms outstretched. The earth continued to crack and open and the people tumbled into the blackness. Everything was pure chaos.

The earth shook violently beneath me and, very quickly, the rock from the mountain rose up behind and around me. Soon it engulfed me in a cave, but left an oval-shaped opening above me, about four feet from my face. When I cocked my head upward, I could see only the sky. It was quiet, blue, and still. I could still hear the rumblings of the earth, but where I sat in my igloo-shaped cave, the ground had stilled.

I heard a voice from the sky say, "Come out, Lynnie."

"No, I'm okay in here. I'm okay to die," I replied.

"It's okay, Lynnie. Come out."

I did not want to come out. I was ready to die. I'd already made up my mind I was dying. I said again, "I'm okay to die." I sat and I did not budge.

Then the voice said, "I have more for you to do."

"It's too hard," I said. "Life is too hard."

"I will help you."

Shrugging my shoulders, reluctantly I crawled out of the hole. I sat down on the steady, still rock just outside, feeling peaceful, and small, compared to the voice I'd heard. Below me, down the mountain, the earth was still rumbling, people were still running with their arms in front of them, and the big black cracks were still opening and swallowing them.

I said, "Okay. I'm here. But I need your help. I cannot do this alone."

"I will help you," came the voice. The soft and loving tone of the voice seemed to understand that it was the only reason I'd come out of the rock cave, and now it would have to take responsibility for that and look after me extra carefully.

When I woke up that morning, I surrendered to whoever still wanted me here on earth.

Laying Claim

Before I left Louisville to move to Hawaii, Dave wanted to come for a visit. I was a little surprised; he'd never been to Kentucky, and I wondered why he wanted to take a week off work to come down. I was actually thrilled to show Dave my life in Kentucky, all the places I knew, where I'd grown up. I thought of him as a good friend. Dave showed almost no emotional reaction to anything the whole time he visited. I found myself wondering what life would have been like with someone who showed so few feelings.

I took Dave to the house and neighborhood where I'd grown up, visiting our old neighbors. All of this was fun for me, but nothing beat taking him to the mountain behind my house. Back on my foot paths, my horse paths, seeing my hollow trees, my Lillyput, my vines, my craters, my old campfire marks, my logs for sitting, my hills, my tall trees, my dirt, my land - my playground. All of this had been mine. It had also belonged to countless others, but that did not matter. What we were now seeing had once been mine. Dave drank it in. I watched him as he looked around. During that week, he'd been spending time, absorbing his surroundings, all of the places that made me - me. I was a bit amazed by this. He'd never been so interested.

He stopped abruptly on the path and turned to face me. He took both my forearms in his hands. Standing in the woods high on the mountain behind my house, he looked at me as the sunshine dappled over us. He lifted his face to the sounds of the leaves in the trees. He closed his eyes and squeezed my arms. All at once, I knew he knew who I'd always been. *I* was the horsewoman he'd longed for and never knew he had. *I* was the country girl.

While we'd dated, he'd lamented the other girl. I wanted to scream, "Can't you see that *I* came by it naturally?" That's what he saw now, in that moment. It was amazing watching him realize this in my Kentucky woods. I knew this man knew me on a deep level to begin with, but now he saw straight through me and realized the wind that was blowing through my trees all around us was the same wind that blew through my veins. It was a profound moment. No words were said. With the look we gave each other, I laid claim to who I was and I was vindicated on the spot.

"Get back into the saddle"

I had a task to do before moving to Hawaii. I needed to talk to Mr. Huggins. I needed to tell him about the Colorado incident. I could not get some thoughts out of my head. *How humiliating for me not to have a letter of recommendation from this school. If my letter of recommendation was so short, it must be bad, right? If I tried to get another teaching job, what would this principal tell them? Would I interview well and then be turned down because they'd later talked to him?* I was afraid I might never teach again. My plan was to go to Hawaii and get a different type of job, but what would bring me back to the mainland? I needed a plan that reached farther. I needed to know I could teach again someday.

Dave came with me. We sat with Mr. Huggins and his wife Phyllis and I told them the whole story before, during, and after dinner, tears and all. In the end, I asked for his advice. He did not flinch. "Wipe it off your resume. Do not put it on. Move on. Act like that job never existed."

"Huh? How can I do that? *Can* I do that? Is that possible?"

He responded, "People do it all the time." This had never occurred to me. "Lynnie, you can't let this one incident take you out of teaching forever. You had a bad run. Things go that way. Go out to Hawaii and get back into the saddle." I left there that night incredibly relieved, but I could not yet imagine being back in the classroom or even sitting down for an interview and ignoring the fact that I'd had this recent experience. *Was I even capable of withholding such information?* I had to grow up and learn.

He Loves Me Knot?

Dave decided to leave Louisville earlier than he'd planned. I was fine with that. He got in the car and traveled all the way back to Virginia. When the phone rang, it was Dave. He told me he wanted to be with me. He wanted me to move to Virginia. He wanted to drive back right then and get me. He wanted me to put Hawaii aside and said one day we'd go on a vacation. I dropped the phone. I walked out to my mother where she was sitting in her blue recliner. I squatted down and squeezed and held her arm saying. "Please don't let me marry him, Mom. Please don't let me marry him." All I could think was here was a man who'd just spent six days with me and in none of that time did I feel affection from him. None. What he was telling me now was that he loved me. He did not come out and say it, but why would he ask me to be with him? Move to be with him? Come to Virginia to live with him and not Hawaii? He wanted all of this from me and had never given me any indication he *thought* these things, had feelings for me, beyond friendship. *How could he hide them? Why had he not told me? Why couldn't he tell me?* All I could think was I did not want to be with a man who could not show me he loved me.

Letting Go

I landed in Maui and, by then, my brother had moved back to New Zealand. I found a permanent spot to live for that year: a renovated garage off a house up in the high country, where the dry country met the wet country. My place was about seven feet by twelve feet, had a loft where I slept, a laundry sink inside, and a shower outside. To use the toilet, I walked the path into the house. One wall was windows and the view from my place was of greenery everywhere I looked. In the yard there were papaya, banana, avocado, and orange trees. My roof was tin and the first night I slept there I wondered what the intermittent thumping was all night long. Oranges falling out of the trees. Each morning, I gathered four oranges, sliced them open and stood over the laundry sink slurping them up for breakfast.

I spent four weekends preparing the bed for a twenty-square-foot garden. I planted on Thanksgiving Day and was harvesting lettuce by Christmas and all else by January. I got about 500 cherry tomatoes off one plant. I grew beets the size of a fist. Carrots and broccoli and herbs galore! Each day I imagined what I'd have for dinner that night.

While traveling the hills on Maui one day, I made sure to drive by and see the school I'd pictured in my dream. I'd always been able to see into the driveway of the school, but not beyond the courtyard. I drove in and saw the cluster of white buildings atop the hill. There it was - the white buildings, the green hills that ran down the mountain and into the sea. It was all there, not exactly like in the dream, but very close.

I interviewed with an assistant principal to be a teacher at the local high school. I was very afraid to sit and look a person in the eye and have the secret of my one-semester teaching stint in Colorado. It did not come up and I was glad to be finished with the interview. I was home an hour when I got the call. I would be teaching ninth and eleventh grade English on Maui.

The assistant principal was very good and did all he could to help prepare me for the culture, but he also had twenty-two new teachers that fall; the turnover rate was great. *Hmmm...* He tried his best to describe the local, island kids, mostly that they did not like to be confronted in any way. "They will not look at you until Christmas, but when they start to like you, they will love you forever." *Hmmm...* I usually taught about the importance of eye contact on the first day.... *Hmmm...* There was a lot to learn, but there was one thing I clearly remembered him saying, "You will have to treat these kids completely differently than you treat kids on the mainland. Whatever you'd do there, you must do the exact opposite here."

Whatever problems I'd had in Colorado, whatever disrespect or cursing or violence I encountered, was not going to compare to life in this school. It was to be far worse. The Colorado school proved only to be my training ground. But a beautiful thing happened. My feelings of humiliation and of being a complete failure at the previous school guided me. I was able to learn readily and change quickly. I was more flexible and more relaxed, more laid back, more soft. That's it. I was soft. Not a softy, but I could feel the softness I had. It was the feeling as if after having a huge sigh of relief, when I knew I'd just totally let go of something big. I had this feeling all the time now. My mental health was a priority in my life. I began to see the stress I felt around things I could not control. I was no longer going to worry so much, try to control so much.

The first day of school began with my standing at the door as each eleventh grader entered the classroom with his or her head down - and the gloomiest feelings I'd ever felt emanating from so many people in one place. Now, I pride myself in being able to bring groups together and facilitate getting-acquainted activities. I have no fear doing this with crowds of people I do not know. But, if I had twenty-five ideas before those students walked in, I threw each and every one of them out the window. I was truly at a loss as to how to deal with this group.

I was called a Haole. It means "without the breath of life" and refers to a pale-skinned person or Caucasian. When a darker-skinned person gets sick, his skin goes much paler, so when missionaries first arrived, the Hawaiians thought they were so pale, they must be dying! Haole was rarely said without the word "Fucking" prefacing it.

Of 160 students, only ten were Caucasians, or Haoles. Students were from all over the Pacific Islands – Samoa, Bora Bora, Tahiti, Fiji, the Philippines, Guam, China, Korea, and Japan. Gangs were formed according to a person's origin. From my classroom I could see the front parking lot of the school where two police cars with flashing blue lights were parked every day. It was a warning.

I had the class list in my hand and began checking off names. Three minutes after the first bell rang, a girl lunged from her seat and yelled, "Fuck you!" as loud as she could to a boy near me and across the room. He said something else to her. Again, she stormed, "Fuck you!" He was teasing her about her real name. "Fuck you!" she screamed for the third time.

Everyone looked to see what the Haole was going to do. I stood there. I did not get upset. I was not riled. I took one fist and patted the palm of my other hand as I swung my straight arms behind me and in front of me, still patting my slightly closed fist into my palm, swaying. "Well," I said. "These are the types of things we are going to talk about this year. Different ways to communicate." And I began class with a discussion about communication skills. I let them talk and I let them teach me. About them. I needed to know more.

At the end of almost every single class, a boy student walked out of the classroom, ripped off his shirt, and jumped around in a circle with another boy, each with his fists held high, ready to fight. Apparently, one had given the other "stink eye" during class. "Stink eye" was looking at someone in his eyes longer than he wanted, or simply to catch his eye. Of course, I thought they were going to fight, and, while many did, if a teacher came behind them and said their names while they were bouncing around like Muhammad Ali and George Foreman, they backed down – for that teacher - and no fight ensued. If a person they respected asked them not to fight, they stopped. This was a way they could save face. Otherwise the fight was on. Stink eye was a big problem. Among the Pacific Islanders there was a wonderful culture of saving face, and it was impressed upon me how important it was to give a person an out. I thought back to Mrs. Warren and the electric toothbrush. That had been the greatest expression of kindness I'd known. After all my lessons in how to use words and confront, in Hawaii I was being shown the gift of balancing that. I knew how to confront. Maybe I needed to learn more about "giving outs." I knew somewhere between the two, was wisdom.

The kids were wild and, as I tried to get my bearings, they tested me in all sorts of ways. They were constantly watching any moves I made concerning how I handled problems with them. We were doing an activity one day, standing in a circle, and I asked a girl two down from me to do something. She looked the other way and ignored me. I did not ask twice. I began to see instantly in some situations how I needed to let go of things as quickly as they occurred, to move on as if nothing had happened. It was a funny idea, but I got it. It had to do with shame. "Me shame," was a common response from a student who did not want to do something, but that was from the student who had the courage to say it. Some, like her, were just silent. "Me shame," meant, "I am ashamed, too embarrassed. Please don't ask me to do it. Please don't draw any attention to me." I understood shame. These kids did not want to stick out in any way. There was not one among them who I could ask to run an errand for me that involved taking a note to a teacher in another classroom. That required walking into a room full of people.

Since I did not push the kids in discipline, they continued to be wild in spirit. The ninth graders had the free spirits of my younger students back East. I remember one day standing at the chalkboard writing. I turned around to see the kids laughing and talking, not seated, and walking around. I felt my anger rise. I turned back to the chalkboard and continued to write. *If a principal in Virginia walked in and saw my classroom running like this, I'd be fired. But I'm not in Virginia. I'm in Hawaii. I am not going to get angry. I am not going to allow myself to get stressed about this. I cannot afford that kind of stress anymore. There is no need. Just let go, Lynnie.* I took a deep breath and it felt like my shoulders dropped five inches. In that dropping of my shoulders, I made a decision that I was not going to get angry. Nothing was worth the stress I went through in Colorado. I turned around to see a wild and popular boy standing there doing all his antics for the class. I clasped my hands together, dangled them in front of me while I stood, and smiled. *Just love them, Lynnie.* And I did. This was not hard. I stood there smiling, and one by one, the students took their seats. I did not move until the last one sat. Then, I began to teach. Without saying a word, armed with only a smile, I was able to get the kids to do exactly what I wanted. Instead of molding them around me, I decided to mold myself around them. It was a defining moment in my teaching. I learned the "letting go" philosophy was actually the basis for a student-centered, rather than a teacher-centered classroom. I rarely, if ever, felt anger or frustration in any of my classes from that day forward. Some decisions are very powerful.

It did not take as long as Christmas for the students to look me in the eye, but it did take until Thanksgiving. I did not take it personally. I wondered how they'd respond to my teaching them affirmations. That meant they had to look one another in the eye, begin with a prompt, and say something positive to another person while mentioning something specific they liked about him or her. I modeled affirmations for them and then it was their turn. They were shy at first but began to take to it. I sat back and listened to some of the most beautiful words being said from one student to another. At the end of our first lesson, I asked if there was anyone else who wanted to give someone an affirmation before we closed. One girl said, "Yes, I want to give one to you."

"Okay," I said.

"I think you are really nice, and I'm sorry I called you a fucking bitch."

My Friend, the Moon

In Hawaii I learned about the healing power of the moon. I'd heard people talk about it. I was particularly drawn to it because of the clouds that moved so fast on Maui. When the moon was full, I took a sheet out into the yard and lay on my back and stared up. It was the brightest fluorescent white. But what was really cool were the clouds that flew past it – in all shades of gray – from the blackest black to the whitest white. And, they flew by FAST. Wow! I lay there with my eyes focused on the moon, while the clouds whizzed past. I could have lain there for hours, but had to get up and go to bed. It was the kind of "television" I think even teenagers would have enjoyed.

Lying there made me feel wonderful, and I began to crave the natural force that drew me to it. I did it every month for the days leading up to and away from the full moon. I have seen some beautiful scenes in nature – the woods behind my house when growing up and in all my travels - but lying still for those hours with the moon and fast-moving clouds was not like any power I'd ever experienced. I felt very blessed to be living in paradise.

I was lonely though, so Dave and I re-connected yet again. There was something between us that neither could let go, nor find in someone else. He planned a trip for late January, still months away.

Just Mauied

Mary called me from Australia in October and asked me to look into the possibility of Kevan and her getting married at Christmas. *Hot diggity dog! A wedding!* I'd not yet met Kevan, but Mary loved him, I could tell. Since we'd both married alcoholics the first time around, I asked her how she knew he was not one. "Because I don't cringe every time he pops the top of a can of beer," which was infrequently. *Yes!* That line was very telling of any dysfunction. I started to watch what made me cringe when I was around people.

Mary did not want any big deal made about the fact that she *might* get married. Kevan had asked her years before, and her standard response was, "Kevan I know I will marry you; I just don't know when." They flew to Maui for a six-week Hawaiian vacation.

I fell in love with Kevan right off the bat. He was a love bunny. Mary described him as "just the nicest person I ever met," and he was. In some cultures there is a belief that people come back in a different body over and over to learn the lessons they were not able to master in previous lifetimes. Mary believed Kevan was in his last lifetime, saying, "He's just that peaceful." It's true. Kevan is still the happiest and most peaceful person I know.

When the three of us were first together, Mary talked a million miles a minute, telling me things about herself that were very personal - like she always had. *Doesn't she know that Kevan is in the room? She must not.*

A couple of times I motioned to her that Kevan was in the room. "Oh, I can say anything in front of him." Mary was one hundred percent herself in front of Kevan, revealing her good, bad, and ugly parts. I did not know whom to admire most - Mary for being so confident in front of him or Kevan for being so accepting of absolutely everything about her. I'd never seen that before, but it was something I craved.

Mary had been living in Australia for over ten years. After college she'd moved to London for ten months to work and live in a flat with ten others. When she'd come home that Christmas, and I whispered in her ear, "Thank goodness you're home. Now you can help me with this crazy family," she decided right then and there she was going to head off again, this time to Australia. No one knew she was not coming back, including her.

After the years of being chained to our house and caring for our mother, Mary was carrying very deep anger and rage about our family life. Hers was particularly directed at our mother. She was resentful and felt like she'd been used as Cinderella during her childhood. Since the last time we'd seen each other, Mary had been to see a therapist, having to make a four-hour roundtrip journey in the outback in order to do so. Mary could always make and save money, so she sent money home to Mom, hoping that would suffice. She did not want to give her any more of her time. Mary bought Mom a ticket to come to Maui to be there for her wedding. She, Kevan, and I spent ten days together before Mom got there, and Mary was fine. Even though Mom was 62 and could walk, she arrived in a wheelchair. The moment Mary saw her in it, her anger ignited. Mary thought, "She's arrived as an invalid! At my wedding! Here we go again!"

The next several days, we spent time together and apart, with Mary needing to talk to Mom about her feelings about her childhood. To her credit, Mom listened while Mary told her how she'd felt. Kevan and I sat right there. I remember thinking I wished a man loved me enough to sit through something like this with me. I was dumbfounded at Mary's honesty, I was mesmerized by Kevan's love for Mary, and I respected my mother for how she helped Mary through this. My mom had enough understanding under her belt about the family disease of alcoholism to not be devastated.

I had made all the arrangements for Mary and Kevan to get married, if they chose to do that, and Mary was feeling like it was a "go." I bought leis for everyone and seven of us headed up to Iao Valley at eight in the morning. We stood by a waterfall as a judge said beautiful marriage vows. We all went to have pancakes afterwards. It was the first time I was a bridesmaid – and it was for Mary! The whole experience was awesome.

Mary and Kevan knew about my on-again-off-again relationship with Dave. Each night I took a shower and stared at the moon, meditating and praying about it, because Dave was planning to arrive in Maui in late January. The last thing Kevan said to me before they left was, "Good luck with Dave's visit."

Lonely Can't Wait Forever

It had been seven months since I'd seen Dave. I was excited for him to come. Very. He'd written me sweet letters expressing his love all fall and I was happy to have him come to a place that was so beautiful. I was lonely for him. I wanted to share paradise. *Maybe we can make it. Maybe he really does love me and just can't show it.* So far away from each other, I convinced myself I could live with that.

The very night Mary and Kevan's left, Dave called to say he'd cancelled his trip and did not know when he'd re-book it. I was shocked. I said, "That's it!" I hung up, looked at myself in the mirror, and said, "Righteo. Get on with your life." I could not depend on Dave. I loved this man, but canceling a trip I'd waited months for was the last straw. He'd rejected me many times, but this one pierced me deeply.

I picked up my laundry basket and headed downtown to do laundry. Within an hour, two guys flirted with me! *Funny, no one has flirted with me in months and the minute I say it's over, they start coming out of the woodwork!* It was true. I had two dates with guys that week. Days later, I received a letter in the mail from Dave. I put it in my pocket and drove to the other side of the island to meet a group of friends. I pulled over to a private beach and took out the letter. I sat on an ocean cliff reading. It was a defining moment. I knew I loved Dave, and I wanted to be with him, but he kept letting me down. Was I kidding myself? Every time I was available to him, he did not want me and when I was not available to him, he wanted me with everything in him. As I read the letter, I knew I had to let him go.

The determining factor in my decision was that I was lonely. I did not know when or if Dave would ever come. People have admired me for being able to do so much on my own, and I do enjoy being alone, but not all of the time. I wanted a man. I still wanted to have a child. I wanted to create a family. At that point, I still thought I could have all that. I was 32. So, I put the letter in my pocket, went to meet my friends, and by the end of the weekend, I'd met a fellow I liked.

I did not hear from Dave until two weeks later – on Valentine's Day. He called to tell me he was sorry and was making plans to re-schedule his trip. He said he'd talked to an old girlfriend who'd pointed out that Lynnie had been waiting for him a very long time, not just those several months, but almost five years. He said he got it. But I was one hour away from getting on a plane to Honolulu for a Valentine's date with another man. I said, "I need you to let me go." He was silent, so I said it again. And again. And again. I meant it this time.

Finally, he said, "Okay."

There is a saying, "a bird in the hand is worth two in the bush." Right now, I had a bird in my hand, and it felt right. I was going to stick with it. Dave and I hung up the phone, and I did not hear from him again. Three months later, I was engaged. This man was a computer specialist, a very spiritual man who'd studied the American Indian culture. He was just plain bright, in every sense of the word. We were also the same height, both blonde haired, blue eyed with bright smiles. When people met us, they took a step backwards. As one of my Hawaiian students said, "You match!" He asked me to move to Oahu to be with him until both of us could move back to the mainland together. But still Dave lingered on my mind, and this relationship would not last. *Ugh!*

I had decided living in Hawaii was not for me. I met several wonderful people on Maui, but my women friends all seemed to be in destructive relationships. One girl was pregnant by a man who was brutal to her, another was marrying an alcoholic, another was having an affair on her husband, and another was miserable with the husband she had. It was very hard for me to find a person who did not drink or smoke pot, even teachers. One teacher I worked with closely spoke so harshly to students, she'd be fired on the spot if she'd worked on the mainland. The administrator at the high school yelled at the faculty in such a way that, at first, I thought it was an act. But the Japanese teachers bowed their heads and listened to him rant. Among other things, saving money for the future or building a retirement and not living for "now" seemed to be frowned upon. It was as if the person who wanted to be prepared had no faith. Many people were into spiritual therapies, but when it came to the same people practicing their spiritual beliefs in their daily lives, I did not see them respecting each other in the way I wanted to be treated. Once a friend said, "You will find a lot of pseudo-spiritualism here on Maui." That's what I felt. It was during this time that I began to long for people who were clear-headed, effective communicators working toward goals.

By the year's end, though, I'd fallen in love with my students and hated to leave them. They had improved in their reading and writing, and they knew how to give affirmations to one another. One eleventh grade boy told me, "Before I met you, I'd never read a book in my life. Now I've read nine." They told me their high school graduation was one of their biggest events in life, as many would never leave "The Rock." In those kids, I met some of the most loving people I will ever meet. Once they saw I loved them and was not there to take from them like others had, they showed me who they were. I have never seen anyone so generous as a Hawaiian student. When a child brought in a bag of candy, he passed it around and let go of the bag and never looked again to see where it landed. There was no longer ownership of it when it left his hand. In the short time I was there, I came to believe their generosity of spirit came from the abundance all around. No one on the Hawaiian Islands would ever starve. Trees were always "going off" with some fruit, and sharing their blessings was the norm. I will never forget the smiles on the faces of those beautiful teenagers.

Three Siblings

Before I left Hawaii for good, I flew to New Zealand to spend a month with my siblings, Mary and Aaron. We spent the first two weeks on the North Island sailing with Aaron, and the second two weeks traveling the South Island in Aaron's van. The first two weeks were difficult because his wife was very emotional and could not make decisions, so everything we did revolved around her inability to commit to a plan. My mother had been a very emotional woman and had been very dependent on our older brother Jeff, so Jeff set out to find and marry a clear-headed, decisive woman. My brother Aaron married a woman who was many times more emotional than our mother.

Traveling on the catamaran was awesome. We swam constantly, ate healthy food, laughed heartily, and soaked up the sunshine and each other. It would have been a dream trip, but Aaron's son was unruly and abusive to his mother and to us, never letting up on his hitting and kicking. When he bit Mary's finger once, she thought he'd bitten it off. And we were all confined on a boat in the ocean. His wife commented to Mary and me that when she and Aaron argued, she feared he might shoot her. *Oh, no! She did not just say that! Holy shit! Do we have to carry this shit with us everywhere we go?* It was the first time Mary and I put ourselves into the shoes of one of our brothers – and what a woman could hang over him. We were furious.

Aaron continued to discipline his son with "No" and his wife continued to rescue him. It confused the boy and devastated his father. This was a classic case of different parenting styles and what happens to kids in a lose-lose situation. I know there are two sides to every story, and Aaron was far from perfect, but a brute he was not. I'd never once seen him be violent in all our lives. He was a kind and loving man, desperately wanting to be a good father to his child whom he loved and adored. It caused me to wonder just how many women were able to paint a manipulative picture such as this of their partners.

Really?

Mary, Aaron, and I headed to the South island together, just the three of us, in Aaron's old van. Whenever I got together with my siblings, and with Mary in particular, they asked me about things when we were young because they knew I remembered. Since the night of the shooting, I'd had a clear memory of most of the events of my life. If a person were ever to a give me a month and a year, I would be able to tell him exactly where I was and what I was doing.

On the ferry from the North to South Island of New Zealand, Mary and I sat chatting. Again, she wanted to know what she was like as a child, what she was doing at a particular age. As we talked, it occurred to me that, in all those years, she'd never told me anything about me when I was young. I said, "What do you remember about me?"

"Nothing."

"Nothing?"

"Nothing. Not a thing."

"Really?" I sat there for several minutes and took that in. It made me feel incredibly sad. *Had I been invisible? How can you not remember me? We lived in the same bedroom; we sat next to each other at dinner each night - for sixteen years! Why can't you remember me?*

I knew Mary did not have clear memories of our childhood, so I tried not to take it personally. Still, I was dismayed. Finally, I said to her, "Well, Mary, if you were going to describe me with one adjective, who I was as a child, what you knew, what you felt about me…what would that one word be?" She scrunched her face, struggling. "Please try."

"Okay, I'll try." She sat there with her head down for the longest time. Finally she looked up and said, "Outcast."

"An outcast? Really? How can that be? I was right there with everybody at the same time. I was always around. How could I have been an outcast?"

"I don't know. That's just the word that comes to me." Mary was a smart woman, and as foreign as that word sounded, I thought I'd give it some time to sink in. We walked around the ferry and got cups of hot tea. While we were people watching, Mary said, "It may have been because you were Pop's favorite, Lynnie."

It was the first I'd heard this. I was 33 years old. Perplexed, I asked, "Me? I was Pop's favorite?"

"You didn't know that?"

"How would I know that? We were all always together. I never did anything separately with him when we were young. I was never singled out."

"Yeah, you were his favorite. I think Mom was jealous of you."

"Really? Jealous of me? Why on earth would that be?"

"Because you were our dad's favorite," she continued, as if to drill it into my head.

I had information to ponder. I had been an outcast, and I had been my dad's favorite? All this was news to me. Neither had I felt, nor had any inkling of. *How could you not know you were an outcast? How could you not know you were a favorite? What did either of these mean? What did both of them together mean?* I was bewildered but began to use this information as I continued to piece together my puzzle.

Words Heard

It had been twenty years since Mary, Aaron, and I had lived in close quarters. Spending twenty-four hours a day with each other was surprisingly easy and fun. We were from a family of campers. Everywhere we went in New Zealand we were close to the ocean, but also inland water. At night we camped next to water and bathed in the rivers and lakes. Each of us was adventurous and outdoorsy. Splurging for a hotel was just not our style.

New Zealand was breathtaking. Every scene was a post card - white sheep on green hills, tall trees, the ice, the fjords, the mountains, the grasslands, the ocean views, and just pure nature. We hiked up a glacier, took in the sights, stopped to talk to people, talked to each other, drove from town to town, and met up with Aaron's friends. Most of all, we were three adult siblings traveling together, sharing at last.

One night after dark, Aaron trekked off. When he came back, he said to Mary and me, "Come here, you guys." We followed him along a creek bed and then along a ledge of rock above it. He stopped and said, "Okay, stand there a minute." He moved his hands up behind a wall of moss, gently pulled it away from the rock cliff and said, "Come here. Look at this." Mary and I edged our way in to see. Underneath this wall flap of moss were hundreds of glowing worms, crawling on the rock. Glowing in the dark! It was just plain cool.

Another night, as we were headed for our next destination, I lay in the back of the van; the bed was high enough to see out the front window. Aaron drove while Mary sat up front. It was pitch black outside and all we could see were the headlights splashing on the pavement in front of us.

Together now, it was not like when we were young and *not* talking about things. Now we talked without measuring what we said. We were free, and each of us had done enough work on ourselves that talking was more comforting than stressful. We wanted to hear what each other thought about living in our house growing up. Talking about our father, Mary and Aaron were surprised to hear that I remembered so much. I began to tell them the story of how he answered my questions that I bombarded him with before I could talk to him on the phone. As I said these words to Aaron and Mary, it occurred to me that they might never have heard him say he was sorry. He'd said it to me many times because

I'd asked him over and over if he was. But they had not. In that silence, I felt so deeply for my siblings who had *not* heard this. I made sure to say it slowly and clearly, "Daddy, are you sorry you shot Mommy?"

"Oh, yes. Very sorry."

I noticed how still they sat. I felt like I was giving them a gift. Almost like I was telling them what our father would have said to them, had he had the chance. The words had been his. Then I told them the story of being able to tell him before he died that I loved him and that I would miss him.

I was glad to be telling it to them because there in the dark it felt like I'd said, "I love you and I'll miss you," for them, too. There we were, the three of us together on the other side of the world, looking out into the distant night, each remembering our father.

The Welcoming Willow

Back on the mainland, I wanted to go back to Virginia because it felt like more of my life was there than in Kentucky. But Mr. Huggins encouraged me to come back to Kentucky to give in-services to teachers about how to discipline unruly children like the child I'd been. That would take telling my story. *How else would anyone listen to me?* I had prepared for this in my training with the Stevens, and I knew it was time to go back to the place where it all started.

Before arriving in Louisville, I'd read about visualizing what you want, so for months I visualized renting a small farmhouse for $400 a month, in or near town. When I got home, I went to see Aaron's friend at a bank. There was a property the bank owned that was, at some point, going to be used to build a subdivision. The previous renter had paid $750 a month and had liked the area so well that she bought the farmhouse across the cornfield from this rental property.

When I went to look at the house, the willow tree's branches hung so low in the driveway they swept over the car's windshield. The swooshing sounds made it feel like I was entering a whole new world. It was a five-bedroom farmhouse with French doors, wood floors, a fireplace, and marble bathrooms on 38 acres, right in the middle of Louisville. "I'll take it!"

"How about $700 a month in rent?"

"How about $400?"

"Hmmm…. Well, okay. It's a deal," the banker said. I now had a place to live. I got a part-time job in a bookstore and set about preparing to do in-services for teachers on dealing with traumatized students. It was time to tell my story.

Building Courage

I had created a situation in which I would tell my story in public. My fear cannot be overstated. I wanted to be a healthy person and I knew what I had to do to get there. I knew my life's calling was to do something with the knowledge I'd gained from the shooting. When I became a teacher, I saw how easily a kid like I'd been could be turned around in the classroom, just by using the very simple techniques Mr. Huggins had used. Not the part about listening to me talk for an hour, but by just using simple words that could easily be taught. I knew there were hurting kids sitting in the seats of classrooms. I wanted to take teachers into the mind of a hurt and traumatized kid. In the past I'd heard colleagues call a kid a jerk or an asshole. My standard line had been, "That kid is not an asshole. That kid is in pain, and it is our job to find out what it is. After talking with teachers, I wanted them to be able to walk away from me and say, "Oh, that's why that kid is doing that," or "Oh, now I know I need to approach this kid from a different angle." Even if a teacher never knew any particular child's trauma, the techniques and words soothed a whole class. We have all been traumatized.

The kid is not bad. The kid is in pain. That was my message.

The mustering of my courage to speak in public took longer than I expected. I was fearful. The great room at the farmhouse was long with a fireplace and a wall of windows that faced nothing but brush and trees. On the other side of the house was a cornfield. No other houses could be seen except for their lights at night. I had the mornings free, so each day from July to December, I sat in a cushy chair and stared out the window, three to five hours a day. Each day a force planted me there, and each day a whirlwind spun itself out in me. At Byron Bay, I had peeled back my onion of sadness. There in that chair, I peeled back my onion of fear.

Part of me was stuck in my fear, but another part loved facing it. I had to purge every judgmental thought and imagined criticism and make peace with every storm that blew through me. I had come back to the town where the shooting had occurred 26 years before, and I was planning to tell my family's story in public. *How would my siblings feel? How would my relatives react?* I needed answers to quiet the noise in my head. *Why do I have to bring this up? Why do I have to rehash an ugly event? Why can't I let things lie? What is the point? How do I explain this to people who criticize people for 'bringing up the past'?* As if this questioning weren't bad enough, I'd hear other criticisms such as *Who do you think you are? No one cares what you think. No one cares what you feel. Shut up. Sit down. Get on with your life. Don't live in the past.*

So many of my friends were long-since married and raising children. From them, I imagined hearing, *Why can't you just get on with your own life and leave this alone?* I'd even sent Nem an apology letter several years before, telling her how ashamed I'd felt about our fight. I asked for her forgiveness. She sent me a note saying she had other and bigger things to worry about, without accepting my apology. I'd spent all those years before not wanting Nem to have information about me, then I wrote my feelings to her. *Would I be equally rejected by others?*

Little by little, my courage grew. I visualized myself in front of people, telling my story. Each night I read *Women Who Run with the Wolves* by Clarissa Pinkola Estes and each morning I meditated on what I'd learned. The author encouraged women to tell their stories; it became my favorite book of all time. I underlined practically every word in the book, but there was one line that burned in me like a brand: "A woman's main source of power is speaking candidly on her own behalf."

It is interesting that in life we are often defined by what we "do" in the world. I sat still for all those hours all those days. It was with a sense of irony that I learned sitting in that chair doing nothing was when I was able to see myself most clearly, learn about myself most deeply, and develop who I was most fully. As the months passed, the noise lessened, and the unshakable essence of what I'd seen in Judy's eyes guided me.

The Holy Terror Returns

With just a healthy amount of fear left, the time came to speak publicly. Mr. Huggins had made the first and only phone call he would make for me, and in the first week of December, I was to give my first in-service training at *my* former high school. On that day, I was ready. A friend came and sat in the back of the faculty of a hundred people. Some of my former teachers and counselors were still there, even the man who had laughed at my mom's "chicken scratch."

When I spoke about who I'd been as a student, they remembered me well. My goal was to help the faculty get into the mind of a traumatized child who had little to no therapy, to share the discipline techniques that worked and did not work on me, and finally, to share the discipline techniques I made up myself or acquired from others over the years. The speech went well, and for the next two years, I worked twice a month visiting schools and businesses giving staff development trainings. My story was out.

A Miracle is a Shift in Consciousness

It was that fall I became enthralled with Marianne Williamson. Oprah had her as a guest on her show several times. While sitting in her own audience, Oprah gave Marianne the stage. The audience members stood up and asked Marianne questions about life. Her responses were the clearest answers to problems I'd ever heard. They all focused on love. She'd written a book called *A Return to Love,* and I remember Oprah holding it up saying that it needed to be in every household in America. It was the first book Oprah ever recommended.

If we each take different vehicles trying to get to the same place on this spiritual journey, this woman's vehicle had been studying *The Course in Miracles.* Her answers to questions from troubled viewers blew me away. I wanted to hear more. I began to go to groups that studied *The Course in Miracles*, and on January first, I started a group in my farmhouse. Twenty people came.

I learned a miracle is the moment a person's consciousness shifts from negative thoughts to love.

Studying *The Course in Miracles* reaffirmed for me what I learned from the buzzing bug years before: the negative thoughts in my head were not real. The loving thoughts in my head were real.

The Course in Miracles reaffirmed for me what I'd learned in all those hours at the butcher paper. A negative thought was a lie that was in my head, usually about myself. I had to find it, rework it, and rearrange it into a loving thought. I tried to imagine what loving words would come from a higher power.

The Course in Miracles reaffirmed for me what I'd learned standing naked in front of the mirror. Those demons in me were just in my head.

There were thoughts and words a person could say that could bring down those demons.

The Course in Miracles reaffirmed for me the healing power of love when I saw the television show of the anorexic survivor whispering into the girl's ear who was still suffering from anorexia, replacing her demonic thoughts.

The Course in Miracles reaffirmed for me what I'd learned from studying Gandhi's life, especially his quote, "The only devils are those running around in our own minds, and that is where our battles must be fought."

I was reminded of when I was a teenager viciously yelling at my mother, and the moment she opened her arms to me. I shifted. I broke. Love broke me. I, the angry person, was not the powerful one. I was the wounded one.

Most of all, *The Course in Miracles* taught me that a miracle is the moment there is a shift in consciousness in another human being, a shift so powerful that it causes him to see things completely differently. When Mary spoke her words of love and hate, "Daddy, I used to love you, but now I hate you. I don't love you anymore. Look what you've done to my Mommy," I knew a miracle had happened. I was there. I was in it. I felt it. I saw it. I heard it. That miracle happened - with a little girl simply having the courage to use words.

Words. Power. There is tremendous power in words.

But if all it took were courage and words, why couldn't these miracles happen everywhere? What, I wondered, stood between courageous words and people's will?

The Course in Miracles taught me how to change each and every one of my negative thoughts, brilliantly referred to as "attack thoughts," into positive, loving ones. I had to read through the course in my own way because some of it was not written in words I could accept. I got the gist of it, though. And wonderfully, the lessons in the course offered me new ways to think positively.

It was then I began to think of ways to talk about healing through words with regular people, and possibly with students. I realized, for every situation we find ourselves in, we have two voices and two choices. Our two voices are one negative voice and one positive voice, and our two choices are one negative thought and one positive thought. Each choice gives rise to words we say, an action we do, an experience we have, and a reality we come to know. Our character and our reputations are formed directly from the choices we make moment by moment.

I began to teach students this in a way they could understand. I'd say, "We have two voices and two choices. We constantly get to choose which one we will listen to."

I attached it to the paraphrased saying of Gandhi, "Your thoughts become your words and your words become your actions and your actions become your character. Your character becomes your reality." Then I added, "You must be very, very careful not to let your negative thoughts come out of your mouth. This will not be easy. In fact, if you are used to saying whatever you want, negative or otherwise, it will be very hard for you. But watch and see. Pretty soon, if you stop *saying* your negative thoughts, they will actually lessen in your head. But they will never go away. You must be on guard. You must constantly be aware of your choices. Every moment of every day, you choose the life you will have, whether you know it or not. Be conscious of what you say. It will show you what you are thinking."

My Hometown

Growing up in my hometown, I had experienced hurt, but I'd also experienced success. Since so much of my hurt had been purged, I thought maybe, by going home, I could regain something I'd lost. Maybe that strong leader in me would re-emerge. My return was to have its highs and very low lows.

That January in Louisville, we had such a big snowstorm that it made national news. Cooped up, I decided I wanted to have a video library of some of my speeches. Someone told me that anyone could have his own 30-minute television show to air on public television. *Wow, that would make it very official. Besides, no one watches public television. I can't embarrass myself too much.* Over the next two months, I taped eight segments that aired at 2 p.m. on Saturday afternoons. I named it *My Hometown*.

I told no one about its airing.

I was surprised how many people watched public television. Two weeks after the first one, a guy walked up to me at the bookstore counter and told me after listening to me, he called his wife who he was separated from. He flew down to Florida and they decided they were going to get back together. He told me he'd committed to getting therapy. Surprising. Others did not tell me anything that drastic, but people did come into the store to tell me they'd watched the show! High school friends called to tell me they'd seen me and were passing the news around.

I had a mixture of being delighted and embarrassed. People laughed when I said I did not mean for anyone to really watch it. I was just practicing! I'd come back to my hometown a different person from the one who'd left, having learned a great deal about the family disease of alcoholism. I used my story as a springboard, and went on to describe the many things I had to do on a regular basis to stay well, most of which had to do with taking care of the body. My yoga friend from Virginia came down to be a guest on a couple shows. That spring I wrote a letter to Oprah Winfrey about the self-esteem workshops for young women I was planning. Being in the middle of all of this – putting attention on myself – was uncomfortable on many levels. The shame was lifting, yes, but my family was still unpredictable, and when I felt bombarded by everyone all at once, I fell off course.

Overwhelmed by Neediness

Coming home hurt. It seemed every time I tried to do something for myself, there was a family member popping up, trying to knock me down. The truth was, I was not emotionally equipped to manage all of my family members' problems. My mom had three operations, one on top of the other, and needed constant care – something I could not give her and stay afloat financially. The guilt was almost more than I could bear. Judy was lurking about when she wasn't in the hospital. I did not feel safe around her. If anyone could sabotage my undertakings, she could. Once a friend and I were at my mother's house when Judy happened to be there. He and Judy sat on the porch together. I heard her ranting through the window but did not hear what she said. I knew some of it had to be about me. Later, he looked at me funny. "What?" I asked.

He told me all the vile names she'd called me. She'd said terrible things, like usual, in her sick and demented way. But I heard something in his voice I didn't understand. It caused me to ask, "What do you mean? What else?"

He said, "Lynnie, she really had me convinced."

"Convinced? Convinced about what? Me being horrible?"

"Yeah! She's pretty good!"

"And you believed her?"

"Uh, well, uh… I didn't know what to believe."

Right there and then I realized I was dealing with fire. It was difficult enough to be talking publicly about the family disease of alcoholism to people without a good understanding of it. For people to question my character through Judy's angry schizophrenic rants, was too much for me. By the way, I ditched that so-called friend.

My brother Aaron was back in town wheeling and dealing. Still, his wild antics left people roaring with laughter but, afterwards, they would not know what hit them. It seemed every time I saw him he wanted to coerce me into doing something. I wanted to shrink and hide when I saw him coming. *Please don't ask me to do one more thing for you. Could you just talk to me instead?* By now Carl and I got along very well even though he was quite cynical, and he was angry with Mom. Jeff and Mary lived far away.

The story I was telling publicly was about craziness and healing it. But craziness was all around me. How could I maintain my own sanity when others didn't have theirs? How could I keep the look of my doubts and insecurities off my face? How could people believe that it was possible to get well from a family like mine when I didn't feel well myself? I was not expecting support from my family, but I was not expecting to be dragged backwards so far. Backwards to what self-examination told me was my biggest fear of all: people will think I am crazy, too. I feared my family was a reflection of me - that I'd be put into the same box, the lid closed, and I'd never break free. Being free and well did not feel like an option while I was still in such close contact with my family. Picture Thanksgiving dinner - every day.

I felt like I was at the base of that fence again, being asked to climb back on top, to walk it again. Instead of walking it gingerly like before, hoping not to fall, I did not even have that chance. From my vantage point, if I went back up on that fence, this time there were many needy arms reaching up to pull me down. I could *not* get back up there. I had to stay on the side of the fence I'd chosen, the one I'd found through therapy. I had to have boundaries. But the emotional pulls - the guilt, sadness, and fear – continued to overwhelm me. I needed days to have breaks, to plan my workshops, but often I could not find them. *I just can't get away from them. No matter what I do, they're there. I cannot hope to make a living working with emotional wellness when my family is still so emotionally ill.* Then one particular night over the phone, a man who'd hired me to do workshops said, "Oh, your brother called me today and wanted me to buy such and such from him…." Too close to home, literally and figuratively.

A while later, I sat in the bathtub feeling bombarded from all sides, and, for about three minutes, I wanted to die. *Now what is it that people kill themselves with? Is it vodka and some sort of pill combination? What is it they say in the movies? I wonder which combination?* When I found myself having these thoughts, I knew I was in trouble. I stepped out of the bathtub and called the one person who would understand the overwhelming feeling I was having, the person who'd taken herself to the other side of the planet to get away from it: Mary. When I heard Mary answer the phone, I tried to speak, but began crying convulsively. Listening to me cry so hard, not being able to speak for some time, Mary said, "I can get on a plane today, Lynnie. I can be there tomorrow." That snapped me out of it. All at once I understood I only needed someone I could count on.

I could count on Mary. Mary and I regularly talked on the phone for two hours at a time. But Mary was not in my daily life. She understood clearly how being around mental illness could make a person feel ill mentally. She had a great line about dealing with mentally ill people. "When I walked away after talking to her, I didn't know if I was Arthur or Martha." That always made us laugh. I calmed down and began telling her exactly what had happened, all the events leading up to then. She listened while I talked it out, and two hours later we were chatting like always. We had a good laugh about all things painful. I knew I was better when I said to her, "Well, I'll be sure to call you next time I feel like killing myself!"

Alarmed at the beginning of our phone call, Mary had nothing to worry about at the end. We both knew how serious thoughts of suicide were. Even with all the pain I'd been through in healing my past, I'd not thought about killing myself since way back when I opened my mom's medicine cabinet at thirteen. Healing my family's issues from my past had been easier on my own, away from them. In present time, in the same town, it was different.

Working

It was around this time I realized what I'd not known consciously. From the moment I saw Mary "resolve the conflict" with my father, it crystallized in me that if a little girl could do that with such a big problem, adults could use eye contact and words to resolve smaller conflicts. Even wars had been started - and ended – with words. Most conflicts are on a smaller scale than attempted murder or war. I wanted to help people resolve conflicts.

I tailored workshops and staff developments to meet the needs of the administrators and bosses who hired me. I knew I could help teachers create happier environments for kids and help staff members get along better. I was a mediator for people in disagreements, helping them articulate affirmations and apologies.

Although my relationships with men were dysfunctional, my relationships with people were not. I was a happy, eager, and enthusiastic person and attracted others to me. I used the communication skills I'd learned on a daily basis. My very nature sought ways to resolve conflicts easier, faster, and more effectively, without damaging the relationships. I also began giving self-esteem workshops and weeklong camps to young girls. I flew to Virginia to give a young women's workshop to eight of my former seventh graders who were now seniors in high school. It was beautiful to see how they'd grown and sad to see the pain some carried. One girl was still a bright and beautiful flower, her eyes still beaming, as they had in seventh grade. A few of the other girls had a hard time looking me in the eye. Over the course of the day, I learned those girls had painful secrets they did not want me to know. Later when they felt safe enough to talk, I learned almost every painful case had to do with feeling shame about a relationship with a boy. I could relate.

Oprah

I called my house sitter from Virginia on a Thursday. She told me there was something there for me from Western Union. "Oh, it's probably just a coupon." I returned home on Sunday night to find it was a telegram from a producer of the Oprah Winfrey show, asking me to call her about the letter I'd written. It had been exactly six months since I'd mailed the letter about my creating self-esteem camps for young women.

I could barely contain myself until nine o'clock the next morning.

When I reached the producer, we talked for 30 minutes, after which point she said, "Can you get on a plane today?"

I responded, "Yes."

"And will you bring your mother, too?"

"I'll try," I answered.

"If not," she said, "it's okay, but we'd like to have her." She gave me the arrangements for the plane, hotel, and show. They were taping the next morning. I needed to get to the airport by one o'clock. *Uh, oh. Here I've put myself out there; that's fine. But my mom?* As "big as life" as my mother had always been to me, she was actually a very shy person in public.

I called her. "Mom, I'm going to ask you something that might be really, really hard to do, but if you say yes, it might be very good for my career working with kids - so I'd *really* like you to say yes."

"Okay," she replied.

In another mouthful, I continued, "Would you please go through your closet and pick out your nicest outfit, pack, and be ready, so I can pick you up in two hours to take you to the airport to fly to Chicago to go on the 'Oprah Winfrey Show'?"

In a small and feeble voice, she said, "Okay." My mom was in. We were off. Plane, hotel, dinner, bed, breakfast, downstairs to be picked up. What surprised me most was, I was calm and peaceful. I was not nervous. This was exactly what I was supposed to be doing.

When we arrived downstairs, we stood with the fifteen other people who were going to be on the show. These people had all witnessed violence between their parents. Oprah devoted the entire show to the aftermath of violence, as it pertains to and impacts children who witness it. It began by highlighting the 911 calls Nicole Brown Simpson made; O.J. Simpson's voice could be heard in the background. Oprah had already interviewed several children privately and early in the show played that tape for the audience. She had other guests – the son and daughter of a man who had stabbed his wife, their mother, forty times with a knife on their kitchen floor. The father came on the show, too, being televised from prison, and denied that he'd stabbed his wife. The son got to confront him and he later told me that was the best part of show for him! There was a daughter who'd witnessed her preacher father beating her mother. Her father was there with her. There was a woman whose father shot and killed her mother on Christmas Day, and Mom and me. Lastly, a psychologist.

When I did speak, it was only for two minutes and thirty seconds, but it was enough to have Oprah kiddingly fall forward with her microphone and say, "Yooooou're a wooooooooonderful story teller!"

Oprah was a delightful person who I only spoke to in tiny bits and pieces. I learned the most about her by talking to the people she'd hired. Every person who guided us through the taping of the show was an excellent communicator. It was as if her staff as a whole had a higher consciousness.

In the early days of Oprah's show, I could not watch it. Although I could see she was a good person, I cringed when she asked people personal questions, then took the microphone back and said something like, "No you didn't!" or "You did what?" or "You're kidding!" or "Why did you do that?" or "What were you thinking?" or "What was wrong with you?" or "Why didn't you just walk away?" These were the exact responses a person was restricted from giving in a support group. It was cross talk. Often I saw the look of shame on the person's face. Whether her eyes dropped or his face just twinged, the moment for growth was lost.

Slowly over time, on camera, Oprah became a miracle in the making. She became more soft, more humble, a better listener. She gave examples from her own life. Oprah was on a tremendous healing journey herself, so I was drawn to her and her struggle. Year after year, she began to open up more about her challenges with food addiction. She brought on guests that spoke quiet truths. As a country, we got to see Oprah question, marvel at, and be skeptical of them. Ultimately, we all got to formulate our beliefs through the spiritual laws presented to us. In essence, we as an audience changed as we watched Oprah transform in front of our eyes. I felt a kinship with her because I knew what we saw on television was just the tip of the iceberg in terms of her development and growth. I knew ugly very well, and I believed she did, too.

Before our nation and the world, Oprah was bravely "doing" B through Y. She began to sit in quiet peace, looking into the eyes of her guests on stage, listening in present time, drinking in every word for her own healing. She modeled healing. Her show highlighted healing from posttraumatic stress better than any show on television. Thank goodness for her courage and strength to withstand years of brutal criticism. The Oprah Winfrey Show is responsible for jump-starting the healing for millions of people, especially women, around the world.

Mediating Parents and Teenagers

My Oprah show appearance may have been brief, but my phone rang the day after its airing. A parent said she was having trouble with her teenager. She described her problem. I told her to bring her husband and teenager to my house. I intuitively knew to use a certain technique. I had the two parents sit on one side of the great room and the teenager sit about ten feet away. I said to the parents, "Okay, tell your daughter why you are here."

Trying to speak straight to their daughter was difficult; they were noticeably agitated. I asked one parent to speak at a time, and combined, it went something like this: "She's a mess! Look at her! Look at you! You're a mess! You look like crap, you won't go to school, we can't get you out of your room, and then you leave and we can't find you to get you back home. She won't come home!"

The tone and the words that came out of their mouths were words that would have turned my stomach as a teenager. Now, as an adult, I knew what they were trying to say. I turned to the teenager and said in a softer, slower voice, "This is what I believe your parents are trying to say: 'We miss you. We love you. We want to spend time with you. We want you home. We miss you terribly.'" After I said it, I turned back to the parents and I said, "Is that what you meant?" Staring at their daughter, their eyes still, they nodded their heads up and down.

After a meaningful pause, I said to the teenager, "Okay, now tell your parents how you feel."

Out spewed, "Ha! They don't miss me. They hate me! They hate how I dress. They hate my friends. You guys act like you are so nice, like you want to 'spend time with me,' and all you really want to do is corner me so you can criticize everything I do and run off a long list of what you hate about me. You don't trust me. You hate me. Well, I hate you both. I hate everything about you."

I listened very carefully to hear what she might really be saying beneath her anger. I turned to the parents and I said, "This is what I think your daughter is trying to say: 'I don't feel your love. I'm afraid if you come near me, you will hurt me. I am in so much pain right now.'" And when I asked the teenager, "Is that right?" she nodded.

I asked the parents to speak to their child again. Again, they used too many ugly words that "creeped out" the teenager. They thought they were being kind. "Afraid of us? Hurt you? We've never hit you. What kind of pain? Of course, we love you. We wouldn't have brought you here. We're tired of looking at your black hair, your black makeup, and your friends who look like drug addicts who don't speak to us when they come through the house. Your room looks like a bomb went off in there."

To the teenager I said, "This is what I think they are trying to say: 'We are so surprised you are afraid of us. We had no idea, and we are sorry. We had no idea we were hurting your feelings so terribly. We brought you here because we love you. When we see you, we do not know you. We are afraid our daughter is gone. We are afraid you do not love us anymore. We are terrified of losing you. When your friends do not talk to us, we become more afraid. We would never want you to be in this much pain. We are so, so sorry.'" And back to the parents, "Is this right?"

Now the parents had tears in their eyes.

I asked the child to speak again to the parents. "Funny way of showing it. You're not sorry. You're only saying that. If you could change me, you would, but I won't let you. I hate you. I hate living in the house with you. You make me sick. I just want to go be with Brian. Just leave me alone."

It was very clear the way they were speaking here in my house was the way they spoke to each other at home. I asked about Brian. It was her brother who'd gone off to college. I turned to the parents, "This is what I think she is trying to say: 'I am in so much pain right now, I cannot feel your love for me. I hurt so badly. I miss Brian terribly. He liked me. I feel so alone. I don't know who I am without him here. I don't really want to be alone. I just want someone to love me. I want you guys to love me like you used to.'" And when I turned back to the young girl, tears were streaming down her face.

The parents, crying, now speaking directly to their child without prompting. "We miss Brian, too. We are so sad to see him gone. And now we feel like we are losing you, too. We do not want to lose you."

I turned to the child and said, "I think your parents are also trying to tell you they would die a million deaths if anything happened to you. They would never forgive themselves, their worlds would come crashing down and life would never, ever be the same without you – the daughter they love. They want you back, and I think if you come back, you will find things can be different among you."

One parent crying said, "We just want our family back."

"I want my family back, too," the daughter responded.

They stood up and hugged, crying.

There was no more to say. The details of their lives and how they worked them out were not important to me. It was important they see the love they had. I suggested they call Brian that night and meet me back in those chairs in three days. I knew a week was too long with those raw feelings. I knew they would forget the love part and be down each other's throats fairly soon. If this method was to stick, the power of the love part had to be felt to its core. Several times. I had to get them to see how much they loved each other in spite of harsh words and outward appearances. We did it again in three days. And in another three days. Each session went about the same way.

They did not come back after that, but the mother called to give me progress reports. She told her friends, and I began mediating parents and their teenagers. Of all the work I've ever done, this is the work that made me happiest.

When people don't have effective words, they use ugly words in their place. Most of the time, that is not what they mean. It turns the other person off so fully, the love they have for each other gets lost. In the words. It was the pain I was listening for in each person. I'd been an angry person. I knew the hurt and humiliation lurking underneath. In all my heartache, I had come to learn that love had always been there. That was the *only* place to put the focus. When the three of them aligned in love, the details would fall into place.

When I have a conflict that is unresolved, I can remember the fine details that surround it, down to the lime green thread that hung off the button of the sweater the person was wearing at the time. But when a conflict is truly resolved, the details vanish, and I even have difficulty retrieving the topic of the conflict. When I know I have been heard, the conflict is resolved. When someone has a conflict with me, I know I must sit completely still and silent to hear his words in my core. I suspect every one of us just wants to be heard.

The Letter

My mom called me after the airing of the Oprah show to say my aunt, another of my father's sisters, had called to scream *at her*. Since she was an active alcoholic herself, I decided to write her a letter. In the letter, I said if my father were here today, he would support me in what I was doing. I knew he would be proud of me. My father knew the damage he'd caused his children and I believed he would have come listen to me speak. Had he lived longer, he may have even come to an AA or Al-Anon meeting with me. *His* was all the permission I needed. I told her not to call my mother again, to call me instead, giving her my phone number. She did not call again.

Thanksgiving at OLC

There was something I'd been visualizing, something I needed to do. For twenty years, over and over again in my head, I thanked all of the people who helped us after the shooting. It was now time to go back to the church where I grew up, to give thanks in person.

That fall I asked the priest at Our Lady of Consolation if I could address the congregation on Thanksgiving Day. He agreed, so I put an invitation in the church bulletin, inviting people who knew my family from the past. It'd been twenty-seven years since the shooting, but many people were still alive. For those that were not, I wanted their family members to know what a large part they'd played in the healing of our family. I asked them all to come.

On Thanksgiving morning, I had not written down a word. All my professional speeches I'd given up to that point, I had written out in meticulous detail. I had studied them, only following the organization, not reading the words. Time had run short. For some reason, I could not write this speech until the very day I was to give it. That morning, I wrote it lickety-split. The words flowed out quickly. I included every visual image of help received from that time period, including the buttons Mrs. Senn sewed up the sides of the dresses she made for Mom, so Mom could get them on over her cast. One had lavender flower bouquets with matching lavender buttons, Mom's favorite color.

Mom no longer attended OLC, but was still friends with everyone.

She and Aaron came with me that morning. Father called me to the podium after communion. I did something I'd never done. I read what I had written, word for word.

I was "pulled" to give this thank-you speech, but I was terrified of saying the specific words I'd said in my head. I realized when I'd said them, why I had to read the speech. My gratitude so overwhelmed me I feared I might not make it to the most important words of all: "Thank you for cleaning up the blood."

Take the F

Tough love was something I believed in and had the boundaries for, but when some people initially saw it, they viewed it as unkind. I respected it from first-hand experience and was always willing to walk someone through its painful process.

I had been giving staff development seminars for a year when in January a principal called and asked if I'd consider coming to teach in an "emergency" situation. A teacher had left in November, and the students had run off two substitute teachers. I agreed to teach eighth grade English for the second semester.

I did not find the kids unruly. It was their parents. This was a very affluent area; one of the parents was on the school board. Apparently, she'd made the first teacher's life so miserable, she'd quit. Fortunately, I had never been impressed with or intimidated by money or prestige.

When I arrived, the school board member's child had earned an F before, and a C since, the original teacher left. I took over with three weeks remaining in first semester. The student, her child, was very smart and capable, but he was lax about his work. In those three weeks, he'd earned an F from me, too. His final semester grade was an F in English.

The school board mother came to see me. She thought her child deserved an A because he was smart, and an excellent reader and writer. That was true, but he did not produce evidence of this and he did not follow instructions. I think, in many ways, he thought he did not have to.

She was livid. At me. Why would I not change the grade? I told her he did not earn an A. She spoke angrily for a while and soon was about to get up and leave. All at once, I drew in close to her and said calmly, "I want you to listen to me carefully. Let him take the F." She scowled.

Again, I said very slowly, nodding my head, "Let him take the F." Her face twitched. She was no longer as angry. Next I said, "I know your son is capable. I know he is an A student, but he is not doing the work. He feels he does not have to." She began to argue, so I let her finish. Then I said, "This is not a reflection of you. He has a lesson to be learned here." Her eyes welled with tears and I said very slowly, "I know this is painful for you. I see that you are very angry. But right now your son is being arrogant and cocky. Let him take this F and let him start anew with me." Tears streamed down her face. We were sitting closely by then. As she cried, I said again, "You can do this. Let him feel the pain of getting an F. Let him see the consequences of his actions." We stared into each other's eyes, and I said one more time, "Let him take the F."

"Okay," she said gently, got up, shook my hand softly and left my classroom. I never heard from her again. Her son came back that semester a different person and earned an A.

I wish I could have explained to this woman that she had to be willing to feel her own pain first before her child could learn the lessons of his own consequences. Painful consequences are vastly underrated.

Wrestling with a Demon, Literally

That spring my eighth graders helped me move Mom into a new apartment not far from my farmhouse, and Jim and Phyllis Huggins came up to go to the Derby with me! It was May in Kentucky. The flowers were blooming, I was teaching and gardening, and all was right with the world. Until it wasn't.

This is my hardest story to tell.

Judy had been in and out of the mental hospital for many years. Mom knew very well that I was genuinely afraid of Judy; merely being around her, I feared for my safety.

One day, Mom's car pulled up to my house and out hopped Mom and Judy. I did not like this from the start. I was surprised. Mom needed to drop off my hoe and later told me she thought Judy was having "one of her good days." She thought it was okay. They came in very briefly to see the house, and then I led us all out onto the porch to sit. Judy's blonde hair was so dark and dirty that it was almost black. It was a very hot day so Judy was in shorts, and I in the old tank dress I wore for gardening.

Judy sat with her legs crossed, bouncing the top leg up and down very quickly while she stared into the cornfield. Mom was acting overly cheerful. Neither of these was a good sign. My awareness sharpened.

All at once, Judy said, "Looneybird, you stole my body parts." I'd heard this line before. "Looneybird, look, you stole my legs," she said more animated.

I went into my let's-talk-down-a-crazy-person mode, realizing anything could happen. "Well, Judy, that's because we are in the same family. We're going to look alike. See our hands." I put my hand up to hers. Her nails were claws, thick like an animal's. "My nails are not as thick as yours. I wish my nails were thicker."

"Uh, huh, uh, huh, uh huh," she began saying, over and over again quickly while bouncing her leg, staring straight ahead. "Uh, huh, uh, huh, uh huh."

I sat back and said, "Mary's hands look like mine too. We all have Mom's hands."

"Uh huh, uh, huh, uh huh." She was rocking in her chair, her leg still bouncing, her eyes fixed straight ahead. I took deep breaths, as I could see she was thinking. The air thickened.

Then, to me, she blurted, "Did you steal my peas and carrots? I think you did! How am I going to fight a war without my peas and carrots? I need more peas and carrots on my side. You stole them, didn't you?" Judy had been having wars with peas and carrots for years.

"No, Judy, I didn't."

"Who took 'em then? Huh? Mom, was it you?"

Mom looked down and shook her head sadly, "No, Judy."

We both knew Judy was headed to a place where, once there, she could not let go. We'd all been in these conversations before. Relentless in her asking, we knew we were in for a barrage of questions. "Well, somebody did. And you're sleeping with my boyfriend, aren't you, Looneybird? You're sleeping with Mick Jagger, aren't you? Go ahead, tell me. I know you are."

I was standing by the time she mentioned "boyfriend," because I knew we were now headed to the point of no return. Mick Jagger was her boyfriend, and everyone was sleeping with him, especially me. "Well, I think I'll get the hoe out of the car, Mom. Let's all walk to the car."

Judy followed me down the sidewalk the whole way, cursing loudly in my ear, "Didn't you, Bitch? You're a whore! I know you did! You probably slept with him last night. You don't want to tell me, do you? Go ahead, tell me. You're sleeping with Mick Jagger. You whore! He's *my* boyfriend! Mine!" Everything about her - her voice, her pace - had escalated. It was clear there was only one thing that would de-escalate the situation – a climax of some kind.

It was the climax I feared most.

Judy continued ranting filthy remarks. Hate was spewing from her mouth. Her body became stiff and angry, with adrenaline pumping through it. I knew I had to hurry. I reached in and got the hoe out of the back seat. As I lifted it, Judy was on the other side of the door next to the driver's seat. She was still badgering me with questions about sleeping with Mick Jagger. I was no longer answering her questions. She did not like this. "Look at me! Look at me!" she screamed. She wanted my eye contact, but I was afraid to look her in the eyes. As I pulled out the hoe, she slammed the door, only half way, as if to hit me with it but she jerked it back to her. She said again, "Didn't you, Bitch?" She had both of her hands on the edge of the door slamming it at me. Judy was in a full-blown fit of rage now. I thought she was going to slam the car door on my arms.

"No, Judy. No," I answered her questions. I looked up at her and then away. She did not like it when I looked away. As I came around the car with the hoe, she grabbed hold of it.

There were three hands on the hoe. Two of mine and one of hers. Her one hand pulled it so forcefully, I knew I had a monster on the other end. I had to get very strong. I felt her ferocious anger. I knew what was in there. I'd gotten mine out in therapy. She had not. She was a bottomless pit of fire. I knew her strength was going to be greater than mine; I was going to have to flex every muscle I had in warding off this force. I knew then I was fighting for my life.

Now Judy had both hands on the hoe. She was stronger. I felt like a weakling compared to her. I did not want to become what I knew I had to become.

I will say, in this split second, I wanted her to get out all her anger. Not on me. I just saw how much was in there as I felt it rising to the top. In another time and place, I would have loved for her to have a place to put this anger. I knew she had stuffed it for too long. Getting rid of my own anger was the key to my becoming well; I felt so sad that she was too sick to benefit from therapy. I felt sad that now that I could see this anger at the surface, I could not help her find a container for it right then and there. To get it all out and put it - somewhere. This was my split-second thought. But I understood my life was at stake.

I had to draw from every part of the heavens and earth to not let her get that hoe.

With four hands on it, it was moving back and forth, to her chest, then to mine. I moved backwards trying to get away. Judy had become a killer. I knew I would be dead if she got it. My life would be over. There was no doubt in my mind that if she were to swing once and land a hit, she would swing a hundred times - or a thousand. Whatever volume of anger had accumulated in there, its measurement would be told in every strike to my skull.

Finally, I twisted the hoe, and it broke free from her grasp. I turned to run toward the house. I got about three steps when she jumped on my back while I simultaneously threw the hoe forward and away. We rolled in the grass; she scratched and clawed me. We tumbled into bushes, rolled across my sidewalk, and through the grass. She chomped down on my thumb. It was the wild and vicious clamp of an animal. It was a death bite, and it seemed impossible that my thumb did not come off. With the vicious biting of my thumb, I knew she was going to kill me in a matter of seconds.

I was going to have to kill her first.

She was not my sister. She was some "thing," and I knew it was either she or I. We rolled more. She clawed more. There were no real fists thrown. I was just trying to get away. It was as if she were glued to me, mirroring my every step. Whichever way I turned, she was still on me, pressed to me, stomach to stomach.

When we rolled into the driveway, I was finally on top of her, holding her arms down while she writhed under me, kicking up dust and gravel. She was viciously stretching her neck off the ground, like a wild beast, trying to bite the insides of my forearms or my neck. Growling. Spewing the vilest words I'd ever heard, words I'd *never* heard and cannot write here, in a deep, unearthly voice. Her words felt like they were motoring up from her chest like an engine. As I pulled my arms away, it brought my face closer to hers, and then I saw it. Her eyes glowed fluorescent green. All at once, I understood: this was not Judy. This was not my sister. Staring into her eyes, I was shaking wildly, frightened beyond boundaries I'd known. I wanted to release and run, but I knew this beast could catch me faster than Judy could. The closer I came to her face, the more it exposed my neck, giving her legs more freedom to kick – and to bring me closer to her. But when I pulled back, it gave her better access to my arms. In my mind, I could see my flesh being ripped away in pieces by her teeth. I was trying to protect myself from the most lethal part of her: her mouth.

As I was on top of her, I could not look away, but was screaming to Mom, "Mom, call 911! Call 911!" She ran to me and told me she already had. "Then go out to the road and stop a car! Bring someone to me! Help. Help! Please, Mom, run! I need help!" Judy's strength was such that I knew I could not keep her pinned long. I saw Mom run down the long, gravel driveway through the willow tree branches.

When I turned back, the deadly motor had been turned off. The engine had died down. The plug had been pulled; the demon was gone. It was Judy. She was saying to me in her soft voice, "I'm okay, Looneybird. You can let me up now. I'm okay. I'm not going to hurt you." I did not loosen my grip, but I felt like I did not have to worry so much about my arms being eaten. She was flatter now, no longer arched or writhing with volumes of puffed air. Now she said in her little girl voice, "Owww, Looneybird. You're hurting me. Let me up. You can let me go now. I'm not going to hurt you. I promise."

Such is the roller coaster of mental illness.

I looked into her eyes and said, "Judy, I can never see you again. This will be the last time I ever see you." She did not say anything. She was just annoyed and wanted to get up and 'get on with her day,' so to speak.

Mom had stopped a van and the woman driver came running down the driveway. She slid onto her knees, leaned in and said to Judy, "Are you okay? What can I do for you?"

I had never heard the tone of voice that came out of me just then. I turned my head to the right. Our hair was dangling over both of our faces, this woman's and mine. Evenly, I said to her, "*I'm* the one that needs help, Lady."

Mom was there now, hovering over us. Judy was saying to her, "Mom, tell Looneybird to let me up. I'm okay now. I'm not going to hurt anyone." She turned to me to say, "I'm not going to hurt you, Looneybird."

Mom said, "We have to wait for the police to come, Judy. You will have to go to jail."

"Okay," she said weakly. She had been there before. She slumped her head to one side and resigned herself to wait with her face lying in the gravel and dust. The police came and brought an ambulance. I got off Judy as they rolled her over, handcuffed her, and put her in the back seat of their car.

There I was with my dress askew. There were cuts on all sides of me, caked with dirt and gravel, with long streams of blood running from them in all directions. The paramedics asked me about my injuries and I told them Judy bit my finger. They wanted me to come with them to the hospital to get my wounds cleaned. I thanked them, but told them I would clean them myself. They told me, since it was a human bite, it could become very infected. I said I'd take a bath and go to the hospital later. I knew what I had to do first. Everyone agreed and off they drove with Judy. I was weak and limping and did not even watch as the police car drove away.

My mother, the nurse, was with me, but I did not want her. I appreciated that she called the police. After the last incident, fifteen years before, I made her promise several times that she would call the police if it ever happened again. She had kept her promise.

I went into my beautiful marble bathroom, ran the bath water, and locked the door. I wanted to do it alone. I began cleaning my wounds. I knew that I had been traumatized. I knew I had the tools to get through this. And so I began. I washed my arms with soap and bubbles and rubbed my arms over and over. Judy had put two four-inch gashes on both my arms. A matching set. They were very deep grooves, and I knew I would be scarred. The other wounds were smaller knicks and cuts of her fingernails going straight into me but not ripping back a trail. They would scar, too.

I was in the bathtub for three hours, crying, praying, rubbing my arms, hoping to heal them with the love I had for myself. I knew I had done nothing in the past or present to make Judy want to kill me. When I came out, Mom was waiting. She took me to the hospital, and we began our long wait. Finally, I got my thumb wound cleaned. We got home at four in the morning.

Eight Mothers

When I woke up the next day, I was weak and, with oozing wounds, very gingerly went out to the video store and rented the movie, "The Exorcist." I had not seen it since I sneaked into the movie with friends in the eighth grade. I remembered it well enough, but I wanted to see it again. I sat very carefully and watched when Linda Blair became the demon. I listened to her guttural voice that obviously was not the voice of Reagan, the young girl whose body the demon had overtaken. I listened to the foul words. And then her eyes glowed green. I had seen enough. After that, whenever I noticed an upcoming program of an exorcism in the television guide, I tried to watch it. They fascinated me because the behaviors they described of the possessed person – the growling voice, the motoring chest, the murderous strength, the foul words, and sometimes even the glowing eyes - were the ones I'd witnessed in Judy. I wanted to hear from other people who'd encountered a beast like this in a human.

I did not want to see my mom after that. I lay in bed for two days and asked two different older friends of mine to visit, one on each day. Each one spent hours with me next to my bed. I once read that every woman needed eight mothers. After reading that, I worked hard to cultivate loving relationships with older women. This was a time I needed a mother, but not my own. It took me a while to figure out why. A constant theme of my healing process was learning how to protect myself. My mom did not leave her husband when he beat his children. It does not matter why. It is a fact. My father did not protect his wife or his children. My brothers did not protect us. Protection comes in words and action. I grew up without protection. I was learning how to provide it for myself. I finally figured out why I was mad at my Mom. She brought Judy to my house that day.

An Answer I Never Wanted to Know

I now know what I'd do if someone attacked me. There is no question in my mind. I would win at all costs. It is a primal act of survival. Before that day, to the question, "What would you do if someone were trying to kill you?" I might have said, "I don't know." Now I do.

It is a question that I really did not need or want an answer to, and I hope most people never get to find out that answer, because just knowing I could have killed someone is frightening.

And my sister? Kill my sister? "She killed her sister." I don't know how I would have gotten over the shame of that.

"I killed my sister." How does one say that?

It is only a sentence. Sometimes one sentence is all you get. Even if I got a chance to add, "She was mentally ill. She tried to kill me. I *had* to kill her." Being able to add sentences does not clean up the act of violence.

The Details

My healing has been in the details. Getting out the details. Not carrying them around in my head. "Judy tried to kill me," is just a sentence. But that sentence does not contain the initial fear, the black hair, the hairy legs, the tiger claws, the body parts, the peas and carrots, the Mick Jagger, the name calling, the hoe, the force, the anger, the actions, the movements, the clawing, the rolling, the grass, the sidewalk, the bushes, the bite, the decision to kill, the gravel, the blood, the words, the neck, the flesh, the forearms, the sound coming out of her, the motor, the engine, the green eyes, and the saddest sentence I ever had to say.

Violence is not a sentence. It is not a sound bite on the evening news. It is actually a *long* story, full of details. And, in my mind those details will stay, if I do not get them out.

People should not have to carry around in their heads all the details of a trauma. They need to get them out. Why does it have to be with just a therapist? Why should we have to pay people just to talk? We must listen to each other to be well. I am not afraid to ask the details. I do not ask them for myself. I believe it is a gift to someone if I sit and listen to his details. I want to hear them. I want the people around me to be well. Because of how long I carried my own details of the night of the shooting before telling a group, I believe they have to come out in order to be well.

When I think of details, I think of soldiers at war. Soldiers at war are special people. Their details are many. It is important even for soldiers to tell the details to someone. All the details. Soldiers used to come home and not share them. It worked for some, but not all. Life is going to throw little traumas at us all the time. For me to live fully in the present I had to get rid of the details; I had to make room in my mind for my present life to happen.

Making Sense

I did not talk about this to anyone except the people who knew me well. How do you say to anyone else, "My sister tried to kill me"? In my head I imagined they would say, *Well, what did you do to make her mad? What made her so angry? Why would she have done that?* I could only imagine that in other people's minds, I must have done something so wrong for her to want to *kill* me. We would be back to, "What could Frannie possibly have done that would make Ed shoot her?" She had done nothing to cause that kind of anger. Neither had I. How could I tell someone this simple statement when I knew I'd have to defend myself answering these questions? There is no defense. It does not make sense. It is a fact that will remain forever. It doesn't matter why.

Mental illness does not make sense.

Judy's anger toward me puzzled everyone for many years. I could not figure it out. All I could think of was the time I'd hit her over the head with a telephone receiver. I'd apologized for that many times even before she got sick. There was nothing I could pinpoint that I'd done to create this kind of anger in her toward me, specifically. Why me?

Many of my friends and family members had theories, but none ever felt right. Then one day that summer talking to a friend, he said, "It makes perfect sense, Lynnie. If she did not remember the shooting, but she stood looking into your eyes with her back to the others, then your eyes may be the only thing she remembers. It may be that when she sees your eyes, you represent something so horrific to her that she has to go into heavy protection mode." I felt much better after hearing that theory. I accepted that as the reason. It felt right then and now.

I never stopped feeling terribly sad that Judy, whom I believed saved my life, had tried to kill me. Judy had not stepped in to heroically "do" something during the shooting, she just heroically "was" something. A person, a human who held my eyes. And I held hers. I did not stop, and she did not stop. I only glanced away to look at the others, but every time I looked back, there were Judy's eyes.

I believe that one act kept me grounded and kept me in present time, which, I believe in the long run, kept me sane. So, in essence, it feels like Judy is the one who gave me my sanity. The irony is that she lost hers. Among the six of us, Judy is the only one who is mentally ill.

Still Looking

I wore long sleeves that summer. My wounds oozed; the grooves were deep and needed attention hourly. I was right about the scarring.

I drove down to see the Huggins', and Jim took me out for a five-hour sail on his boat. As we swam in the water, I told him the story of Judy's attack. When I finished, he asked me something that surprised me. "Why do you tell me your stories, Lynnie?"

A little lost, I thought about it for a minute, and I told him what occurred to me. "I guess because you are the first person I ever told my stories to." He just shrugged his shoulders.

When I thought about it later, I realized I felt embarrassed by his question. Here I was at thirty something, and I was still telling him gruesome stories of my life. He was such a normal guy, married to an angel, and the two of them were raising five wonderful teenagers to adult children. There I was still telling stories about attempted murders.

It was hard not to feel ashamed.

I realized there were many people who just could not relate to my situation. It was high drama and many people felt uncomfortable with it. None more so than myself. I longed to be with someone who could understand me, not pity me, but admire me for what I'd come through, and just accept what I had yet to heal. I had begun to think of myself, and each of my siblings, as miracles. I longed to be a whole person in a relationship with a nonjudgmental, gentle someone. I knew it would take a special person.

Something important about relationship dynamics was brought home to me through interacting with my siblings. When we were each in our youth and early adulthood, we were critical of each other, especially in the areas of how we handled our individual stress. Stress showed up differently in each of us and I learned we couldn't expect people to handle stressful situations exactly as we would. What some people can cope with easily, others become zombies around. As we siblings grew older, I came to understand that when a person is not coping well with stress *that* is when he needs to be loved the most, helped the most. That is not the time to become critical or belittle the person. That is the time to throw judgment aside and pitch in to do the thing that he cannot. I came to see that as one of the highest forms of love a person could give another person. Pitch in and do the thing that he cannot. Sometimes we just have to accept that a person is *never* going to function well under certain circumstances.

Once I had dinner with friends, and one couple had recently become engaged. When the fellow left the table to go to the restroom, he took a huge whiff of his gal's hair, as he skirted off. It was not a dramatic move for everyone to see, but I saw it. *There is something missing from my relationships with men.* I wanted someone to love me like that. Someone, too, who'd pitch in and help me the moment he saw I was stressed. While I had come far, I still had not broken open the "bed scene," and I intuitively knew I would not be able to attract that kind of love until I had.

The Five of Us on the Porch

Mary was worried for my safety. She came home from Australia, and we agreed it was time for me to move back to Virginia. Before I left my farmhouse that summer, a beautiful thing happened. Five of the six of us siblings were in town. Aaron and Mary were in the country, and Jeff had traveled to town with his family. Carl lived in town. We all met at my farmhouse. It just happened that we had a legal case about our family's land to discuss, so the five of us sat on the porch to talk. All but Judy.

It was the first time we had all been together in eighteen years.

It has always made me incredibly sad that my siblings and I do not get together like many families, but I could tell that night, it was not for the lack of love. We had to discuss a problem, to make a decision about a court case, whether to fight it, or let the court decide. We'd come from all over the world, each one of us separately having come to the exact same decision. Basically, "Let's let the judge decide."

This could easily have been something other siblings would have fought over. We were not fighters. We'd all grown up to be wonderful people. Each one of us was college educated and functioning in the world with good jobs. Not one of us drank alcohol or smoked cigarettes. Two of my brothers were raising children they adored. We were peaceful people. From a violent beginning, we had created peaceful lives.

There was a softness as we sat in a circle that night. The love and respect we had for one another was apparent. All had long since been forgiven. What remained was the reverence we held for each of us, knowing what we'd been through to make it in life. Mary said the sense she had on the porch that night was an overwhelming feeling of safety. We were all safe now, protective of each other.

My Biggest Fan

Before I moved to Virginia, Mary came with me while I taught a three-day faculty in-service for teachers in Kentucky before school started. It was the first time she'd sat in on a staff development. I talked about the shooting, as that is how I let people know the "why" behind my recommended forms of discipline. Mary loved it. She beamed with a mixture of pride and relief.

Mary would not, in a million years, speak in front of an audience, especially about our difficult story, but she became my number-one fan. She knew the importance of educating people about the disease of alcoholism and the havoc it could wreak on a family. We loved Judy so very much, and, although we did not know the exact causes, we thought the shooting contributed to her mental illness. If we could facilitate other family's knowledge of the disease of alcoholism, maybe we'd spare them a casualty such as Judy.

The cool thing about that three-day gig was that in the audience sat my eighth grade teacher, Mr. Gossett, the man who'd made me love English class. He was going into his twenty–seventh year of teaching.

Almost all of the teachers lived in the more affluent parts of Louisville. They drove long miles to teach in the south end, near where we grew up, but in a rougher area. Most rewarding was a woman standing at the end who said, "I did not know any of the kids I'm teaching could really 'make it' out of here. I thought my efforts were being wasted, but now, I don't feel that way. I will try harder to make a difference for them." She believed what I believed – that a child anywhere could make it with the right kind of guidance.

Mary and I loaded up the car and drove to Virginia by way of the Blue Ridge Mountains, camping along the way. Our old digs. We even saw a black bear lumbering across the road. Mary loved to swim in fresh water lakes because she did not find many in Australia, so that's what we did.

No matter how many times we parted, it was always excruciatingly painful for us to say goodbye. Mary had a full life in Australia, but we lived on separate ends of the earth. We had to accept we were never going to be like normal sisters living near each other. Each time we got close to the point where we knew we'd have to say goodbye, we stopped seeing anyone else. We "hid" ourselves away to soak up and absorb the last bits of each other, neither wanting to share the other with anyone else. Mary and I know each other's histories, what makes each other tick. Whenever one of us is stressed to the max, we will say only two words: "Dig deep." We draw from firsthand knowledge and understand just how deeply a person can and sometimes must dig in order to find the place where peace will follow. Mary has more depth than anyone I know. She can be so much fun and, on a dime, go to the depths of a conversation, to hit the mark of any point to be made. She is constantly seeking people who can go there with her. We often say we do not know how women survive without having a sister. It has been important to our mental health to stay emotionally close. It is always painful when we say goodbye and head off to our end of the world.

Because I laugh at all her jokes, Mary calls me *her* biggest fan.

A Diagnosis

When I returned to Virginia, I went back to see Patrick and Carrie, my bodyworks therapists, several times, just to talk about my transition. Patrick said, "Lynnie, if you'd ever been diagnosed, it probably would have been for posttraumatic stress disorder." No one had ever said that to me. *Diagnosed? How does one get diagnosed?* He told me that in today's age, if the shooting had happened, I would have immediately been referred for counseling for PTSD. *Wow, you mean there is a name for what's wrong with me?* I was happy. I now had a label that made sense of the chaos I felt, especially so long ago. After that, when I heard PTSD mentioned, I became more alert and, over time, read bits and pieces about it. It fit.

On Being Effective

While still living in Louisville, I'd been recommended by a principal to become an instructor for Thomas Gordon's graduate course, *Teacher Effectiveness Training*. The principal said he could see that I was already living the TET win/win philosophy. I was honored because this course was modeled from the book I'd read the summer before my first year of teaching, the one that eased my insecurities because it gave me permission to be authentic in the classroom. It encouraged me to use all of the communication techniques I'd learned from Mr. Huggins, which I intuitively knew to be the most effective ways to reach the most difficult students. I'd been on both the giving and receiving end, witnessing the success of these techniques. If anyone could teach this class, I could.

The course manual warned the instructor that he would meet considerable resistance from teachers in the course. The TET course could stand on its own, but I decided to cut to the chase and tell my story to the group up front - to set up my credibility as a traumatized, angry, bitchy, energetic, and unruly student who was ultimately full of pain. I knew firsthand of the techniques used on me, which ones had worked, and which ones failed miserably. Telling my story first laid a foundation that prompted immediate listening. I was not messing around. People soon gathered I was no sissy when it came to personal growth, and this would be no ordinary course. So much of what I needed as a teenager were words I never heard from teachers I never had. Thomas Gordon's book guided teachers to using language students could hear. He was a genius.

I had found a passion and a purpose. Even talking about the most difficult subjects, I'd often have the audience howling with laughter. My approach to life had always been, had I ever said it out loud, "I'm going to get through this crap and come out on top and have a great life." Clearing out the gunk of my life paved the way for laughter. I was in my element when I was talking about getting through pain to come out on the other side to meet joy. I was essentially teaching the same techniques from my workshops, but someone else was setting up the classes. I just had to show up with my manual. This helped me physically and financially. Class time energized me emotionally, mentally, and spiritually. Depending on the honesty of the teachers, the classes could be used for life-changing personal and professional growth. The course was filled with activities that produced "Ah ha!" moments. Several of the men told me their wives had been trying to tell them something for years, but they'd only "got it" when they heard it in the course. One man always credited me with "saving" his marriage. Another man stood in class once and said, "I would follow you into battle."

To be an excellent teacher, I believe one has to look at it as a spiritual journey. Whatever demons come up for a person, they have to be examined in the teacher's mind and dealt with there. Whenever I hear a teacher using sharp criticism while describing a student, I know that teacher has a lot of personal growth to do. It is normal to have negative thoughts about a child when he is often not doing what we want him to do. When those negative, or "attack thoughts," are turned around in the teacher's mind, the student will turn around. I knew with the right attitude, tone, and particularly in the stringing together of the right words, a teacher could create miracle after miracle in a classroom. Many believed in the approach of being affirming, yet straightforward in disciplining unruly kids and returned to look at that child differently, which is exactly what I wanted.

Instead of being a secondary English teacher right away, I taught graduate courses for a year. I began teaching *Teacher Effectiveness Training* when I arrived in Virginia, traveling to four different states, ultimately teaching over forty graduate courses in the ensuing thirteen years. As the company added them, I taught nine other courses such as *Self-esteem for Educators, Resolving Conflicts in Classrooms and Schools, Stress Management for Teachers,* and *Reaching Today's Students.* Many teachers took several classes from me over the years and we got to know each other well. Through the years, hundreds of teachers told me I had to write a book. I felt some day I would. And here it is.

An Invitation to the Deepest Stone

In all these years, I'd continued to be on again off again with Dave. For ten years. He had visited me again in Kentucky. I had been very vulnerable when moving back to Virginia. We were still very connected spiritually, and we knew we loved each other. We moved in together, and tried to make a go of it. But still, we were not getting our emotional needs met; his distance and shutting down *still* made me pretend to be overly happy and my pretending to be overly happy *still* made him shut down. We lived together for ten months and although we were dysfunctional, we were trying to make our relationship work.

Then a blow came that unlocked the bed scene. In all the years I'd prayed for it to be unlocked, never did I imagine it would be dynamite detonating inside me. Never did I imagine the work I had yet to do. There would be no more pretending with men when I came out of this one.

After facilitating a weeklong self-esteem camp for young girls in Kentucky, I came home on Monday. Dave picked me up at the airport. From the moment he gave me a half hug, I knew something was wrong. After dinner he told me he wanted to tell me something. *Uh, oh.* We sat down on the couch, and he told me he'd just spent the weekend at the beach with a woman he intended to marry. He'd known her five years before, when I'd lived in Hawaii, but she'd been dating another man then. He'd found out she was single again ten weeks prior to this, and they'd been communicating and visiting each other. She lived about four hours north, so they'd rendezvoused in the middle.

"So, let me get this straight..." and I repeated back to him all he'd told me. He was going to marry another woman. I asked him several questions and tried to process it. He was adamant that he wanted to remain friends and asked me to agree to tell people we'd decided to be "best friends."

I did not rant, I did not rave, and I did not fight. I did not leave, I did not tell him to leave, and I did not flee in any way. I did what was natural for me to do in a trauma with a man. I froze. I sat paralyzed. With all my natural instincts cut off, the seal on my victimhood had been so tightly glued into place, I could not budge. To react would have been to protect myself from this now stranger who I'd trusted with my well-being. That was not happening.

Soon I'd be shown, step by step, that to react, to regain those instincts lost, I'd have to go back into that bed with my dad, and face the fear that had stolen a part of me and locked it away. It was a piece I'd needed all my life and, up to this point, had been operating without. Yes, I wanted it back, but was I prepared to engage this thing? This was the demon that possessed such strength it had clung to me through all my previous purgings. To find the courage I needed and lost in the depths of my suffering on that night, I would have to travel that same path to retrieve it. Into the murky waters I would have to go. It laid there somewhere on the bottom, waiting for me to come get it. I'd vaguely heard it calling, reminding me it was there. It had been the tight seal that kept me deaf to its voice. This was no job for a wimp. I was going to have to become a very strong swimmer to reach that depth. It was as if all the therapy work I'd done prior to this had been a walk in the park compared to what faced me now.

Dave continued to say, "Let's just tell everyone that Dave and Lynnie decided to be 'best friends.'" He wanted to use that explanation, because it sounded better than "Dave found himself another woman." That way we could both keep our friends in tact. Ten-years worth of mutual friends.

Each time he said it, I said, "I did not decide this. You did." I walked around numb, dumfounded, a zombie. Dave took off from work the next two days, Tuesday and Wednesday. I was not well, and in his friendship to me, he was going to "help me" through this. I walked around. I lay around. I was sinking. With every unanswered question, I was sinking. Somehow, I'd built a world around me that was not real, only a pretense of happiness. I'd done it again. His dishonesty revealed to me now, felt real, but it was very dark. *How could this be real? Had I been in that much denial?* The answer was yes. *How was it that I did not know what real love was? Why was I so blind? How could I not see? And… what in the world was wrong with me? Something must be terribly, terribly wrong.* Here was a man who knew me so well, yet he did not want to marry me after all these years. I was jealous. I was hurt. I was humiliated.

But I was not mad. Not until the third day.

Dave had been in and out, running small errands. I was sitting in deep water in the bathtub when he returned. I heard him come up the stairs. At the door, he said, "Are you okay?"

"Yes."

He opened the door, and stood talking through the wide crack. "Lynnie, if you told me you would never see me again, I would not see this woman again. I would drop this whole thing. Your friendship is more important to me than anything. I do not want to lose you. You are more important to me than her."

Of all the years of going back and forth with "Dave and Lynnie," I could see it coming again. It felt to me as if he tore me down this low - and then popped back in to say he was now willing to "keep me." What a great prize I was. Here I sat, naked in the bathtub, completely demoralized, in the deepest hole I'd ever been, and he was giving me his hand, ready to pull me out, sacrificing his new love, for me. *How pathetically grateful I would have to be!* I could hear myself now: "Dave picked me! First he picked another girl, who he really loved, far more than me, but he was willing to lose her and come back to me because he did not want to lose our friendship. You know, that one we had where we always told each other everything, the whole truth, even if it hurt? You know, the truth you tell even if you fear you may lose the relationship? You know, that one. Sure, he'd lied. He'd deceived. He'd withheld. But now he was willing to let all of that go and take *me* back. Just to keep me, he'd give up this other woman, the 'love' of his life."

At last, I had had it.

I took my fists and I banged them on top of the deep water in the bathtub. The water flew straight to the ceiling. How dramatic! I banged my fists on the water again. Again the water flew to the ceiling. I gritted my teeth and snarled, "Oh, no you don't! You are not going to have me make this decision for you. I will not be responsible for breaking up you and this other woman. This is your decision. You have made this decision. You are not going to pull me into this. This is your doing and your doing alone."

Finally, I was angry. I had words. For a man.

He scrambled away, and when I got out of the tub, he was gone. My anger had cracked inside me. I was able to feel. I was able to feel, all right. As I rounded the corner coming into the kitchen, I had the distinct feeling my cells were eating each other. That's how fast my body was moving on the inside. Like little Pac Men running around, chomping, eating everything in sight. That is the visual picture I had. I stood at the refrigerator. It was Wednesday evening. I'd not even had a glass of water in two days. I'd not eaten in two days. Time had stood still. I stood there holding onto the door of the unopened refrigerator in a state of alertness. My body needed something - and quickly. The anger had jarred me back into my body.

I guess for those two days, I'd wanted to believe it was all a dream, that I'd not be losing the man I'd loved for ten years, he'd be picking me over this woman, and he'd not be going away. But away he was going, and on Thursday, he got up and went to work. Just like that. His life went back to normal. He had taken off the obligatory two days. He'd done his job. He'd done the best he could to console me. Now it was up to me to face this. Alone. His going off to work that day was a turning point.

Beginning with the End in Mind

I knew the grieving process so well by then, that even at the onset of this trauma, I knew one day I would be at the acceptance stage. I also felt the full force of my anger moving in. It was a tsunami I could see from a distance. I realized this incoming anger would cause me to be "gone" from Dave for a very long time. I also knew I'd one day be out of it. I would honor it and let my body move through it. But on a spiritual level, this was the most important human being I'd known. As torn apart as I was, I knew I would forgive and be whole again. I knew his significance in my life would never be altered. No matter the anger settling in, we had moved mountains together.

Because I knew the love I had for him was real, because there was a part of me that could look past all the pain I was in, because I knew one day I'd be past all my hurt and have another love, I wanted him to know what I might not be there to say later. "If you get to be an old man, and you don't have anyone to take care of you, I want you to call me. I will come help you, and I will be there for you until you die." I made him promise he would call me if he ever knew his death was coming. With that, I opened the gates for the full separation of Lynnie and Dave to begin. The waves of my anger came crashing in.

My Mole

Although the break up was the shock to release what I needed, an unlocking of this sort does not happen suddenly. It's as if someone has taken a key and turned the lock on the other side of the door, but does not tell the one inside. She only finds it on her own, as she wanders around the room and reaches up by habit to check the door once more, and by chance finds that the knob turns freely.

On Thursday, I laid in bed almost the entire day. I called close friends and told them about the split. It was time to make a plan. As I lay on the bed, there was a bump about the size and shape of half an egg, inside my skin, running up and down my torso, from my pelvic bone to my sternum. Running frantically. Almost like it had tiny little centipede feet. It ran and ran and it did not stop. It had the energy of a chipmunk. I lay there observing, fascinated by this little animal - but I was not scared. By this time in my life, I was not surprised by much. I knew the body was an extraordinary tool to guide me, so I figured I would be shown what it was trying to tell me.

Talking to my friends, I even told them about it. I lay there curious for most of the day, allowing it to wind itself down. I even took my first telephone interview survey for a job while this "thing" was running around in my torso. I felt calm speaking on the phone. I was still grounded in who I was as a teacher in the classroom with kids.

This little guy was a running bump. A bump I could see. It seemed frantic. I wondered what in me was frantic. Over the course of the day, I tried to meditate on what it was. Nothing came to me. I talked intermittently on the phone. I closed my eyes. I listened and listened. Was this "thing" trying to tell me something?

It hit me. Very hard. So hard it scared me. After watching this bump running around inside me for the better part of six hours, it struck me that he represented the thing that was supposed to protect me. Always there, but buried too deep *to matter*. My voice. My instincts. My anger. The thing I'd lost on *that* night. There. In the bed.

This thing was mad, mad, mad – and trying to tell me something. "You don't protect me. You don't know how. You have gotten us into all kinds of situations that have hurt us. You continue to let me be hurt. I don't trust you anymore. I'm not listening to you any more. I no longer respect you. I am up. I am awake now. I am taking matters into my own hands because you won't. Look what a mess you've made just because you would not let me out! You stuffed me in every time I wanted out. I will not take it anymore. *I* matter now. *I'm* coming out, whether you want me to or not. I am overriding your decisions because you do not make good ones for us."

This thing was telling me he was coming out whether I liked it or not. My anger. Unleashed. Unbridled. I wanted to say, "Now, wait a minute. You can't do that. You could hurt someone. You might come off wrong. You could embarrass me. You will humiliate me."

It was no use. This thing had made up its mind. There would be no stuffing it anymore. I had been cautious and timid with my anger. I'd not let it out enough to protect myself in the face of hideous abuse. This was exactly the reason he was going to override me. I was frightened. All these years of being a doormat, a victim, a pleaser, of not speaking when appropriate. It was going to have me do what I feared worst: speak up, fly off the handle if I had to, make me look like a fool, make me look like "other" angry people. I knew what anger had done to me when I was young. I knew it had hurt me and hurt others and I never wanted to go back there. But this thing was not telling me it was going to hurt anyone. Not *anyone*. Me. It was going to humiliate me. It was telling me, "I can't trust you any more, so I'm coming out when I have to. Don't you dare try to stop me, because you won't be able to."

This "thing" had my back against the wall in a whole new way. I was going to have to speak up and tell the truth every time I was annoyed or irritated or angry with someone. This was not good. Since I'd learned my new skills, I still picked the opportunities to assert myself. Many things I still let slide, did not confront. Someone once tried to explain to me that a person could not be fully healthy until he allowed himself to be totally unreasonable. Unreasonable? I did not want to be that. I wanted to be controlled, able to handle my anger, address it with words, not hysteria. But he tried to explain to me that unreasonable did not mean hysterical. It just meant reacting in present time - and sometimes reacting in present time, *without all of the facts*, made a person appear unreasonable. *Oh. My mole would not know all of the facts because he is - a mole! Emotions living inside of me! But he is something internal that can sense when something is wrong – outside me. Hmmm...*

I had no other choice but to respect it, placate it. I said, "Okay, I promise you. I will not make you stay underground any longer. I realize I have hurt you badly, and I have not respected you. I have stuffed you, and I have hidden you, and I have betrayed you. I see that now. But I promise you, whenever I feel someone has done something to hurt me, I will speak up."

I knew then I would have to work overtime to figure out how to speak up before this "thing" inside me took over and did it anyway, in *any way* it knew how. It wanted me to make good decisions so it could live happily and *not* have to get mad. It wanted *me* to protect *it*. I called this thing my mole – because that is what it felt like. This thing was crazy in an electric way. Energy I'd not had in present time. Underground, present-time, angry energy.

I made a promise and a deal to my mole that day and he believed me and died down. I knew he knew I'd heard him - and I believed him. I also knew he was still in charge. I call my mole a he because it felt (and still feels) like the warrior in me, the part of me that will fight to stay alive. I have never respected any man, woman or thing so completely in my life as I have that little guy who represented my protective anger, my natural instincts. This little guy came to guide me very well for the next many years. I never saw him again as the half egg-shaped bump on my torso, probably because I respected and listened to him. In the future he only let me know he was there by the adrenaline pumping through the muscles of my stomach. The more fierce the throbbing, the faster I knew to take care of business - any conflict at hand.

In the days ahead, I said goodbye to the doormat I was. I did not do it intentionally. I did not mean to do it at all. I had been a little girl walking around all this time and now this mole rose out of me like a dragon. It was all of the fire and ferocity I'd never been. It was all of the fire and ferocity no one had been on my behalf. And now the injustice of three little girls in bed with a would-be killer spun me like a tornado.

Get Out of My Way

My new anger was not the anger I'd had before, the private anger at the butcher paper, of dealing with what *had been* done to me. It was the anger of knowing what *was never going to be* done to me again. Never again, was anyone going to get away with hurting me, or anyone in my charge, like they had that night. After my initial hesitance, I welcomed this mole and let him guide me. If B through Y had been ugly before, this fire I walked through now had no face at all. And worse, it did not care. I was trained now to believe we stored trauma and stress somewhere in our bodies. When something happens to us in present time, we get a stiff neck or a tummy ache. When a trauma happens to us, it surges through our bodies and takes up residence somewhere. My bodyworks therapy had trained me to go in and find it, talk to it, bring it out, understand it, and rework it - to give it a new face. But this recent trauma, and the anger that accompanied it, needed no coaxing out. It was out in all its glorious form. Uninvited, it stormed out with its arms held high – upward into the light of day. Sure to embarrass me.

This dragon was not looking for a fight, only to be there *to* fight, if needed. People had been doing and saying things to me that were wrong for so many years, the victim in me hadn't stood a chance. She'd had her chance and lost it. Now, not only did I have a chance, I had a "fighting chance." The dragon, the beast, the mole in me, registered wrongdoing quickly and mightily. The natural instinct I'd lost was crashing ashore, slapping me to the side. I meant very little to it. It was coming, whether

I got out of its way or not.

Moving Forward, Sort of...

I'd called a good friend that Thursday after the break up, and by that evening, she was at my house with food saying, "Get packed. I'm taking you to my house. You're not staying here any longer." It was a wonderful gesture and I was grateful.

The next day I was supposed to fly to New York to teach a graduate course to a room full of teachers - all weekend. I called a friend, wondering if I should find a substitute, but she advised, "It will probably be the best class you'll ever teach." That gave me strength. It was true. I was filled with a humility that came from being in a very low spot. I not only survived the weekend, I thrived. Very vulnerable and serene, I arrived in the classroom. I started with parts of my story, like always, and everyone sat quietly. The chemistry of the class was remarkable. At the end of the third night and first half of the course, when I dismissed the class, the students stood and clapped for what seemed to be two minutes. Amazing. They were clapping for *me*. No students had done this before. When I returned, I told my girlfriend about the clapping. "Had you told them about your break up?" she asked. I told her I had not. "Oh, so you mean it wasn't a 'pity' clap?" We both laughed. I knew they had felt something very powerful in all the words they'd heard among classmates in discussions that weekend. My last prayer before leaving the hotel room to teach was, "Please, when I open my mouth, let my words be yours." I knew I had held hands with a higher power all weekend. Every step I took, every word I said, were words I received in the prayers I said as I led these discussions. The folks in that class kept in touch with me for years, including a couple who'd just met in class and connected so strongly, they later married.

I would like to say that I never went back to Dave, but I had more zigging and zagging to do with him. We'd already RSVP'd to a wedding, and he called to ask if I still wanted to go. It was crazy for him to ask, and crazier still for me to go. I could not yet let go. After the wedding, I drove out to the shore in Maryland to attend a wedding with the Huggins. I walked in that night to see Jim sitting around the table with his kids, having a good time. I started to cry, and my crying cleared the room. I was not well, clearly an emotional wreck. He'd raised five beautiful children, and they were all in their late teens and early twenties by then. I was not one of them. I was of a different breed. He'd called me his adopted daughter. I knew he and his wife loved me dearly, and his children were kind to me, but I would have to find my own way in the world with these emotional issues of mine. It clearly scared the girls; they did not want to be me. Once again, I felt the humiliation of living B through Y.

Confronting Trauma

I lived in my friend's house now and moved my stuff from Dave's, little by little. I'd said I would never read Dave's notebooks again, but as sick as I was, when they beckoned, I did not resist. I knew where they were. I was out of shock and wanted answers as to why this had happened. I opened one. I flipped through it, barely stopping on any one page. I read his anger. I opened another one. Did the same: flipped through it quickly, stopping only for a few seconds. More anger. I read the thoughts he was purging onto the pages, similar to the thoughts I had purged onto the butcher paper. We had both been taught how to do this work. When I read anything about me, I was able to look past it and say, "This is not about me." I was not any of the things he'd written. They were just thoughts he'd had, given to him by demons.

I flipped through three notebooks in a total of five minutes and then put them down. I realized Dave was a tortured soul, just like me. I felt sorrow for him. I'd done nothing to torture him. I was just not the person he needed in his life. He'd done nothing to torture me. His decision to leave me, as Mary said it best, "Saved me from a fate worse than death." He was not for me either.

I talked to Mary every single day for the first ten days after I left the house, for two to three hours a day. Again, when I first called, I was miserable, but by the time I hung up, my newfound anger gave me power, and we were both laughing our heads off. I was healed by my best friend's spirit and love.

A couple of weeks went by, and I became angrier and angrier. I had a vision of going back into Dave's house and smashing china plates on the hardwood floor, watching them shatter and bounce. I walked around for days thinking I should go to a thrift store and buy fifty china plates. It felt wonderful to imagine myself doing this, but it was violent and I knew I would not.

I had visions of hitting Dave! Actually hitting him. I couldn't believe it. In the past, I'd hurt myself, either by imploding, overeating, or thinking of hurting myself. Thoughts of hurting someone else were new. I'd been suicidal, but never homicidal. In those few days during which I had those thoughts, I heard a DJ on the radio say someone had cut him off in traffic that morning. He wanted to take a baseball bat to his head. *There! He said it! You mean other people have thoughts like these?* Flashes of myself hitting Dave over the head with a baseball bat came to me. I was that angry. I wanted to hurt him. For the victim in me, that was good news. Anything to bring me out of the place where I just sat there while people hurt me. I was relieved to hear what the DJ said. I was not alone. When I told Mary, she said casually, "Oh, that's just you killing him off." It was my psyche that was so mad, wanted revenge, but still these new feelings continued to scare me. My anger felt like power. I came to see it was a phase of my healing. I allowed myself to watch it pass through me, but that would take all summer.

A weekend came when I knew Dave's new girlfriend was visiting, and they were going to church. My church. His church. Their church. There they'd be - moved on. And here I was with all these "buzzing" emotions running through me. *When will they ever stop? Will I ever tame this beast inside me? Will this anger pass? When? What if, after working so long to be calm, I am walking down the sidewalk, a year from now and I see the two of them together on the sidewalk?* I knew it would send me back into a spin. I would be right back. *I need to see them together. I need to get this over. Finish it. See them together, feel the whole miserable lot all the way through now and, if I see them again in a year, I will not be traumatized - again! I will walk through this trauma myself.*

I called a very bright girlfriend and told her what I was thinking. She was an actress and said, "You know what, Lynnie? Some actors gather all the papers with their reviews, go into a room, and read each one all the way through. They go through the trauma, reading the critiques - in private. They do this rather than hiding from them and hearing bits and pieces of stinging negative reviews from others over the course of weeks. It makes all the sense in the world for you to do this. If you're going to be traumatized by seeing them together again, you might as well put yourself through it now and be done with it. That way you're in control."

I'd be in control. I would see it with my eyes. I would face it. It had nothing to do with the two of them anymore. It had to do with my healing. I went upstairs, put on a dress, and drove to the church. I went in and stood in the back. One leg was shaking so hard I could not stop it. I just let it shake. I did not see them. He was nowhere around. I did not know what she looked like. Soon church ended. I waited for the minister to leave and asked her on the way out if she'd point out Jenn to me.

I went up to Dave's new girl, Jenn, and stuck out my hand, "Hi, I'm Lynnie."

"Oh," she said.

"Would you mind sitting down with me?" Slightly hesitant, she decided it would be okay. We sat down in a pew.

As we sat together, I looked at her. Her hair was my color. Her eyes were my color. She was my height. What pained me so was I'd imagined her to be a more spiritually evolved person than I, a much *better* person. I had to remind myself that she was the one who agreed to meet a man at the beach for a weekend, knowing he was "with" someone else. She saw me looking at her. I said, "I just wanted to see you. I really have nothing to say. I really just wanted to make this real for myself."

"I understand," she said.

"I had really wanted to see the two of you together. Hey, Jenn, would you do me a favor and come over to Dave's house with me, so the three of us can sit down together?"

She thought we'd better call Dave first to warn him. I did not care if we surprised him. She, of course, was thinking more loving thoughts toward him. We walked into the church office and, on the phone, she said, "Dave, Lynnie would like to come over and have the three of us sit down together. Would that be okay with you?"

There was a long pause. I motioned for her to give me the phone. I said to Dave, "It's okay. I'm fine. I just want to sit down with the two of you."

"Okay," he agreed.

I followed her to the house. She drove a truck like the one I'd driven for years. She was obviously an outdoorswoman, like me. I found all of this fascinating. We drove up to the house where Dave and I had lived together. The two of us walked in. They hugged each other. I sat on the couch that faced the windows. With the curtains I'd made. Each of them sat in a chair, facing me. Dave began to talk and talk. I just sat there and listened. Then she began to talk and talk. I listened. I said nothing.

All the while, both of them were explaining what had happened, how they'd stumbled upon each other again.

I realized none of their story mattered. The only thing that mattered to me was me. I'd brought myself there. I was proud of that. I was sitting there in the room, seeing them together. I was peaceful. It was just like many years back when I was visiting the high school where Rudy taught, looking at him against the lockers. He'd been befuddled. These two were befuddled. I have found it is an interesting way to confront. To just "be there."

When ten minutes had passed, and they'd talked themselves out, I guess my silence became apparent to them. It became quiet. There was now room for me to talk. If I wanted to. I just stared at them. Not a creepy stare. I just looked at them. When I spoke I said, "I really don't have anything to say. I just wanted you guys to see me. I just wanted to come here and sit with you. I wanted you to see there's a third person here. When you are together, there are only two of you, and it may look like that is all there is. I want you to know there's a third person here that has been affected by your coming together. It's me. I am part of this picture, too."

I just needed to be seen.

I think it is so easy to hurt people when we cannot see them, cannot imagine how they are feeling. If we do imagine it, it is fleeting. But hurt lasts longer than that. Sometimes it sticks around for days, months, and even years. We three just sat there. I said, "I just wanted to be here. I just wanted you both to see me and see that your coming together has impacted my life."

When Dave realized the heavens were not going to fall from the sky, he got up and went to get something to drink. Jenn came over and sat next to me. I tried to imagine Dave and her together. It was hard. It hurt, but I tried not to let myself feel that for too long. She tried to make small talk. I couldn't. I asked, "At the beach that weekend, did you ever think of me?"

"I did for an instant, and then I blocked it out."

It was an honest answer. I did not hate this girl. A few minutes later, I got up to leave. We all hugged each other awkwardly.

Pain

Having a relationship that revolved around personal growth, Dave called me that night to tell me what I'd done was a "stroke of genius." I knew what he meant. What I'd done by sitting down with them had the effect I'd intended: to let them know that my life had been affected by their new, budding relationship, and to make myself feel better and more whole. I did. He didn't say so, but it felt as if my visit did not exactly make the two of them feel "better." He asked me how I was doing. I said, "I'm in a lot of pain. But pain is pain, no matter where it comes from. It's been brought up for a reason and I will go in and find where it leads me." At that point, I was not yet aware enough to say it would lead me back to the "bed scene."

He acknowledged the fact that I was going through this trauma completely consciously – without the use of food, drugs, or alcohol to numb my pain. He knew the difficulty in feeling pain all the way through. Going through trauma consciously is a lot different than going through it unconsciously. When I thought of all the dramatic chemical changes to a body during high stress, I often wondered about my own reaction and what must have surged through me on the night of the shooting. Whenever I see a seven-year-old girl, I think of how small her body looks and how the surging of chemicals did not have far to travel, confined in a tiny space. Maybe if I'd been able to "feel" back then, or if anyone had asked me, maybe this current pain was what it might have felt like.

On the second page of *The Road Less Traveled*, Scott Peck described what he believed was the most valuable gift an adult could give a child: let him see you walk through pain – un-medicated – without any drug of choice. Basically, after a loss, model what it is like to get up, take a shower, eat, go to work, all the while sad, talking about it, yet moving on, little by little.

Had I had someone walk me through the blood scene and the bed scene, and talk about its impact and ask me how I'd felt, shortly afterwards, I think the lasting effects of that night would not have been as severe. I think the toxins trapped in me would have "broken" up faster had I been able to get my story out with words and tears. When the school system began hiring counselors for schools, I heard colleagues complain, as if they were not needed. I knew better.

I had long since learned not to take out my anger on anyone, including myself. Going through this time period, was not like any other since I'd begun this journey. The agony was more severe and prolonged. I was not overeating, doing drugs, drinking, or doing anything to excess, except talking, crying, and feeling. There would be no medicating this pain. I had prayed for it to come up and I was not going to stuff it down. I knew a treasure of some sort awaited me on the other side. I knew the only way to get through this was to let it all happen - and work to contain it when it was not appropriate to show my emotions. I was not "all over the place" emoting. I waited until I felt safe enough, either alone or with someone I trusted, and then I said how I felt.

Choosing Laughter

Escorted into the office by the principal, I sat down while she finished writing something at her desk. She was a tall, very well groomed woman with short hair, beautiful fair skin, and a serious attitude. It was my first interview to be an English teacher and this position was to teach seventh grade. When ready, she turned to me and said, "This is a very competitive position. I have already interviewed three highly qualified candidates, all with master's degrees." She hesitated a moment and said, "But, I'm looking for the very best person!" She turned back to her papers to write. *Oh, great, here I go. This will probably be my first of thirty interviews. Just sit back and relax and enjoy yourself.*

I took a deep breath. She asked, "If I were to walk into your classroom, what would I see?" *Well, blow me over with a feather. This is the easiest question I could get!* I began telling her about the smiling kids, the enthusiastic teacher, the colors in the room, the energy, the manners, the discipline, the students working diligently, their student papers hung everywhere, their projects hanging from the ceilings. Mostly, I talked about how she would see a very productive, energetic environment.

The interview continued with many good questions, and her last one, "Why should I hire you?"

"Because I will make your life very, very easy. You will have a very motivated teacher, and you'll never have to worry whether or not I am doing my job, and I will rarely need you to discipline a child for me."

I got a call from the principal that afternoon, telling me I had the job if I wanted it. I told her I would deliberate over the weekend and call her on Monday. The next day I met with a friend. He asked me why I even had to think about it. A part of me was still holding out to teach high school again. He asked, "Tell me the difference between teaching high school and middle school."

"Well, teaching high school, you exert less energy during the day, but more at night. It's very time consuming to read, research, and prepare tests. But you do get the chance to form awesome relationships with young people. They can be very serious."

"Okay, now tell me about teaching middle school."

"Oh, teaching middle school, you exert more energy during the day with them, working with discipline and such, but the workload is easier in the evening. I would have more time to have a life after school. Plus, the kids are so funny, all you do is laugh all day long with them and their antics."

"Okay, let's get this straight. More work at night and more serious people during the day versus less work at night and laughing all day. Seems like a no-brainer to me."

I decided to accept the job.

Wanting the Cake and the Horizon, Too

On Sunday, I was going to drive to Pennsylvania that evening to teach a weeklong graduate course beginning Monday morning. I was packing and getting ready when Dave came to see me. The weirdest thing happened. He wanted to be affectionate and intimate with me. This was very confusing. *Does he want me back? What is happening? He has just crushed me. He is with another woman. What is he doing?*

He hounded me. I kept saying, "What are you doing? What about her?"

"Oh, she's on the horizon."

"The horizon? But aren't you with her? Isn't she your girlfriend? What do you mean?"

"She's on the horizon. She won't be moving down for a while."

"But you are *with* her? And you want to be with me? That does not make sense."

He just kept saying, "She's on the horizon." I thought this was absurd and I was disgusted. I said goodbye and drove to Pennsylvania. It was the last time I ever saw Dave.

On the Run

It is an adventure to move, to travel, to meet new people, to see what you're made of, to venture out and, through research, luck, and serendipity, find a place to live, a car, and a job. All of that is wonderful. Once or twice. Or more over long periods of time. But I'd had six major moves in five years, all without a cushion for landing. Each had been very difficult to maneuver mentally. Stressful. I had posttraumatic stress disorder, something I did not even know until the sixth move.

I had left Virginia essentially because of a man, and I'd come back five years later for that same man. I'd run away from something only to come back to find it. Saying "No" to Dave was scary and difficult. He was harsh, no doubt, but I thought a stronger woman might have held her own with him. I was not she.

I thought moving away would be my final "No." It was not. It did teach me something about running away. Like "the chair" I sat in to learn spiritual truths, I learned each conflict I found myself in could teach me hard lessons, too.

I'd gotten pretty good at sitting through conflicts, but looking at that night in the bed with my father felt like more pain than I could bear. I know we cannot measure or compare one person's pain to another's, but when we measure our own pain, I think we know which is worse. I knew. As hard as it had been for me looking at the "blood scene," reliving the pictures that had been with me in my mind everyday, bringing them up willfully and examining them piece by bloody piece, there was no comparing the two. For me, in the "blood scene," my mother, as she was, had died that night. In the "bed scene," my natural instincts, what made me fully human, had died that night. They had disintegrated. The agonizing pain of the loss of them that I felt now, I could not run from. It was with me 24 hours a day.

Principal Appreciation

One often hears of a person who is very effective professionally, but is a train wreck when it comes to her personal relationships with the opposite sex. In my lowest points, this was who I felt I was. I managed to use my personal stress to dig deeply into my spiritual beliefs, to channel it instead into communication skills. Each stressful episode convinced me more that there were better ways to communicate. Humiliated by my failures, I seemed to be able to use my ups and downs to motivate people through the joy and pain I described from my own life.

I had always dreamed of gathering all the principals and counselors, who'd helped me in the past, into one room to show them my appreciation. When I was asked to give a staff development session that summer for a group of principals in Kentucky, I decided it was time. I invited the now-retired James Taylor, Jim Huggins and his wife Phyllis, Lynn Nixon, and Nancy Ohyler Parker to sit in the front row of my three-hour motivational speech and workshop to a group of eighty professionals.

Teacher Appreciation Day happened annually, but there was no special day to celebrate principals. I decided to use my speech to show these gathered principals just how important they were in the lives of their students. In my mind, two principals had saved me. Had they not come into my life at the right time, and not known what to do, I did not believe I would have been able to choose and commit to the path that had led me back to them now.

And so I told our story and there sat my former principals looking up at me, smiling. It was a wonderful feeling to be able to tell the story of how they'd helped me, to give them the appreciation they deserved. One of my principals sat with tears running down his red face. I don't think his crying was entirely about what I was saying. I believe it was jarring his memory of all the struggling kids he'd loved all those years as principal and had acted on his instincts to help.

I wanted to let all the principals know they had very important jobs. I wanted them to know that the lessons they taught teenagers in their offices when in trouble might be the only lessons the teens were capable of learning at the time. I wanted to bring educators into the minds of kids in pain, possibly from dysfunctional families like mine. I wanted to create a paradigm shift in them from possibly looking at a kid as a jerk to someone who was in pain. I wanted them to know that if they *respected the child's pain* and gave it equal weight in their decision-making process, their kindness and firmness could become a great beacon to the child. I knew the child's pain needed to be respected in order for the adult to be successful with him - like Jim Huggins having me write down my feelings, but also giving me firm instructions. If hearing my story made just one principal give himself an "attitude check" in heading into the new school year, I considered my job done. I knew the kind of disciplining these great men used on me required an attitude shift, one that kept me from reacting in anger first. By then, having experienced all types of discipline, I knew *how* someone was disciplined was far more important than the fact that he *was* disciplined.

Through knowing Mr. Huggins, I came to believe kindness and firmness mixed with instruction was the best discipline a person could give a child. Tough love was a rarity in my life and it was noticeable when it came along. His kindness matched my inner voice. His instructions were the first time I'd heard such things in detail. I knew of things, but I did not know "how to do" them, step by step. Again, the B through Y, in the how to do many things was an empty hole for me. No matter how much I tried to imitate the actions of my peers, it wasn't until the explanation of them – helping out the teacher, taking on chores, being a leader among my peers - that I fully understood the reasoning behind the actions.

After the staff development session, I had dinner with the Huggins and told them about my recent break-up. When I told Jim that Dave had continued to say we should tell everyone we decided to be best friends, he told me that was mentally abusive. *Fancy that. Mental abuse.* It was always instructive to hear the vocabulary other people labeled words or actions that continued to befuddle me.

Triggered

I drove to Louisville and spent time with my mom and my dear friends. To each one I told the story of the break up. The anger spewed from my mouth. I heard it come out of me. I wanted to stop talking. I was embarrassed. Here I'd been trying so hard to revise the victim in me, and I felt like one - more than ever. But all this was a different sort of victim. At least now I was an angry victim.

Time was getting short. I only had ten days left before starting my new job. I began to feel certain I would not be able to release this valve of anger. Would I carry my ripped-apart life into my new job with me?

All summer, my shock and anger remained revved into high gear. I lost all my body fat. My body was "churning" at such a rate that, even though I ate normally, my metabolism must have been very high. It seemed my cells were eating each other - literally. Still. My body was spinning. My head throbbed. I was trying to make sense of it all. The bargaining, the questions I still had, went off in my head day in and day out. I tried to talk to anyone who'd listen. I'd been betrayed. I'd been hurt. I'd been left. For another woman. I was humiliated. I was angry. *I was triggered.* I was a woman scorned. I just wanted someone to know how hurt I was. But, of course, as always, the world moved on.

I later learned that my experience had all the ingredients for a severe trigger. I'd had the rug pulled out from under me. What had been stable in my life was no longer. I'd lost my best friend, my trust of him, and my home. I had all new surroundings in my new home and planned to start a new job.

Each new school year I made sure I was well prepared and in a good mental state to begin. It was August now and no matter what I did to calm myself, the anger returned with its original intensity. With that kind of anger, I was not able to build up the reserve I needed to enter a new school year.

Even though I knew my anger was normal, I did not want it to continue. I began collecting and reading all the information I could on forgiveness. It was a joke. None of it made sense to me. I could not feel it a bit, but I knew I needed it. Just the thought of forgiveness felt like a million-mile journey.

In the Glow of the Campfire

On the way back to Virginia, I stopped at my favorite campground on a large lake in Kentucky. I was going to stay at that spot until the last possible moment, if that is what it took for me to feel well. I loved the spot. It was on a small hill with high trees above. I had my usual routine. Each morning I woke up from a very deep sleep around nine and did yoga at my shady site. I ate breakfast on my picnic table. I went for a swim. Then I sat in my lounge chair with a box of books and papers and pencils and pens and tissues next to me. Reading forgiveness materials irritated me. I did not expect myself to be magically healed, I just wanted my anger to lift somewhat, just so I could function.

I went to work writing down everything I thought and felt, replacing the negatives with positives, just as I'd done on the butcher paper. I sat and wrote, cried, read, cried, slept, cried, stared up into the leaves of the trees, cried, prayed, cried, got up to pee, cried, wrote, cried, read, cried, prayed, cried, listened to the wind in the trees, cried, and begged God to help me. Crying. I did this for days. Every day. All day.

Each night, I waited until twilight and I went down to the lake and sat on the rocks and, guess what? Cried. Then I slipped into the water and swam, waiting for the first star. When I found it, I treaded water and waited for the others to arrive. Everything I did became a prayer. I was trying to make contact with every living thing in nature that I knew could cure me, heal me, and relieve me. Back at my tent, I curled in and felt the weight of my body sink into the earth. My body was heavy and tired. The throbbing crickets in my head were the loudest prayers of all. Some people go to the ocean to get their bodies in sync with the sounds of the waves. My body gets in sync with the sounds of the crickets. The louder the better. And waking from the deepest sleep, a new day of the same began.

As good as this was for me, as wonderful as it felt, as much progress I felt I was making, I still felt that buzz inside me that I could not tame.

All the days I was there, there was a large, extended family in the campsite near mine. I could see them over at their site and they could see me, but they did not bother me and I did not bother them. I only spoke to them with a friendly nod, and I think they sensed I wanted to be alone. But twice a day, without fail, they sent one of their littlest members running over with a plate of something for me to eat. It was the smallest of the biggest blessing I was to receive from them.

I left the site to go to a wedding one day and did not return until very late, nearly midnight. I saw the adults of the family sitting around the campfire. I wandered over. They were glad to have me and we all sat together by the glow of the fire. Although I was very comfortable with them, I was still not right with myself.

It had been six or seven days by now and I still did not have the peace I came into the woods to find, the same peace I'd never left the woods without. I had known how to get it. I had known how to fix myself. I'd done it many times. In fact, I was a pro at going into the woods and coming out whole. But there I sat at the fire with this group of people I'd never really had any meaningful conversations with. What had been a sweeter, but silent, conversation was their sending over plates of food to me, someone who they'd watched and wondered about sitting for hours and hours in a chair. My smile and wave had been enough for them to continue "talking," with the sharing of their food.

I'd only been sitting for a few minutes. They'd asked me a few questions just to be polite. I don't know if it was the sweet glow of the fire on their faces, the sparkle and glow of the embers, the comfortable relationship of privacy they'd built for me, the loving ways I'd noticed among them toward each other, or the fact that I knew my time in the woods was ending that caused me to open my mouth and speak.

Out it came. I told them I had been sitting there all week trying to relieve myself of a terrible anger I carried. Immediately a woman in the circle said, "Oh, Honey, we know exactly what you mean." She explained that her husband was a Vietnam Vet. He jumped in to continue the story, describing his anger. He'd had nightmares for years and had woken up many nights beating his wife. Their marriage suffered and had almost ended, but they stayed together and he worked through his anger. They didn't go on and on about details. They just told me this brief story to relay that yes, they knew anger very well – and its consequences.

I felt comfortable with them. But something happened that would alter that comfort to a new level. Another man, a younger man, looked at me from across the fire and said, "May we pray for you?"

I said something that changed me forever. "Yes." Almost before I could get the word out, the entire group of about eight adults stood. One, on either side, took my hand. In the first moment the younger one spoke, something happened to me that I'd never experienced. If I try to use words here, I know I will fail. It was a turning point, not just for that summer, but for my life. These people were standing up, praying for me. Not for anyone else. Just me. This was not church where everybody prays, just to pray. These people had heard what I'd said, understood what I'd said, took in what I'd said, and now in the culminating of our week together, were putting out a prayer for my anger to be released. The chemistry of my body changed. I was "touched" to my core. Everything in me was rearranged.

I'd allowed myself to be vulnerable. It was beautiful. Funny, whatever releasing of my anger I had prayed for came when others prayed for the releasing of my anger. I was sold. This was the coolest tool I was to collect in my basket of effective means of moving from one place to another: pray with other human beings. Any other time if I'd been asked that question, I probably would have said, "Nah, that's okay." I'd grown up Catholic. We didn't really do that kind of thing – actually pray making up the words. Most of our prayers were memorized prayers. Even the prayers my family said about our family were memorized. A "present time" prayer? Spontaneous, at that? What a concept!

By this time in my life I'd had many professional massages. During them, I remember thinking, *What an interesting trick God has played on us. Our backs are the thing that itches the most, gets sore the most, needs rubbing the most – and we can't even reach it! To get real relief, we need to ask another human being to scratch it or rub it.* (Of course, we could rub against a tree like a deer!) This made me wonder about prayer, too. Here, I could pray until the cows came home, but those cows never really came home until someone prayed with me, for me.

Praying Out Loud
I drove back to Virginia feeling like my old self again.

I still had sadness and anger that came with losing Dave, but I never went back to the buzzing feeling of being triggered so severely. Two months had been long enough with no relief.

I immediately went back to my women's group in Virginia and asked a woman if she'd pray with me. She suggested we do it each morning on the phone before going to work. Initially, I could not open my mouth, so she prayed. One day I said a short prayer. I had never done this – prayed out loud with someone. It was embarrassing. It felt humiliating. *How does one do this? I did not know how. How does one do it right? What is the right way?* I was to find there was no right way to pray.

Early on, I decided to read a prayer about forgiving a betrayal from Marianne Williamson's *Illuminata.* The sound of my voice reading it made it easier to continue speaking on my own after I finished reading it. Each time I prayed with someone, I felt lifted up like nothing else had done for me. It felt as if I'd taken a magic pill.

Landing in Heaven – and Hell
The clientele at my new school was wonderful. I'd never worked in a school where almost every child had either a mom and a dad, or at least a mom and a male figure, such as an uncle, to assist, or a father and a female figure, such as a grandmother to help. There was a supportive consciousness in the people that was phenomenal. I received homework from ninety-five percent of my population. A miracle. I was now in my

seventh school. I felt for the first time in my teaching career, I'd become a real teacher. I could teach. Each day I arrived at school prepared. My students were also prepared. They were clean, clothed, fed, and had been instructed and schooled at home. They were teachable humans. It was any teacher's dream come true.

My classroom had a carpet, a TV, a video player, five windows, lots of supplies, books, and more. All of a sudden I had respectful colleagues, students galore, and an exciting career. My life was full speed ahead.

One of the teachers asked if I wanted to rent her nearby townhouse that had been empty and on the market since spring. I moved in October 12, but the house sold and I had to move again by December 30. That would be my fourth move, living in five different places, in eight months. *Ugh.*

Knowing more about managing my own stress during a huge transition period, I decided to keep a low profile at work, observe for the first year, and not open my mouth during meetings.

My neighbor teacher was an angel and I told everyone I felt like I'd landed in heaven, being next to her. She had more class in her pinky fingernail than most people have in their whole bodies. Her spirit was calm; she spoke slowly and commanded respect wherever she went. She told me she'd had a schizophrenic mother and her childhood had been difficult. She'd made a conscious decision to transcend it all, and she had. I wanted to be like her.

Two other colleagues I had to work with closely that year turned out to be from a land far from heaven. One turned out to be the meanest person I'd ever met, and the other, the most vicious person I'd ever met, if I may differentiate the two. Let's call them Meanie and Vicsh.

Meanie was Alfred Hitchcock mean. An older woman with an I-must-have-been-a-child-star bow in her hair, a smile on her face, and a queerly sweet tone to her voice, Meanie made sarcastic comments. Her smile confused everyone, including me at first, but I soon recognized it as razor blades. When anyone least expected, there she'd be, finding people at their most vulnerable and she'd start slitting away - all with a smile, and all with a bow in her hair. Disease-ridden with negative thoughts, she was just plain mean.

Visch was blatantly a holy terror, driving 50 miles an hour across a parking lot, drinking heavily, ignoring rules, cursing out people left and right, and taking pride in it. She told stories of getting out of her car at stoplights and banging on another driver's window to rant and rave. I knew she drank because early on she'd called me on the phone several times at five in the evening with slurred speech. I could hear the ice cubes clinking on the sides of the glass. She did not make sense, went from one extreme on the emotional scale to the other, and the next day did not remember she'd called me. Although this woman had many so-called friends, she targeted select people to torment. She referred to almost everyone as a "Bitch." I knew it would just be a matter of time before I, too, was the bitch on her list, so I stayed clear of her, except when we had to meet for work, which was far too often.

I was given all this, as if I'd not had enough hard times, on the way to my brand new life! I guess life is not that simple. I know there are difficult people everywhere, but every now and then, wouldn't it be nice to have a break from them?

I was to endure Meanie for another two years and Visch for quite a few more. It was comforting to know that my colleagues in my new school saw all of this, one telling me Visch had "ripped to shreds" the group she'd worked with the year before. I heard many horror stories from ones who'd washed their hands of the two of them. I later learned no one else had wanted to work with them. Being the new girl, I was "it."

Stressors. Count them. Being recently triggered by the unlocking of the bed scene. Losing Dave and our ten-year relationship. Knowing he'd left me for another woman. Moving. Brand new job. Working with 130 new students in a new school and in an unfamiliar community. Keeping my mouth shut in department meetings. Having to open it and figure out what to say back to these two mean and vicious women, because of course, my mole was not going to be oppressed anymore. All of this made for the most stressful year of my adult life.

Any time I wanted to call Dave or get in touch with him, I stopped myself. Knowing what he'd done for 74 days – kept a secret from me about another woman, something I could not have done to him for ten minutes - helped. Dave had explained that several male friends had said over and over, "Don't tell Lynnie until you're sure." Not good advice. Each of the men had been a friend of mine. I never respected any of them again.

A Woman Scorned

As crazy as it sounds, when I was feeling sad at night, I often thought of being comforted by both Dave and Jenn. I wanted to run back to them and tell them – again – how sad I was. Although my zigging and zagging were not extreme, and by now I was living in the second half of the alphabet of B through Y, I did have a major slip that fall. To get to a meeting, I had to use a major road that connected to the street where Dave and I had lived one block up. Each time I drove down that highway, I said to myself, *Don't look, Lynnie. Keep looking straight.* And I did. Until one day, four months after I'd last seen Dave, I looked.

Just looking triggered in me the need to know more. There was a car I did not recognize in front of the house. I made a U-turn and drove up the street slowly and stopped one house away. I sat and stared. There were foreign plants in the window. The house looked different. *Was he still living there? Was she living there with him? Had he moved?* I had to know. All at once, I felt like a stalker. I *was* a stalker! Then somewhere in my head I had a vision of Bette Midler's feisty character in the movie, *The Second Wives' Club.* All of a sudden, I did not feel scared. I decided to go knock on the door. Jenn opened it, calming her barking dogs. I looked at her. She had something cooking on the stove, but she saw the look on my face and came out to sit with me on the porch. There I was, taking it all in - again. Their lives had moved on. My handmade curtains still hung in the windows, she was cooking dinner on my stove, he would be home soon, her new plants were all around, gone were my two cats, in were her two dogs.

I was no longer a part of Dave's life. She was moving her stuff down from up north intermittently and would live there fully the following month. They *really* were in love. I *really* was gone from Dave's life. I sat there in disbelief. And cried.

Jenn sat there with me. I said, "This is really not about you. It's about me. I am just so sad. I just cannot believe Dave and I are not together!" I think she was relieved to find I was not mad at her. She put her arm around me. I broke lose and cried harder. Between my sobs, I told her about the string of events that occurred just before we broke up: about friends divorcing and Dave saying, "Oh, that could never happen to us. We've been through too much and we have come out stronger." I told her about the diamond earrings he'd just given me, our excitement about moving into a new house, planting a garden, and the huge party we'd had! I think I was trying to get across to her how shocked I was by our break up.

While I cried and talked, she talked too. She told me how disappointed she'd been in Dave, in how he'd led her to believe that he and I had not really been that close, that we were not that serious. I was not even sure he'd let her know we were living together. Seeing me at church and at the house and then seeing me now convinced Jenn more than ever that he had not fully represented our relationship to her. I could tell that she regretted coming into this new relationship, before the one before had been finished. I respected that.

And then, in my burst of anger, I did something I should not have done. Maybe some say it would have been okay to do, but my intent was wrong. I wanted revenge. I wanted to plant a seed with her. Previously, when I'd moved my things from the house, I'd seen her birthday marked on his calendar – the last day I'd seen Dave. As I cried, I told her that even after we'd broken up, he'd come back trying to be intimate, and I'd said, "But Dave, what about her? Wouldn't you be doing to her what you did to me?" I told her his response each time was, "But Lynnie, she's on the horizon."

And then I moved in for the kill, "Even on July 15, he wanted to have sex!" I said the date a few times. I told myself this was okay to say, because it was true. And it was true.

She did not know that I knew July 15 was her birthday. It is the only time I can think of, besides the pie-ing of Ms. Darby, that I purposefully and intentionally exacted revenge. I did not go there knowing I'd say this. I did not know I'd say this when we sat down. It only came to me as we talked back and forth. Somewhere in that conversation, I made a conscious decision to say it.

I was angry. He had wanted us both. I had stopped feeling special when he wanted someone else. How could she still feel special after knowing that while they were together, he still wanted someone else? I knew the minute I said it, it would be a death sentence to something she felt for him.

There's an expression that when someone is miserable, he wants others to be. That fit. The path to their relationship had not been all sunshine and roses and I opened my mouth to prove it. But what had I done? I told myself it was okay, but later when I tried to tell the story, I was not proud. I'd been a person I never wanted to be. Although I'd given her information I would have wanted had I been in her spot, I'd not been straightforward. It was backhanded and wrong and I felt ashamed.

On My Knees in the Bathtub

I found little tricks to keep me balanced that year. During the fall, the words and antics of Meanie and Visch were escalating and their behavior was seriously affecting my frame of mind. It was during this time I began a daily practice of yoga. In the past, when things got rough, I took a two-hour bath. When things got really rough, I got down on my knees and prayed. It was this year that I found myself on my knees, in the bathtub, on a regular basis.

Active alcoholics do not like me. Visch hated me. I had done nothing to hurt or provoke her, so I could only guess at the reasons she found me despicable. First, listening to her, she found most people despicable. Secondly, I think she despised my positive energy. I confounded her. Thirdly, I was vulnerable under stress in a new school; her unpredictable and volatile nature jarred me. To her, I was a wimp. It was true, I was afraid of her. I did not counter her attacks with the same venom she carried. But, remember, my mole was on the loose. I was just as afraid of him as I was of her, so I spoke my words every single time, not letting him down. There is an expression: "Never wrestle with a pig. You both get dirty, and the pig likes it." She was a pig, at her height of happiness describing her angry antics. I was too confused in a new job to match her anger, and she seized upon that vulnerability. Had I been able to bare and grit my teeth at her, as my mole would've liked, she probably would have left me alone. If it's true that a person shows her character in how she welcomes a newcomer, she'd shown me who she was. Vicious.

The biggest reason I think Visch did not like me was because she knew I knew what she was desperately trying to hide: she was an active, although high-functioning, alcoholic. I became her target for bullying. Daily. I believe she knew instinctively, that in order to be friends with me, in order to have anything to do with me, even have an honest conversation, she would have to put down her bottle.

I'd heard, "What you say to one person, you say to all people. Who you are to one person, you are to all people." I watched Visch laugh with her friends and experienced her simultaneous cruelty toward a few others and me. In my mind, I knew who she was at her lowest common denominator.

Remembering to Remember

During that year, I was hit over the head with a hammer five times. I picked up a book, opened it randomly, and read the words, "Ask and you shall receive." The next week, in a meeting, I heard someone use the phrase, "Ask and you shall receive." Another time I picked up a magazine, opened it randomly, and glared at the same words. Listening to the radio I heard them. This happened *five* times in a period of five weeks. It was uncanny. I'd rarely run across these words in my life.

I had come to believe that prayer was the best way for me to find a calm space. Throughout this break-up trigger, though, I kept forgetting. Forgetting to pray during the day. I'd always believed in a power outside myself, but I was not in the habit of *relying* on it. Now, I was in such a state, I had to. Between my heartache and the viciousness at work, I was squeezed into a spot where I needed constant help just to get through my day. I had to *remember* to remember to pray.

I'd been broken down, trying to get back up, but feeling kicked down again. I was weak. I remembered the prayer, "Help!" That often jump-started me into using more words. "I have failed miserably at this, and I am at a loss. I have tried and tried on my own, but I cannot do this alone. I need you. Please show me the way." Into this spot where I'd been squeezed, I came to see that there was little else that could heal my soul.

The Key

I'd read every piece of literature on forgiveness I could get my hands on. Whole books, magazine articles, pamphlets. Each time I saw the word "forgive" on a piece of literature, I grabbed it. *Okay, maybe this will be the thing that helps me forgive. Maybe this will have the magic words and I will be healed. This horrible feeling of anger will lift from me.* But each time I read words about forgiveness, they seemed to be the words I might feel, once I crossed over to that side, once I *got* there. It seemed like everyone wrote about their perspective of forgiveness *after* it had come to them. *Okay, maybe someday I will feel that, but not now.* All I wanted was to feel better.

I knew the grief process; I knew I would be through this some day, but that did not make the pain cease. I was still in the wretched-in-the-middle part - the anger and resentment. I instantly filled with hatred if I *thought* of forgiving Dave. There's a piercing feeling when, life is going along just fine and then abruptly, something makes you think of the one solitary person you haven't forgiven. You think you are fine and when that topic comes up, you're aghast at how fast your feelings heat up and you have switched to that dark place again. That is where I was. I needed help from *that* place.

I found it. It was not the "all light and lovely" feeling of the "after" part. This was something that met me where I was – in that sinister place where *I* wanted to feel better, but cared little about the person for whom I was to forgive. I was led by someone to read a passage in the AA book. I read that in order to forgive someone, I needed to pray for *his* happiness, *his* prosperity, and *his* health. All of the things I wanted for *myself*, I was to pray for *him* to have, too. *Ugh!* The thought repulsed me. *No! I could never mean that!* Thank goodness the passage went on to say to pray for all of this, even if you do not mean it. *Well, that's right. I don't mean it!* Ah ha! I had an out! I did not have to mean it! *I can do that!* But then it went on to read that I would eventually come to mean it. *Fat chance. That will never happen.*

The passage continued. If I prayed for this person for two weeks, I would come to mean it. I already knew I was a hard sell. I was told that about affirmations, too. "Say them for a month and they will become a part of you; they will change you." Ha! Nothing ever came to me in two weeks. My mind was too tricky. It would revert to its former state. It was stubborn. It did not want to be trained. I was used to having negative thoughts and my ego fought to keep them. When I was angry, it was easier to hate. So I overlooked the "two week" part and opened my mouth to speak. To pray for Dave and Jenn to have all the treasures I wanted for myself, for them to be happy and in love, prosperous, and healthy was hideous and absurd. I could barely get it out. But I did. I forced myself to feel that pain, so I would get better. I threw in a prayer for the alcoholic lady who was cruel to many, but especially to me.

I knew as I prayed, I did not mean it. It was a comfortable way of forgiving – pretending. At least I was on my way. In that not-meaning-it prayer, was a hand that reached down to save me from my miserable self.

The moment I prayed for Dave and Jenn to have all that I wanted for myself, I dripped with hatred. The beauty of the you-don't-even-have-to-mean-it part was that I could gradually come up. I got to stay down and wallow in my hateful feelings, where I was comfortable, as long as I wanted, all the while holding a steady grip. I could pretend to think good thoughts, test the waters of what it felt like to forgive them. I continued to hold the hand, and, while continuing to slop around in my muddy hole of hate, I said the prayer. And I continued not to mean it.

Good Grief!
That fall, a fellow heard me talking at a 12-step meeting. He came up to me afterwards and acknowledged my grief. He said, "You've heard the expression, 'Time heals all things,' right?"

"Yeah."

"Well, not in most cases. In cases like yours, it will probably take more than time." I looked into his eyes. He was trying to be gentle.

Like working to stay physically fit, I was going to have to work harder to stay mentally fit. He told me about a book called *The Grief Recovery Handbook* that was used in large groups at some churches. He'd just finished the handbook with a group that had ninety people in it. He told me the book was so powerful that in it, the authors asked the reader not to read ahead, because if he did, he would be too frightened by the process and possibly quit early. The exercises, he said, were not meant to be done alone, hence the large groups at church. This man did not go to that meeting regularly, so he took my address and mailed me the book! I must have been one sorry case.

The man went through so much effort to reach out to me, I knew there had to be something to this. There was no group starting up that I could find, so I asked a girlfriend to do the exercises with me. Louise had just had a long-time, older girlfriend die, one who'd been a surrogate mother.

In February, Louise and I set about working through the exercises of the book. We met faithfully each Thursday night and sometimes the exercises required us to meet more often. There was nothing like working with a partner who was as determined as I. Like an exercise partner who pushes, I wanted a spiritual partner who pushed me, too. Neither of us wavered from our goal.

One of the exercises required my drawing a horizontal timeline down the middle of paper and "drawing" out my ten-year relationship with Dave. On one side I had to write down the positive experiences. On the other, I had to write down the negative experiences. This timeline took me weeks and several feet of butcher paper to complete.

These authors were brilliant. In the beginning, I had no idea what the exercise would do for me, but in the end I saw. I came away calmer. There had been equally good and bad experiences in my relationship with Dave. What I had been angry about were the bad. It immediately gave me the perspective I needed.

I realized I'd been angry because I'd felt so betrayed by my best friend, someone I thought loved me, someone I trusted, who had always been honest with me. What was behind the anger was the fact that I felt stupid for feeling so fooled, so lied to, so believing. When I wrote out the timeline, I realized that our relationship, amidst the bad times, had been filled with, love, trust and honesty, and I had not been fooled or lied to - until the end. That was a doozey for me.

As foolish as I'd felt for staying with and going back and forth with Dave all those years, I realized that, given the information I had about myself at the time, those were the same choices I would have made. The calmness I felt then was the same kind I felt in the past when I had looked at our relationship, before the "big" hurt.

Another exercise made me write down all the losses I thought I had that were associated with the one big loss of Dave. I did. That was very painful, too, considering how much I'd lost. Another exercise had me write a letter to him and go back to a place where we'd been together - and read the letter to Louise. We did that. Those were the simple exercises. There were harder ones.

As the months went on, Louise worked on her loss and I worked on mine. We were diligent with our exercises and loyal to each other. I could see that I was moving away from my ugly thinking about the breakup. I could see the change in me was, indeed, not "time" healing me, but the *internal* work I was doing. That fellow had been right. I had needed a bulldozer and he gave me the heavy-duty tool to do the shoveling.

The one-year anniversary of our breakup came, June 24. For some reason, I thought I would miraculously *be better*. I wanted to be better. In fact, I felt no movement at all. I was disappointed. Then on June 27, just three days later, Louise came over and we did our final exercise of the book. We sat down in the same room and completed our part separately. I sat on the couch. This lesson had me go back to the beginning exercises and look at all of the things I thought I'd lost, associated with my relationship with Dave.

When I re-read each presumed loss, I heard a strong, resounding affirmation about each. I had lost nothing. I had gained – in every area! The voice was clear and strong. It showed me all I had in a different light. This light flooded me, showing me the abundance in my life. In that moment, I saw. I was as filled with havingness as I'd ever been.

The essence of the feeling I got was that I was free.

I had been set free. Something – while sitting there on that couch doing the last exercise – set me free. As the days went by that summer, I said to my friends, "I think something happened to me on the couch that night" or "I think something happened to me on June 27. I'm not sure what, but I felt something." It was a clear but subtle turning point. So clear, I knew it was powerful, but so subtle, I did not know how to mark it. I just knew something had changed.

To Build My Life Upon

My plan was to teach a graduate course, go camping for two weeks, and go to a weeklong yoga retreat.

When the course ended, I headed to the Pennsylvania mountains. Each day I sat and felt the wind come off the lake. Each night I sat under the half to full moon, staring at its glow. By day I picked blueberries and went swimming and sat and played cards with neighbors. Once I was sitting with a family at a picnic table and someone asked me what I did for a living. "Uh…uh… oh… oh, yeah, I'm a teacher." I was so relaxed, and so completely away from my busy school life in Virginia, I'd forgotten my profession, if only for a second or two! *How cool to have a job that I get to leave for so long and do something so completely differently that I forget what I do!* I decided I should do something each summer that made me forget what I did for a living. That's how I'd know I'd be completely relaxed. I'd go back completely refreshed, ready for a new school year.

A fellow, my age, came to camp at the campsite just across the way from me – for a week. He had a beard and played a guitar and lived nearby in the mountains. I called him Mountain Man. He and I talked and chatted and flirted and it was the first time I'd been around a guy I was interested in, in a year. It felt good and just a little scary.

On Saturday, the day before I was to leave and head to the yoga retreat, I sat at my campsite with the campground host. She felt the wind kick up and scrambled back to her camper. I got my things together to go take a shower. I rounded the corner on the dirt road and realized I did not have my socks. I turned around to go get them. When I opened my car's trunk, I glanced down at the lake and saw choppy black waves, like one might see in the ocean. *That's weird.* Then I walked back to the shower house, but this time, when I rounded that same dirt path, a wind came up under me that buckled my knees. I thought it was going to scoop me up, so I grabbed a tree trunk and clung to it. As I did, I heard trees cracking all around me. High up where the branches shot off into a V shape, the right–side V branch cracked and fell from twenty trees. Massive branches echoed, "Crack! Crack! Crack!"

The trees were pixie sticks and I was completely insignificant. My body was so small compared to this force. If it wanted to take me, I'd have been gone in a flash. I saw the camp hosts run into their RV. I wanted to be with them, so I ran and knocked on the door. The man grabbed me, threw me onto his wife already on the floor and jumped on top of us. The three of us laid there in a pile and listened to the "train" roar through.

It was a tornado. Over in minutes.

When we went out, branches were down everywhere, trees across the roads, one sideways next to my car. A hundred foot tree outside the shower house struck a 15-year-old boy. In the aftermath, we talked to the man who had tried with his father to revive him. The teenager died. It was a very sad day.

Mountain Man, who'd gone home, came back to check on all of us. The next morning, we campers went to the amphitheater for church service. We prayed for the teenager who'd been killed the day before. There was a closeness among us that fear had created.

A family of campers in two boats had been separated during the tornado. They stood and talked about how wonderful it felt to find each other afterwards. They sang a family church song. I asked them if they'd teach it to me. We all sat around and sang it over and over. Many knew the song, but it was the first I'd heard it. Some of the words were: "Looking back now that little mountain church house has become my life's cornerstone. It was there in that little mountain church house I first learned the Word to build my life upon."

"I first learned the word to build my life upon." That line struck a cord right through me. In my earlier life, I'd had no words to "build my life upon," only Mary's. But hers had been enough to guide me to find my own.

My two-week camping trip ended on a solemn note, but when I left, I felt the wind coursing through my veins again, and my respect for nature heightened. At the yoga retreat I slept to the sounds of throbbing crickets, spent seven days doing yoga, walking in the woods, and eating vegetarian food. It was magic. In my annual school picture taken that fall, I saw the twinkle in my eye again, and even a trace of my rascal.

The Glass Vase

All summer, through my teaching, camping by the lake with the moon, doing yoga, and being outdoors, I kept having the same vision.

At first, I did not understand it.

In my mind's eye, I saw a large, very tall, cylinder-shaped glass vase, at least ten feet tall and ten feet wide. At the base of the glass vase were beautifully round-shaped stones of different earth-toned colors, and sizes, all lying on top of each other, filling the bottom. The water was almost clear, with little particles of algae dissipating in the water and floating to the top. As the little pieces got to the top, the sun took care of them, evaporating them.

My interpretation was this vase represented the arduous task of cleaning up my life. At the bottom had been stones that had once been gross and disgusting, caked with algae and mud and muck. I had swum to the bottom of the vase with a scrub brush, picked up each one and scrubbed it hard. While being scrubbed, the muck and the mud created a storm of turmoil in the vase, a tumultuous swirling filth that rose to the top. The water in the vase had been green and mucky and thick with debris.

No matter how much turmoil this scrubbing made, I continued until the stone was clean and I placed it down. Then I picked up another gross and slimy one. I began doing the same scrubbing on the next stone. In all my time cleaning the stones, the water in the vase had not been clear. Always green, mucky and murky. I'd never seen this vision before.

I only knew it now, as the vase was clean, with clear water, and with the particles floating upward. I realized each stone had been an event in my life that I had to clean and purge. My scrub brush represented talking in groups, writing in notebooks or on butcher paper, growling into the mirror to find my demons, praying for the right words to say to a bully, and fighting all the ugly words I'd once believed about myself.

When I watched this vision unfold, my heart ached as I saw myself scrubbing. The woman in the water was so determined, but the inevitable green filth that swirled around her was a fact that had to be, in order to get clean.

The green murkiness and filth was my B through Y. No matter how I'd looked to others, I could not think of that when I was healing. No matter how embarrassed or ashamed that I did not know things, no matter how many times I tripped over my own feet, my own words, I could not stop just to look good. I could not pretend I wasn't in the pain I was in. I knew I'd made some people uncomfortable. There had been times I'd been abrasive and abrupt in my lack of knowledge of how to do or say things. My emotions had made some ill at ease. Anyone in tune with himself could probably have seen the turmoil that lay just beneath my surface.

I still had to move on to find healthy people who listened to me and shared their wisdom with me. People who believed in me, who allowed me to practice my words on them. I had done the work. No longer trapped, my stones were clean. I could see them clearly. I could now see the whole cylinder. It was my life, now clean. I would not know this or believe it for some time, but the feeling I had on the couch that night marked the end of eleven years of hard work. My inner turmoil had lifted.

I knew now my job was to keep that cylinder's water clear and clean. I came to see any ugly thing said to me as a dirty stone that was thrown into my vase. I promised myself I'd catch it before it hit the bottom. I'd confront the person who threw it in my water, and I'd spend time getting out what dirty residue had been left. I called these people bumps. I figured nothing or no one could be as fierce as what I'd dealt with in the sum total of eleven years. By now I knew my demons well. I had slain them, even befriended them. I had tools. I had courage. I had words. The biggest parts of my natural instincts were restored.

That fall, I rode with Phyllis and Jim Huggins to their daughter's wedding. I sat in the back seat of their truck and leaned forward and described to them the glass cylinder vase. Finally, a good story to tell.

Unlocked by the Brutal Bargain

If the "blood scene" I worked out, the "bed scene" I prayed out. A powerful force had not allowed me to feel completely safe with a man. With the clearing of the water in the vase, came the lifting of the fear I'd held from that night in bed with my father. The fear – as it had been – lifted.

I heard from a mutual friend that Dave and Jenn broke up the following spring. Dave tried to reach me on several different occasions to tell me he still wanted to be friends. I did not respond. He dropped me notes every now and then, and called to leave messages when each of his parents died a year apart. A couple years later, one note said, "I want you to know that if I look back over my life and think of the people who have had a huge and positive effect you are always in the top five. I think of you often, especially when I see mountains or out of doors or have a "secretary" problem. You have a great appreciation for the natural (outdoors) beauty and gave the best advice on dealing with people in the work place that I've ever gotten. Your students are fortunate. For two decades you have and will likely continue to be important in my life. I think you know all this, but I wanted to make sure."

Another year later an email said: "I woke up thinking of you and decided to drop you a note. I learned as much or more from you in my life as any single person. I often tell stories about this wise woman I once knew and the many things she taught me. I hope your life is as good as the last time I heard from you. This may seem like crazy stuff to you but I will share it anyway. When I think of you and me, the feeling is of separation. It is not as mates but as something quite different – "sister" is all that comes to mind. It is like you were my sister, and we were joined at the hip in another era. I think of you often. I know that by the ways of the world I did a horrible thing with you, but............I feel a long time ago in another era we made a bargain with each other: that we would spend time together when we went into the next world and at one point I would leave you in a brutal way. That this would trigger horrible feelings in you but they would be ones that I was not the root of. I would be the catalyst that allowed them to surface so you could deal with them and see something you wouldn't otherwise see. We smiled when we made the bargain knowing it would be brutal but also knowing that was what life on earth was like. Anyway, take it for what it is worth. I know we will be friends again in another time and know that you are often in my thoughts."

It was true that I had prayed to be "unlocked," because I could not do it myself. I truly was cracked open by the emotionally brutal event of our break up. The finality of losing Dave ignited in me a firestorm I could never have predicted, one that propelled me into a year-long whirlwind of traveling to my ugliest depths, snaking out that long-ago frozen fear I'd assumed would always be a part of me. My victimhood, sealed and delivered to me, a helpless child, on that night, would not remain. I had surrendered to it then because there was no one to protect me. As an adult, I'd developed tools to protect myself. In perfect timing, that brutal event came my way, giving me a second chance to run the victim out. I was ready when it came. My warrior came out in full force to fight against it, using every tool in my arsenal.

There Comes a Time

Ten years after our breakup, I arrived home weary from leading a twelve-hour field trip with a hundred students and parents. I fell into bed that night relieved, the stress melting off me as I sunk deeply into my sheets. In that sinking, I forgave Dave. Many years before, I'd stopped praying for this forgiveness to come, believing it would come when it was ready. I never knew when it would show up. There it was. I got out of bed in the middle of the night and wrote Dave a note telling him I forgave him and had four conditions for our friendship: One, he always had to tell me the truth, no matter what; Two: he could never say anything harsh to me again; Three: we would never be lovers again; and Four: if he had a girlfriend and we were ever to meet for lunch, she had to be informed. He called me days later and agreed to all. He had a girlfriend, so we decided to just talk on the phone every now and then.

I can never underestimate the value of having people around me who know me. Dave knows me. When I have a difficult situation now, he is one of the people I call. He does the same with me. We probably speak on the phone every three to six months. That's all. It's enough.

Fight or Flight... or Fright

When encountering a stressful situation, the body moves into the fight or flight mode, releasing chemicals into our bodies that help us do one or the other: fight or flee. On the night of the shooting, my brothers did the instinctive thing: they fled. My sister did another instinctive thing: she fought.

What did I do? If the first two things are instinctual and natural and protect you, what I did was unnatural. With all of the adrenaline flowing through my body, I froze. Where would I have gone? To some place safe? I was in my house. The only safe place I knew. Who would I have fought? How would I have fought? With what would I have fought? There were no real answers to these questions, so I remained in what I now see as the third category – the fright mode.

All those chemicals that flowed through my body on that night had nowhere to go – not into the grit of a fight, not into movement of travel. They just stood, and later lay there with me, forming a cesspool of toxicity, creating a little unnatural, suspended-in-time statue. Me. Hardened to the core. The victim statue.

When a trauma happens and a person is not able to fight or flee, but instead freezes, that freezing can retard his or her natural instincts. This person gets a lot of criticism in our society. People judge victimhood mercilessly. All I can say is anyone who judges it harshly has never really been in a situation devastating enough to cause the freezing.

In victimhood, the victim is A. Nobody wants to be A. No one has respect for A. The fighters and the fleers are Z. Everybody wants to be Z. Everyone has respect for Z. But how does one get from B through Y? It is difficult. When does one get from B through Y? Slowly. Where does one get from B through Y? Internally. With whom does one get from B through Y? Yourself only. How often does one get from B through Y? Daily.

In order to heal, I had to do B through Y with my head held high even when on my insides, my head was hanging very low. I had to do B through Y slowly, daily, internally, and in the face of skeptics and arrogant people.

The good news is that I can share with anyone who wants to know, how I found my way out of a living hell. I felt my feelings. Think about it. A feeling is invisible. It carries no sword. It points no gun. But the fear that feelings bring up is the dying kind of fear. *I am going to die.* But think of it. It is not real. I learned in bodyworks therapy that if I just let a feeling come up, it will move through me and it will dissipate. Fear and grief and painful feelings can only move through me if not squelched by my drug of choice, so I had to know my drug. It may take a long time to feel an event through. That is why being willing to be well takes determination in a world that is so fragmented and that runs so fast. To be well, a person must slow down. A person has to sit – with nothing to do. A person has to invite the uglies into his life. A person has to be conscious of the uglies being there, to not react to them, to not take them out on other human beings. I know if I ask for it – to be well around an issue - it will come, in all the universe's great force. And feeling this invisible threatening feeling will not kill me. It will not defeat me. While it is up and passing through me, I may want to attack every person I come across, but I have to know that these people are the gift of my being able to feel and heal. They are in my life to help bring up what I have asked to come up. I must bless them. And I must virtually ignore them to get well. I cannot take what they say personally, but I must direct this energy of hatred to the demon still living inside me, still wanting to take up space and conquer me, still laughing at me for being so foolish as to believe the ugly sentences it has put there and nurtured.

The best tool in my toolbox for becoming mentally well, to conquer and starve any demon, was to not let a negative *thought* cross my *lips* when speaking to or about other humans with whom I came into contact. I held those thoughts. I looked inward to find the source. I went there, met it, and beat the tar out of it. Someone's words, some act I experienced somewhere in the past, gave me those ugly thoughts. They were not real – they were in past time - and no one deserved to hear them from me. I looked for what they had morphed into: "I am not enough." "I am useless." "I am worthless." "I am ugly." "I am fat." "I am not worthy of life." "No one loves me." "No one wants me here." "I am not worthy of love." It took time to crack these codes. I found the words I carried, growled with muster until one day the demon took me seriously and knew it could no longer infiltrate my soul. It was possible to banish, but I had to be dedicated, in it for the long haul. In my lowest times, I held these words in my mind: "I was given weakness so that I might feel the need of God." Once I found their source, the sentence that haunted me, I had to then listen for the words to replace them, the words that lived inside me naturally, and the ones the negativity had been suffocating.

I knew if I wrestled long enough, each negative sentence would be replaced with phrases such as these: "I am enough. I am quite enough. I am all there is. I am a precious child of God. I am everything in the universe. I am full of worth. God loves me. I am his precious child. I am a gift to everyone around me. I am so beautiful. My body is gorgeous and loving and strong and full of goodness. I deserve to be here. Everyone wants me here. I am worthy of everyone's love." No matter how strong the negative force appeared to be, it was the positive force that won.

If and when negative thoughts did cross my lips, they needed to be spoken in a conscious effort to be well. This was only to be done with another person or group that did not buy into and agree with me about my negative opinions of another person. I knew their agreement would not heal me, but their guiding me to the demon that brought them would. Through this often-long process, *feeling* words came to me and *those* were the words I eventually needed to say out loud. I learned to never speak the negative, ugly words directly to the person I believed to be my problem. That, I came to know, was a made-up lie. I came to know that in present time we are all wonderful and we are all doing the best we can. If someone was negative, I saw him in pain first. I saw him as unwell, as limited. I came to see how the anger someone acts out under stress and in conflict is indicative of his mental health. Wrestling with a pig. His own demons are revealed in that moment. My job was to not react to the attacker, but to see all the oceans and seas, valleys and mountains of the world in his presence. If his anger was unreal, a lie, I had to reflect back to him what was real, the truth.

I asked the universe to unlock this freezing-in-fright for me, and it eventually happened. My mole was released. I suspect most people have this "mole" in them and naturally react to protect themselves when "he" tells them to. My fight or flight instincts kick in now, but, miraculously, what I have found is I still do not want to fight and I certainly do not want to flee. I want to stand my ground, speak candidly, and resolve a conflict. With words. I can be at peace in the midst of conflict. I believe it is possible to grow beyond fight or flight. I think the universe gives us this gift, if we do our part. Once I saw a little girl stand up to a monster.

I always thought Mary was the lucky one, the one who stood up to the gun and paved a way for her life to be free of the victimhood I carried. But I learned I had another task on earth. My task was to find, in the midst of the most shattering chaos, that peace I found in Judy's eyes. To know it is there and that it has never left the room. It exists in present time, simultaneously with the madman. All I have to do is pick which one I want to believe. Not knowing how to bark down an attacker was a source of great shame to me. I thought I was weak, even pathetic. I so wanted to be Z, the person who could scream down a beast. Something in me could not attack a person verbally. Now I know why. Finding love in the midst of conflict is even better.

A Fitting Piece of the Puzzle

Whenever people asked me how old my mother was, I always said her age, but added that her body was really twenty years older than she was. With all her operations and medications, Mom's body wore out long before her mind, and she has needed 24-hour care for many years. One day Mary and I took Mom out of her facility for an all-day outing. We traveled in a car with her for eight hours. After having been in a confined space for that length of a time, Mary saw the sharp disparity in how our mother talked to each of us. With Mary, Mom used soft, loving, and gentle tones. Her words were filled with praise and admiration. With me, her tone was harsh and sharp. Her words were critical, however subtle. I had always known this, but when Mary experienced it so glaringly, in such close quarters, she walked away from the experience saying to me, "Lynnie, I am so sorry. I am so sorry. I had no idea." She never had to tell me what she was sorry about. We both knew what she meant.

Mary said to Mom the next day, "Mom, how come you have such a problem with Lynnie?"

Without flinching, Mom spit out these words: "She was your father's favorite. He loved her. And look what he did to me."

Mary, replied, "Stop right there." She got out a piece of paper, wrote it down, word for word, and brought it to me that afternoon. When she handed it to me, she said, "Here you go. I got it from the horse's mouth." She knew she was giving me something of value. Mary had always told me I was our father's favorite and I told her I had no idea. She always questioned, "Really?"

When she gave me this information, I told her, "See. I can prove to you that I did not know I was our father's favorite!"

"How?"

"Because I did not know I was our mother's least favorite!"

It seems that it might be difficult to learn that you are a parent's least favorite child, but for me, I was ever so grateful for the information. I always thought something was wrong with me. *Why is everyone so critical of me? What is going on? What have I done? Why can't I get this right?* All of these thoughts ran through and messed with my mind.

Turns out, I was a very eager and enthusiastic little girl. My mother always said, too, that I'd been conceived in love and was born at a time when my parents were their happiest. It seemed I had a happy and giggly spirit that people gravitated toward, even my father. Mary had been withdrawn and admitted that she could see why it was so much more difficult to get close to a timid and reserved child, as she'd been.

Those three sentences Mom spoke to Mary on that day were good for me to hear. I could finally realize there'd been a reason for my feeling criticized. It was not just I who thought something was wrong with me. Mary gave me a huge piece to lay down in my puzzle. I asked her this question: "If your father was an abusive person to everyone around, but you were his favorite child and your mother was a very loving and affectionate person to everyone around, but you were her least favorite child, how do you think that would affect you as a person? How do you think you would have turned out?"

I asked Dave the same question, but at a different time. Mary and Dave both gave me virtually the same answer. "I think it would give me very bad judgment in both male and female relationships."

Well said, I thought.

Three Women

Mary's clear-headed "No!" launched her into the world knowing how to say no. Although brilliant and educated, she chose to work for herself, by herself, in construction. Mary said she'd already raised a family, and did not want to have children. She was able to find a new companion, forge a team, and have a wonderful marriage. As for Judy, on one of their recent visits, she asked Mary, "Does Kevan love you, Mary?"

"Yes, he loves me very much."

"Oh, I never had that. I never had anyone love me." Mary's sadness at hearing this could have wilted a field of flowers. Judy never progressed into the adult world and found a partner to love. She was too ill to ever have children. Her entire life consists of living in a facility where she has the freedom to walk around her small town.

I have loved men and I have had men love me, but not the whole me. It has taken me a long time to find, and come to love, the whole me. I may still find that love with a man. What I did get to do is heal my anger. I learned how to be angry without being violent or silent. I learned how to communicate my simplest and deepest emotions in a healthy way. My closest friends always saw me as being a mother some day, as did I, but that did not happen. I intuitively knew I would need the help of a partner in a solid, healthy relationship. I did not find him or become that healthy person early enough. If my writing all this down helps someone find that healthy place sooner, bless you.

There's a saying: "You can have *anything* in the world that you want; you just can't have everything. Above all else, I have wanted to be well. I've learned it takes work to be well.

My Siblings

Everyone asks about my siblings. How is everyone else doing, how are they coping? Out of respect for their privacy, I only speak in generalities. They are good, loving people. They did not ask for the shooting to happen to them any more than I did. Of the three of us who stayed in the house, I was the only one whose memory was clear enough to recount this story. I did it because I had to. This is a project that has lived inside me all my life. It is probably not something any of my siblings would ever have done. No one wants his or her story told by someone else. I never did. Please think of this as my story and mine alone. I hope and pray that it does not harm my siblings. I love them dearly. So, please, dear readers, be kind to my brothers and sisters and let go of any of your questions about them. Know that they lived several lifetimes of pain before my father left, and I do not want to stir up more for them in their later years. If this document is to be used for good, use it to direct your questions inward for self-exploration. Instead of seeing the shooting as a sensational, overly extreme event, juxtapose it over any painful event of your own. Look for any underlying negative message that is still being fed to you by any of your demons inside who would so ferociously love for you to believe them. I saw that demon in living color in Judy's fluorescent green eyes that day on the gravel driveway. But I did not believe it. It could not conquer me and get its wish for me to never tell this story. I had once seen the beauty in those same eyes so long ago, a beauty that transfixed me and held me alive, held me in love, and held me floating in time and space, showing me the way into the universe. If you take anything away from us, please take only the love in this story.

Only One Thing

In present time, I wake up every day of my life and walk into a classroom I love, filled with kids I love, teaching what I love. I love my life, I love being here, and I'm glad I stayed. I have people who treat me with love and respect. Ironically, I was later the head of the sunshine committee at my school for fourteen years, so I guess you could say I did get the title of "Miss Sunshine" after all! Willingly. I still help set up and attend every high school reunion – every five years - and get to see all the people who familied me in my darkest years, including Nem.

Nothing is perfect and never will be. I will always have posttraumatic stress, but I can manage it instead of it managing me. I had to work to get my anger and fear to a manageable place. If I hang around with crazy people, I will be crazy. There is no doubt. But if I hang around with wonderful, loving and kind people who understand that I, like everyone else, have special needs under stress, then I am in the clear.

I still have my ups and downs, but my continuous suffering ceased the summer the particles in my vase reached the top and evaporated in the sun. My judgment is still skewed and I make unwise choices every so often. I have the tools to get myself away from people who misrepresent themselves, or from situations where I find myself unloved. A long time ago I read that self-esteem is measured by the amount of approval we give ourselves. Now, when I make a mistake, amazingly, my reactions of embarrassment, humiliation, and mortification are replaced with a very easy, gentle, and surprisingly quick forgiveness. I still have a voice that follows me wherever I go saying, "I love you, Lynnie."

My life is not about the shooting. There are far worse things that have happened to far better people than I. My life is about the hard work it has taken to change negative thoughts to positive ones, and doing my best to deal with negative, crazy, and angry people. For the first half of my life, I felt very lonely. I want the second half of my life to be filled with people who are like me: full of love and energy and who want to stay mentally, emotionally, physically, and spiritually fit. I hope they find me.

I will continue to catch the stones thrown into my well, hopefully before they reach the bottom, and I will scrub them clean and lay each one down peacefully. Success, for me, is giving service to others, resolving conflicts with love and words. It is also living a life that will stand up to truth detectors: kids. To all of the kids in my classroom, past, present, and future: I love you.

As times change, I find I have to modify my boundaries to find peace. I think computers and cell phones are great inventions; I love the chime that comes in when I text someone I love, back and forth. I can see these machines connect us with each other and with all parts of the world. But speed and fragmentation can lend danger to my life, leaving me harried and taking my attention away from my inner voice. I understand I must manage and control how much fragmentation I can allow. But I wonder how our younger generation will learn that the off switch is in their control. I try to remember that slow is real. Speed fools us and sets us in motion for what is unreal. Real needs time. Eyes. Words. Tone of voice. Speed is only for when slow has already done its magic. Speed ruins relationships. If we want respect and good, solid relationships, we have to listen to our intuition when it tells us to take long breaks from machines. When lost, the best boundaries to have are manners. We do not have to be – and should not be - available to everyone, all the time. We must make ourselves available to ourselves first, staying awake to our inner voices, our communication with what is inside us, or to whom we pray. There is no substitute for present-time eye contact, touch, uninterrupted listening, speaking, skipping over the trivial and insignificant, and sharing from our individual depths. When a person is moved to tears, we must lend that person our utmost respect. If we seek respect from our loved ones and those whose lives we touch daily, we must be present enough to connect with attention. "The best compliment we can pay is attention." This attention can be applied to any aspect of our lives, especially our intuition, health, and relationships.

Everybody supposedly wants to know the meaning of life. I am not the wisest person in the world and I am not the dumbest, but I know what the meaning of life is for me. It's only one thing: love. I don't need to know any more than that. I found that answer long ago in Judy's loving eyes. Though I may stray from it for a time, nothing I've learned since has upstaged it. I gravitate toward loving people, as if someone were pinching my T-shirt at the sternum and pulling me in the right direction.

Somewhere along this whole journey it hit me that God wants me to be happy every single moment, every single day of my life. If I am not happy, not laughing, if I am suffering, if something is wrong, not right, not real, I need to do whatever it takes to bring my life back to a place of joy. Stand up, speak, confront, leave, move, go find, let go, forgive, address a situation, whatever it takes to get back to that place of joy and love. Quickly. That was helpful to realize.

Grieve it and Leave it
There, but for the grace of God, go I.

There's a saying that God never gives you more than you can handle. After watching what Judy was given, I don't believe it. The human body reacts to loss, and must go through a process to get out of grief and, yes, some people do use prayer during this time. But if many big losses are piled on top of each other all at once, the stress can become too great. Not being able to pass through the stages of grief naturally, especially getting stuck in anger, the person can become mentally ill.

Had I known about the grief process at a young age, I believe my lonely suffering could have been far less. Through the teaching of literature, I teach my students the grief process. They take to it like the thirsty. In almost every story or novel we read, there is loss and often a tragedy. I do my best to cultivate their emotional intelligence by helping them connect to a character, to follow how he moves through the natural, normal process of loss. We have created a culture where children experience far more adult language and scenes on the screen than they can process. We owe it to them to cultivate their emotional intelligence so they can find their way through this quagmire, help them make sense of the world that spins so fast. I show my students how they can experience the grief process in a short amount of time in their everyday lives. It can play out the moment they feel the shock of realizing they have forgotten their homework. Then to the anger they feel after remembering their younger sibling went rummaging through their backpack. They understand the bargaining stage of wondering if the teacher will cut them a break, and then the depression they experience when going to lunch feeling defeated, knowing that F is going to stick. With friends rallying around them, though, they can come to an acceptance of not getting credit for the homework. And all of this – their process – takes about an hour.

Or the grief process can be a long process of years, such as when losing a grandmother to death, a parents' divorce, or moving away from friends. The point is when a child can pinpoint when and where he is in the process, he knows he is a normal, functioning human being. *There is nothing wrong with him.* At the end of the school year, my students tell me that above anything else they learned in class, learning the grief process helped them most. Children need to know it before they reach their teenage years. Experiencing a loss in teenage years, most still have not had enough losses to know they will "come out of this one, just like all the rest." Depression overwhelms them and we lose our teenagers to long bouts of depression and sometimes suicide. We can save a lot of pain and suffering in our children if we cultivate their emotional intelligence by teaching them the grief process, early in their lives.

I ask my students to remember that every time they see a homeless person, to understand that person was probably not always homeless. That person probably once had a job, a home and a family, and maybe, one by one those things were lost – *too close together.* It is important to grieve losses, so that we can handle the stress of the next ones, because loss is a part of everyday life. Think of the people who have lived to one hundred years old. They have had many losses. In order to get that far and still live a positive life, they have had to learn to grieve well. At some point, they learned how to experience a loss without becoming debilitated, moved through it, and continued forward. Grieving well means not having to be ashamed of the natural feelings that come with loss, and staying with those feelings until the loss is resolved.

Mental illness is the result of unresolved grief.

None of us was able to save Judy but, if she leaves a legacy, I hope it will be to demonstrate the importance of eye contact. She gave me a treasure that night and I have tried to put into words just how her gift impacted me. If this book helps you in some small way, please consider it a gift from Judy. The happy, generous little girl she was would have wanted you to have it.

Thank you, Judy. Love, *Looneybird*

Words from Mary

Reading this has been hard. If I ever feel like I lack character, all I have to do is remember what I did on that night. It helps me know what I'm made of. Standing up to that gun is a big part of me.

Lynnie had to tell this story. It was never going to be me. There should be no shame in what happened to us, but there always is with violence. As my mom said, "This is what alcoholism can do to a family." I miss the family we could have been. I miss Judy. We're all great people, but this shooting splintered us. We were told not to talk about it and get on with it. That's what we did. But in doing so, we went our separate ways. Me, all the way to Australia. I did what I needed to heal. We all did. It is very hard to think about what we could have become - instead of struggling with the violence inflicted upon us. It could not have happened to a more wonderful group of people than my brothers and sisters. *That* is the real shame.

The six of us have never sat down and talked about the shooting. I'd love to think this writing would bring us together to finally talk about that night. I love my husband for a hundred different reasons, but I love my brothers and sisters for no reason at all.

Mary Vessels

Acknowledgments

I would like to thank all who have helped me along my way, especially my students over twenty-five years, who may have also known me as Ms. Nielson/Hower. Thanks to JudyAnn Gray, Larry and Lisa Clarke, Gracie Loveall, Les Johnson, Peter Crockett, Connie Ridgeway, Karen Kelleher, Kim Donahue, Brother David Petry, Smokey, Janice, and Jillene Bolt, Sylvia Warren, Jim and Phyllis Huggins, Jim Taylor, Lynn Nixon, Nancy Ohyler Parker, Claude Hentchey, Suzanne Simon, Sid Simon, Connie Herrman, Sharon Fulkerson, Julie Deane Nash, Keith Richardson, Geoff Gilbert, Kelly Owens, Mitch Jones, Debbie Schaefer Russell, KB and Kevin Beckman, Reenie Vandergrift, Ned Smith, Sharon Grimner, Susan Graceson, Ruth Furpahs, Roy Knapp, Dick Wynne, Kevin "Arnie" Norse, CJ Arban, Aaron Edmondson, Beth Pierce, Furman Riley, Elaine Ryan, Sue Coryell, Kim Madill, Dave Graham, Lynn Ward, Becky Meyer, Juli Jergensen, Donna Koerbel, Jim Cunningham, Judy Butz, Frannie Lucid, Mimi and John Totten, Cynthia and Paul Roye, Joseph Armstrong, Ras and Tina in Colorado, Anita and Andre in Hawaii, Peter Kafka, John McKay, Betty Petersen, Kevin Kemble, Sandy Robinson, Betty Bibbins, JJ Gormley, Dennis Gormley, Mary Salins, Peggy Fink, Jane Wagner, Kim Feather, Midge Flaherty, Kristi Kampschafer Chin, Susan Bryant Raque, Donnie Wright, Dahna Cannon, Karen Wathan Nelson, Sherri Marlow Barnard, Maureen Weber Ahmadi, Kathy Massie Lightle, Lisa and Moe Garvin, Judy Dumbstorf, Pam Lewis, Mark Mulanax, Amy and Steve Goldberg, Sue and Larry Hamlet, Kevan Goodall, Lance Kallenberg, Sumitra, Dominic, and Andrew Raj, Julie Bohon, Vernelle Boykin, Anne Ferranti, Ann Marie Mochen, Becky Jones, Shannon Hicok, Catherine Kent, Fritz Heinzen, Dan Stone, Bob Sellers, Debbie Scott, Laurie Redfern, Pam Hickenbotham, Clarissa Pinkola Estes, Oprah Winfrey, Marianne Williamson, Maya Angelou, and my Pennsylvania girls Bobbie Strausbaugh, Beth Stump, Kathy Schrann, Marti Vaughn, and Margaret Hope.

And a special thank you to all of you whose voices rang in my head for years after you walked up to me in my courses and said, "You have to write a book!"

Lynnie Vessels

About Author

Lynnie Vessels has a master's degree in Secondary Education and has been teaching English in the public school system more than twenty years. She has taught over forty graduate education courses in the areas of communication and discipline, including *Teacher Effectiveness Training, Self-esteem for Educators, Resolving Conflicts in Classrooms and Schools, Stress Management for Teachers,* and *Reaching Today's Students*. She appeared as a guest on the Oprah Winfrey Show and has traveled the country as a surprisingly candid motivational speaker. She lives in Virginia with her Maltese, Okie. Visit www.lynnievessels.com for more information.

Book cover design by Allison Lee
Interior design by Brandi Phipps
Poster photographs by JudyAnn Gray

Judybird
Publishing